Affirmative action in the United States and India

A comparative perspective

Thomas E. Weisskopf

Routledge
Taylor & Francis Group

LONDON AND NEW YORK

First published 2004
by Routledge
2 Park Square, Milton Park, Abingdon, Oxon, OX14 4RN

Simultaneously published in the USA and Canada
by Routledge
270 Madison Ave, New York NY 10016
1009230875
Routledge is an imprint of the Taylor & Francis Group

Transferred to Digital Printing 2006

© 2004 Thomas E. Weisskopf

Typeset in Bembo by
Taylor & Francis Books Ltd

British Library Cataloguing in Publication Data
A catalogue record for this book is available from the British Library

Library of Congress Cataloging in Publication Data
A catalog record for this book has been requested

ISBN10: 0–415–70002–7 (hbk)
ISBN10: 0–415–77107–2 (pbk)

ISBN13: 978–0–415–70002–3 (hbk)
ISBN13: 978–0–415–77107–8 (pbk)

For my parents

In memory of
Ellen and Victor Weisskopf

"Effective participation by members of all racial and ethnic groups in the civic life of our Nation is essential if the dream of one Nation, indivisible, is to be realized."

Justice Sandra Day O'Connor (opinion in *Grutter et al. v. Bollinger et al.*, 2003)

"The absence of empirical studies of the achievements of reservation, and changes resulting from these in the larger social situation, is one of the many reasons why it becomes difficult to conduct an informed debate."

Patwardhan and Palshikar (1992: 4)

Contents

Illustrations

Figures

Tables

Preface

My interest in writing this book has two primary sources – one going back to the early years of my academic career, and the other much more recent. During the 1960s I spent a total of four years in India, teaching economics at the Indian Statistical Institute and working on problems of economic development planning. During that time I developed great affection for and appreciation of the people and the cultures of India; and for many years thereafter my teaching and research was oriented to the political economy of that fascinating sub-continental nation. By the early 1980s, however, my focus had shifted to other parts of the world; and I did not visit India for two decades after a brief trip to New Delhi in 1980.

In 1996 I accepted an appointment as Director of the Residential College at the University of Michigan. One year later, two lawsuits were filed against the affirmative action admissions policies of the university, and the growing national debate over affirmative action came to be focused on the Michigan campus. As a social scientist as well as an administrator, I became increasingly interested and involved in issues relating to racial/ethnic diversity in higher education. I was certainly predisposed to favor affirmative action policies; but I was also conscious of some of the negative consequences to which such policies could give rise. I began to acquaint myself with the literature on the subject and found myself participating increasingly in discussions and debates about affirmative action.

In looking forward to a year of leave in 2001–2, I had been hoping to start a new research project that would renew my acquaintance with India while drawing on my background as an economist and my interest in controversial policy issues. I was aware of the fact that India had been practicing a form of affirmative action for a considerably longer time than the US; but in my earlier years I had never paid much attention to issues of race, caste, or ethnicity – much less the details of India's "reservation policies" on behalf of "backward classes." Here, then, was a marvelous opportunity for me to return my attention to India. I would undertake a research project designed to shed new light on a controversial contemporary issue through a comparative analysis of affirmative action policies in the US and reservation policies in India. After two trips to India (in December 2000 and September 2001), and after exploring several possible research directions, I resolved to write the present book.

By coincidence, just as I was finishing the manuscript, the US Supreme Court handed down its rulings on the two lawsuits filed against the University of Michigan's admissions policies. In the context of the general rightward drift of US politics since the 1970s, and mounting attacks on affirmative action in particular, many observers expected – and not a few fervently hoped – that the Court would decide in the Michigan cases to end affirmative action preferences in educational admissions once and for all.

In fact, in the decisions issued on 23 June 2003, the Court came down firmly in support of affirmative action. Although it ruled against the particular procedures used by the University of Michigan to implement preferences in undergraduate admissions, it strongly endorsed the basic rationale for such preferences in upholding the admissions policies of the Law School. Speaking for the Court majority, Justice Sandra Day O'Connor stated unambiguously that the nation has a compelling interest in promoting racial/ethnic diversity in higher education and that racial/ethnic identity may be taken into account in determining who should be admitted to selective colleges and universities.

How can this surprising outcome be explained? The answer is that affirmative action won the day not as a policy promoting social justice for America's disadvantaged racial/ethnic minorities. Instead, it prevailed because it serves the interests of a wide-ranging coalition of the US elite in the effective management of America's major institutions in an age of globalization. This coalition includes a substantial majority of the top executives of American multinational corporations, most of the top US military brass, many US political leaders, and almost all of America's higher educational administrators.

Some members of the pro-affirmative action coalition (especially the educators) are genuinely committed to the group-egalitarian goals that affirmative action policies can help to promote. But what unites most coalition members into a politically powerful partnership is the understanding that the US cannot expect to prevail in the heightened competition of an increasingly globalized multicultural world if its leadership remains predominantly and visibly White. As so many CEOs, generals, and politicians in the US have come to realize, they cannot win from America's growing non-White population the legitimacy and trust they need to achieve their goals so long as they monopolize society's most esteemed positions. Nor can they and their White colleagues and subordinates effectively engage the cooperation, confidence, and commitment of their fellow citizens of color – unless they are seen as genuinely appreciative of racial, ethnic, and cultural diversity. How much more important are these considerations when one is dealing not with a minority of the US population, but with a majority of the world's population?

The contrast between the US and India is illuminating. Most Indian business, military, and educational leaders – especially those representing the most elite institutions – line up firmly against reservation policies in higher education and employment. They argue that these policies weaken India's ability to compete in a globalized world, because they provide opportunities to typically under-prepared and culturally deprived members of marginal groups, who are likely to perform poorly, at the expense of well-prepared and culturally sophisticated members of mainstream groups, who are primed for success on the world stage. From this perspective, preferential policies are seen as a costly luxury rather than a good investment.

Globalization puts a high premium on the capacity to speak articulate English, which is hard to attain in India without attending English-language schools. So it is from the uppermost Indian social strata that effective players on the world stage are most likely to be recruited. Moreover, India does not need to look for members of under-represented racial/ethnic groups in order to show the world an assemblage of leaders who reflect the diversity of the world's population, rather than looking like members of a privileged club, and who can therefore be expected to inspire more confidence and less suspicion around the globe.

The effect of globalization on high-level support for preferential policies is just one of many issues into which insights may be gained by a comparison of the experiences of the US and India with policies favoring under-represented racial/ethnic groups. In this book I undertake a systematic comparison of US affirmative action policies and Indian reservation policies, focusing attention primarily on the consequences of those policies. In so doing, I hope to contribute both to a general understanding of preferential policies and to a specific understanding of how affirmative action and reservation policies have been working in the US and India over the past half-century.

In ruling on the Michigan affirmative action cases, a majority of US Supreme Court justices shied away from taking a moral position on the fundamental rightness or wrongness of preferences for under-represented racial/ethnic groups. Instead, their decisions reflected a concerted effort to balance considerations weighing for and against the use of such preferences. In this book I adopt precisely such a pragmatic approach to affirmative action and reservation policies, treating them as policy options entailing possible benefits and possible costs. Indeed, I seek also to draw from the comparative experience of the US and India lessons that will be helpful in designing preferential policies so as to maximize their potential benefits and minimize their potential costs.

T.E. Weisskopf
July 2003

Acknowledgments

In writing this book I have received help of many kinds from a great variety of old and new friends in both the US and India. Among my colleagues at the University of Michigan I am especially grateful to Elizabeth Anderson, Carl Cohen, Patricia Gurin, and Ramaswami Mahalingam. Among colleagues elsewhere in the US I am indebted to Margery Davies, Donald Heller, Thomas Kane, Glenn Loury, Arthur MacEwan, and an anonymous reviewer of an early version of the manuscript. During two trips to India, and in subsequent correspondence, I benefited greatly from the hospitality and advice of Mrinal Dattachaudhuri, Ashwini Deshpande, Satish Deshpande, Amitabha Ghosh, Viney Kirpal, Ravivarma Kumar, and G.G. Wankhede; and I am also grateful for the helpful suggestions offered by Karuna Chanana, V.K. Ramachandran, Srinivasa Rao, A.R. Vasavi, and Padma Velaskar. I thank Satya Chakravarty, Jean Dreze, and Anjan Ghosh for organizing seminar presentations of my work at the Indian Statistical Institute, the Center for Studies in Social Sciences, and the Delhi School of Economics. I thank also Krishna Raj for encouraging me to publish in his *Economic and Political Weekly* some articles based on my work for this book. Chandan Gowda provided me with excellent research assistance in the early stages of the project. Finally, I gratefully acknowledge the support of the University of Michigan, in the form of a year of sabbatical and off-campus duty leave from the College of Literature, Science, and the Arts, as well as financial support for research and travel expenses from the Office of the Vice-President for Research, the Rackham School of Graduate Studies, and the International Institute.

My greatest debt is to my wife, Susan Contratto, who not only gave me unstinting encouragement at all stages of this project but also helped me to improve the clarity and readability of the book.

T.E. Weisskopf
July 2003

Abbreviations

Note: only frequently used abbreviations are listed here.

AA   affirmative action
GPA   grade-point average
IIT   Indian Institute of Technology
OBC   Other Backward Class
PD   positive discrimination
RP   reservation policies
SAT   Scholastic Aptitude (or Assessment) Test
SC   Scheduled Caste
SES   socio-economic status
ST   Scheduled Tribe
UM   University of Michigan
UREG   under-represented ethnic group

Introduction

The US and India are in many obvious ways very different; but in some important respects the two nations are similar. Both have functioning democratic electoral systems and are constitutionally committed to preserving civil liberties and individual rights. Both have large, multicultural populations including significant minority groups with a long history of deprivation and disadvantage, whose members are quite disproportionately under-represented in the upper socio-economic strata of the society. And both nations have sought to address the needs of these under-represented ethnic groups via certain forms of positive discrimination, labeled "affirmative action" in the US and "reservation policies" in India.

The policies of positive discrimination in favor of under-represented ethnic groups, enacted initially with strong public support, have proven increasingly controversial in both India and the US. In each country the debate over these policies has become sharper, as participants wrestle with the inherent tension between the individual right to equal treatment and the societal goal of overcoming profound inequalities of opportunity. And in each country the issue of positive discrimination looms large in the political arena and in the judicial system.

These similar circumstances suggest that much can be learned from comparative analysis of affirmative action in the US and reservation policies in India. There have indeed been quite a few such comparative studies published in recent decades.[1] For the most part these studies address the origins and the development of positive discrimination policies in each country, focusing on the political and judicial context in which the policies have taken shape over the years. Much less attention has been paid to assessing the consequences of positive discrimination policies. This is not surprising, for these consequences are multifaceted and generally very difficult to measure. Yet it is surely a matter of considerable importance to evaluate whether affirmative action policies in the US and reservation policies in India have in fact been achieving their objectives, or whether they have made matters worse – as the critics claim.

My approach to the analysis of positive discrimination policies is a pragmatic one, which recognizes that such policies are likely to have some good and some bad consequences. To evaluate a set of positive discrimination policies requires both a clear understanding of their potential consequences and a systematic investigation into the benefits and costs to which they give rise. For reasons that I will elucidate later, it is too much to expect that a comprehensive benefit-cost analysis can be carried out on any given policy of positive discrimination – much less on the whole gamut of such policies implemented in any country over a period of time – in such a way as to yield a clear-cut judgment about its success or failure. One can, however, make use of the logic of benefit-cost analysis to shed comparative light on how affirmative action in the US and reservation policies in India have been working. That is one of my main objectives in this book.

My second major objective is to provide a general model for the comparative analysis of positive discrimination policies, wherever they may be practiced. I believe that one can make real progress in the endless debates about affirmative action and reservation policies by putting the claims of proponents and opponents into a framework of balancing benefits and costs, by identifying claims capable of empirical testing, and by putting those claims to the test of empirical evidence. This means that one should be genuinely open-minded about the value of any given positive discrimination policy, prepared to change one's mind about it depending on what the evidence shows. It implies, too, that it is possible and desirable to fine-tune such a policy so that it attains the best possible results.

In Part I of this book I will describe the differing contexts for positive discrimination in the US and India; and I will analyze how these differing contexts can be expected to affect the prospects for the success of positive discrimination policies in the two countries. In so doing, I will develop a theoretical methodology for qualitative comparative analysis of positive discrimination policies. In Part II I will narrow my focus to one important sphere in which such policies have been implemented – admissions to higher educational institutions – and I will review and compare the evidence available from the US and India on the consequences of affirmative action and reservation policies in this sphere. I hope that in so doing I will provide a road map for dispassionate empirical assessment of the consequences of positive discrimination policies in any context. In the one chapter in Part III, which concludes this book, I will draw from my comparative analysis of the US and India some general lessons about the rationale for, and the optimal design of, positive discrimination policies.

Part I

The differing contexts and potential consequences of positive discrimination in the US and India

*My major objective in this part of the book is to analyze, in a systematically compara-
tive framework, the way in which differences in the social, cultural, economic, and
political contexts of the US and India are likely to affect the prospects for the success of
positive discrimination policies in the two countries. In order to address this question, I
begin in Chapter 1 by reviewing the historical development of the relevant policies in
each country. In Chapter 2 I discuss the debate over positive discrimination in each
country, which is helpful for understanding both the context and the potential consequences of positive discrimination in each country. I then go on in Chapter 3 to
organize the arguments advanced in such debates into a comprehensive list of arguments
and claims for and against positive discrimination, defining the potential benefits and
costs of positive discrimination policies in terms of claims of beneficial and costly consequences. In Chapter 4 I develop a model for qualitative comparative analysis of the
relationship between the context and the consequences of positive discrimination policies,
which I apply to the cases of the US and India in the following two chapters. I explore
in Chapter 5 key differences between the two countries in the context for positive
discrimination. Finally, I undertake in Chapter 6 an analysis of the way in which these
differences are likely to affect the comparative benefits and costs of positive discrimination policies in the US and India.*

The subject of positive discrimination is beset with much controversy and strong feelings. It is also beset with much misunderstanding, due in no small part to lack of clarity
in the meaning of key terms and concepts. Before proceeding to my substantive discussion and analysis, I believe that it will be helpful to define as clearly as possible how I
will use certain important terms that will recur throughout the book.

The meaning of "affirmative action" has evolved over time in the US. When
President John F. Kennedy first used the term in 1961,[1] he meant an affirmative
effort to assure equality of opportunity to all Americans and to end discrimination
against members of groups that had historically been exposed to a great deal of
discrimination – most obviously African Americans. Affirmative action policies in the
following years consisted of vigorous efforts to assure that no person would be denied
opportunities simply because of the group he or she happened to be born into. By the

late 1960s, however, affirmative action had come to mean stronger efforts in support of members of groups that had been (and were often continuing to be) discriminated against. More specifically, the term came to denote policies that provided a certain degree of preference, in processes of selection to desired positions, for members of groups that were under-represented in such positions. Such preference could come in the form of extra weight in a selection process or quotas to be filled with members of under-represented groups; in either case, the objective was to reduce the extent of their under-representation. Thus affirmative action came to encompass a form of discrimination in favor of under-represented groups, as opposed to an effort to abolish all forms of discrimination; and this is how the term continues to be understood today.

The meaning of "reservation policies" has not varied over time in India. This term has always been understood to denote the reserving of a certain number of seats or positions, in a desirable institution or occupation, for members of groups that were under-represented in such positions. Here too the underlying objective is to reduce the extent of the under-representation of these group members. It has always been clear that reservation policies involve an effort to discriminate in favor of members of such groups; such policies have also been labeled "compensatory discrimination" or "protective discrimination."

I will use the term "positive discrimination" to encompass the practice of preferential selection of members of under-represented groups to widely esteemed positions – in other words, when membership in such a group increases one's likelihood of being selected to such a position. Positive discrimination thus includes both affirmative action as practiced in the US and reservation policies as practiced in India.[2] Any kind of discrimination involves making distinctions between people according to their group membership and selecting members of a particular group for special attention. What makes discrimination "positive" is that it is designed to favor members of groups that are under-represented in widely esteemed positions and (hence) under-represented in the upper strata of their society. Positive discrimination is therefore a policy aiming at the inclusion *of members of groups whose members have gained relatively limited access to society's most esteemed positions. Negative discrimination, by contrast, denotes a policy of* exclusion *of members of such groups.*

There are various kinds of groups that might be deemed eligible for positive discrimination. In practice, however, positive discrimination policies are almost always oriented to (members of) an "identity group" – i.e. a group that is defined in terms of characteristics that are not a matter of voluntary choice, generally determined at birth, and rarely alterable or altered. The defining characteristics of an identity group are typically physical or cultural, such as "race,"[3] caste, tribe, ethnicity, and gender.[4] This is certainly true of the beneficiaries of affirmative action in the US and reservation policies in India.

Although positive discrimination policies have been implemented in favor of women in the US and – to a considerably lesser extent – in India,[5] I will confine my attention in this book to positive discrimination in favor of members of identity groups defined in ethnic terms (defined broadly to include race, caste, and tribe). Because the relationship between women and men is in important respects very different to that between under-represented and over-represented ethnic groups, the issues raised by gender-based positive discrimination are qualitatively different from those raised by ethnicity-based positive discrimination. I will use the term "under-represented ethnic group" to denote the kind of identity group that is the focus of my attention in this book. The groups of this kind that have been favored by affirmative action in the US are African Americans, Hispanic Americans, and Native Americans. In independent India the under-represented ethnic groups favored by reservation policies have included Dalits (the former "untouchables," officially classified as "Scheduled Castes"), Adivasis (tribal groups who generally live in somewhat remote geographical areas, officially classified as "Scheduled Tribes"), and a variety of "Other Backward Classes."

Members of any given under-represented ethnic group are identified as belonging to it according to certain physical and/or cultural characteristics that they inherit from their parents. Which physical or cultural characteristics determine membership in such a group is a matter of social construction: it depends upon the conventions of the larger society in which the group is embedded. Over the course of time the larger society sometimes redefines the boundaries of an under-represented ethnic group, thus changing the group identity of some individuals; but an individual is rarely in a position to change his/her own group identity by means of individual action. In some cases one may disguise or misrepresent one's group identity, but always at the risk of discovery. The permanence of group identity contrasts with the malleability of socio-economic status. A poor and uneducated child may be able, through hard work and/or good fortune, to rise later in life to a high position in society; but an African American or a Dalit will virtually always remain an African American or a Dalit throughout his/her lifetime.

1 On the origins and nature of positive discrimination policies in the US and India

I begin this chapter by reviewing briefly the historical origins of positive discrimination in each of the two countries. Then I go on to compare the nature, the legal basis, and the scope of current policies of positive discrimination in the US and India. Finally, I consider possible cultural and historical sources of the differences in these policies as between the two countries.

A brief history of positive discrimination policies in the US

Contemporary positive discrimination (PD) policies in the US owe their origin to the Civil Rights Movement of the 1950s and early 1960s.[1] Some preferential policies on behalf of emancipated Blacks[2] – former slaves – were enacted during the Reconstruction Era immediately following the Civil War; but this brief effort to restructure the racial balance of power in the South was soon abandoned, and the "Jim Crow" era of White domination took over with a vengeance. For almost 100 years after slavery had been formally abolished, all kinds of negative discrimination and related injustices were imposed upon formally free African Americans – then known as "Negroes" – throughout the South. In the North, Blacks did not suffer quite so many indignities, but their lot was generally poor, and they were largely ignored by the White population. By the middle of the twentieth century, after Blacks had played important roles in two world war victories, and many Blacks had migrated from the rural agricultural South to northern industrial cities, American society was forced to come to terms with its continuing mistreatment of the Black population.

In the years following the Second World War growing numbers of Blacks (as well as sympathetic Whites) rallied to the cause of the Civil Rights Movement, which called for an end to the injustices perpetrated against Blacks (especially, but not exclusively, in the South) and for the participation of Blacks in American society as full citizens. The struggle to achieve these goals was led by the Reverend Martin Luther King, Jr., whose effective strategy of civil disobedience and non-violent resistance was inspired by that of Mahatma Gandhi in the struggle for Indian independence. By the late

1950s and early 1960s, the Civil Rights Movement succeeded in prodding the US federal government into taking action against the segregation of Blacks into inferior schools and public facilities and providing Blacks with access to rights and opportunities that had long been denied them because of their racial identity. Following the example set by Blacks, other under-represented ethnic groups – such as Hispanic Americans and Native Americans – began to mobilize in the late 1960s and early 1970s to push for an end to various forms of discrimination that they faced in American society.

The most important legislative step in response to the Civil Rights Movement was the 1964 Civil Rights Act, championed by President Lyndon B. Johnson and passed by both Houses of Congress in the wake of the assassination of President John F. Kennedy. This Act, based on the Equal Protection Clause of the US Constitution, formally outlawed discriminatory practices in almost all public – as opposed to personal or private – spheres of American life. The Civil Rights Act was followed by a series of executive orders, issued by the Johnson Administration, to promote equal opportunity in employment and education. It was hoped and expected that the assertion of formal legal equality of all citizens, the removal of overtly discriminatory barriers, and a much wider diffusion of relevant information would lead to significant increases in the representation of Blacks and other under-represented minority groups in desirable jobs and educational institutions. In this context the term "affirmative action" was applied to active outreach efforts made by organizations and enterprises to assure that members of under-represented groups would have the same kind of access to jobs and educational opportunities as their more advantaged fellow citizens – without any regard for their ethnic status.

The legal authority for affirmative action in its original form was embedded in Titles VI and VII of the Civil Rights Act of 1964. These two titles ban discrimination (whether negative or positive), on grounds of race, color, religion, sex, or national origin, in federally assisted activities and in employment, respectively. To reinforce these provisions President Johnson issued Executive Order No. 11246, which directed government contractors to actively seek out Black candidates for jobs, and called for colleges and universities to recruit more Black students and faculty members, "without treating them differently when making actual decisions." The Order also created the Office of Federal Contract Compliance Program to monitor and enforce the policy directive.

It soon became apparent, however, that affirmative action of this kind would not have an immediate and significant impact on the numbers of Blacks in most professions and educational institutions in which they had always been greatly under-represented (in proportion to their population). There was much debate over the extent to which the continuing under-representation was due to continuing (if on the whole subtler) forms of discrimination against Blacks, as opposed to lack of sufficient qualifications for specific positions. On the premise that the former was indeed a significant part of the problem, the US Labor Department began to measure progress in ending discrimination in terms of quantitative increases in the percentage of Blacks in various fields and work forces. Public organizations, as well as non-profit institutions and private companies supported by or otherwise linked to the federal government, came under pressure to increase the representation of Blacks in order to demonstrate that they were operating in a non-discriminatory manner. Such pressure increased as courts began to accept statistical information on the low percentage of Blacks employed, in relation to their proportion of the population presumably qualified for a position, as evidence of racial discrimination.

By the late 1960s these developments had led many government agencies, as well as some private organizations, to discriminate in favor of Black candidates for jobs or contracts. Such positive discrimination most often took the form of giving some degree of preference – in relation to traditional or conventional qualification criteria – to Black candidates in order to overcome their under-representation. In some cases, efforts were made to fill target quotas of Black representation or to set aside a certain fraction of contracts for Black-owned firms. Moreover, many educational institutions – both public and private – and some other non-profit organizations sought to increase the representation of Blacks by applying preferences in admission or selection. During the 1970s such preferences were generally extended to members of other under-represented ethnic groups as well – notably Hispanic Americans and Native Americans. In this context the term "affirmative action" (AA) took on a new meaning – which it has retained ever since – of positive discrimination in favor of under-represented groups.

Federal government measures, issued both by President Johnson's Administration (1963–8) and by President Richard M. Nixon's Administration (1968–74), helped to spur the transition from the original to the stronger form of affirmative action in the sphere of employment. For example, in 1971 the US Labor Department issued regulations directing government contractors to adopt "goals and timetables" to hire minorities and women, and it announced that it would soon impose mandatory racial hiring quotas on certain federally sponsored construction projects. In the late 1960s and early 1970s the federal courts were also supportive of strong AA efforts. In 1970 a federal district court established the legitimacy of quotas as a way of implementing Executive Order No. 11246; and in 1971 the Supreme Court ruled that an employer could not require certain minimum credentials before hiring a person if such a requirement had the effect of a "built-in headwind" for minorities. In the sphere of education, the application of AA preferences in admissions, to increase the numbers of students from under-represented groups, was not so much a response to government or court action in support of such policies. Rather, such practices were undertaken voluntarily by educational leaders and administrators, in a political climate resounding with calls to reduce racial and ethnic inequalities.

Since the early 1970s AA policies have increasingly been contested, and disputes over affirmative action have frequently been adjudicated in court. As the political and judicial climate of the country shifted in a more conservative direction, federal government agencies became less assiduous in promoting affirmative action and a series of US Supreme Court rulings gradually narrowed the permissible scope of AA policies.[3] In the employment sphere, quotas have been ruled out; and other forms of preferences have been deemed permissible only if narrowly tailored to offset discriminatory practices by the same organization or enterprise.

In the sphere of admissions to educational institutions, the most critical AA court case until recently was that of Alan Bakke.[4] Bakke sued the University of California at Davis Medical School for denying him admission even though his conventional academic qualifications were superior to those of many admitted Black students. The Supreme Court issued its decision on the Bakke case in 1978, ruling out the use of quotas in admissions but allowing the use of other forms of preference for students from particular racial/ethnic groups – provided that the institution has a compelling interest in a racially/ethnically diverse student body as a means of carrying out its educational mission and that race/ethnicity is only one of many factors taken into account in the admissions process. The support that this ruling provided for affirmative action in educational admissions was tenuous, because it rested on the solo opinion of Justice Lewis Powell; the rest of the Court was split 4–4 between justices who favored stronger preferences for racial/ethnic minority groups and justices who opposed any such preferences.

The Bakke ruling enabled educational institutions to continue to apply AA preferences in admissions, and most selective colleges and universities did so. From the mid-1990s on, however, some university regental actions, a few state referenda, and several federal lower-court rulings struck down affirmative action in educational admissions – on the grounds that not just quotas but also other ways of preferring applicants from particular racial/ethnic groups violate the Equal Protection Clause of the 14th amendment to the US Constitution (banning discrimination on the basis of race, national origin, religion, or sex) as well as the related Titles VI and VII of the 1964 Civil Rights Act. Two lawsuits filed against AA admission polices at the University of Michigan (UM) in 1997 were ultimately taken up by the US Supreme Court for a definitive ruling on the future of affirmative action in educational admissions in the US.

In June 2003 the US Supreme Court issued its long-awaited decisions on the Michigan cases.[5] The Court voted 5–4 in favor of the system of admissions preferences for under-represented minorities utilized by the UM Law School and 6–3 against the system used by the UM undergraduate admissions office. Speaking for the majority in the Law School case, Justice Sandra Day O'Connor argued forcefully that the nation has a compelling interest in promoting racial/ethnic diversity among students at selective higher educational institutions, and that the Law School's procedures for granting preferences to under-represented minority applicants – involving holistic and individualized consideration of every application – were appropriately narrowly tailored to achieve that end. On the other hand, a Court majority (including Justice O'Connor) found that the procedures used by the UM undergraduate admissions office to increase the racial/ethnic diversity of the student body were too mechanistic and formulaic to pass muster. The main impact of these rulings was to provide a firm judicial basis for the practice of affirmative action in US colleges and universities, reinforcing the rather tenuous support provided for the previous twenty-five years by Justice Powell's solo opinion in the 1978 Bakke case.

A brief history of PD policies in India

The history of PD policies goes back much further in India than in the US.[6] It begins in the late nineteenth and early twentieth centuries, with the development of organized movements, especially in the southern part of India, designed to reduce the power of Brahmans. Although they constituted only about 3 per cent of the population in these areas, Brahmans dominated those elite positions – in the civil service and in related professions – that were open to Indians under British colonial rule. The anti-Brahman movements led to increasing pressure to establish reserved seats for non-Brahmans in public service and also to provide aid for non-Brahmans in educational institutions. The non-Brahman communities included relatively well-off upper-caste Hindus as well as members of various religious and ethnic minority communities and Hindu outcastes (the then "untouchables"). Not surprisingly, the non-Brahman movements were generally led by members of the better-off communities and oriented to their interests, as distinct from those of the poorest groups. These latter, including India's aboriginal tribal groups as well as the Hindu outcastes, were commonly labeled "the depressed classes."

In the 1920s the pressure for positive discrimination in favor of non-Brahmans was translated into action in the Princely State of Mysore as well as in the Bombay and Madras Presidencies (directly controlled by the British). The Mysore Government in 1921 instituted a system of reserved places in public service positions and in higher educational admissions for "backward communities," defined as all but the Brahman community. Similar reservations (for a slightly less extensive grouping of "backward communities") were introduced in Bombay in 1925. The most systematic effort to redistribute access to elite positions was undertaken in Madras by the anti-Brahman Justice Party, which used its political strength after local elections to get British approval for government orders classifying public servants according to community and allocating new public service appointments and promotions so as to increase substantially the representation of various non-Brahman communities. In 1926 specific quotas were established for public appointments, according to which every fifteen appointments should be allocated as follows: two to Brahmans, two to "backward" (i.e. low-caste) Hindus, six to other Hindus, two to "depressed" (i.e. untouchable) castes, two to Anglo-Indians and Christians, and one to a Muslim.

In the 1930s, reservation policies were implemented in the political arena throughout British India. A new round of major constitutional reforms had come under discussion in the late 1920s and the early 1930s, as the colonial authorities sought to establish a federal assembly, as well as provincial assemblies, to which Indians would elect representatives whose leaders would exercise substantially expanded powers under overall British rule. The British proposed, and the Indian nationalist movement led by Mahatma Gandhi ultimately accepted (grudgingly), the establishment of separate electorates and seats for four of India's minority communities: Muslims, Christians, Sikhs, and Anglo-Indians. Dr. B.R. Ambedkar, who had risen to prominence as the greatly revered leader of India's untouchables, strongly advocated the same arrangement for the untouchable community. Gandhi was totally opposed to any kind of separation of the "Harijans" (literally "people of God," a term Gandhi coined for the untouchables) from the rest of the Hindu community. The two leaders struggled intensely over this issue, but they ultimately agreed to a compromise (the 1932 "Poona Pact") in which there would indeed be reserved seats for the depressed classes in the federal and provincial legislatures, but candidates for these seats would be elected by general electorates rather than by separate untouchable electorates. This compromise was incorporated into the Government of India Act of 1935, which established the new federal and provincial assemblies. The Act established a system of reserved seats, but not separate electorates, for two communities – the untouchables and the tribals, now officially labeled "Scheduled Castes" (SCs) and "Scheduled Tribes" (STs).

The raised consciousness of the untouchables – and, to a lesser extent, the tribals – had led them by this time to part ways with the better-off caste of Hindus in the non-Brahman movements and to call for a variety of measures designed to end the particularly oppressive discrimination and remedy the related injustices they had suffered over the centuries. The Indian provincial governments that came into power in 1937 maintained and, in some cases, expanded previously enacted reservations in public service jobs and educational admissions for religious minority groups and for depressed classes; additional special measures were also adopted to aid the latter. At the federal level, however, reservations were adopted only in the public services and only for religious minorities.

After India became independent in 1947 (and the separate nation of Pakistan was formed from many of the Muslim-majority areas of British-controlled India), the issue of reservations came to the fore in the context of the drafting of the Indian Constitution. The establishment of India as a secular state undermined the case for continuation of the reservations for religious minorities introduced under the British. Jawaharlal Nehru, as well as most of the other leaders of the Indian National Congress that had won independence, were committed to improving the lot of India's impoverished masses; but they were opposed to group-based reservations as a means of accomplishing this.[7] However, Nehru named B.R. Ambedkar as law minister and chairman of the constitution-drafting committee of the Constituent Assembly; and from that position Ambedkar was able to press for a constitutional basis for reservations favoring India's SCs.

In the end, the Indian Constitution that came into force in 1950 (and subsequent amendments) proved to be highly ambivalent about the role of positive discrimination. On the one hand, drawing on the spirit, if not the letter, of the US Constitution and its amendments, the Indian Constitution provides for fundamental rights such as the guarantee to all citizens of equality before the law (Article 14), the prohibition of discrimination on grounds of religion, race, caste, sex, or place of birth (Article 15), and the assurance of equality of opportunity in matters of public employment (Article 16). On the other hand, the same Constitution also includes − as a "Directive Principle of State Policy" − the oft-quoted Article 46:

> The State shall promote with special care the educational and economic interests of the weaker sections of the people and, in particular, of the Scheduled Castes and the Scheduled Tribes, and shall protect them from social injustice and all forms of exploitation.

Pursuant to this directive, there are a series of provisions that allow for positive discrimination in favor of members of under-represented groups − as detailed below.

In the political sphere, the framers of the Constitution dropped the notion that religious minority communities deserved any kind of special status; but they retained the system of reserved seats (with common electorates) for SCs and STs that had first been established by the Government of India Act of 1935.[8] Articles 330, 332, and 334 of the Constitution of 1950 require that a certain number of parliamentary constituencies, both at the national and at the provincial level, be represented by an SC member, elected by all eligible voters in the constituency, with the number of reserved seats proportional to the SC population in the constituency; and likewise for STs. Article 331 limits the period of such reservations to twenty years; but, in the event, the reservations have been regularly extended by amendment for additional ten-year periods.

In the sphere of employment, the Constitution's apparent general ban on discrimination in public service jobs is qualified by Section 4 of the relevant Article 16, which permits the state to make "any provision for the reservations of appointments or posts in favour of any backward class of citizens which, in the opinion of the State, is not adequately represented in the services under the State." Moreover, Article 335 asserts that "the claims of the SCs and STs shall be taken into consideration, consistent with the maintenance of efficiency of administration"; and it calls for the central government to reserve for SCs and STs a certain percentage of jobs in the civil and technical services, in state-run and semi-autonomous enterprises, and in private as well as public technical institutions.

In the arena of education, the Constitution originally banned any kind of discrimination in government-aided educational institutions (Section 2 of Article 29). Following two early Supreme Court decisions rejecting discrimination in educational admissions, however, the Constitution was amended in 1951 to add a new provision to Article 15. The new Section 4 qualified the Article's general declaration of non-discrimination by explicitly asserting that nothing in the Constitution "shall prevent the State from making any special provision for the advancement of any socially and educationally backward classes of citizens or for the Scheduled Castes and Scheduled Tribes."

Thus in independent India since 1950 there has been a clear constitutional basis for positive discrimination in favor of backward groups, defined to include explicitly SCs and STs and potentially other "weaker sections" or "backward classes" as well. Reserved seats for SC and ST members in elective legislative bodies are mandated, whereas reservations in employment and education are authorized and indeed encouraged. The latter kind of reservations were enacted by some pre-independence provincial and local governments, mostly in the South and generally in favor of a broad range of non-Brahman castes and minority religious groups. Such reservations were maintained by post-independence authorities only in the states of Madras and Mysore (now Tamilnadu and Karnataka, respectively). What is qualitatively new in the post-independence era is that employment and educational reservations in favor of SCs and STs, in particular, have been introduced at both the central government and the state government level throughout India. To promote and enforce these reservations, as well as to oversee various related forms of aid to these communities, the office of Commissioner of Scheduled Castes and Tribes was established in government administrations at the central and state levels. The central government is also enjoined (by Article 275) to provide separate allocations in national development plans for the improvement of the SC and ST communities.

Identification of which groups to include among the SCs and STs, officially eligible for reservations, has not been unproblematic.[9] To implement the related provisions of the Government of India Act of 1935, lists of officially scheduled castes and scheduled tribes were drawn up in 1936 on the basis of information collected in the 1931 census of India about respondents' ethnic and/or caste status and about the kinds of disadvantages associated with different ethnic and caste communities. In principle, SCs were to be identified as communities that were backward because of untouchability, defined essentially in terms of their ritually "polluting" status in Hindu society. There was also an admixture of economic and educational criteria, as well as some consideration of local politics; and it was generally the socio-economically lowest groups of Hindus in any given area who were ultimately included in the SC list. The designation of STs was less problematic; spatial and cultural isolation was the key, and these characteristics were closely correlated with socio-economic backwardness. The 1936 lists of SCs and STs were largely duplicated in independent India, with some minor additions (e.g. to include a few "backward" Sikh and neo-Buddhist castes) in the early 1950s and at several times thereafter.

Reservations in political assemblies, though originally considered temporary, have become for all intents and purposes permanent in contemporary India. There is no serious controversy about this. Reservations in educational admissions and public employment, however, have become much more controversial. The impetus for the heightened contention has come not so much from the SC and ST reservations, in particular, as from efforts to expand the range of reservations granted to "Other Backward Classes" (OBCs). As noted above, in a few parts of southern India many OBCs had long been favored by forms of positive education in employment and education. National reservations for OBCs were rejected by the ruling Congress Party Government in 1961; but state governments were given the discretion to grant reservations to groups they deemed deserving.[10] As SC and ST reservations became more firmly established, more and more low- and even middle-caste Hindus began to agitate for similar reservations on the grounds that their communities were no less socio-economically disadvantaged than those benefiting from positive discrimination. Their demands met with some positive responses at the state level in the 1970s, but they were not seriously entertained at the national level until the publication in early 1981 of the report of the Mandal Commission.[11]

The Mandal Commission was appointed in 1978 by the then ruling Janata Party (the first non-Congress Party to win a national election), which catered to agitation by lower-caste Hindus for more reservations. The Commission was directed to consider the matter of extending reservations to OBCs at the national level, along the lines of the reservations already granted to SCs (15 per cent of the population) and STs (7.5 per cent of the population). In its report the Commission recommended that OBCs be granted employment reservations in central government services and public sector undertakings (e.g. public enterprises and educational institutions). The Commission also recommended a series of measures designed to upgrade the education of OBC students, but it called for reserved seats for OBC students only in scientific, technical, and professional institutions. On the basis of a complex combination of social, educational, and economic criteria, the Commission classified as OBC sub-groups not only a great number of lower-caste Hindu sub-castes but also a substantial number of Muslim sub-groups and other religious/ethnic minority communities, amounting to an estimated 52 per cent of the Indian population.[12] Because prior Supreme Court rulings had set a limit of 50 per cent on national reservations, however, the Commission recommended that reservations be extended only to the (most deserving) OBCs amounting to 27 per cent of the population – bringing the overall percentage of reserved seats in public employment to 49.5 per cent.

The Mandal Commission report gathered dust for a decade, as the Janata Party lost power in national elections and subsequent Congress Party administrations (under Indira Gandhi and Rajiv Gandhi) showed no interest in pursuing the matter. In August 1990, however, Prime Minister V.P. Singh – prime minister of a shaky new coalition government led by the populist Janata Dal – stunned the nation by announcing that his government would actually implement the recommendations of the Mandal Commission. This announcement set off a firestorm of demonstrative opposition – including riots in the streets as well as some self-immolations – mainly in the northern regions of India, where many middle- and upper-caste Hindus were adamantly opposed to any extension of reservations. In the face of the continuing uproar, the Singh Administration decided not to push through the entire set of Mandal recommendations; but it did propose to implement the principal recommendation to extend reservations in central government services and public sector undertakings to OBCs. This plan was challenged in the courts and ultimately resolved in November 1992 by the Indian Supreme Court, which ruled in favor of employment reservations at the national level for OBCs amounting to 27 per cent of the population.[13]

The significant negative response to V.P. Singh's Mandal announcement in 1990 contrasts sharply with the general acceptance of plans for SC and ST reservations in the early 1950s. The reasons for the difference in reactions are many, but the following are among the most important. First, OBC members were more likely than SC or ST members to be able to fill positions reserved for them in the most desirable institutions, so they were a greater competitive threat to high-caste Hindus (especially in the North, where state-level reservations for OBCs had not proceeded very far). Secondly, in the 1950s the Congress Party was in full control of the central government as well as most state governments, and its (predominantly Brahman) leadership was widely respected, whereas in the 1990s government power was divided among a variety of parties at the central and state levels, many of which owed their political strength to the mobilization of lower castes included among the OBCs.

Although opposition to the extension of reservations remains widespread – especially among the Indian elite, including many political leaders – none of India's political parties are prepared to alienate the various groups of voters supporting reservations by publicly opposing them. As a consequence, the Mandal recommendations for employment reservations at the central government level have been increasingly put into effect since the Supreme Court ruling in 1992.

Previously established reservation policies in employment and education remain firmly in place in contemporary India. While the Mandal controversy focused the spotlight on reservations for OBCs, some new light was inevitably cast as well on the issue of reservations for SCs and STs. Support for the continuation of employment and educational reservations for SCs and STs is no longer as widespread as it was several decades ago; but few Indians – and no politicians – advocate their termination.

The current state of PD policies in the US and India

It is clear from the foregoing that the nature as well as the origins of positive discrimination in the US and India are very different. Reservation policies in India have a longer history, and they have become both deeper (more interventionist) and broader (affecting more societal arenas) than AA policies in the US.[14]

In the US, AA policies now generally take the form of preferential boosts, which improve the competitive position of eligible candidates, rather than quotas, which reserve seats or opportunities for such candidates. In the early decades of affirmative action, however, quotas were sometimes used. The size of the preferential boost extended to eligible candidates has varied widely, from modest to quite substantial. In India, positive discrimination has from the beginning taken mainly the form of reserved seats or positions, to which eligible candidates can gain access without competing with candidates from non-eligible groups. Moreover, in India beneficiary groups are often entitled to their proportion of reserved seats or positions over and above the number that they gain in open competition;[15] so reservations establish a minimum desired percentage of representation. However, in many cases reserved seats and positions go unfilled, because of a lack of eligible candidates who meet established minimum qualifications.

In the US, government actors played the key role in initiating affirmative action in the 1960s; but since then non-governmental organizations have played an increasingly important role in extending its scope. Because affirmative action is not addressed – much less mandated – in the US Constitution, the range of allowable AA practices has been wholly dependent on judicial opinions; these in turn are influenced by the general political climate and, more specifically, by pressures from groups favoring or opposing positive discrimination.

In India, by contrast, reservation policies are much more firmly grounded on a constitutional basis – even though the authorization of preferences for particular groups coexists uneasily with the Indian Constitution's general affirmation of individual freedom, equal opportunity, and non-discrimination. Much more than in the US, the impetus for positive discrimination in India has come from governmental actors. Reservations are mandated from above by the central and state governments; they are often resisted by lower-level public sector institutions, and they are virtually absent in private sector institutions. Many of the details of reservation policies are dependent on judicial interpretation of the Constitution, so the Indian courts have played a significant role in shaping the way in which these policies are implemented – but not in determining whether they can exist at all. As a practical matter, both in India and the US, the strength of the commitment to PD policies tends to depend on the vigilance of beneficiary groups and pressures from their political representatives.

In both the US and India, PD policies have been applied in the spheres of employment and education, and in both countries these are the spheres in which such policies are most contentious. In the US, affirmative action in employment is practiced not only by public sector agencies and organizations but also by many non-profit institutions and many private enterprises, whether or not they are dependent on government funding. The implementation of some non-governmental AA policies is conducted under pressure from government authorities (or in order to avoid legal liability for discrimination); but some of it is due to voluntary efforts on the part of organizational and business leaders to increase the representation of minority groups in their ranks. Even more so in the sphere of admissions to educational institutions, AA practices in the US are due to decentralized voluntary actions rather than to governmental mandate or pressure: many educational administrators (in both private and state schools) have embraced the goal of increasing the representation of under-represented minority groups in their institutions, and they often utilize preferential AA policies in an effort to achieve this goal.

In the Indian case, reservations in jobs and in educational admissions are mandated throughout most of the public sector – including government services, government enterprises, and government-controlled colleges and universities – with just a few exceptions (e.g. in key strategic areas such as national defense).[16] On the other hand, reservation policies do not apply at all to private enterprises, and the Indian private sector has never been concerned about minority group representation. The fact that non-governmental policies of positive discrimination are important in the US but virtually non-existent in India does not mean that the scope of positive discrimination is greater in the US. To the contrary: because the public sector looms much larger in India, the reach of positive discrimination in employment and education is proportionately at least as broad in India as in the US.

In both the US and India, positive discrimination in educational admissions is practiced mainly at the level of higher education – though it can be found at a few (relatively elite) secondary schools as well. Moreover, it is mainly at the more selective and prestigious higher educational institutions that PD preferences are systematically applied; at lower levels of the higher educational hierarchy there is generally room enough to admit all interested and minimally qualified applicants. Along with preferential boosts or reserved seats for under-represented ethnic minority groups, many colleges and universities in both countries make available various forms of aid – such as scholarships, subsidized living quarters and meals, special programs, and textbook loans. In India this kind of aid comes almost entirely from government sources, since most educational institutions are funded by government at the central or state level. In the US, private contributions play a major role in such funding.

The scope of reservations in India extends also to the political domain: seats are reserved for candidates from eligible groups in central and state legislative assemblies, in constituencies where those groups form a relatively significant (though still a minority) part of the population. These reserved seats have unquestionably enabled Dalits and Adivasis to gain far more positions of political power than would otherwise have been possible; and this represents a significant advance for these marginalized groups.[17] In the US there are no such reserved seats, nor any kind of AA preferences for minority candidates. There has been, however, court-sanctioned pressure for electoral districts to be defined geographically in such a way that in areas where minorities are concentrated, they will be able to vote together in a single district rather than having their votes split among several adjoining districts (where minority voters would form a much smaller proportion of the electorate).

Positive discrimination plays a greater role in India than in the US not only in that it is more interventionist (reserved seats rather than preferential boosts) and broader in scope (including the political arena as well as employment and education). It is also the case that the proportion of the population represented by ethnic groups eligible for positive discrimination is greater in India than in the US. The primary Indian beneficiaries are the SCs (now more commonly referred to as Dalits) and the STs (or Adivasis),[18] who now constitute about 16 per cent and 8 per cent of the Indian population, respectively.[19] But a substantial population belonging to OBCs, defined differently in different areas, is in many states also eligible for reservations in public sector employment and in admissions to higher educational institutions. Since the adoption of some of the Mandal Commission recommendations, OBCs amounting to roughly 27 per cent of the population are now eligible for employment reservations at the all-India level too. Thus roughly 50 per cent of the population in India is now eligible for reservations of one kind or another; though the proportion of the population with reserved legislative seats will remain a little below 25 per cent for the foreseeable future.

In the US, Blacks were the first beneficiaries of affirmative action (in the 1960s). Since the 1970s, however, the beneficiary ethnic groups have usually included also Hispanic Americans and Native Americans. These groups represent (as of the year 2000) roughly 12, 12, and 1 per cent of the total US population, respectively.[20] Taken together, their proportion of the population is close to that of the SCs and STs in India – but much less than that of the SCs, STs, and OBCs combined.

Whereas the designation of beneficiary groups in India is fixed by governmental authority, in the US it is often decentralized to non-governmental organizations and enterprises, who make their own judgments about which groups are under-represented and deserve AA preferences. In the US, certification of individual beneficiary status depends simply on self-identification (which is rarely challenged). In India, certification of beneficiary status is an official government process, handled by officials in the locality where the individual was born and/or raised.

Sources of the differences in PD policies in the US and India

A distinguished Indian sociologist has contrasted the origins of India's reservation policies with the origins of the US's AA policies as follows: "What took about 200 years to make a tentative appearance in the US emerged fully articulated and theorized almost at the instant that India became a sovereign and democratic nation-state" (Gupta 2000: 99). This is perhaps a bit of an exaggeration, inasmuch as there was an important prehistory of Indian reservation policies during the last half-century of British rule. It is certainly true, however, that India was constitutionally and politically much more deeply committed to such policies at the time it gained independence than the US has been at any time. The differences in the nature and scope of positive discrimination in the US and India are understandable in light of the very different cultural and historical backgrounds of the two societies.

The US is a country whose dominant social and political culture has always been strongly oriented to individual rights and responsibilities. Although its citizens have come from many different ethnic backgrounds, and often still identify strongly with their community of origin, Americans typically see themselves as constituting a nation in which the most important characteristic of a person is his/her individuality and not his/her community. Efforts to spur collective action of any kind, and especially to press claims on behalf of an ethnic community, have typically encountered suspicion, if not outright hostility; only under unusual historical circumstances have such efforts succeeded in making some headway.

Positive discrimination in favor of under-represented ethnic groups thus clearly cuts against the American grain. It could only have been brought about on a significant scale under special conditions demanding attention to a group cause. Indeed, affirmative action arose in the US in the 1960s in response to the broad and compelling grass-roots Civil Rights Movement. By focusing attention on the egregious pattern of social injustice done to African Americans, the collective actions of the Civil Rights Movement forced the nation and its leaders to recognize and respond to the claims of African Americans, not only as individuals, but ultimately also as a group. The success of African Americans in achieving AA preferences provided a model for Hispanic Americans and Native Americans, in turn, to press successfully their claims for AA preferences in the 1970s.

In Indian society, in contrast to that of the US, groups or communities defined in ethnic or religious terms have always been highly salient. Community identity has for most of India's history been more important than individual identity; and even now that remains true for a substantial majority of Indians. Concern for one's community is second nature, and collective action to promote community interests is commonplace. The salience of community identity – and therefore also community rights – can be attributed to the highly multicultural nature of Indian society and to its complex stratification into different groups over a very long historical period of time. The stratification is multidimensional. Cultural, linguistic, and/or religious differences stratify the society horizontally. The caste system – whose influence extends well beyond Hindu society to minority religions as well – stratifies the society vertically (as well as horizontally). Moreover, the "divide and rule" policies of the British colonial authorities accentuated and aggravated some of the most important differences among communities (notably those between Hindus and Muslims, which led to the partition of British India). Thus group differentiation, and not infrequently discrimination, has long been the norm in India.

In this context, it is not surprising that positive discrimination – in the strong form of reservation policies – became an important means by which Indian leaders responded to pressures to improve the lot of the disadvantaged. In the US, the first group to press successfully for positive discrimination was the minority group that had suffered most from negative discrimination. In India, it was a large coalition of groups, neither at the top nor at the bottom of the socio-economic scale, who formed non-Brahman movements in the South and successfully pressed for better opportunities vis-à-vis the dominant Brahmans.

The most downtrodden of India's ethnic groups – the Dalits and the Adivasis – did not have the means to organize a grass-roots movement comparable to that of Blacks in the US. Instead, an absolutely critical role was played by Dr. Ambedkar. His leadership capacity and strong personality enabled him to bring the plight of the untouchables forcefully to the attention of both the British colonial authorities and the Indian nationalist leaders. The influence of Ambedkar, combined with the determination of such Congress Party leaders as Jawaharlal Nehru to address profound socio-economic inequalities in Indian society, and the example of earlier reservations on behalf of non-Brahmans, led to the constitutionally based establishment of reservations in favor of the SCs and STs.

Representatives of India's OBCs did not do so well at the constitutional table, for many reasons. They were regionally divided rather than nationally based, they lacked a commanding leader like Ambedkar, and there was no clear way of limiting the proportion of the Indian population included in their constituencies. Thus the (predominantly upper-caste) Congress Party leadership held off additional reservations for OBCs – until the Congress Party began to lose political power, first at the state and then at the central level, to rival regional parties with strong political bases among the lower castes. Such parties provided the impetus first for the expansion of OBC reservations in many states and then for the implementation of Mandal Commission recommendations for OBC reservations at the national level.

2 The debate over positive discrimination in the US and in India

When policies of positive discrimination in favor of under-represented ethnic groups were first introduced in (independent) India and in the US, they enjoyed a great deal of public support. Over time the extent of the opposition has grown significantly in each country; positive discrimination has become an increasingly controversial issue and the subject of increasingly heated debate.

In this chapter I begin by reviewing in more detail the evolution of public opinion about affirmative action in the US and reservation policies in India. Then I go on to explore the particular arguments that have been made by proponents of positive discrimination (PD) policies, and those that have been advanced by opponents of these policies, in each country. In discussing the arguments made for and against positive discrimination, I will necessarily refer primarily to what people have written about the topic, i.e. what members of each society's elite have to say. Precisely because they express their views in writing, however, these elite are influential in shaping public opinion. Finally, I offer some observations about how and why the debate in each country about positive discrimination has changed over time. In this chapter – and in the rest of the book – I will focus attention on PD policies in the spheres of employment and education, where positive discrimination has proved to be most controversial.

Public opinion on positive discrimination in each country

In the early years after India gained independence there was clearly a great deal of public support for reservations in favor of Scheduled Castes (SCs) and Scheduled Tribes (STs). The idea of reserving places for members of disadvantaged groups, as a way of doing justice to those groups, had been legitimized and popularized during the British Raj. The extent to which positive discrimination was embedded in the constitution of independent India, in tension with its commitment to individual liberty, testifies to the degree of support it enjoyed.

The political leaders and constitution-makers of the Indian nationalist movement were mostly from the upper castes and in many ways rather elitist in outlook. Their institutionalization of reservation policies in favor of the most under-represented groups – the Dalits and Adivasis – was not merely a matter of *noblesse oblige* in response to demands from below. They recognized that the strength of India as a nation would depend partly on its ability to bring together people from vastly different ethnic and socio-economic backgrounds, and they saw positive discrimination in favor of the most under-represented groups as a way to accelerate this process. In articulating these objectives they not only responded to but also helped to strengthen popular support for the idea that India's former "untouchables" and "tribals" – unquestionably the most victimized and disadvantaged groups in the Indian population – should receive special consideration.

At the time of independence, popular support of special consideration for other under-represented groups was by no means so widespread. This is reflected in the fact that the Indian Constitution is much vaguer about the appropriateness of positive discrimination for such groups, and in the fact that no reservations for any groups other than Dalits or Adivasis were adopted at the all-India level. Reservations for "Other Backward Classes" (OBCs) at the state level enjoyed strong support among their beneficiary communities; but they also elicited strong opposition among the non-beneficiary communities most directly affected.

In the US, policies of positive discrimination were introduced in a far less explicit manner than in India. The process whereby the term "affirmative action" (AA) came to denote policies that granted preferences to members of under-represented groups was for the most part obscure to the general public, for it involved a series of little-publicized decisions by government officials and non-governmental administrators – notably in colleges and universities. Only by the early 1970s, after some of these decisions came to be tested in the courts, did the general public begin to become aware of the meaning and significance of affirmative action.

Public opinion about positive discrimination in the US has always been divided, but it is probable that, at least until the late 1970s, a majority of the American general public supported the kind of AA policies that were then being implemented. It was significant – as a barometer of public opinion – that the administration of President Richard Nixon, elected as a Republican highly critical of policies pursued by his Democratic predecessor, Lyndon Johnson, chose to continue and even to strengthen the AA policies that had been introduced under President Johnson. To be sure, voices opposed to these policies could always be heard – even among members of the beneficiary groups, the great majority of whom have supported affirmative action from the beginning. AA policies never enjoyed in the US the kind of society-wide positive consensus that characterized reservation policies for Dalits and Adivasis in India; but affirmative action resonated with a majority of Americans as an appropriate response to the past injustices and current disadvantages suffered by Blacks in particular and Hispanic and Native Americans as well.

In both India and the US, controversy over positive discrimination – and opposition to it – began to grow in the late 1970s. In India, political pressures for reservations on behalf of previously excluded OBCs had been gradually mounting in various states, and they burst upon the national scene with the publication of the Mandal Commission report in early 1981. The extension of reservations to new groups was vigorously opposed by most high-caste Hindus, concerned that any new reservations would come at their expense. Moreover, India's intellectual elite – writing in English-language newspapers and periodicals – increasingly addressed the reservations issue and, for the most part, deplored its extension. Support for the extension of reservations remained strong, however, among actual and potential beneficiary groups and the increasing number of politicians and political parties who counted on their votes.

The controversy and contention escalated further in 1990, when the then prime minister, V.P. Singh, announced that his government would put the Mandal recommendations into effect. This resulted in increasingly heated and acrimonious debate between proponents and opponents of extended reservations, in public forums and in both the vernacular and the English-language press. The mainstream English newspapers and periodicals were predominantly opposed to the implementation of the Mandal recommendations – often aggressively so.

The controversy over reservation policies in India has focused primarily on reservations for OBCs in public employment and in admissions to education institutions (especially the most elite ones). Reserved seats for SCs and STs in legislative assemblies seem to have been accepted on all sides as a permanent feature of the Indian political landscape, even though they were not established in perpetuity by the Constitution but must be extended every ten years by parliamentary action. Reservations for SCs and STs in employment and education have not been directly targeted by opponents of reservations for OBCs, but support for those longer-standing reservations has also been adversely affected by the vocal opposition to OBC reservations – as the two sets of beneficiary groups are increasingly conflated by the general public.

Overall support for positive discrimination, in any sphere other than parliamentary representation, has been waning in India for several decades. The great majority of India's intellectual elite (whether or not they happen to be high-caste Hindus) is opposed to any expansion of the groups eligible for reservations in employment and education; and many also oppose existing reservations for OBCs. Elite opinion is not so hostile to the reservations currently in place for SCs and STs. As Andre Beteille has written, "the moral basis of claims for special treatment of the Harijans and Adivasis is quite different than the moral basis of claims by the various castes and communities which seek inclusion among the Other Backward Classes" (Beteille 1981: 10); "Only the Harijans and Adivasis have suffered collectively the kind of social abuse and psychological injury that justify very special measures of redress in their case, including the reservation of jobs" (Beteille 1990: 41).

Yet support for reservations benefiting OBCs as well as SCs and STs remains strong among Indians from the lower and middle rungs of the socio-economic ladder. Studies have demonstrated a very strong correlation between an individual's caste and his/her opinion on caste-based reservations: most Dalits and (actual or potential) OBC members tend to support reservations, while members of the remaining "forward" castes tend to oppose them.[1] The fact that the former constitute a significantly larger share of the Hindu population than the latter no doubt helps to explain why not a single major politician or political party in India has opposed the extension of reservations, let alone proposed their curtailment.[2]

In the US, the growth of opposition to positive discrimination became highly visible when Ronald Reagan was elected to the presidency in 1980. Reagan's supporters were on the whole hostile to the AA policies put into effect or supported by his predecessors, and he replaced key officials who had promoted those policies with new appointees who opposed them.[3] In the 1980s and 1990s, US Supreme Court decisions also became more skeptical of AA policies, as they narrowed the grounds for which – and the extent to which – such policies could be applied. In the 1990s, the curtailment of AA policies reached new heights, as several state legislatures, boards of university regents, and federal district courts ruled against any consideration of the racial/ethnic status of applicants for admission to public educational institutions (and, in some cases, candidates for public service jobs). These changes in the official and legal status of AA policies reflected corresponding changes in the views of the American public as a whole, which was becoming increasingly skeptical about positive discrimination.

Affirmative action has been a highly controversial topic in US public life since the early 1990s. Many books, articles, and newspaper reports have addressed this topic; and one can find both passionate proponents and passionate opponents among those who are most widely read and heard on the subject. In the 1960s and 1970s, US "opinion-makers" appeared to be predominantly in favor of AA policies in general, if not in every detail. At present, however, the intellectual elite appears to be quite divided on the subject. In ruling in 2003 narrowly in favor of AA policies in admissions to higher educational institutions, the US Supreme Court was responsive to the pro-AA views of many of America's business, military, and educational leaders. Polls of the general public, however, suggest that a majority of Americans are now opposed to positive discrimination.[4] This is not the case among members of the underrepresented groups themselves: most Blacks, Hispanic Americans, and Native Americans continue to believe in the need for AA policies; though among them one can hear prominent dissenting voices too.

Arguments for positive discrimination most prominent in each country

In the US the case for positive discrimination in favor of African Americans developed initially out of the case for affirmative action in its original sense of assuring formal legal equality and equal opportunity without granting any preferential treatment. When it became clear that this kind of affirmative action was not sufficient to overcome long- and well-entrenched patterns of discrimination against Blacks, those determined to assure equal opportunity began to expand the range of policies undertaken in the name of affirmative action to include preferential policies in favor of Blacks.

The first argument made in the US in favor of positive discrimination was thus that it is necessary *to assure truly equal opportunity* to all applicants for desired positions. Advocates of affirmative action on these grounds claim that, in the current social context of the US, selection processes determining who gets access to schools, jobs, etc. are inherently biased against African Americans (and other under-represented ethnic groups such as Hispanic Americans and Native Americans), in a way that cannot generally be overcome simply by appeal to "color-blindness" on the part of decision-makers or recourse to anti-discrimination laws. It is claimed that use of conventional (and supposedly objective and non-discriminatory) indicators of an applicant's qualifications – such as standardized test scores – in fact biases selection decisions against members of under-represented ethnic groups, either because of biases inherent in the indicators[5] or because the performance of members of these groups tends to be relatively better in dimensions of ability for which it is difficult to find good indicators. It follows, therefore, that in order to really level the playing field, it is necessary to give preferences in educational, employment, and other selection processes to members of under-represented ethnic groups.

Another argument very frequently invoked by advocates of affirmative action in the US is that of *compensatory justice*. There can be no denying that African Americans have endured a long history of injustice at the hands of White Americans; and a comparable case can be made for Native Americans. Whether Hispanic Americans, or other communities of color, have endured on a similar scale is not so clear; but they have certainly faced discrimination of various kinds, and to varying degrees, by Whites. In this context, AA preferences are seen as compensating (in a small but important way) for a history of mistreatment and discrimination on the part of Whites, which has had the effect of disadvantaging Blacks and members of other such under-represented ethnic groups in the competition with Whites for desirable positions in contemporary American society. This argument is passionately felt and articulated by a great many – no doubt a substantial majority of – Blacks and Native Americans, if not other Americans of color; it is also shared by a minority of White Americans.

A related argument for affirmative action as a mechanism of compensatory justice operates on a somewhat different plane. As Sunita Parikh has observed, "Ascriptive policies, despite their obvious problems and potential for controversy, signal as do few other policies a recognition by ruling elites that bedrock characteristics of groups are recognized and valued" (Parikh 1997: 197–8). From this perspective a policy of positive discrimination in favor of under-represented ethnic minority groups can be seen as an important symbolic affirmation of society's commitment to overcome the effects of past injustices and to welcome all its citizens as full and equal members. This variant of the compensatory injustice argument is especially likely to animate those members of the majority White population who see affirmative action as a good way to provide redress for past (and continuing) patterns of discrimination against people of color in the US.

The two arguments just discussed are surely those most widely believed and voiced by members of the US general public who support affirmative action. American intellectuals supporting affirmative action have raised a number of different arguments to buttress their position. Perhaps the most significant of these is the case for affirmative action – especially in the spheres of higher education and high-status jobs – as an important means *to integrate the societal elite.* Here the key benefit of AA preferences for members of under-represented ethnic groups is seen as promotion of the legitimacy and vitality of a democratic society. In the absence of such preferences, decision-makers in professional, business, and political circles would likely remain overwhelmingly White; so members of under-represented ethnic groups would feel poorly represented and unable to exercise their rights and responsibilities as citizens and full members of the society. Elizabeth Anderson, a very forceful exponent of this argument, concludes that

> there is no way to achieve a society in which one's race does not profoundly affect one's life chances, and in which racial antipathies do not rend civil society, without integrating society at its highest levels. Without this, America can be neither just nor truly democratic.
>
> (Anderson 2000: 305)

Several related points are also often articulated by advocates of affirmative action: First, in a multicultural society, certain kinds of jobs are best performed by members of minority ethnic communities – especially jobs involving significant interaction with members of the same communities. Furthermore, members of these communities who achieve some degree of success can serve as role models to inspire younger group members to do better in their own lives; and they are also more likely than other members to make voluntary service contributions – especially for the benefit of members of their own (relatively needy) communities.[6] It follows that the efficiency of the economy as well as the functioning of the democratic system can be significantly enhanced by measures designed to increase the representation of under-represented minorities as students in top educational institutions who, as graduates, can be expected to enter professions of high respectability and responsibility.

Another argument for affirmative action advanced by intellectuals has to do with the *motivation to improve one's lot in life* on the part of members of under-represented ethnic groups. The people in question are on average well behind their White fellow citizens in terms of virtually all socio-economic indicators of well-being – e.g. per capita income, health, education, housing. Much of this has to do with circumstances well beyond an individual's control. Some of it, however, is also due to "effort pessimism," i.e. the notion that efforts to better one's life chances through hard work, determined study, positive goal orientation, and other such means of self-improvement are highly unlikely to pay off. In this context affirmative action, by opening up opportunities previously unavailable to most members of an under-represented ethnic group, can improve the odds that effort will pay off; thereby it can serve as an incentive for members of those groups to apply themselves more seriously and more fully in a positive direction.

Finally, two additional arguments for affirmative action have been put forward to justify preferences for members of under-represented minority groups in admissions to educational institutions.[7] The first argument has been voiced with increasing frequency and conviction by administrators in prestigious US higher educational institutions since the early 1990s, when such preferences began to be challenged more sharply and more effectively by their opponents. Thus Neil Rudenstine, former president of Harvard University, has stated and written that "the most fundamental rationale for student diversity in higher education [is] its educational value. Students benefit in countless ways from the opportunity to live and learn among peers whose perspectives and experiences differ from their own" (Rudenstine 2001: 31). And Patricia Gurin, the then chair of the University of Michigan Psychology Department, wrote that "Racial diversity has the features – novelty, unfamiliarity, discrepancy from pre-college experience, a source of multiple and different perspectives, contradictory expectations – that increase engagement in thinking" (Gurin 2001a: 5). The argument for *diversity as a source of higher-quality education* holds that one cannot become well educated in a multicultural society without having interacted in significant ways with members of other ethnic groups. Colleges and universities provide an ideal setting in which constructive inter-cultural interactions can take place, given that most students have experienced very little diversity among their school-mates in primary and secondary schools because of the high degree of residential segregation in the US. Increasing the representation of under-represented ethnic minority students on college and university campuses therefore contributes in an important way to the education of all the students.

The remaining argument in favor of affirmative action in US colleges and universities is voiced rather less frequently than the diversity argument. This one begins with the observation that a good higher educational experience not only augments students' "human capital," by increasing their knowledge and skills, but also provides them with more "social capital," in the form of useful contacts and networks that increase their awareness of and access to good job opportunities.[8] Members of an under-represented minority group are particularly likely to lack such social capital, precisely because their own community is under-represented in high-status jobs and positions of responsibility. Thus affirmative action helps to *spread social capital more broadly* throughout a society, thereby ameliorating an inequitable distribution of social capital that is linked to the history of past injustice done to minority group members.[9]

In India the arguments most often made in favor of reservations for SCs and STs include several – but not all – of those advanced in support of affirmative action in the US. Unquestionably the most frequently and passionately voiced argument – ever since the concerns of the then "untouchables" were first brought to bear forcefully on Indian national consciousness by Dr. Ambedkar in the late 1920s – is that of *compensatory justice*. Anyone inspired by principles of equal treatment and equal opportunity cannot but be overwhelmed by the span of historical time, and the scope of societal arenas, in which such equality was denied to India's outcastes. The extent of the injustices done to the indigenous tribes of India varied over time and across different regions and groups; but if these groups suffered less at the hands of India's mainstream population, it was only because their isolation limited the extent of their interaction with the dominant groups of the subcontinent.

The significance of the compensatory rationale for positive discrimination in favor of India's Dalits and Adivasis is suggested by the terms often used to characterize reservations for SCs and STs – "compensatory discrimination" and "protective discrimination." Those leaders of the majority population most responsible for instituting reservation policies have clearly seen them as an affirmation of their desire to recognize and welcome the beneficiary groups as full – if not in all respects equal – members of Indian society. The fact that they have often been motivated by the hope and expectation of gaining the political support and electoral votes of Dalits and Adivasis detracts only a little from the significance of this affirmation.

Members of the beneficiary groups have clearly seen reservation policies – and the related measures taken by Indian governments for the "uplift" of the SCs and STs – as a form of compensation for their long history of mistreatment and discrimination on the part of the majority population (especially caste Hindus). For example, a survey of Dalit and Adivasi students at a prominent medical college in Pune showed that they were almost unanimously in support of SC and ST reservations, on the following grounds:

1   they have a constitutional right to reserved seats;
2   their communities have suffered for thousands of years and deserve compensation for just as long;
3   this long history of systemic discrimination has made it impossible for them to compete on the basis of exam-revealed "merit";
4   they benefit from reservations only at college entry and still have to meet same standards to graduate; and
5   they overcame all kinds of obstacles to gain entry to a top medical college, which testifies to their hard work as well as their intellectual ability.[10]

It should be noted that positive discrimination is seen as just compensation not only because it enables individual Dalits and Adivasis to move up the social and economic ladder. Also important, in the Indian context of group rights, is the fact that reservations and related policies have been generated in a process by which these highly under-represented communities – like other communities before them – have been able to articulate the collective interests of their members and gain a share of society's spoils.

In the US the other argument for affirmative action widely held and voiced by its supporters among the general public is that it is needed *to assure truly equal opportunity* for citizens from under-represented ethnic groups. This argument is also heard in India, though less often. More significantly, the argument is developed along rather different lines. In the US, AA preferences are seen as counterweights to certain inadequacies of conventional measures of applicant qualifications, which cause conventional evaluation procedures to be biased against members of under-represented minority groups; so positive discrimination is seen by its proponents as improving the accuracy with which applicant merit is assessed. In India, this claim is somewhat less tenable because reservation policies are typically much blunter instruments of positive discrimination than the preferential boosts provided by affirmative action.

Furthermore, Indians tend to have much less faith than Americans in the prospect that the true merit of applicants competing for a position can and will be the basis for selection. As Dharma Kumar has written: "A particularly Indian view is that the existing procedures of selection and promotion are so corrupt or nepotistic that merit is irrelevant" (Kumar 1992: 300). From the view that the system is not really meritocratic, but instead dominated by the privileged and the powerful, it is a short step to the conclusion that the less privileged and powerful should have an opportunity to benefit from non–merit-related advantages too.

Many proponents of positive discrimination reject the very notion of measuring merit on some quantitative scale – especially one based on a single test or indicator, which is often the way it is done in India. Others are deeply suspicious of the kinds of indicators most often used to measure "merit," if only on the grounds that they typically put a considerable premium on knowledge of the English language (which is largely a privilege of the Indian elite). Thus Kancha Ilaiah, a Dalit academic, activist, and author,[11] has written:

> We need to debunk the present theory of merit which makes for a relative position in rank list based on marks in written examination. Securing good marks in all such examinations depends to a large extent on having the advantage of educated parents, availability of books, and providing coaching at a young age. If [O]BC, SC and ST students get lower marks than the upper class/caste students this does not mean that they have less intelligence or capacity to learn…If you scrutinize the issue carefully, scoring high marks is directly related to acquiring proficiency in English.
>
> (Ilaiah 1990: 2309)

In general, the sense in which proponents of positive discrimination in India argue that it can contribute to equal opportunity is not that it serves to improve the accuracy of measurement of applicant qualifications. Rather, it is that reservations serve directly to promote fairness in the distribution of benefits by assuring that under-represented groups are better represented among those who attain desirable positions.

The argument that reservation policies can help *to integrate the societal elite* is also voiced by advocates of positive discrimination in India. Thus Nirmal Mukarji, arguing against the notion that the Dalit and Adivasi children from well-off families should be excluded from the benefits of reservations, points out that the development of a Dalit and Adivasi elite is one of the key objectives of positive discrimination, designed to strengthen and give hope to under-represented groups: "it takes more than a single generation for an elite fashioned out of communities oppressed...for centuries to stabilize itself" (Mukarji 1981: 18). The case for integrating the elite here, however, tends to stem more from prospective economic efficiency gains than from enhancement of democratic legitimacy and vitality. Some intellectuals – not necessarily very sympathetic to reservation policies – have noted the likelihood that under-represented communities themselves will be better served if more decision-makers come from their own communities and that a greater number of success stories from such communities will serve as good role models for the young.[12] The fact that benefits of reservation policies for the functioning of a democratic system are rarely stressed is probably due to a widespread sense among Indian intellectuals that party affiliations and voting patterns are already so tied up with caste and community identity that policies like reservations, which further stress that kind of identity, may well weaken rather than strengthen democracy in India.

Indian proponents of positive discrimination have also alluded on occasion to the argument that it will increase the *motivation to improve one's lot in life* on the part of members of under-represented ethnic groups. Reservations for SCs and STs clearly open more doors for Dalits and Adivasis in the spheres in which they are applied – in educational institutions, in public employment, and in representative legislative assemblies. Surely, the proponents argue, this must have the effect of encouraging some Dalits and Adivasis to believe that their personal efforts at betterment will have a higher chance of paying off; and in this way reservations can serve as an incentive for such efforts.

The argument advanced by American educational leaders for positive discrimination in the sphere of admissions to higher educational institutions is simply not heard in India, for it has no resonance in the context of the Indian system of higher education. With the exception of some smaller private institutions (to which Indian reservation policies do not apply), and a few of the most elite public institutions at the all-India level, Indian higher educational institutions involve large lectures and impersonal classroom environments in which there is precious little room for active and meaningful student participation – let alone meaningful inter-cultural interactions among students.

Residential quarters and campus facilities are poorly equipped and not at all conducive to bringing together students from different backgrounds. Even in the elite institutions where smaller classes and better facilities offer more opportunities for student interaction, Dalit and Adivasi students (virtually all of whom are admitted by virtue of reserved seats) tend to be residentially segregated in their own hostels and socially shunned by "general entry" students.[13]

Proponents of positive discrimination in favor of OBCs, as distinct from SCs and STs, have articulated much the same kinds of argument. The fact is, however, that OBC members cannot claim a history of oppression of their communities anywhere near as profound as that experienced by most Dalit and Adivasi communities. As Aditya Nigam has written: "the worst forms of social oppression based on caste, like untouchability, have been practiced over hundreds of years…The case of the OBCs, however, is entirely different…they have never been victims of the type of caste-based social oppression like untouchability" (Nigam 1990: 2652). Nor, in most cases, can OBC members claim as great a degree of contemporary disadvantage. K. Balagopal has noted that: "The poor among the forward castes – who are undoubtedly numerous – have one advantage which Dalits do not, *viz.*, the use of caste links with the rich to obtain a small job or a petty loan" (Balagopal 1990: 2232). As a consequence, arguments that OBC reservations are needed for compensatory justice ring somewhat hollow; and the case for OBC reservations is more often made in terms of fairness in the distribution of benefits – by assuring that OBCs are better represented in the distribution of desirable positions in Indian society.

Arguments against positive discrimination most prominent in each country

By far the most common argument raised against positive discrimination in the US is that it is fundamentally unfair – as well as unconstitutional – because, quite simply, it constitutes *reverse discrimination*. Opponents of AA policies appeal to the US constitutional commitment to equality of treatment of every individual, reinforced by the language of the Civil Rights Act of 1964 banning any form of discrimination by race or color. They assert that in order to combat negative discrimination in a fair and constitutional manner, one must eliminate that discrimination rather than engage in another form of discrimination. Thus Carl Cohen, in a characteristically forceful critique of affirmative action, wrote that: "What was once the name for the active pursuit of equal treatment regardless of race has become the name for instruments designed to give deliberate preference on the basis of race" (Cohen 1995: 4). This view is held by almost all opponents of AA policies in the US, and it is also the basis of the many lawsuits that have been brought against such policies over the decades in which they have been implemented.

Closely associated with the argument against affirmative action as reverse discrimination is the claim that it is *poorly tailored to help the most disadvantaged*. Beneficiary groups are identified largely on the basis of their degree of socio-economic disadvantage; but the benefits of preferential access go to individual members of those under-represented groups. Many critics contend that the individual beneficiaries of AA preferences actually tend to be among the best-off members of their respective groups, and therefore have little if any legitimate reason to be preferred ahead of individual members of more advantaged groups. This claim is based on the fact that AA preferences are applied mainly in the selection of candidates for high-status positions and high-quality institutions, for which it is reasonable to presume that plausible candidates will be found in under-represented groups mainly among those who are relatively well off – because they would be the most likely to have received adequate prior education and sufficient preparation to meet even the minimum needed qualifications.

An implication drawn by some who raise the "poorly tailored" critique of affirmative action is that policies seeking to overcome disadvantage ought to be directed not at (any and all) members of under-represented ethnic groups, but at under-represented individuals. Thus calls are issued for "class-based" rather than "group-based" AA policies, where the relevant under-represented class consists of everyone whose family background puts them in the lowest socio-economic strata of the society.[14]

Two other arguments are also frequently raised against AA policies in the US, each of which focus on the allegedly negative consequences of such policies. One is that they are divisive because they serve *to heighten consciousness of irrelevant ascriptive distinctions* between ethnic groups, exacerbating Balkanization of the society rather than promoting harmony and cooperation among members of different ethnic groups. Not only is this seen as generating conflict and weakening the structure of democracy; it is also charged with causing resentment among members of the dominant group(s), which makes it all the more difficult to sustain efforts to help members of under-represented groups. As Cohen put it: "Racial hostilities in the United States are exacerbated, not appeased or mitigated by giving favor. Majorities become resentful while minorities are demeaned" (Cohen 1995: 231).

The second such consequentialist argument often voiced against AA policies is that the policies generate allocational inefficiency because they result in the deliberate *selection of less qualified candidates* ahead of more qualified candidates – with the result that the quality of work done will be inferior. Critics expect that applicants admitted to educational institutions by virtue of AA preferences will not do as well as the displaced applicants (with better conventional qualifications) would have, and that the same will be true of candidates selected for jobs by virtue of such preferences.

A closely related argument has been raised (mainly in academic circles) by critics of AA policies applied specifically to the admission of applicants to higher educational institutions. This is the argument that preferences enabling members of under-represented groups to enter higher-quality colleges and universities than those which would have admitted them without preferences result in a *mismatch between students and educational institutions*. It is claimed that AA beneficiaries will be prone to failure in competition with better-qualified peers at high-quality institutions, and that the beneficiaries would have been better off attending lower-quality schools. Similar arguments have been made in the context of preferences in selection to jobs.

Many prominent critics of positive discrimination in the US have made the mismatch argument, especially with reference to Black Americans in higher education.[15] Thus Thomas Sowell wrote that: "the actual consequences of admitting blacks to institutions where they do not meet the usual admissions standards have been educationally disastrous for those students" (Sowell 1990: 109). Sowell went on to assert that

> black students who failed to make it to graduation at Berkeley were perfectly capable of graduating from an average American college. Their failure was due to their being mismatched with Berkeley. This pattern is neither new nor peculiar to Berkeley…Once the process of mismatching begins at the top-level institutions, the second-tier institutions find that the minority students who meet their normal standards of admission have been siphoned off and so must take minority students whose qualifications are more appropriate for lower-ranked institutions. Once begun at the top, the mismatching process continues down the line.
>
> (Sowell 1990: 110)

Some opponents of AA policies in the US have argued that such policies lead to *complacency and dependence* on the part of the actual and potential beneficiaries. It is claimed that members of under-represented groups, confident that they will be able to take advantage of preferences in access to higher education and employment, will be correspondingly less motivated to work hard to improve their knowledge and skills. As Shelby Steele, a prominent African-American critic of positive discrimination, has put it: "the worst aspect of racial preferences is that they encourage dependency on entitlements, rather than our own initiative" (Steele 1990: 90).[16]

One final argument against AA policies in the US has been articulated mainly by some highly successful African Americans. They point out that when AA policies are widespread, it is only natural that the *achievements of beneficiary group members get devalued* by others. This is because these achievements are likely to be attributed to a significant extent to arbitrary advantages conveyed by AA preferences rather than to genuine personal abilities and accomplishments. This presumption may well be applied to successful members of under-represented ethnic groups who have not in fact benefited from any preferences, under circumstances in which an environment of affirmative action suggests that they might well be among the beneficiaries. As Stephen Carter put it: "Small wonder…that every black professional, in our racially conscious times, is assumed to have earned his or her position not by being among the best available but by being among the best available blacks" (Carter 1991: 55).[17]

Turning to criticism of positive discrimination in India, I should first note that there is little opposition to the reservation of legislative seats for SCs and STs. As the distinguished Indian sociologist Andre Beteille (1981, 1990) has stressed, the case for reservations is much stronger in representative institutions like political assemblies than in institutions where academic or professional expertise is at a premium. Criticism of reservations in India is thus aimed primarily at reserved jobs in the public sector (widely regarded as the most important sphere of positive discrimination in India) and reserved seats in educational institutions. Moreover, most of the criticism has been leveled against reservations for OBCs, as distinct from SCs and STs, for these are the kinds of reservations that have been at issue over the last several decades. Yet such criticism is, at least implicitly, also relevant to reservations for SCs and STs – albeit with less force – insofar as the greater degree of past mistreatment and current disadvantage of Dalits and Adivasis makes them worthier candidates for benefits.

As in the case of arguments for positive discrimination, many of the arguments against positive discrimination raised in India are the same as those put forward in the US. The relative frequency with which different kinds of argument are raised, however, is different in the two countries.

In India the most frequent complaint about reservation policies is that they conflict with considerations of merit and result in the *selection of less qualified candidates* ahead of more qualified candidates. Thus most critics point to the poorer quality of government service, and poorer academic performance, to be expected from the beneficiaries of reservations. In a sharp critique of the Mandal recommendations, Ashok Guha (1990a, 1990b) has written that reservations in public employment impair the efficiency and quality of public services by reducing the average competence standard of civil service entrants, reduce their incentive to perform well and their motivation to improve, undermine the morale of workers and supervisors, and stimulate caste conflict in public institutions, thus harming teamwork and cooperation. In a similar vein, A.M. Shah wrote that:

> Efficiency or merit is not a fetish of the elite, as frequently alleged. It is in fact an essential ingredient in every field of life…The policy of job reservations needs to be replaced by effective programmes of affirmative action to promote efficiency, merit and skills among the weaker sections of society…This does not mean that we abandon the goal of social justice but use different methods to achieve the same goal.
>
> (Shah 1991: 1734)

Some critics have even suggested that the failure to allocate key jobs on a strictly meritocratic basis has resulted in very serious harm as well as gross inefficiency.[18]

The most important and contentious arena for reservations in India is public sector employment; and the debate over reservations in this sphere has a special salience in India because of the widespread perception that Indian public sector job-holders are likely to use whatever discretionary decision-making authority they have so as to steer benefits to members of their own community, rather than to carry out their mission in a community-neutral way. From the perspective of critics of reservations, this makes it all the more important to insist on strictly meritocratic hiring practices and impartial fulfillment of responsibilities in government service and public institutions. From the perspective of supporters of public employment reservations, however, it makes it all the more important that jobs be allocated in such a way that assures that all groups are sufficiently well represented. In an effort to reconcile the competing demands of efficiency and social justice, Aditya Nigam expressed the opinion that

> A left position need not necessarily be identified either by its crusading ardour against merit and efficiency or by its messianic zeal for reservations. What it certainly needs to recognize, in no uncertain terms, is that merit and efficiency are largely socially determined and therefore, any consideration on merit alone works inherently against the underprivileged.
>
> (Nigam 1990: 2652)

A second very commonly voiced argument against reservation policies, in India as in the US, is that the reservations are very *poorly tailored to help the most disadvantaged*. Indeed, an entirely new term has come into everyday use in India to highlight the thrust of this argument: "creamy layer." This term refers to those members of the under-represented groups eligible for reservations who are very well off in socio-economic terms and who, according to the critics, monopolize the opportunities opened up by reservation policies. Especially among the candidates who are not eligible for preferences, and who are concerned about being displaced by beneficiaries of reservation policies, there is a widespread belief that the beneficiaries come from a creamy layer that is, if anything, more privileged in socio-economic terms than those whom they displace. Thus a (general-entry) student at one of the elite Indian Institutes of Technology opined that

> The present policy of reservations is ridiculous, because an IAS [Indian Administrative Service] officer's son who is academically weak has a preference over a lorry driver's son who is bright and academically sound, just because the former is from the reserved caste and the latter from the non-reserved caste.
>
> (quoted by Rao 2002: 57)[19]

Linked to this concern is the criticism that the benefits of positive discrimination have simply not reached the most under-represented and deserving members of the under-represented groups, for whose benefit they were ostensibly enacted. For example, Aditya Nigam writes that

> As many studies have shown, [reservation policies have] only resulted in the creation of a small stratum of elite, who have been able to distribute patronage to their caste-brethren. Essentially, it has resulted in a democratisation of patronage distribution, without so much as touching the frills of caste-exploitation.
>
> (Nigam 1990: 2652)

The creamy layer argument leads some critics of positive discrimination in India, as in the US, to call for the use of socio-economic class or income-based criteria – rather than caste or ethnic group status – as a means of identifying and helping those under-represented persons most in need of aid. Many observers of the Indian scene have pointed out that far greater economic gains have come to the masses of Dalits and Adivasis from enlightened social policy oriented to the needs of the poor (as in the state of Kerala) rather than from reservation policies.[20] And some argue that the focus on reservations has deflected attention from other measures that would do more for Dalits and Adivasis – e.g. programs to combat poverty, illiteracy, etc.[21]

The third argument most often raised in India by opponents of positive discrimination is that it serves *to heighten consciousness of irrelevant ascriptive distinctions* between ethnic groups – especially invidious caste distinctions, which have been such an important and (at least to the Indian modernizing elite) lamentable part of India's history. Whereas a few of India's intellectuals have argued that "if you want to bring caste to an end, provide more reservations for the backwards" (Rajni Kothari, quoted by Kumar 1992: 299), many more take the position that "by making caste a criterion for social benefits, government will in effect perpetuate the caste system" (Kumar 1990: 12). The critics anticipate further related problems as well. Drawing the line between the deserving and undeserving is a precarious exercise, fraught with potential for unfairness, squabbling, deceit, and litigation. And, once started, reservations will be expanded (mainly for political gain) to more and more groups with less and less reason for such assistance – thus further exacerbating inter-group divisions and tensions.[22]

The claims that reservation policies undermine merit, favor a creamy layer, and perpetuate invidious caste distinctions are unquestionably the points most frequently raised in India by critics of reservation policies. Two other points of criticism are also voiced, but rather less frequently. First, it is claimed that reservations lead to *complacency and dependence* on the part of the beneficiaries, who do not have to work very hard to gain access to good higher educational institutions or good government jobs because (if they have at least minimal qualifications for such opportunities) they are assured of a good placement.

Thus R. Shetty has written that: "The system of reservation…kills the beneficiaries' initiative, drive and capacity" (quoted by Galanter 1984: 74).

Secondly, critics of reservations allude to a *mismatch between students (or employees) and educational institutions (or job settings)*, although this critique is not as prominent a part of the critique of positive discrimination in India as it is in the US. Certainly much attention has been focused on the allegedly inferior performance of holders of reserved positions in Indian educational institutions and public sector organizations. The mismatch argument is especially likely to be raised by those who find that the competitive struggle for admission to good schools, and selection to good public sector jobs, is more difficult because some of the places have been set aside for members of reservation-eligible groups. The concern about bringing under-prepared Dalit and Adivasi students into higher educational institutions is also voiced by many faculty members and administrators at elite institutions, who find it a considerable challenge to cater successfully to under-represented students. Thus P.V. Indiresan wrote that

> In higher education we are trying to mix up two widely divergent groups, which are not in a position to interact in a healthy manner. The consequences have not been happy even to those who are expected to be the beneficiaries.
>
> (Indiresan 1982)

The related claim that poor performance by beneficiaries of reservation policies will exacerbate negative stereotypes about the under-represented groups is rarely heard in India, perhaps because such stigmatization is already so deeply ingrained in Indian society that it is hard to imagine how it could become any stronger!

Another argument heard from time to time in India – though also less frequently there than in the US – is that the *achievements of beneficiary group members get devalued* by others because they are attributed to arbitrary advantages resulting from reservation policies. Thus Dalits themselves have drawn attention to the characterization of Dalit occupants of reserved positions as inferior to their peers in ability and performance. Patwardhan and Palshikar report that doctors who have benefited from reservations do feel devalued by that status; and they would prefer to see investment in primary and secondary education to bring under-represented groups into a competitive position in applications for higher education. Moreover, they would be ready to give up caste-based reservations for well-off members of under-represented groups, but not for the great majority who remain economically backward and hence deserving of help.[23] Because reservation policies in India (unlike affirmative action in the US) leave little doubt as to who are the beneficiaries, it is much less likely that a Dalit or an Adivasi who has not benefited from positive discrimination will be erroneously presumed to have done so; and it is hence correspondingly unlikely that the achievements of such a person will be devalued by the presumption that they are attributable to arbitrary advantage rather than true ability.

The charge of *reverse discrimination* – probably the most widespread complaint about affirmative action in the US – is occasionally leveled at reservation policies in India, primarily by those who are competing for positions in elite educational institutions or high-status government jobs. However, this charge is not often mentioned – and even more rarely given much prominence – by intellectual critics of reservations.[24] No doubt the difference here in argumentation between India and the US has much to do with the different constitutional status of positive discrimination in the two countries. In the US, positive as well as negative discrimination appears to be prima facie unconstitutional (though one can make a case that certain forms of positive discrimination are constitutional in certain situations). In India, positive discrimination is explicitly sanctioned by the constitution, so a critic does not get far with simply a charge of reverse discrimination; one must appeal to substantive arguments as to why it is bad policy.

Observations on the evolution of the debate over positive discrimination in each country

When they were first adopted, policies of positive discrimination in favor of under-represented ethnic groups enjoyed strong public support in both the US and India. In recent decades, however, critiques of PD policies have become increasingly widespread and increasingly vociferous. The critics are most often members of the elite from the dominant ethnic groups; but in each country criticism has also been heard from a number of under-represented group elites as well. Advocates of positive discrimination have been increasingly on the defensive; and overall public support for positive discrimination has been diminishing in both countries. In the US, court rulings have led to some cutbacks in the scope of AA policies, whereas in India the scope of reservation policies has expanded. In spite of these contrasting trends, however, PD policies are now highly controversial in each country.

In the US, the trend in public opinion away from support for positive discrimination since the 1970s is no doubt due in part to the concurrent rightward drift of public discourse and political life in the country. But it is surely also due in some part to the visible success of a significant number of under-represented ethnic group members, over the past several decades, in entering the "middle class" and even the upper strata of American society. One can debate how widespread such success has actually been, and to what extent it is attributable to AA policies. In any event, many contemporary critics of PD policies are inclined to argue that while such policies may have been needed in the past, they are "no longer" needed to assure that members of under-represented ethnic groups have sufficient opportunities to improve their lot nor to assure that they are adequately represented in the societal elite. Such voices are now added to those who have always opposed preferential AA policies on principle.

Critics of positive discrimination in India are much less likely to argue that reservation policies are no longer needed because their objectives have largely been achieved, since there is much less evidence that a significant proportion of members of the beneficiary groups have joined the middle and upper classes in India than in the US. It is often argued in India, however, that the actual beneficiaries of reservation policies are much less in need of positive discrimination than was the case in the past. This argument rests on evidence that the beneficiaries are now a good deal more likely to come from the creamy layer – in particular, the children of earlier beneficiaries of PD policies – than was true in the past. On these grounds, one can expect calls for exclusion of the creamy layer from the benefits of positive discrimination rather than calls for an end to PD policies altogether.

An explanation for the growth in vocal opposition to positive discrimination in India must therefore be found elsewhere. There can be no doubt that the announcement in 1990 by Prime Minister V.P. Singh that the Government of India would adopt some of the Mandal Commission recommendations was the impetus for a huge wave of criticism of reservation policies in the 1990s. For one thing, such a large-scale extension of eligibility for reserved seats (to OBC members) strengthens the credibility of several of the main claims of critics of positive discrimination – notably that positive discrimination undermines the quality of key institutions by diminishing the scope for merit in appointments; that it exacerbates rather than alleviates inter-caste tensions; and that, once started, reservations will invariably be expanded to more and more groups with weaker and weaker grounds for preferences.

The bitterness of the criticism following the V.P. Singh announcement, and the public demonstrations against the Mandal Commission recommendations, were clearly linked to a perception on the part of higher-caste Hindus that their competitive position in the struggle for good jobs would be seriously undermined by such an extension of reservations. This points to an underlying reason why PD policies have become increasingly controversial in India, especially among the upper classes, over the decades since independence. During the past half-century there has been a rapid expansion of higher education in India, together with relatively slow growth of the economy as a whole. This has resulted in a steady deterioration of employment opportunities for highly educated youths, at the same time that under-represented group members have been given preferential access to both higher education and desirable public sector jobs. As Patwardhan and Palshikar have put it: "As employment opportunities have shrunk…new elites from the middle order of castes along with the high castes have become more stridently opposed to reservations in education and employment" (Patwardhan and Palshikar 1992: 3).

One final difference between the debate over positive discrimination in the US and in India is worth noting here. In each country three under-represented ethnic groups have been recognized (for different periods of time) as deserving of eligibility for PD benefits – African, Hispanic, and Native Americans in the

US; Dalits, Adivasis, and OBC members in India. Yet in the US debate it is rarely argued that any one under-represented group is more deserving of AA preferences than the others, whether on grounds of historical priority, greater negative discrimination, or greater socio-economic disadvantage. In India, however, it is not uncommon – especially since the announcement regarding implementation of the Mandal Commission recommendations – for someone to support the continuation of reservations in favor of Dalits and Adivasis but to oppose reservations for OBC members.

3 The potential benefits and costs of positive discrimination

In Chapter 2 I discussed various arguments raised in the US and in India in support of or in opposition to policies of positive discrimination (PD). In this chapter I seek to organize these arguments systematically into a comprehensive list of arguments for and against positive discrimination. I begin by considering two common arguments that are based strictly on principles of justice; and then I turn to the many arguments that make the case for or against PD policies on the basis of their anticipated consequences.[1] These latter arguments involve claims that certain benefits or certain costs will result from PD policies. In the last section of the chapter I discuss the societal goals that underlie the benefits and costs anticipated from PD policies by their proponents and opponents.

Positive discrimination as due compensation or reverse discrimination?

For some participants in the ongoing debate over positive discrimination, the matter can and should be settled on the basis of moral principles alone. Thus many proponents contend that it is a matter of fundamental social justice. Members of under-represented ethnic groups (UREGs) have been victimized in many ways and, as a result, they find themselves on average in a relatively poor socio-economic position. To give them some degree of preference in processes of selection to desired positions in a society seems a small but eminently reasonable form of compensation for past injustice. On the other hand, many opponents of positive discrimination object that it results in the selection of applicants from the favored ethnic groups at the expense of other applicants who are more qualified or meritorious, thereby violating elementary procedural justice. From this perspective, preferential selection of UREG members appears to constitute reverse discrimination against the rest of the population – a form of discrimination against the latter just as arbitrary and morally unjustifiable as (negative) discrimination against the former.

These two irreconcilable arguments from basic principles of justice represent probably the most widely held – and certainly the most passionately held – positions on positive discrimination. Yet, as I will argue in this chapter, neither one of them can survive close scrutiny, in the forms in which they are usually articulated. What's wrong with them?

Compensatory social justice

The case for PD on grounds of social justice views it as a desirable form of (partial) compensation to victims of gross historical injustices – injustices that have extended in some cases to such extremes as slavery and virtual genocide. Even in the case of an ethnic group whose members are no longer exposed to a great deal of injustice and overt discrimination, the adverse effects of past victimization remain significant. Contemporary UREG members continue to suffer both from relative socio-economic deprivation – due in considerable part to lower rates of accumulation of capital of all kinds[2] as a result of past victimization – and from deeply entrenched forms of social exclusion, invidious stereotyping, and stigmatization. Surely they are deserving of some compensatory advantage when it comes to access to higher education at a good university or a desirable and well-paying job!

Some critics reject this argument on the grounds that injustice can only be done by – and redress can consequently only be due to – individuals, not groups; so that no group-based compensation can ever be justified. This position, however, is surely too rigid. The possibility of inter-group injustice has been recognized, and corresponding inter-group remedial compensation has been widely approved, in a number of historical circumstances: cases of war reparations, and the compensation of Jews by post-Nazi German governments, come to mind. One should therefore entertain the possibility that there are historical reasons – i.e. slavery and its aftermath – why UREG members as a group might be owed compensation by other groups.

The issue then turns on the appropriateness of PD as a mechanism for compensating UREGs for the historical injustice done to them. Here some serious problems come to the fore. First, those UREG members who gain directly from PD are at most a small number of all those who have been victimized by historical injustice. Moreover, they are very probably not among those who have suffered most – because they are well enough positioned to be applying for selection to a desirable position in the first place. Secondly, those applicants who are displaced by PD from selection to such a position are at most a very small number of those who are likely to have benefited from the historical injustice, and not necessarily among those who have benefited most (even though they may owe their relatively privileged position to some extent to the past injustice).

Proponents of PD as a remedy for injustice might respond by arguing that the UREG applicants who gain from PD deserve to be the specific recipients of compensation, since the historical injustice done to their community has had – among other effects – the specific effect of disadvantaging them in competition for selection to desired positions. For corresponding reasons, those applicants who lose from PD deserve to bear the burden of that compensation. It remains true, however, that the applicants involved constitute a very small proportion of those who have been either disadvantaged or advantaged by the historical injustice; and it is very hard to see why they should be singled out for remedial compensation. Thus PD should really be judged an inappropriate form of compensation: it violates basic principles of justice in requiring a small number of those owing compensation to shoulder the whole burden and in benefiting only a small number of those owed compensation.

If compensation to UREG members for historical injustice is indeed called for, there are clearly much better ways of doing it than via PD – ways which would target much better those UREG members deserving compensation and which would spread the cost much more widely among those people who have benefited from it. For example, one could suggest some kind of redistribution of income from taxpayers in general to the UREG population, structured so as to favor the most disadvantaged members of that population. Such redistribution need not result in cash payments to the beneficiaries; it could instead take the form of resources invested so as to raise the minimum levels of schooling and health care available to UREG members. Critics who argue that PD cannot be justified as compensation to remedy historical injustice are therefore on solid ground.

Reverse discrimination

The case against PD on grounds of procedural injustice views it as reverse discrimination against those non-UREG applicants for desired positions who are rejected in order to create room for those UREG members accepted by virtue of PD. This argument is rooted in the presumption that there is a legitimate set of selection qualifications on the basis of which all applicants are entitled to be considered, and that PD introduces an illegitimate characteristic – status as a UREG member – into the mix of qualifications that determine an applicant's merit for selection. If UREG status is indeed an illegitimate qualification, then its use to enhance prospects of selection does arbitrarily discriminate in favor of UREG applicants and against other applicants, thereby violating the important procedural principle of equal opportunity for all applicants.

But what makes a qualification legitimate for the purpose of selection decisions? Those who see PD as reverse discrimination tend to argue that, in order to be legitimate, a qualification must reflect some kind of "merit" reflecting voluntary action by the applicant rather than an involuntary characteristic ascribed to the applicant by virtue of his/her family background.[3] For most of these critics it seems self-evident that merit should be based on an applicant's past record of achievement. Some go so far – at least implicitly – as to identify merit with an applicant's score on standardized qualifying examinations. They see prima facie evidence of reverse discrimination in the fact that PD enables UREG applicants to gain access to universities and desirable jobs with lower scores on standardized examinations than their non–UREG competitors.

But this fact would imply unequal opportunity only if such scores constituted, in and of themselves, an appropriate criterion for determining who is qualified for admission. More sophisticated critics of PD recognize that such standardized tests may not be the best available measures of achievement; so they endorse more refined measurements taking into account other evidence of a candidate's achievement. What all the foregoing measures have in common is that they are based on performance with respect to an absolute standard of achievement. I will characterize them as indicators of "realized achievement."

There are several ways in which one might justify using only measures of realized achievement in assessing the merit of an applicant for a desired position, in which good performance is important. One might argue that applicants who show the greatest prior realized achievement will be most likely to do well in the position for which they are applying. One might argue that rewarding greater realized achievement with selection to a better position will provide a strong incentive for applicants to achieve. But these are consequentialist arguments, making the case that selection criteria restricted to measures of realized achievement will lead to good results. As such, they cannot be used to rule out a priori the use of other qualifications, like UREG status, on the grounds that they are illegitimately discriminatory – for it might well be shown that, under certain circumstances, the use of UREG status as a qualification leads to the best results.

The only way in which PD could properly be rejected a priori as a form of reverse discrimination is if UREG status could be shown to be an inappropriate qualification for selection decisions, whatever consequences its use might entail. In other words, one would have to show that the use of UREG status as a qualification violates some fundamental entitlement of every applicant to be evaluated on criteria that in no way involve his/her group identity. Some adherents of an a priori reverse discrimination view of PD do believe that it is immoral to use categories like racial, caste, tribal, or ethnic identity in any selection process. But skeptics are certainly justified in asking why this moral imperative should always trump others – for example, the moral imperative to assure that people are not disadvantaged by virtue of their UREG status.

The most compelling moral basis for entitlement to be selected for a good position is what an applicant has earned through his/her own prior effort and exertion. This is indeed the reason why measures of past achievement are often believed to be appropriate qualifications for selection, whereas qualifications assigned by virtue of family background (like UREG status) are not. A person's realized achievement, however, reflects not only that individual's effort and exertion, but also the individual's innate abilities and surrounding situational circumstances. Surely being born with great talent, or being raised in an affluent household with access to all kinds of opportunities, cannot be a basis of moral desert. Thus realized achievement fails to qualify as a basis for moral entitlement to selection. Some combination of realized achievement and UREG status might well come closer to reflecting the individual effort and exertion on which moral desert can legitimately be based, since UREG members who attain a given level of achievement are likely to have had to overcome more adverse situational circumstances than their non-UREG competitors.

I conclude that appeals to morality and justice are simply not adequate as a basis for assessing the desirability of positive discrimination. Concerns about morality and justice generate a good deal of the passion in debates about this controversial topic (as do, no doubt, considerations of self-interest). And concerns about morality and justice draw on deeply held values that people very much want to express. But there are many ways in which to express one's values, other than through support for or opposition to positive discrimination. In assessing whether or not positive discrimination is desirable, it is best to consider it in the form of a particular policy, undertaken in specific circumstances, with certain consequences. Some of these consequences may be good, providing benefits; some of them may be bad, incurring costs. The desirability of the policy will depend on the extent to which the benefits exceed the costs. From here on I will therefore focus attention on the consequentialist arguments made for or against positive discrimination.

Consequentialist arguments and claims in favor of positive discrimination

A variety of different kinds of consequentialist arguments have been put forward to justify PD policies. I organize them below into six basic arguments, each of which entails one or more claims about the beneficial consequences of PD. The six basic arguments can usefully be divided into three categories, according to whether they are concerned primarily with the effects of PD on (a) the society as a whole, (b) the organizations or institutions where PD policies are being applied, or (c) the welfare of members of the UREGs eligible for PD.

The most common argument in favor of PD sees it as fulfilling a broad social justice objective by compensating UREG members for a historical injustice done to their community:

1   *PD represents due compensation from the rest of society to UREG members*

I have rejected this argument in the sweeping form in which it is usually articulated. This does not, however, dispose of the case that a PD policy may have consequences that contribute in some significant compensatory way to the attainment of social justice. The following is a variant of the compensation-for-injustice theme that is a consequentialist and potentially valid claim:

1.1   *PD affirms society's commitment to reduce the continuing disadvantages experienced by UREG members as a consequence of past injustice*

Here it is claimed not that PD provides redress to individuals who have been harmed, but that it serves as an important way of signaling that the leaders of a society are committed to reducing the continuing disadvantages associated with UREG membership. There can be no doubt that the sorry history of past injustice done to people simply because of their UREG status is a major reason for the low levels of wealth accumulated by most UREG families (not only in the form of physical and financial assets, but also in the form of human and social capital). Lower levels of accumulated wealth are, in turn, a major source of contemporary UREG disadvantage. It would be impossible to determine in the case of each UREG family the precise amount of wealth lost because of past injustice; so there is no question here of precise compensation for harm done. But policies that serve in a general way to benefit UREG members can be – and often are – represented and perceived as an effort by society at large to recognize and redress a significant source of UREG disadvantage. As such, they can help to ease tensions and promote social harmony by showing UREG members that they are welcomed as equal and integral participants in the life of the society.[4]

A second argument for PD is also concerned with the welfare of the society as a whole:

2   PD promotes the integration of society's elite

This argument rests on the premise that society is made up not just of an aggregation of individuals but also, in a significant sense, an aggregation of groups. By ensuring better representation of previously under-represented groups in elite positions, PD is seen as having consequences that generate significant social, political, and economic benefits – not only for UREG members but also for the whole society.[5] The prospective benefits are articulated in the following claims, for each of which I provide a brief explanation:

2.1   PD strengthens the legitimacy of society's leadership

The legitimacy – and therefore the effectiveness – of a society's decision-making elite depends to a considerable extent on the degree to which it is perceived as representative of the groups that constitute the society. The strength of a democratic political system will therefore be enhanced if responsibility for decision-making is distributed among members of all relevant groups rather than dominated by members of just one or a few groups.

2.2   PD increases the number of UREG decision-makers, who are likely in turn to offer more and better opportunities to other UREG members

The opportunities available to members of any group will arguably be enhanced when more decision-making positions are occupied by members of that group.

2.3   *PD increases the number of UREG role models and mentors*

Such role models and mentors can be especially effective in motivating younger UREG members to study well and to work hard to develop their abilities.

2.4   *PD improves the performance of jobs in which quality of performance is enhanced if the job-holder is of UREG status*

Jobs serving a multicultural clientele are often best carried out by people with experience in multicultural situations; and jobs serving mostly members of a particular UREG are often best carried out by people from the same UREG.

2.5   *PD generates greater contributions of community-oriented service*

Because they themselves come from disadvantaged communities, members of the UREG elite are especially likely to contribute leadership and voluntary services – not only to their own communities, but also to the wider society. Such service contributions can be expected not only to increase the availability of services, opportunities, and resources to people at the lower end of the socio-economic ladder – including many UREG members. The improvement and expansion of service-oriented organizations can be expected also to strengthen institutions of civil society that are central to a successful democracy.

2.6   *PD helps to dispel negative stereotypes of UREG members*

By increasing UREG representation in society's most honored roles, PD can help to dispel stereotypical perceptions of UREG members as tending to be inherently incapable of meeting the responsibilities and demands of such positions. More generally, an integrated elite can help to overcome inter-group antipathies associated with persisting social, economic, and political disparities along ethnic lines.

   The next two basic arguments in favor of PD see it as improving the effectiveness of organizations or institutions that implement PD policies. The first of these two arguments addresses the process of selection of individuals from a pool of applicants:

3   *PD improves accuracy in the appraisal of applicant qualifications*

This argument begins with the presumption that conventional criteria for assessing the qualifications of applicants for positions in an organization or institution are deficient as measures of applicants' true potential – especially in the case of UREG applicants. This is attributed to the fact that conventional criteria (like scores on standardized tests) favor applicants who have enjoyed a situational advantage in their past preparation or (broadly defined) education – e.g. a good home environment for learning, high-quality schooling, special coaching in exam-taking skills. Applicants who have not had the benefit of such advantages are penalized with less impressive conventional credentials, even though their innate capacity for achievement may be high. It might be possible to offset this bias to some extent by using additional selection criteria less likely to be influenced by situational advantage. Even if some such measures are obtainable, however, they are unlikely to control adequately for the deficiencies in situational advantage experienced by UREG members as a consequence of their group identity. The use of PD is therefore needed in order to "level the playing field" for all applicants and to identify the most capable among them.

Two different claims of benefits are associated with this argument:

3.1   *PD improves organizational performance by increasing the average quality of individuals selected*

Selection processes will increase the average quality of selected applicants because highly capable UREG applicants (who would otherwise be rejected) will be selected in favor of less capable other applicants (who would otherwise be selected). Organizational performance will be enhanced both by the involvement of more capable individuals and by the higher overall performance standards that their presence will enable the organization to enforce.

3.2   *PD dispels UREG member cynicism due to perceived unfairness of selection processes*

Confidence that selection procedures do not discriminate unfairly against UREG applicants reduces resentment on the part of UREG members against others and fosters better inter-group relations.

The other argument oriented primarily to organizational or institutional efficiency is premised on the putative advantages of diversity in personnel:

4   *PD contributes to valuable diversity in an organization*

Here it is claimed that by assuring that the set of occupants of certain key positions is ethnically more diverse, PD enables an organization or institution to provide better-quality goods and/or services; thus:

4.1   *PD enables organizations to perform better by virtue of greater diversity in their personnel*

This claim is based on the premise that diversity among personnel provides a wider range of ideas, greater perspective, more productive interactions, and in general a more innovative and dynamic environment than could be expected from a more uniform group of individuals. The case for PD as a source of diversity presumes, of course, that diversity with respect to ethnic status, in particular, is an important source of the positive contributions just noted.

The last two basic arguments in favor of PD are oriented primarily to the welfare of members of the UREGs eligible for PD. The first of these arguments envisages benefits accruing to a broad range of UREG members:

5 *PD increases motivation on the part of young UREG members*

PD policies increase the range of opportunities available to UREG members, who would otherwise tend to be discouraged by their prospects of advancing in a society that has been in various ways inhospitable to them. Thus it is claimed that:

5.1 *PD motivates UREG youths to work harder to develop their human capital*

PD policies are expected to stimulate young UREG members to invest more often and/or more fully in the development and improvement of their human capital – their skills and capabilities – in order to take advantage of the greater opportunities for advancement made available to them.

The final argument for PD is also oriented to the welfare of UREG members – in this case, those who are the direct beneficiaries of a PD policy:

6 *PD spreads social capital to those who most need it*

UREG members striving for advancement tend to be disadvantaged by a relative lack of contacts and networks with people who can smooth their way to good career opportunities. In this context it is claimed that:

6.1 *PD helps to offset deficits in social capital that handicap UREG members*

By providing UREG applicants with preferred access to desirable educational institutions and job opportunities, PD can help to overcome their social capital deficit vis-à-vis their peers and enable them to get access to opportunities that would otherwise be denied them.[6]

Arguments and claims made in opposition to positive discrimination

The consequentialist arguments advanced to reject PD policies can be organized into six basic arguments against PD, most of which make several different claims. I again distinguish arguments according to whether they are concerned primarily with the effects of PD on (a) the society as a whole, (b) the organizations or institutions where PD policies are being applied, or (c) the welfare of members of the UREGs eligible for PD.

I have already rejected the procedural injustice argument that PD represents a form of discrimination on the basis of ethnic identity, which is *ipso facto* unacceptable. Rejection of this reverse discrimination argument, however, does not dispose of the possibility that PD may unfairly and inappropriately reward members of its beneficiary groups and penalize members of other groups. A consequentialist variant of the reverse discrimination argument is that PD policies are poorly tailored to help those who have been most victimized by discrimination, because they tend to benefit well-off UREG members:[7]

7   *PD is poorly tailored to help the most disadvantaged*

This argument is concerned with the implications of a PD policy for society as a whole. It leads to the following two claims about undesirable redistributive consequences of PD:

7.1   *PD exacerbates inequalities among UREG members*

7.2   *PD redistributes opportunities from less-well-off others to better-off UREG members*

In support of the first claim it is argued that PD beneficiaries are likely to be among the most privileged and best-off UREG members (the "creamy layer"), since the typical downtrodden and needy UREG member is not likely to be in a position even to apply for the kind of position where PD is applied. The second claim rests on this as well as a second premise, to the effect that those applicants who are displaced by PD from selection find themselves on the selection margin because they come from families that are not very well off. Any resulting inequitable redistribution from non-UREG to UREG members may well aggravate inter-group tensions.

A second basic argument against PD that is also oriented to the welfare of society as a whole is the following:

8   *PD exacerbates consciousness of distinctions between ethnic identity groups*

This argument – in sharp contrast to the corresponding argument 2 in favor of PD – rests on the premise that society ought best to be viewed by everyone as an aggregation of individuals rather than, in any significant sense, an aggregation of groups. Those who make this argument do not deny that many people may see themselves, in important ways, as members of a particular identity group; but they view this as a legacy of the past that ought not to intrude on political or economic decision-making. Ethnic categories like race, caste, tribe, etc. are especially suspect in this light: the greater is a society's obsession with ethnic group identity, the greater is the need to avoid the use of such categories to distinguish between people. If any positions are filled on a basis that includes consideration of a person's ethnic status, this will perpetuate invidious distinctions and serve to disintegrate rather than to integrate society.

In focusing attention on ethnic distinctions, PD is seen as generating a variety of adverse consequences – as reflected in the following claims:

8.1   *PD leads to more divisive identity group politics and the Balkanization of society*

Inter-group divisiveness will undermine the stability and legitimacy of a democratic system, and it will worsen relations between UREG members and other members of a society.[8]

8.2   *PD encourages deceitful efforts to claim UREG status in order to gain the resulting benefits*

This kind of deceit will worsen relations between UREG and other members of a society and lead to widespread cynicism.

8.3   *PD generates snowballing demands for preferences from members of groups not currently eligible for PD*

Preferences favoring some groups inevitably lead to demands for preferences in favor of other groups, with ever-weaker grounds for special consideration. Such consequences can certainly be expected to undermine social harmony.

The next basic argument against PD is, like argument 3, oriented to the effectiveness with which organizations or institutions function; but its logic is precisely the opposite:

9   *PD generates inaccuracy in the appraisal of applicant qualifications*

Like argument 3, this one rests on the premise that there should be a "level playing field" for all applicants in a process of selection to positions in an organization or institution. Proponents of each of these arguments seek to assure equal treatment of all applicants, so that their true qualifications are assessed fairly and appropriately, without being biased by irrelevant characteristics. The contention is over what it takes to assure equal treatment. Proponents of PD assert that this cannot be done without adding some positive consideration of UREG status to the selection process. Critics reply that, far from improving the accuracy with which applicants' potential for achievement is appraised, preference given to anyone with UREG status will result in an arbitrary and unfair distortion of the selection process.

Two different claims are associated with this argument, each of which directly counters the corresponding claim of argument 3:

9.1   *PD worsens organizational performance by reducing the average quality of individuals selected*

9.2   *PD causes resentment at the unfairness of selection processes by those who are ineligible for preferences*

The perception by non-UREG applicants that PD-oriented selection procedures discriminate unfairly against them will surely foster antagonism on their part against UREG members, which can lead not only to general deterioration in inter-group relations but also to greater non-UREG opposition to any effort to improve the lot of UREG members. Indeed, in a context where PD policies are operating, rejected non-UREG applicants often erroneously attribute their rejection to PD. As Kane (1998: 453) has noted, many more unsuccessful applicants for admission to a college or university attribute their rejection to PD than the actual number of applicants displaced by PD – in the same way as many more unsuccessful drivers attribute their failure to find a parking space to the existence of spaces reserved for handicapped drivers than the number of the latter who are actually able to park in a reserved space.

The remaining three arguments against PD all focus on alleged harm done to UREG members, for the benefit of whom PD policies are presumably enacted. The sharpest such argument is the following:[9]

10   *PD creates a mismatch between its direct beneficiaries and their organizational settings*

Opponents of PD claim that it does a great disservice to the beneficiaries themselves by creating a serious mismatch between their capabilities and the expectations of them in the positions to which they are given preferential access. Because PD places its beneficiaries in an educational or work setting in which they are likely to do very poorly, critics suggest that they might well have been better served by placement in a less challenging position.

The following two claims are made on the basis of this mismatch argument:

10.1   *UREG members generally display poor performance and are likely to fail in positions to which they have gained access by virtue of PD*

10.2   *PD exacerbates negative stereotypes of UREG members as innately inferior*

The second claim follows from the first: if the level of performance of most UREG members is significantly below that of most of their peers, this can be expected to strengthen already existing predilections to view UREG members as innately less capable than non-UREG members.

The next argument against PD is a direct counterpart to pro-PD argument 5:

11   *PD induces complacency on the part of young UREG members*

Like the corresponding argument 5 in favor of affirmative action, this argument focuses primarily on the way in which PD affects the structure of incentives faced by young UREG members. It is claimed that:

11.1   *PD inhibits UREG youths from working hard to develop their human capital*

This claim draws attention to the fact that PD's enhancement of opportunities for UREG members has a double-edged effect. At the same time that it increases the number and the scope of rewards available to UREG youths, it also enables them to advance more easily than would otherwise be possible. While the former effect may stimulate more effort and hard work on the part of young UREG members, the latter effect could lead them to slack off in the expectation that their UREG status will help them move up with less effort than their peers. Opponents of PD claim that this latter effect will dominate the former.

One final basic argument is advanced against PD, usually by successful UREG members themselves:

12   *PD results in devaluation of the accomplishments of UREG members*

This argument holds that any notable accomplishment of a UREG member is likely to be credited with less value in a context in which PD policies are applied than it would in the absence of PD. This is because such an accomplishment will be attributed at least to some extent to the preference conferred by PD rather than to the innate ability and effort of the UREG member – whether or not the person actually benefited from PD. This may not be fair, in cases where PD has played no role in the UREG member's accomplishment. But if PD serves to reduce rather than to increase the accuracy of measurement of UREG applicant qualifications – as is claimed by argument 9 against argument 3 – then it is rational for an observer to infer that selected applicants from a group that receives PD preferences will on average be less qualified, and less likely to achieve success on their own, than selected applicants from a group that does not receive such preferences (or other equivalent preferences).

Several kinds of adverse consequences are claimed to result from PD-induced devaluation of UREG member accomplishments, as follows:

12.1   *PD results in under-appreciation of the true capabilities and achievements of some UREG members*

Those UREG applicants who would have been selected without any PD preference will at times be erroneously presumed to have lower qualifications and skills than they really do. Apart from experiencing hurt feelings, they may find their opportunities limited because they are under-credited for their true capabilities and genuine achievements. This not only hurts those UREG members; it can also lead to inefficiency in organizational performance.

Table 3.1 **Arguments for positive discrimination, related claims of benefits, and societal goals linked to each claim**

Argument and related benefits		Societal goal
Involving overall societal well-being		
1	*Compensation for historical injustice*	
1.1	Affirmation of society's commitment to reduce UREG disadvantages	Harmony
2	*Integration of society's elite*	
2.1	Greater legitimacy of society's leadership	Democracy
2.2	More UREG decision-makers offering opportunities to UREG members	Equity
2.3	More UREG role models and mentors	Efficiency
2.4	Better performance of jobs if job-holder is of UREG status	Efficiency
2.5	Greater contributions of community-oriented service	Equity, democracy
2.6	More dispelling of negative stereotypes of UREG members	Harmony
Involving the effectiveness of organizational performance		
3	*Accuracy in appraising applicant qualifications*	
3.1	Increase in the average quality of individuals selected	Efficiency
3.2	Decrease in UREG cynicism about unfairness of selection processes	Harmony
4	*Contribution of diversity to organizational success*	
4.1	Better performance with more diverse personnel	Efficiency
Involving the welfare of UREG members		
5	*Motivation of young UREG members*	
5.1	More development of human capital by UREG youths	Efficiency, equity
6	*Spread of social capital*	
6.1	Greater offsetting of UREG member deficits in social capital	Equity

Table 3.2 Arguments against positive discrimination, related claims of costs, and societal goals linked to each claim

Argument and related costs	Societal goal
Involving overall societal well-being	
7 *Poor tailoring to help the most disadvantaged*	
7.1 Exacerbation of inequalities among UREG members	Equity
7.2 Redistribution from non-UREG to better-off UREG members	Equity, harmony
8 *Exacerbation of ethnic group consciousness*	
8.1 More divisive identity group politics	Democracy, harmony
8.2 Deceitful efforts to claim UREG status to gain resulting benefits	Harmony
8.3 Snowballing demands for group preferences	Harmony, democracy
Involving the effectiveness of organizational performance	
9 *Inaccuracy in appraising applicant qualifications*	
9.1 Decrease in average quality of individuals selected	Efficiency
9.2 Increase in non-UREG resentment about unfair selection processes	Harmony
Involving the welfare of UREG members	
10 *Mismatch of PD beneficiaries and organizational settings*	
10.1 Poor quality of performance, frequent failure by PD beneficiaries	Equity, efficiency
10.2 Exacerbation of negative stereotypes of UREG members	Harmony
11 *Complacency of young UREG members*	
11.1 Less development of human capital by UREG youths	Efficiency, equity
12 *Devaluation of the accomplishments of UREG members*	
12.1 Under-appreciation of true achievements of some UREG members	Equity, efficiency
12.2 Stigmatization of UREG members as not deserving their placement	Harmony
12.3 Low expectations of UREG members by others	Equity, efficiency

12.2   *PD results in the disparagement of UREG members in general as not really deserving to be placed in the positions to which some have gained access by virtue of PD*

Because many UREG members will have been selected by virtue of PD preferences, others will be likely to conclude that most UREG members of an organization are not as capable as their peers. This can result in the characterization of most UREG members as not really belonging in the positions that they hold.

12.3   *PD results in low expectations for UREG members on the part of others*

Whether this leads to neglect or to patronization of UREG members, it is likely to discourage them from developing their capabilities and realizing their full potential.

Societal goals underlying the benefits and costs of positive discrimination policies

In Tables 3.1 and 3.2 I list all of the arguments discussed above, as well as the claims that each makes about the consequences of applying PD policies. There are surely other arguments and claims that some proponents and opponents of PD have advanced in support of their positions. But I believe that the ones I have presented on each side of the debate encompass the most important consequentialist arguments and claims that have been made wherever PD has been debated.

Several of the six arguments for PD have more or less precise counterparts among the six arguments against PD. Thus the argument for PD as a means of achieving greater accuracy in the evaluation of applicant qualifications (argument 3) is directly opposed to the argument against PD as a source of inaccuracy in such evaluation (9). Likewise, the argument that PD improves the motivation and effort of UREG students (5) is directly contradicted by the argument that PD induces complacency and dependence on the part of UREG students (11). The argument in favor of PD for integrating society's elite (2), and the argument against PD for exacerbating group consciousness (8), come to opposite conclusions about the usefulness of making group distinctions based on race, caste, tribe, religion, or ethnicity. And the argument for PD on grounds of compensation for disadvantages due to historical injustice (1) can be juxtaposed with the argument against PD to the effect that it is poorly tailored to help the most disadvantaged (7). The remaining arguments on each side do not have such counterparts.

The claims listed under each argument presented in Tables 3.1 and 3.2 point to various possible beneficial and costly consequences that may result from a PD policy. In general, a policy of positive discrimination can be expected to generate some (if not all) of these possible beneficial and costly consequences, to an extent that depends on the specific nature of the policy

and the conditions under which it is applied. A full benefit–cost analysis of a
PD policy would require not only an assessment of the magnitude of the
various consequences ensuing from the policy, but also determination of the
way in which – and the extent to which – each consequence affects overall
societal well-being. A critical step in this kind of analysis is the specification of
the particular societal goals to which each beneficial consequence contributes
positively and to which each costly consequence contributes negatively.

In conventional benefit–cost analysis, societal well-being is equated with
the level of societal wealth; all benefits and costs are measured in terms of
their money value, and there is a single implicit societal goal – efficiency in
generating societal wealth. My discussion in this chapter of the arguments and
claims for and against positive discrimination makes it clear that in assessing
the benefits and costs of PD policies, we are dealing with a very broad set of
valued societal goals. The following four goals appear to be sufficient to
encompass the kinds of benefits and costs that proponents and opponents of
positive discrimination have in mind:

> *Social harmony* is enhanced when different groups in a multicultural society
> accept and respect one another, and when previously marginalized
> groups are welcomed into the mainstream of the society.
> *Democracy* is fortified when a democratic political system is stable and its
> leadership is perceived as legitimate, when the institutions that make
> up civic society are strong, and when people are empowered to
> participate constructively in democratic processes.
> *Productive efficiency*[10] is improved when society's resources are allocated
> and used more efficiently (i.e. less wastefully) in the production and
> utilization of goods and services, so that more net output is obtain-
> able from the available resources.
> *Distributive equity* is increased when opportunities, resources, or services
> are redistributed from a group that is relatively well off to a group
> that is relatively poorly off – e.g. from rich to poor or from non-
> UREG members to UREG members.

In Tables 3.1 and 3.2, following each possible (beneficial or costly) consequence of a PD policy, I indicate the main societal goals to which that
consequence contributes (positively or negatively).

The multiplicity of relevant goals makes it difficult to carry out a comprehensive benefit–cost analysis of PD policies.[11] People may well differ on how
much weight should be placed on contributions to the achievement of
greater social harmony, to a more vital democracy, to greater productive efficiency, or to redistribution in favor of the disadvantaged. The difficulty of a
formal benefit–cost analysis is compounded by the fact that some of the relevant goals are highly qualitative in nature, so it is virtually impossible to
measure in any precise way the magnitude of the associated benefits and costs.
How should one measure the value of the contribution to social harmony

made by affirmation of society's commitment to reducing the disadvantages of UREG members, or the value of the contribution to democracy made by strengthening the legitimacy of society's leadership?

Although a systematic benefit-cost analysis of any given PD policy is surely beyond reach, a benefit-cost framework of analysis can nonetheless be helpful in illuminating the consequences of a PD policy. For one thing, it can guide empirical investigation of the actual consequences of specific PD policies and thereby shed light on the desirability of those policies, even if it does not determine precisely the extent to which a given policy generates benefits and costs. In Part II of the book I will pursue such an empirical investigation of US and Indian PD policies in the sphere of admissions to higher educational institutions. A benefit–cost framework analysis can also guide qualitative assessment of the relative magnitudes of the benefits and the costs likely to be generated by different types of PD policies carried out under differing circumstances. This is my objective in the remainder of Part I.

In the following three chapters I will seek to analyze comparatively how well PD policies can be expected to work in the US and in India – given the very different contexts for positive discrimination in the two countries. How will I define "working well," in view of the multiplicity of relevant underlying goals and the difficulties of measuring contributions to those goals? I will consider a PD policy to be working well if significantly more of the potential benefits of PD (the claims listed in Table 3.1) than of the potential costs of PD (the claims listed in Table 3.1) are realized. I will infer that this is the case if significantly more claims of benefits than claims of costs are validated, or if – for the most part – claims of benefits are more strongly validated than claims of costs.

4 A theoretical analysis of the consequences of positive discrimination policies

My objective in this chapter is to develop a general model for comparative analysis of the way in which the context of a positive discrimination (PD) policy influences its likely consequences – i.e. its benefits and costs. I will then utilize this model in the following two chapters to undertake a qualitative comparative analysis of PD policies in the US and India.

Modeling the relationship between the context and the consequences of PD policies

The success or failure of a PD policy favoring an under-represented ethnic group (UREG) will clearly depend upon the context in which it is applied. In analyzing any given PD policy of this kind, we would like to know the extent to which the potential benefits and costs listed in the previous chapter will actually be realized. In some cases, under some conditions, there may be many benefits and few costs; under other conditions, in other cases, the opposite may be true. In order to analyze how variations in the context of a PD policy affect its chances of success or failure, it will be helpful to formulate a qualitative causal model linking various kinds of conditions to different kinds of potential benefits and potential costs.

What kinds of conditions are likely to affect the extent to which a given PD policy generates beneficial as opposed to costly consequences? First of all, the *characteristics of the PD policy* itself – its procedures, how they are implemented, etc. – will surely be important. As well, certain *characteristics of the under-represented ethnic group* favored by the PD policy are bound to matter. Furthermore, some *characteristics of the societal environment* within which the PD policy is applied are likely to make a difference. These three kinds of characteristics I will label "primary factors"; they are primary in the sense that they define the PD policy and the relevant context in which it is being carried out. Some or all of these primary factors may differ as between different PD policies and, as I will show below, variations in the characteristics of each primary factor have predictable effects on the consequences of a PD policy.

Two other kinds of circumstances associated with a PD policy seem highly likely to affect the benefits and/or costs it generates. The first and most obvious is the (average) *quality of performance by PD beneficiaries* in the positions to which the PD policy provide them access. Proponents of PD policies tend to argue that prospective beneficiaries will do very well, because they have suffered more from lack of access to good opportunities than from lack of ability to perform when given an opportunity. Critics of PD policies, conversely, tend to argue that prospective beneficiaries will do poorly, because they are not adequately prepared for the opportunities provided by positive discrimination. The extent to which a PD policy actually realizes many of its potential benefits and avoids many of its potential costs clearly depends on how well the beneficiaries of the policy actually do, once they get access to an educational or work setting by virtue of positive discrimination.

A second kind of circumstance is also likely to influence the consequences of a PD policy, but not so obviously. PD policies are motivated by a desire to overcome profound social and economic inequalities in a society – and thereby to enable people who have historically been excluded or marginalized to participate to a much fuller extent in the opportunities and resources of the society. On the face of it, it would seem most sensible for a policy aimed at overcoming such inequalities to provide benefits to those who are the most disadvantaged socio-economically – since socio-economic disadvantage is clearly a very important source of marginalization in a modern society. Indeed, PD policies are controversial in large part because they define beneficiaries not in terms of indicators of socio-economic disadvantage, but in terms of ethnic group identity. It follows that the desirability and the success of a PD policy will depend on the strength of the *need for a focus on ethnicity* – defined broadly to include race, caste, and tribe – as the basis for targeting beneficiaries of social welfare policies. A strong need for a focus on ethnicity, instead of (or in addition to) socio-economic class, will strengthen some of the benefits and weaken some of the costs anticipated from a policy of positive discrimination.

The above two kinds of circumstances I will label "intermediate factors," because they occupy an intermediate position in a causal chain running from the primary factors to the consequences of PD policies. Primary factors not only have a direct influence on the potential benefits and costs of any given PD policy; they may also exert an influence on intermediate factors, which in turn are likely to have a significant impact on the consequences of a PD policy.

The structure of my proposed model of the consequences of a PD policy is depicted by the diagram in Figure 4.1, which is arranged to show causal influences running from left to right. On the left-hand side are three boxes representing, respectively, characteristics of the PD policy, characteristics of the under-represented ethnic group eligible for PD, and characteristics of the larger societal environment in which the policy is carried out. Together, these three boxes account for the primary factors of the model.

On the right-hand side of the diagram is a circle representing the potential consequences of a PD policy – both positive (benefits) and negative (costs).

PRIMARY FACTORS   **INTERMEDIATE FACTORS**   **CONSEQUENCES**

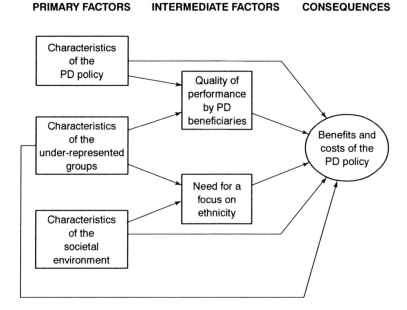

Figure 4.1   A model of the consequences of a PD policy

The potential benefits include all the favorable consequences claimed by arguments for positive discrimination – as discussed in Chapter 3 (see pp. 45–9) and listed in Table 3.1 (see p. 54); the potential costs include all the adverse consequences claimed by arguments against PD – as discussed in Chapter 3 (see pp. 49–56) and listed in Table 3.2 (see p. 55). Arrows running from the boxes representing different primary factors to the benefit–cost circle indicate that some characteristics of these factors have a direct influence on the magnitude of some of the benefits or costs resulting from the PD policy.

In the middle of the diagram are boxes representing the two intermediate factors of the model. The first is the quality of performance by PD beneficiaries, which depends on characteristics of the particular under-represented group and also on characteristics of the PD policy that is at issue. The second intermediate factor is the need for an ethnicity focus, which depends both on characteristics of the under-represented ethnic group in question and on characteristics of the societal environment. Each intermediate factor, in turn, has an important influence on the potential benefits and costs of positive discrimination – as indicated by the arrows running from these factors to the benefit–cost circle.

In the preceding paragraphs I have made a series of assertions about relationships between variables associated with a PD policy. These assertions are represented by the causal arrows in the diagram in Figure 4.1. It remains for me to justify the structure of causality depicted in the diagram. To do this I must first provide more detailed descriptions of the characteristics of the primary factors in the model, just as I have already done (in Chapter 3) by categorizing the potential benefits and costs of positive discrimination.

Characteristics of a PD policy

The first of the three primary factors in the model comprises characteristics of the PD policy itself – as opposed to the group or groups to which it is applied, or the societal context in which it is carried out. Each of these characteristics can vary across different beneficiary groups within a particular society, so that a given society can have as many PD policies operative at one time as it has beneficiary groups. In practice, however, societies tend to maintain certain common characteristics in the PD policies that are applied to different beneficiary groups. In the following paragraphs I identify variable characteristics of PD policies that seem likely to be important for comparative analysis. I began by considering what may appear to be the most important defining characteristic of a PD policy: whether it involves *quotas* or *preferential boosts*.

A PD policy may involve the establishment of a quota – a certain number or proportion of positions reserved for members of a UREG – and thus divide the overall competition for selection into two separate competitions: one open to UREG members only and the other open to all other applicants. Separate quotas and competitions may of course be established for members of different UREGs. Whatever the criteria for ranking applicants, these criteria are applied separately to each group of applicants; and the highest-ranking applicants in each group are selected until the available positions are filled. In this kind of selection process, the number or proportion of selected members of any PD-favored UREG will equal the size of the quota for that UREG (unless fewer UREG applicants actually apply). A variant of this kind of selection process is one that excludes from the reserved quota those UREG applicants whose conventional qualifications (i.e. those qualifications not linked to an applicant's ascriptive characteristics) enable them to be selected in competition with all other applicants. In this case, all the UREG applicants who are selected to reserved seats rank lower, by the relevant ranking criteria, than those selected in the general competition; and the overall number of UREG applicants selected may exceed the quota reserved for them.[1]

The principal alternative to such a quota system is one in which there is a single general competition for selection, but members of a UREG are given a preferential boost in the form of more favorable consideration in the determination of the ranking of candidates. In the case of quantitative selection procedures, in which an applicant's qualifications are summarized in an overall point score in order to determine his/her position in the rank order, the preferential boost could take the form of a certain number of additional points credited to UREG applicants. In the case of qualitative selection procedures, in which a variety of applicant qualifications are taken into account but not formally aggregated into a single overall point score, the preferential boost would take a less precise form; for example, UREG applications could be viewed in a rosier light or given extra credit for signs of unrealized potential. Different degrees of preferential boost may of course be given to applicants from different UREGs. In any kind of preferential-boost system, one cannot be certain in advance how many applicants from each UREG will be selected.

The difference between a quota system and a preferential-boost system is not as great as it may first appear. Corresponding to a quota system that selects any given number n of UREG applicants for a particular position, there is bound to be some amount of preferential boost that leads to the same outcome. In the case of a selection process in which applicants' qualifications are summarized in a single point score, the amount of preferential boost that would do so is the number of points needed to bring the nth UREG applicant's score up to the level that would make him/her the last applicant admitted in the general competition.[2]

Notwithstanding the formal correspondence between quota and preferential-boost systems, there remains a substantive difference between the two systems insofar as the parameters of each kind of system – the size of the quota or the amount of the preferential boost – are held constant for a period of time. A preferential-boost system assures that the gap in conventional qualifications between UREG applicants selected and other applicants selected does not vary much over time, while the number (or proportion) of UREG applicants selected will in all likelihood vary from one competition to the next. A quota system assures that the number – or the proportion – of UREG applicants selected will remain constant (unless the quota is not filled), while the gap in conventional qualifications will likely vary considerably over time.

In practice, quota systems are often constrained by specification of minimum conventional qualifications (e.g. a minimum qualifying score) below which UREG applicants will be rejected, even if their quota is not filled. Whenever such a minimum conventional qualifications requirement serves to keep the number of accepted applicants below or equal to the quota, this kind of constrained quota system has the same effect as a preferential-boost system in which the size of the preferential boost is equal to the gap between the minimum conventional qualifications required of a successful UREG applicant and the conventional qualifications of the last applicant admitted in the general competition.[3]

From this discussion we may conclude that a pure quota system is considerably more arbitrary than either a constrained quota system or a preferential-boost system of positive discrimination. By focusing on a target number or proportion of UREG applicants to be selected, a pure quota system ignores problems likely to arise if the conventional qualifications gap between UREG and other applicants selected becomes substantial. At the same time, however, it should be clear that the choice among a pure quota system, a constrained quota system, and a preferential-boost system is not the most critical choice for the success or failure of a PD policy. Several other characteristics of the selection system employed by a PD policy are likely to have more significant effects on the consequences of the policy.

Magnitude of the preference   An obviously important dimension of any PD policy is the extent to which it intervenes in and perturbs the allocation of available positions between UREG and other applicants, as compared with the allocation that would obtain in the absence of the policy. This could be measured by its displacement impact – defined as the proportion of desired positions that are shifted by a PD policy to UREG applicants who would otherwise not have been selected. An alternative way to measure the impact of a PD policy focuses on the magnitude of the preference extended to PD beneficiaries.[4] The magnitude of preference is easy to measure for selection procedures that are quantitative, in the sense that applicants' qualifications are summarized in an overall point score. In the case of a quantitative preferential-boost system, it is simply the number of additional points granted to UREG members. In the case of a quantitative quota system, it is the difference between the point score of the marginal applicant selected in the general competition and that of the marginal applicant selected in the UREG competition.

When a PD selection procedure is qualitative, involving consideration of a variety of qualifications that are not scored and aggregated into a single overall point score for each applicant, the average amount of preference extended to PD beneficiaries is implicit in the process and much harder to measure. In such situations one can only try to estimate the magnitude of the preference by *ex post facto* construction of a numerical scoring framework within which relevant applicant qualifications can be quantified and aggregated into a single overall attributed point score for each applicant. (An applicant's standardized test score alone could serve as a simple, if crude, measure of such a point score.) The magnitude of the preference extended to PD beneficiaries can then be approximated by the difference between the average attributed point score of the lowest-scoring subset (say 20 per cent) of UREG applicants selected and that of the lowest-scoring subset (of the same number) of non-UREG applicants selected. The reason for choosing subsets of applicants rather than marginal individual applicants is that, in the context of a qualitative PD selection procedure, there is bound to be a good deal of overlap between the bottom ends of the distributions of attributed point scores for UREG applicants and non-UREG applicants.[5]

Insofar as the conventional qualifications of an applicant are a good predictor of his/her performance in the position at issue, the magnitude of the preference extended to UREG applicants is the best measure of the impact of a PD policy for the purpose of evaluating its effect on the likelihood of successful performance by beneficiaries – and on any PD consequences linked to beneficiary performance. On the other hand, the displacement impact of a PD policy will be the most relevant measure of PD impact when it comes to the effect of such a policy on the non-beneficiaries and, in particular, the extent to which they are disturbed and resentful about its impact on their own fortunes. For these purposes, what is most relevant is not the displacement impact of a single PD policy favoring members of one UREG, but the overall displacement impact of the PD policies for all favored UREGs operative in a society at a given time. This is really a characteristic of the societal environment, not of a PD policy applied to a particular UREG, so I will include it in the discussion of societal characteristics below.

Sensitivity of the selection process   PD policies vary greatly with respect to the sensitivity – as opposed to the rigidity – of the process whereby UREG applicants are selected. The most rigid type of process involves a quantitative procedure in which all applicants take some kind of standardized test and are ranked simply by scores on that test. In a quota system, the test rankings are used to select UREG and non-UREG applicants in separate competitions; in a preferential-boost system, a certain number of points are added to UREG applicant scores before all candidates are ranked for selection in a single competition. A somewhat less rigid selection process would take account of several different qualification criteria, not just a test score. This kind of process would assign scores on each criterion to every applicant and then aggregate every applicant's scores into a composite quantitative index for purposes of ranking, prior to the selection of UREG applicants via a quota or preferential-boost system.

A selection process becomes progressively more sensitive – or nuanced – the greater is the variety as well as the number of criteria involved in ranking applicants. Even more important, a selection process becomes more sensitive – or nuanced – the more the process of evaluating an applicant's standing with respect to relevant criteria is a qualitative rather than a quantitative one, involving considered judgment by selection personnel rather than mechanically determined scores fed into a composite index. A highly sensitive PD selection process could not only include qualitative evaluation of the extent to which a UREG applicant satisfies various relevant criteria; it could also treat UREG status as a signal to look especially hard for evidence of additional applicant characteristics suggesting a strong potential for good performance.

Sensitive selection processes are harder and more costly to administer than rigid ones, since they require that more information of various kinds be gathered from applicants and that more people be employed to implement the selection process. On the other hand, more sensitive selection processes are likely to be able to discriminate more accurately between those UREG applicants with the potential to succeed and those more likely to fail in the positions to which a PD policy could provide them access.

Identifiability of the PD beneficiaries   The existence of a PD policy means, of course, that some individuals selected in a competition will owe their selection to that policy. Depending on how the PD policy is implemented, however, the identity of the beneficiaries – as well as their total number – may or may not be known to anyone other than those administering the selection process (and sometimes not even to them). This is not a trivial matter, because both the self-esteem of a beneficiary and his/her treatment by others may be adversely affected by knowledge that he/she would not have been selected in the absence of the PD policy. Thus one characteristic of a PD policy relevant for its consequences is the extent to which PD beneficiaries are made identifiable.

One might at first presume that a quota system necessarily makes PD beneficiaries identifiable and a preferential-boost system does not. The fact that a quota system channels UREG members into separate competitions for reserved positions, however, does not require that those chosen in each competition be separately identified. And even when the number of positions reserved for a particular UREG is known, that does not mean that an equivalent number of UREG members owe their positions to positive discrimination; for it is always possible that some of the successful UREG applicants did not need positive discrimination to be selected and/or that some of the reserved positions went unfilled. Conversely, the fact that a PD policy is based upon a preferential boost does not always preclude the selection administrators from revealing who required such a boost in order to be selected. Under a preferential-boost system it is not always clear precisely which successful UREG applicants owe their selection to the PD policy, so identification of PD beneficiaries is less likely to occur under such a system than under a quota system. But whether or not it occurs under any selection process is really a policy variable.

Extent of support for the PD beneficiaries   Whether or not a PD beneficiary is able to meet the challenges of the position to which positive discrimination has provided access may well depend significantly on the extent to which support is made available after the person is selected. Policies of positive discrimination can stop once the selection process is over (costing no more than the administrative expenses of that process), or they can involve various forms of subsequent support for PD beneficiaries (costing a good deal more in resources). There are several kinds of support at the organizational or institutional level that can be helpful for PD beneficiaries, whether in an educational or a workplace setting. These include both human resources, such as favorable attitudes on the part of supervisors and mentoring on the part of colleagues, and financial resources made available for programs and activities that help PD beneficiaries to adjust to their new settings and to work productively in them. Resources of these kinds will no doubt be most plentifully available in well-endowed elite institutions. Note that the provision of such support to PD beneficiaries either requires that they be publicly identified as beneficiaries or that the support be extended to a broader group, including non-beneficiaries as well, which is correspondingly more costly.

Characteristics of a UREG

The second primary factor in the model comprises characteristics of the UREG favored by a policy of positive discrimination. By definition, such a group must be one whose members share a virtually inalterable ethnic identity and are under-represented in society's desirable positions (see introductory definitions, pp. 4–5). Different UREGs, however, can differ considerably with respect to a number of characteristics likely to be relevant for the consequences of a PD policy.

Degree of homogeneity   Members of a UREG may share certain common traits distinguishing them clearly from others, and they may identify themselves strongly with one another as against other members of the society, in which case the group is highly homogeneous. Alternatively, a UREG may be quite heterogeneous – encompassing a set of distinct sub-groups, whose members identify more closely with their sub-group than with the group as a whole.

Degree of recognizability   Members of some UREGs are distinguished by physical markers that are easily recognizable by others. Members of other groups may be distinguished primarily by cultural differences that are difficult for an outsider to gauge.

Extent of socio-economic disadvantage   Since the point of PD policies is to benefit members of ethnic groups who are under-represented in society's desirable positions, it is almost certainly the case that members of these groups will be disproportionately over-represented in the lower socio-economic strata of the society and socio-economically under-represented relative to the rest of the population. UREGs, however, can clearly differ in the extent to which their members, on average, are socio-economically disadvantaged.

Extent of mistreatment   UREGs are typically characterized by a history of mistreatment by other groups, ranging from identity-based discrimination against their members to persecution of them. In some cases such mistreatment may be continuing in the present time. But different groups will surely differ in the extent to which their members have been and still are mistreated.

Extent of stigmatization   Mistreatment of a UREG is generally accompanied by – and often rationalized by – an invidious ideology that stereotypes its victims as innately inferior and unworthy of equal treatment.[6] UREGs can and will differ in the extent to which their members are exposed to such stigmatization.

Extent of segregation   Both because of their socio-economic disadvantage and because of their stigmatization, UREG members are likely to find themselves residentially segregated – whether by regions of a country or by neighborhoods of a locality. Such residential segregation implies also a significant degree of "social segregation," i.e. separation from the social networks, institutions, and activities that constitute a society's social capital. Clearly there can be considerable variation across groups in the extent of their segregation; this variable is likely to correlate with the extent of a group's socio-economic disadvantage as well as the extent of the stigmatization to which its members are exposed.

Characteristics of a societal environment

The third primary factor in the model comprises a few key social and economic characteristics of the societal environment in which a PD policy is carried out. There are many such characteristics that could conceivably influence, directly or indirectly, the consequences of a PD policy; but the following seem likely to be most important.

Societal salience of ethnicity   The kinds of PD policies under study here are those that favor particular ethnic groups over others. In some societies people are highly conscious of one another's ethnicity and deem it an important personal characteristic; in others there is far less ethnic consciousness. It stands to reason that the salience of ethnicity will influence the extent to which PD policies can achieve benefits associated with gains for favored under-represented ethnic groups while limiting costs associated with inter-ethnic conflict and disharmony – such as divisive identity politics.

Degree of societal elitism   The justification for PD policies in favor of certain under-represented ethnic groups has much to do with the desire to overcome traditional hierarchies of wealth, power, and influence that divide the elite from the masses along ethnic lines. It follows that the extent to which hierarchy is ingrained in a society – or the strength of its elitism – will be likely to play a significant role in influencing the need for and the consequences of a PD policy.

Job prospects for educated youths   PD policies involve preferential selection into higher educational institutions that position graduates for highly desired jobs or preferential selection directly into jobs that typically require a good higher education. The stiffer the competition for such jobs in a society, the greater will be the stakes in getting access to the opportunities affected by positive discrimination. Thus the state of the market for well-educated youths will surely influence the benefits and the costs of a PD policy.

Overall PD displacement impact   The consequences of any given PD policy will also surely depend on the extent to which the society as a whole is affected by such policies. More precisely, it will depend on the extent to which a society's PD policies, taken together, change the allocation of desired positions as between members of UREGs benefiting from PD policies and the rest of the society's members. If only a relatively small proportion of desired positions are reallocated by PD policies from the latter to the former, then the impact of positive discrimination is bound to be quite different than if a very substantial proportion of positions are displaced in this way. Thus a final highly relevant characteristic of the societal environment in which any given PD policy is carried out is the overall proportion of positions displaced by its PD policies.

Justification for the causal structure of the model

In the remainder of this chapter, I will address in detail the way in which variations in the conditions under which a PD policy is applied are likely to affect the consequences of the policy – i.e. the potential benefits associated with the favorable claims listed in Table 3.1 and the potential costs associated with the adverse claims listed in Table 3.2. I will do so by exploring in detail the causal paths represented by each of the arrows in the model depicted in Figure 4.1; I will then summarize the results of this analysis in Table 4.1.

Determination of the quality of performance by PD beneficiaries

Performance quality is relevant not only in the educational institution or work position to which a UREG member directly gains access via positive discrimination, but also in any subsequent program of study or career path on which the UREG member embarks after completing the initial academic program or job. Some of the benefits and costs claimed for positive discrimination show up only at the latter stage; and how well a UREG member does at that stage is not completely dependent on how well he/she does at the first stage. One can distinguish three levels of performance at the first stage: one that leads to a good subsequent career; one that allows progression to an adequate subsequent career; and one that precludes moving on to a satisfactory career. Only the latter level of performance is unsatisfactory, in that it entails a significant cost – to society, and very probably also to the UREG member him/herself.

It is a real challenge for PD beneficiaries to perform satisfactorily, given the variety of obstacles they are likely to face when they gain access to an educational institution or a job via PD. Not only are their conventional credentials weaker, but their socio-economic background is often poor, and the new environment is usually unfamiliar (given the likely lack of any family tradition in this area). Moreover, they may well be exposed to various forms of discrimination because of their UREG status. One must therefore be concerned about whether the social experiment set in motion by positive discrimination will actually work in most cases. Is opportunity, combined with talent and desire, enough to overcome the obstacles? The following characteristics of the context of a PD policy are likely to have an effect on the proportion of PD beneficiaries who perform satisfactorily; I address these characteristics (roughly) in the order of the significance of their influence.

First of all, the performance level of PD beneficiaries will vary positively with the degree to which they are prepared by previous training for the challenges of their new task. Under the reasonable assumption that conventional qualifications for selection – such as standardized examination scores – reflect to some extent the adequacy of such preparation, PD beneficiaries will on average be better prepared the more closely their conventional qualifications approach those of other successful applicants. This means that they can be expected to perform better, the *smaller* is the *magnitude of the preference* given by the PD policy.

In order to overcome the kinds of obstacles to good performance noted above, many PD beneficiaries are likely to need access to support mechanisms in their study or work environment – over and above what is routinely available to all students or employees. Thus the average quality of performance of PD beneficiaries will surely vary *positively* with the *extent of support for the PD beneficiaries* – in the form of facilities and programs provided by the institutions into which they are selected and special attention from the personnel under whom they are performing.

Although PD beneficiaries will generally be weaker in conventional selection qualifications than are other selected applicants, they may well be more capable than is reflected by such measures. The level of performance of a PD beneficiary will thus vary positively with the extent to which he/she has capabilities not reflected in the conventional measures. The chances that PD beneficiaries will indeed have such hidden potential will vary *positively* with the *sensitivity of the selection process* employed by the PD policy. Insofar as the process is rigid and mechanical in identifying PD beneficiaries, it will be less likely to succeed in determining whether an individual applicant has promise unrecognized by his/her formal qualifications. From this perspective, an ideal PD policy is one in which selection committees can assess on a case-by-case basis (including personal interviews with applicants) whether or not each such applicant is likely to have the drive, initiative, and perseverance to succeed in a challenging new environment.

The ability of PD beneficiaries to perform well will likely also vary *inversely* with the *extent of socio-economic disadvantage* of the UREG. High family socio-economic status provides a good home environment, access to good schooling, and contacts with high-status friends and relatives – all of which are conducive to developing patterns of behavior that are helpful for successful performance in higher educational institutions and high-level job settings. Furthermore, in order to perform well (or even just to maintain one's position), one must be able to concentrate on the task(s) at hand – without being too much or too frequently disturbed by personal, family, or community problems. The degree to which one can expect to be troubled by such disturbing distractions is likely to be highly correlated with low socio-economic status – not only because there will be more problems to address, but also because there are likely to be fewer other members of the family or the community well placed to deal with such problems. Some PD beneficiaries may well come from families of high socio-economic status; but the more the UREG as a whole is socio-economically disadvantaged, the more this is likely to be true of its PD beneficiaries.

The ability of a PD beneficiary to perform well is likely also to be affected by whether or not he/she is readily identifiable to others as a beneficiary. If the person's status is evident to one and all, he/she is likely to feel greater pressure to perform well in order to justify his/her presence; this can easily lead to counter-productive anxiety. Thus performance quality is likely to vary *inversely* with the *identifiability of the PD beneficiaries*.

The extent to which conventional selection criteria understate the potential of UREG applicants is likely to be greater the greater the degree of anxiety – and consequently poor performance – exhibited by UREG members when their performance is being evaluated for the purpose of establishing their qualifications. As recent psychological studies in the US have shown, members of groups widely stigmatized as inferior are particularly subject to such anxieties, which are described by the term "stereotype threat."[7] It follows that the amount of hidden capabilities to be found in applicants from any particular UREG is likely to vary *positively* with the *extent of stigmatization* of that UREG in the society.

How the quality of performance by PD beneficiaries affects PD outcomes

The quality of performance of PD beneficiaries is obviously important for the results of PD policies. But which potential benefits and costs does it affect, and in what ways? Good quality of performance of PD beneficiaries is important for realizing the benefits claimed by several of the arguments in favor of positive discrimination (arguments are identified below by the number used in listing them in Tables 3.1 and 3.2):

2   For PD to succeed in contributing to the integration of UREG members into the societal elite, PD beneficiaries must do well enough in their educational institutions so as to complete their programs of study and graduate with a degree, or well enough in their first job setting at least to keep the job and – better yet – to be a candidate for promotion or a move to a higher-level job.

3   For PD to have succeeded in improving the accuracy with which applicant qualifications are assessed, PD beneficiaries must perform well in their studies or in their jobs. Indeed, the performance criterion is more demanding in the case of this argument than in the others listed here: PD beneficiaries must perform at least as well as those displaced by PD would have done. Since this "catch-up" level of UREG performance is very difficult to achieve, one must expect that the benefits claimed by argument 3 will not often be realized.

4   For PD to succeed in improving organizational performance via greater diversity in personnel, PD beneficiaries must do well enough in their studies or their jobs so as to remain in good standing.

5   For PD to succeed in increasing motivation and effort on the part of young UREG members, PD beneficiaries must do well enough in their studies or jobs to encourage UREG youths to believe that they will be able to succeed when given preferential access to such opportunities.

6   For PD to succeed in enabling UREG members to benefit from additional social capital, PD beneficiaries must do well enough in their
educational institutions so as to complete their programs of study and
graduate with a degree, or do well enough in their first job setting, so as
to be eligible for a promotion or a move to a higher-level job.

All in all, the stronger the quality of performance by PD beneficiaries, the
greater will be the *benefits* claimed by most of the arguments in favor of positive discrimination.

At the same time, good quality of performance of PD beneficiaries is
important for limiting the costs claimed by some of the arguments against
positive discrimination:

9   For PD to avoid generating inaccuracy in the assessment of applicant
qualifications, PD beneficiaries must perform well in their studies or in
their jobs. Indeed, as noted above, PD beneficiaries must perform at least
as well as those displaced by PD would have done – a stiff challenge.
10   For PD to avoid generating a mismatch between its direct beneficiaries
and their organizational settings, beneficiaries must do well enough in
their educational institutions so as to complete their programs of study
and graduate with a degree, or well enough in their first job setting so as
to keep their job and remain in good standing.
12   For PD not to result in devaluation of the accomplishments of UREG
members, PD beneficiaries must perform at least as well as those
displaced by PD would have done. This is the same demanding criterion
that must be satisfied in order to achieve the benefits claimed by argument 3 and to avoid the costs claimed by argument 9.

In sum, the stronger the quality of performance by PD beneficiaries, the *lesser*
will be the *costs* claimed by several of the arguments against PD.

Determination of the need for an ethnicity focus

The need for a society to define beneficiaries of social policies in terms of
ethnic identity depends primarily on certain characteristics of the ethnic
group(s) targeted for positive discrimination; but some characteristics of the
general societal environment may also be relevant. The particular characteristics that are most likely to affect the need for an ethnicity focus are discussed
below (roughly) in the order of the significance of their influence.

The case for identifying a particular ethnic group as a deserving beneficiary of social policies is clearly stronger the *greater* is the *extent of mistreatment*
to which its ethnic identity has exposed it. Indeed, one of the main sources of
the demand for positive discrimination is the desire to remedy the historical
injustice done to a group victimized by negative discrimination and other
forms of mistreatment. Past victimization has negative consequences that can

and do persist for generations. The case for an ethnicity focus is all the stronger to the extent that a group's ethnic identity continues to subject it to unfair treatment in the present. Under such circumstances its ethnic identity has been and is a significant liability, independently of socio-economic status (though it is often linked with low socio-economic status for most group members).

The justification for focusing on ethnic identity is also stronger the *more* powerful and entrenched is society's *extent of stigmatization* of the ethnic group as inferior. This characteristic is clearly closely linked to the weight of the burden borne by an ethnic group because of its exposure to unfair treatment, since belief in the inferiority of a group is an important source of – and often a rationale for – mistreatment of it.

The need for defining beneficiaries in ethnic terms is a *positive* function of the *degree of homogeneity* of the members of a given ethnic group. The justification for focusing on ethnicity clearly hinges on the significance of a common ethnic identity as a source of a common pattern of disadvantage for group members. To the extent that the ethnicity of group members is heterogeneous, group members have less in common and are less likely to be victimized to the same extent because of their common group identity; by the same token, the rationale for treating them the same way in a PD policy is weakened.

The need for defining beneficiaries in ethnic terms would appear to be stronger the *greater* is the *societal salience of ethnicity*. The more that a person's ethnic group identity is salient for the rest of the population, the more likely it is that members of disparaged ethnic groups will continue to be stigmatized as innately inferior and discriminated against by members of other groups. It follows that societies in which ethnicity is highly salient are also particularly likely to need ethnically based remedies to combat ethnically oriented injustices and inequalities. This is the basis for the assertion that "in order to get beyond racism, we must first take race into account."[8] To be sure, a high societal salience of ethnicity can also put a premium on reducing attention to ethnic distinctions – a point I will return to below.

Finally, a particular ethnic group has a stronger case for an ethnicity focus the *greater* is the *extent of segregation* of its members from the rest of the society's population. Residential and social segregation from society's mainstream enhances the degree to which members of an ethnic group share common disadvantages and are marginalized in common ways, irrespective of their socio-economic status.

How the need for an ethnicity focus affects PD outcomes

Like the quality of performance of PD beneficiaries, the need for focusing on ethnic identity affects both the benefits and the costs of a PD policy. The stronger the justification for defining beneficiaries of social policies in ethnic

– as distinct from socio-economic – terms, the *greater* will be the value of the *benefits* claimed by several of the arguments in favor of positive discrimination:

1   Affirmation of society's commitment to reduce the continuing disadvantages of UREG members is all the more important, insofar as UREG identity is a major source of such disadvantages.
2   Integration of UREG members into the societal elite is all the more important, insofar as UREG status is more significant as a group marker and a barrier to social mobility than low socio-economic class.
4   Greater diversity in personnel is all the more likely to contribute to improved organizational performance, insofar as membership of a UREG is more likely than membership of a low socio-economic class to be a source of perspectives that differ from those of the mainstream.
6   UREG members are likely to benefit all the more from additional social capital, insofar as UREG status *ipso facto* serves as a barrier to integration into mainstream networks and institutions.

The stronger the justification for defining beneficiaries of social policies in ethnic – as distinct from socio-economic – terms, the *lesser* will be some of the *costs* claimed by a few of the arguments against positive discrimination, for the reasons discussed below:

7   Redistribution in favor of well-off UREG families (the "creamy layer") is likely to be much more limited, insofar as the families of UREG beneficiaries are less likely to have made it into the upper strata of society.
8   Inter-ethnic tensions arising from heightened consciousness of ethnic distinctions are likely to be more limited, insofar as UREG beneficiaries are perceived as deserving of special benefits because of the disadvantages their UREG identity has caused them.

Thus far I have examined how characteristics of each of the three primary factors can affect PD outcomes *indirectly* via their effect on the quality of performance of PD beneficiaries and the need for a focus on ethnicity. Next I consider how certain characteristics of each of the three factors can *directly* generate PD benefits or costs.

How differences in the context of a PD policy directly affect its consequences

The following characteristics of a PD policy, a UREG, or the societal environment are likely to have a direct effect on some of the potential benefits and costs of positive discrimination. Once again, I address the characteristics (roughly) in the order of the significance of their influence.

Degree of homogeneity   The greater is the degree of homogeneity characterizing a UREG favored by positive discrimination, the more significant are the likely benefits from integration of members of that UREG into the societal elite (argument 2). The reason for this is that the gains from such integration are largely dependent on the ability of the integrated PD beneficiaries to represent, in a significant sense, their less-well-off fellow UREG members. If the UREG is quite heterogeneous – consisting of a collection of distinct subgroups – then any given UREG member is likely to think of him/herself, and to be perceived by others, as representing his/her sub-group much more than the UREG as a whole. As a consequence, the trickle-down or spread effects from the elite PD beneficiary to less fortunate UREG members would be much more limited; indeed, they might well affect only members of the same sub-group. This is especially relevant to claims of PD benefits involving provision of opportunities to other UREG members (claim 2.2) and service as role models and mentors for other UREG members (claim 2.3).

A high degree of homogeneity in a UREG also tends to reduce the costs of positive discrimination associated with adverse redistributional effects (argument 7), because PD beneficiaries are then less likely to come disproportionately from certain relatively privileged sub-groups within the UREG as a whole. When a UREG is heterogeneous, PD policies may not only redistribute income and opportunity toward the best-off individual UREG members (the creamy layer); they may well also redistribute income and opportunity disproportionately to members of the best-off sub-groups of the UREG.

Overall PD displacement impact   The greater is the extent of displacement by PD beneficiaries of applicants from groups ineligible for positive discrimination, the more such applicants will perceive themselves to be displaced by PD policies, and the more will positive discrimination be experienced by those excluded from its benefits as threatening to their interests. This, in turn, is bound to increase the degree of antagonism felt by ineligible group members toward eligible group members (claim 9.2), and it is likely to heighten problems associated with attention to ethnic distinctions (argument 8).

Magnitude of the preference   The larger the size of the preference given by a PD policy to get UREG members selected, the greater is likely to be the degree of resentment on the part of applicants who were – or who believe themselves to have been – displaced by the PD beneficiaries (claim 9.2). Not only will the costs of positive discrimination resulting from such resentment be heightened; but the same is true of the costs of positive discrimination associated with exacerbated consciousness of ethnic distinctions (argument 8).

Job prospects for educated youths   The better are the overall job prospects for educated youths, the less will members of groups ineligible for positive discrimination have to worry about competition from PD beneficiaries. It follows that in a society with good job prospects for educated youths, PD policies will entail less resentment by non-beneficiaries about the unfairness of selection processes (claim 9.2). By the same token, there will be fewer costs associated with exacerbated consciousness of ethnic distinctions (argument 8).

Degree of societal elitism   The greater the degree of elitism in a society, the more difficult it is for those not among the elite to achieve upward social and economic mobility. This point does not strengthen the case for an ethnicity focus, since the argument applies equally to a focus on socio-economic class. It does, however, imply that any policy that increases the upward mobility of members of groups under-represented among society's elite – like positive discrimination – is likely to produce more significant benefits from integrating the elite (argument 2) than would be the case if the society were less elitist to begin with.

Extent of support for PD beneficiaries   Higher levels of organizational and personal resources committed to support of positive discrimination and its beneficiaries make it more likely that benefits associated with two kinds of pro-PD arguments will be realized. First, such support enables organizations to take greater advantage of ethnic diversity in their personnel, by generating more opportunities for ethnic interaction and more programs and activities designed to engage members of under-represented ethnic groups in the life of the organization (argument 4). Secondly, this kind of support also increases the likelihood that UREG members will be able to acquire and make good use of the social capital afforded by the organization in which they are studying or working (argument 6).

Societal salience of ethnicity   The stronger is the salience of ethnic group identity in a society, the more important it is that people understand how to operate within a multicultural environment. This puts a higher premium on the benefits of positive discrimination claimed to ensue from greater diversity of personnel in organizations and institutions (argument 4). More significantly, however, greater salience of ethnicity is likely to exacerbate some of the costs of positive discrimination. When ethnicity is highly salient, positive discrimination in favor of some under-represented group(s) will lead to more divisive identity group politics (claim 8.1) and may well generate snowballing demands for positive discrimination in favor of other groups – even if the latter are not so obviously or significantly under-represented (claim 8.3).

Sensitivity of the selection process   Greater sensitivity in the selection will make it less likely that PD beneficiaries among UREG members will come predominantly from socio-economically privileged families. This is because greater sensitivity means less dependence on standardized test scores and other conventional qualification criteria; and applicants from relatively affluent home environments, with access to good schooling and coaching options, are better placed than other UREG applicants to do well by such conventional measures. More sensitive PD policies are therefore likely to incur lower costs associated with redistribution to a relatively privileged creamy layer of UREG members (argument 7).

Greater sensitivity of selection processes may also enhance the motivation for UREG youths to do their best (argument 5), because these youths would have more reason to expect that selection processes would be capable of recognizing and rewarding their true potential for achievement – even if their standardized test scores were not very high and their conventional qualifications not very strong.

Extent of segregation   The greater the extent to which UREG members are residentially segregated, the greater will be their social segregation from members of other groups. Such segregation isolates its victims from informal social networks governing access to economic opportunity – e.g. word-of-mouth notice of jobs. Furthermore, it makes it more difficult to build multi-group political coalitions that can improve living conditions and access to public services, facilities, and development programs. Because social segregation in effect deprives UREG members from much-needed social capital, the capacity of PD policies to enhance their social capital is all the more significant and valuable (argument 6).[9]

Degree of recognizability   The more a UREG member is recognizable (by outward appearance), the easier it is to draw the line between those eligible and those ineligible for PD preferences. Thus a high degree of recognizability makes it harder for an individual to succeed in a deceitful effort to claim UREG status and thereby take advantage of PD benefits (claim 8.2).

Summary of the determinants of PD net benefits

In Table 4.1 I present a summary of all of the identified effects of primary factor characteristics on the consequences of a PD policy. The characteristics are listed in the first column, under the appropriate primary factor heading. Their effects on PD consequences are shown in the other three columns – one for indirect effects via the quality of performance of PD beneficiaries (QP), one for indirect effects via the need for an ethnicity focus (NEF), and the third for direct effects. A positive sign indicates that more of a given characteristic will lead to greater net benefits (greater benefits and/or lesser costs); a negative sign indicates the opposite. The presumed relative strength of each effect is indicated by the number of times the relevant sign is repeated – three times for the strongest effects and just once for the weakest.

Table 4.1 **How characteristics of each primary factor influence PD outcomes**

Primary factor characteristics	Effect on PD net benefits		
	Via QP	Via NEF	Direct
Characteristics of the PD policy			
Magnitude of the preference	– – –		– –
Sensitivity of the selection process★	+ +		+
Identifiability of the PD beneficiaries	–		
Extent of support for PD beneficiaries★	+ +		+
Characteristics of the UREG			
Degree of homogeneity		+ +	+ + +
Degree of recognizability			+
Extent of socio-economic disadvantage	– –		
Extent of mistreatment		+ + +	
Extent of stigmatization	+	+ + +	
Extent of segregation		+	+
Characteristics of the societal environment			
Societal salience of ethnicity		+	–
Degree of societal elitism			+ +
Job prospects for educated youths★			+ +
Overall PD displacement impact			– – –

Note:

★ Characteristics dependent on the society's level of economic development.

As shown in the table, the primary characteristic with the strongest influence on the quality of performance by PD beneficiaries is the magnitude of the preference: the smaller it is, the better performance is likely to be. Net benefits associated with the need for an ethnicity focus are most likely to be realized when the UREG in question is relatively homogeneous and exposed to much mistreatment and stigmatization. Of the characteristics with direct effects on PD net benefits, those with the strongest effects are the degree of UREG homogeneity (positive) and the overall PD displacement impact (negative).

Note that one primary factor characteristic has a contradictory effect on the net benefits from a PD policy: the societal salience of ethnicity. The greater is the salience of ethnicity in a society, the stronger is the need for defining beneficiaries of social policies in ethnic terms (which enhances PD net benefits). On the other hand, the greater is the salience of ethnicity, the greater are the costs of PD associated with heightened attention to ethnic distinctions. The overall impact of this characteristic on PD net benefits could thus be either positive or negative.

In Table 4.1 I have also indicated with asterisks those characteristics of a PD policy and a societal environment that are most likely to be related to the wealth of the society. In general, one would expect greater wealth to enhance the prospects for success of a policy initiative: the richer a society is, the better it can afford the kinds of operational and monitoring expenses that enable a policy to be effectively implemented. More specifically, there are three characteristics relevant to the consequences of a PD policy that are surely dependent to a significant extent on a society's level of economic development.

The *sensitivity of the selection process* used to implement a PD policy depends on the amount of resources that can be devoted to the effort; the richer a society is, the more resources its institutions and organizations are likely to be able to deploy for the purpose of selecting qualified candidates. By the same token, the *extent of support for the PD beneficiaries* that a country's institutions and organizations will be able to provide will tend to be greater the greater is the overall wealth of the society. Furthermore, the ability of a society to assure good *job prospects for educated youths* is also likely to be positively related to its overall level of economic development. Each of these characteristics has only positive effects on PD net benefits. Thus the level of economic development can be considered another characteristic of the societal environment that influences the outcome of PD policies, working indirectly through the effects of several different primary factor characteristics; and its influence is always a favorable one.[10]

In Chapter 6 I will apply the model developed in this chapter to the differing contexts of positive discrimination in the US and India, with a view to comparing the likely consequences of PD policies in each country. First, however, I must provide a description of the relevant primary factors in the two countries.

5   The differing contexts of positive discrimination in the US and India

My objective in this chapter is to compare, as between the US and India, the various conditions that are most likely to influence the consequences of positive discrimination (PD) in each country. In other words, I intend to compare what I described in the previous chapter as primary factor characteristics. I address first the characteristics of those under-represented ethnic groups (UREGs) that are favored by PD policies in each country, because some of the other characteristics differ not only between the two countries but also among the different groups. Then I consider, in turn, the characteristics of the PD policies themselves and the characteristics of the general societal environments. Finally, I will summarize the comparison in Table 5.1. My intention throughout is to contrast the ways in which the characteristics of these three basic factors manifest themselves in the US and in India.

Characteristics of the UREGs in each country[1]

The beneficiaries of positive discrimination at issue here are those UREGs officially recognized as eligible for preferential selection. These are African Americans, Hispanic Americans, and Native Americans in the US, and Dalits, Adivasis, and members of the "Other Backward Classes" (OBCs) in India. By definition, members of these groups share several basic characteristics.[2] First of all, they are conspicuously under-represented in desirable positions and in the upper strata of society. They also have in common a virtually inalterable group identity, based on a social construction of inherited physical and/or cultural characteristics.

UREG identity, in the US and India as elsewhere, is sometimes signaled by easily recognizable physical characteristics; thus black skin serves as an indicator of African American identity. Native Americans and Adivasis are also generally distinguishable by their physical appearance. But this is often not the case with Dalits; and it is virtually impossible to distinguish on the basis of physical characteristics alone either Hispanic Americans or those Indians officially recognized as OBCs. In the many cases where racially linked physical characteristics are not decisive, one's group identity depends on social conventions – such as the American convention that a person is considered Black or

Native American if he/she has any known African or indigenous American ancestry, no matter if the ancestral fraction is very small or the skin color very light.

Skin color is not decisive in determining group identity in either the US or India, but in both countries darker color is associated with UREGs. Indeed, a hierarchy of skin color looms large in the consciousness of both the US and the Indian population, in which light skin color is associated with those in the upper strata and dark skin color with those in the lower strata of the society. Dark skin color is somewhat less a marker of group identity in India[3] than it is in the US. It is noteworthy that the three US UREGs at issue here are precisely those with discernible African or indigenous American ancestry, for in the case of Hispanic Americans the relevant under-represented group is really the "Mestizos" – those Hispanics with discernible indigenous American, as opposed to European, ancestry.[4]

There are many significant differences in characteristics among the UREGs of the US and those of India, and these differences are important for comparative analysis of positive discrimination in the two countries. Among the key differences are the following.

Degree of homogeneity   On the whole, the US UREGs are considerably more homogeneous than those of India. Blacks are united by their (at least partial) African ancestry. There are cultural, and sometimes linguistic, differences between African Americans whose ancestry goes back directly to Africa and those who have immigrated from the Caribbean Islands or Latin America; but the latter constitute a relatively small proportion of all US Blacks. Moreover, Blacks of any geographic origin (and, to a considerable extent, of all socio-economic backgrounds) face certain common presumptions and stereotypes on the part of much of the rest of the US population about the implications of their Black identity. Unlike Blacks, Hispanic Americans are divided into a number of groups, according to geographic origin, which are fairly distinctive in background and culture. Thus those of Puerto Rican origin, those of Mexican origin, those from Cuba, and those from various other Latin American countries have rather different senses of their Hispanic identity.[5] Native Americans are divided into a much larger number of different tribes, which differ to varying extents not only culturally but often in their native language. India's Adivasis are in this – and many other – respects rather comparable to Native Americans, though their proportion of the overall population is significantly greater and they are divided into many more different (and more distinctive) tribal groups. It is India's Dalits and OBC members, however, who are by far the most heterogeneous of the under-represented groups at issue here.

The Hindu population of India is traditionally divided vertically into a caste hierarchy of five broad strata, known as *varna*s: these are, from top to bottom, the *Brahmans* (priests), *Kshatriyas* (warriors), *Vaisyas* (traders), *Sudras* (laborers), and *Ati-Sudra*s (those who do the "unclean" work, who are ritually

"polluting"). Hindu social relations revolve around one's *jati* – a term referring to caste of a much finer definition – of which there are several thousand,
which are further differentiated into even more thousands of different sub-
castes. Some of these castes and sub-castes are confined to a small area; others
extend across substantial parts of the Indian subcontinent. In principle, each
caste is associated with one of the *varna* strata, and there is an especially strong
demarcation between those castes belonging to the top four strata (the "caste
Hindus") and the bottom stratum (the "untouchables"). In practice, however,
there is considerable contention over where in the hierarchy a given caste
belongs, and in some cases even uncertainty about whether or not a given
caste or one of its sub-castes is "untouchable" – for untouchability criteria
vary by state, region, and even over time. Thus there is an almost infinitesimal
vertical as well as horizontal differentiation of castes in India, and even among
the officially Scheduled Castes (SCs) there is a great deal of differentiation of
both kinds.[6]

The various groups constituting India's OBCs are even more heterogeneous than those constituting the SCs. Indeed, it has never been clear just
what should distinguish a Hindu or non-Hindu group belonging to the
OBCs from one that does not. Hindus among the OBCs are roughly, but not
precisely, identifiable as *Sudra*s – i.e. belonging to a *jati* associated with the
lowest of the caste-Hindu strata, and the only one whose members are not
considered to be "twice-born." A variety of government commissions established to tackle the question of defining OBCs eligible for positive
discrimination have come up with different answers, basing their findings on
various mixtures of ethnic and socio-economic criteria. As a consequence, the
OBCs that actually have access to reservations are defined quite differently in
different Indian states and at the national level. They include castes, sub-castes,
and non-Hindu groups that are just as poor as most SCs; but they also include
not a few fairly well-off castes and sub-castes. The heterogeneous Dalits at
least have in common their "untouchable" heritage – as well as a growing
sense of a common political identity. The heterogeneous OBC members have
very little in common other than a keen sense of entitlement to reservations.

The myriad horizontal and vertical distinctions characterizing Dalits and
OBC members in India mean that they have much less of a sense of society-
wide solidarity than Blacks or even Hispanic Americans in the US. Adivasis in
India are likewise culturally considerably more diverse than Native Americans
in the US. As a consequence, the distribution of the benefits of positive discrimination among recognized UREGs in India, not only as between people from
different socio-economic strata within a UREG, but also as between different
(ethnically defined) sub-groups of the eligible population, has become much
more of an issue in India than in the US. Thus demands have also been raised
among Dalits and Adivasis for more finely honed reservation categories within
the two eligible sub-groups of SCs and Scheduled Tribes (STs).[7]

Because of problems of heterogeneity, drawing the line between groups
and individuals eligible and ineligible for positive discrimination has posed

difficulties both in the US and in India. In the US the most significant source of such difficulty is the growing tendency for cross-group intermarriage, which makes it more difficult to associate the offspring of such couples with any one group.[8] A unique problem in the case of Hispanic Americans is that it is sometimes difficult to distinguish between those of European origin (who are presumably no more deserving of preferences than other White immigrants) and those with some Native American or African ancestry (the Mestizos, who are presumably more deserving). Cross-group intermarriage is far less common in India, especially on the part of isolated Adivasis, than in the US.[9] In India, cross-group intermarriage between groups eligible and ineligible for positive discrimination is relatively rare. The main source of difficulty in drawing the line separating Dalits and Adivasis from similar groups not classified as SCs or STs is the uncertainty and variability (across space and time) of "untouchable" status in the case of some castes and sub-castes – not only among Hindus, but also among counterpart groups with other religious affiliations. In the case of potential OBCs, as noted just above, there are myriad problems in deciding which should be eligible for positive discrimination and which should not.

Degree of recognizability   African Americans are on the whole much more recognizably distinct from White Americans than India's Dalits or Adivasis are from other Indians – even though Dalits and Adivasis tend to be darker-skinned than caste Hindus. Physical distinctions usually suffice to identify Blacks, whereas behavioral and/or cultural distinctions may often be needed to distinguish Dalits and Adivasis from other Indians. Adivasis are on average somewhat more distinctive in their physical features than Dalits; OBC members are considerably less so, and indeed they are often indistinguishable from higher-caste Hindus. (The fact that most OBC members and many Dalits are physically indistinguishable from higher-caste Hindus may help to explain why private corporations in India have not emulated US corporations in illustrating the diversity of their work force via the public display of photographs in advertisements and public relations brochures.) Native Americans and Hispanic Americans are on average somewhat less readily recognizable from their physical characteristics than Blacks, largely because of a significant degree of intermarriage with Whites.[10] Overall, members of India's UREGs are not as physically distinct as their American counterparts.

The limited degree of physical recognizability of Dalit identity has a number of consequences that make Dalit status in India somewhat different than Black status in the US. First, Dalits who manage to leave their traditional rural settings are less disadvantaged simply by their appearance than is the case for Blacks; so a modern, urban, anonymous environment provides more protection for Dalits than for Blacks against casual discrimination by strangers. (Once their Dalit status is recognized, however, the likelihood of discrimination by others is a good deal greater for Dalits in India than for Blacks in the US.) Secondly, Dalits have a greater chance of "passing" among the majority group members of their society than do Blacks. In order to "pass," a Dalit needs mainly to acquire the behavioral mannerisms and the speech patterns of a "caste Hindu"; this can be an almost impossible task for a typical Dalit of low socio-economic background, but it is not beyond the reach of Dalits from more advantaged families. As a consequence, Dalits confront more often than Blacks the question of whether or not to reveal their caste status (which they often frequently prefer not to do).[11] The ability of a Black to "pass" depends almost entirely on whether he/she is quite light-skinned and otherwise resembles a White – hence on birth rather than anything under his/her control.

In India, Dalits also have the option of converting from Hinduism to another religion in order to avoid "untouchable" status. But such efforts are most often unsuccessful, because of the tendency of caste status to be carried over from Hinduism into other religious groups. This can occur as Dalits become a bottom-rung group in another religion's hierarchy – for example, in the case of some ex-Dalit groups converted to Sikhism, who were recognized as SCs in the 1950s, and in the case of groups of ex-Dalit Christians and Muslims lobbying for SC or OBC status in recent decades. It can also occur when Dalits become a newly defined religious group – as in the case of the "neo-Buddhist" Dalits who followed Dr. Ambedkar's conversion to Buddhism in 1956.

Extent of socio-economic disadvantage   The members of any UREG are, on average, socio-economically disadvantaged; but the extent of such disadvantage differs among groups and across the two countries. Within the US, Hispanic Americans as a group are somewhat better off than Blacks and Native Americans on most socio-economic indicators.[12] Within India, OBC members are on average better off than SC or ST members, and Dalits as a group are slightly better off than Adivasis.[13] All three of the UREGs in the US are on average considerably better off economically, and considerably better educated, than the UREGs in India. This is true not only in absolute terms, but also relative to the majority population in each country.

Over the past half-century, members of PD-favored UREGs in the US have made more significant socio-economic gains than their Indian counterparts. A small proportion of Blacks, Hispanic Americans, and Native Americans have moved into the upper rungs of the socio-economic ladder in the US, whereas an even smaller proportion of OBC members, Dalits, and Adivasis have been able to do the same in India. In neither country, of course, does the socio-economically disadvantaged segment of the population consist predominantly of UREG members. There are many Whites in the US and higher-caste Hindus in India who are as disadvantaged as their UREG counterparts; but the incidence of socio-economic disadvantage (however measured) is significantly lower in the non-UREG than in the UREG population.

Extent of mistreatment   Mistreatment of UREG members, simply on account of their ethnic status, remains a fact of life in both countries; and in both countries it is often linked to disparagement of the groups in question. There are, however, significant differences in the extent of the mistreatment in contemporary times. Various forms of overt discrimination against and mistreatment of Dalits remain common occurrences in India; indeed, in rural areas they can rise from the level of personal indignities to outright atrocities. In the US, Blacks – and, to a lesser extent, Mestizos among Hispanic Americans – suffer from discrimination and mistreatment that is now most likely to be covert or institutional (e.g. "racial profiling" as crime suspects, and disproportionate likelihood of incarceration or execution). Overt mistreatment of members of these groups is nowhere near as frequent, nor as intense, as in the case of Dalits. Members of India's OBCs are also exposed to much less mistreatment than are the Dalits. Both Native Americans in the US and Adivasis in India are more often ignored and neglected than subjected to discrimination or mistreatment by members of mainstream society.

The history of Black slavery in the US South was no doubt at least as degrading as that of Dalit untouchability in Hindu society, though its duration was shorter – even if one includes the Jim Crow era. Native Americans were subjected to the decimation of a significant part of their population, and deprived of the vast majority of their land, by White settlers. The extent of past injustice, and quite possibly the burden placed by past injustice on contemporary life, is arguably comparable for Blacks, Native Americans, and Dalits. Adivasis in India were not deprived of their land to any comparable extent; but their interests and concerns were largely ignored – if not violated – by mainstream Indian society. The Mestizos among Hispanic Americans have historically been poorly treated by dominant groups in the US, but their mistreatment is of much shorter duration than that of Blacks and Native Americans, and it never reached the depth of enslavement or massive displacement and illness. India's OBCs have suffered at the hands of high-caste Hindus, but among the UREGs they have the weakest claim to a history of victimization based on their ethnic status.

Extent of stigmatization   In India a traditional set of Hindu religious beliefs – associating "untouchables" with ritual "pollution" and thus stigmatizing them as inferior beings – has been used to justify a rigid system of social stratification that subordinates Dalits. Even though this belief system conflicts sharply with the principles on which the secular constitution of independent India is based, it still carries strong force in many sectors of society (if only because it has prevailed over a much longer period of time). In the US an ideology of racial inferiority – not based on ritual impurity – has been used as a justificatory rationale for the subordination of Blacks. As in India, this ideology conflicts sharply with the country's constitutional principles. In the US, however, the constitutional principles have much more widely permeated the society as a whole and are a good deal stronger than the conflicting racist ideology – not only because the constitution is of much longer standing, but also because the ideology was firmly held by a considerably smaller fraction of the population than in India. Thus the stereotype of Black inferiority has rarely been openly voiced since the demise of the segregationist South, in the wake of the Civil Rights Movement of the 1950s and 1960s; and this kind of stereotypical thinking appears to be weakening. The more recent Dalit Movement in India, though inspired in part by the Civil Rights Movement in the US, has yet to achieve a corresponding degree of success in changing stigmatizing beliefs among the population as a whole.

The Mestizos among Hispanic Americans, as well as Native Americans and India's Adivasis, also frequently encounter perceptions by others that they are inferior. Their alleged inferiority, however, is less often ascribed to inherent and inherited characteristics than to the particular histories of these groups, which has isolated them to varying degrees from the mainstream culture. Thus the ideology of their inferiority is somewhat weaker and less widespread than in the case of Dalits and Blacks. In the case of India's OBC members, there is some degree of inferiority attributed by "twice-born" upper-caste Hindus to those OBC members who belong to *jatis* considered to be of the *Sudra varna*; but the strength of the negative stereotype here is far weaker than in the case of the Dalits (viewed as outcastes by most *Sudra*s as well as upper-caste Hindus).

Extent of segregation   In spite of the continual process of modernization and urbanization taking place in the US and in India (at different levels and paces, of course), residential segregation remains an important characteristic of most of the under-represented groups. Virtually total regional separation is the norm for a large proportion of Native Americans (those living on "reservations" established by the US government for indigenous inhabitants of the continent) and of India's Adivasis (who are defined partly in terms of their remote geographical locations). Some Blacks and some Hispanic Americans living in rural areas also find themselves living among residents primarily of their own group. Much more often, however, Blacks and Hispanic Americans in the US, as well as India's Dalits and OBC members, live in diverse urban, semi-urban, or rural areas, where they are not separated regionally from the rest of society. In many cases, however, members of these groups live in fairly compact areas within much larger agglomerations, within which they constitute the great majority of residents; thus they find themselves locally segregated. Local residential segregation of UREGs may be diminishing both in the US and in India, but at best rather slowly. It remains most entrenched in the case of African Americans and Dalits, and least so in the case of India's OBC members.

Characteristics of the PD policies in each country

There are a number of significant differences between the US and India with respect to the nature of the PD policies implemented in the spheres of education and employment. Although in each country such policies have been applied to several different UREGs, they have been applied within each country in the same general way to each such group.

In the US, some organizations and institutions initially established quotas for selecting UREG applicants. The 1978 Supreme Court ruled in the Bakke case, however, that quotas are unconstitutional in the case of admissions to higher educational institutions; and since then PD policies in the educational sphere have almost always taken the form of preferences for UREG applicants in single competitions open to all.[14] The same is largely true in the employment arena. In India, PD policies have almost always taken the form of quotas – hence the use of the term "reservation policies." In some cases all UREG applicants contest for the corresponding quota of reserved seats; more often, however, the quota is limited to those UREG applicants who fail to be selected in the general competition. For positions requiring non-trivial qualifications, there is usually a minimum level of entering credentials below which a UREG applicant will be rejected – even if a quota has not been filled. Indeed, quotas for Dalits and Adivasis in high-level jobs typically are not filled, for lack of minimally qualified applicants.

Magnitude of the preference   In the US the magnitude of the preference extended to PD-eligible applicants has varied widely – over time as well as between institutions – from quite substantial to fairly modest. The same is true of India. It is a fair generalization, however, to suggest that in India the magnitude of the boost has tended to be somewhat greater than in the US. This is due to the fact that Indian quotas of reserved seats are generally set so as to reflect the proportion of the relevant UREG population in the whole country or the relevant state; whereas in the US the implicit targets for UREG applicants implied by affirmative action preferences are usually less than the corresponding UREG proportion of the overall population. It is true that reserved seats for Dalits and Adivasis in the more demanding Indian educational institutions and high-level jobs often go unfilled. Nonetheless, the existence of unfilled reserved seats puts pressure on the relevant authorities to increase the size of the boost for a UREG in order to have a better chance of filling the quota.

The magnitude of the preference imparted by PD policies can vary not only by country but also by under-represented group. In India, the reservation of desirable positions roughly in proportion to a UREG's overall share of the population means that the amount of the boost varies inversely with the extent to which a UREG would be represented in the absence of positive discrimination. This inference is weakened, but not invalidated, by the fact that reserved seats for Dalits and Adivasis in elite institutions often go unfilled. In the US, because PD policies are framed in terms of preferential boosts rather than quotas, and because implicit targets tend to be set in terms of the proportionate representation of all three UREGs rather than each one separately, the magnitude of the preference tends to be much the same for each UREG favored by positive discrimination. There may be some adjustments at the margin to bring representation of UREGs closer to their shares in the overall population; but the resultant variation across UREGs is surely much smaller than it is in India. It follows that among all the UREGs at issue, it is Adivasis and Dalits who receive the biggest preferences from PD policies. It is difficult to generalize about how the magnitude of the preference given to India's OBCs compares with that given to the UREGs eligible for positive discrimination in the US, because the sizes of these preferences have varied significantly across institutions and over time. In the absence of a strong presumption one way or the other, one must assume that the magnitude of the preference given to OBCs does not on average differ greatly from that given to Blacks, Native Americans, and Hispanic Americans.

Sensitivity of the selection process   It is hardly surprising that the selection processes associated with PD policies in India have tended to be substantially less sensitive and more rigid than those applied in most instances in the US. For example, selection processes in India tend to be much more dependent on applicant performance on standardized tests than is the case in the US.[15] This lesser sensitivity is due in large part to India's relative poverty, which limits the resources that institutions can deploy in their selection processes. It is also due to the tendency, in a densely populated as well as relatively poor country like India, for competitions for desired positions to attract huge numbers of applicants, which makes it all the more difficult to undertake careful scrutiny of each application.

Identifiability of the PD beneficiaries   The fact that Indian reservation policies make use of quotas, while US affirmative action policies have mainly involved preferential boosts, makes it likely – but not necessary – that Indian PD beneficiaries are made more easily identifiable than US beneficiaries. Other differences in the characteristics of PD policies assure that this is indeed the case. In India, UREG students and job-holders are often provided with separate facilities – e.g. living quarters – and special programs to help them overcome the challenges they face. Although it is conceivable that some of the UREG members who take advantage of these opportunities do not actually owe their position to a reservation policy, the probability is so high that a UREG member is in fact a beneficiary, at least in the case of Dalits and Adivasis, that those UREG members who do avail themselves of such opportunities are almost all correctly identified as PD beneficiaries. In the US, by contrast, the use of complex and nuanced PD selection processes, as well as the tendency not to exclude non-UREG members from special facilities and programs, makes it much harder for anyone to determine precisely which UREG members do in fact owe their position to affirmative action.

Extent of support for the PD beneficiaries   Clearly, richer societies, and correspondingly better-endowed institutions, can provide more financial resources to aid PD beneficiaries. One would expect the same to be true with respect to human resources, though these are also very much a function of cultural traditions. As well, the amount of resources made available to support PD policies will depend on the extent to which the need is recognized and the extent to which effective ways have been found to apply the resources. In both these respects things have been improving over time in both the US and India, as people working with PD beneficiaries have gained knowledge and experience about what it takes to achieve success. But the vastly greater wealth of the US and (on average) its institutions has meant that PD policies in the US are generally accompanied by significantly greater supporting resources than in India.

Characteristics of the societal environment in each country

The US and India share certain common features, such as a large size, a multi-cultural population, and a democratic political system. Beyond these general similarities, the societal environments of the two countries are in many ways very different; and that is certainly true for the characteristics most relevant to the consequences of PD policies.

Societal salience of ethnicity   As noted at the end of Chapter 1, Indians are on the whole much more community-oriented than Americans, who tend to place a higher premium on liberal individualism. One author has character-ized the Indian orientation as a "collective passion for group equity, for group rather than individual rights" (Bardhan 1999: Epilogue). Groups in India are typically defined in ethnic terms – whether based on language, religion, caste, or tribe. Ethnicity (broadly defined) is thus more salient in India than in the US, and it is quite visible in the sphere of politics. In India different parties compete avidly for bloc support from particular ethnic groups (especially caste groups). In the US the "race card" is played from time to time, and Blacks largely support the Democratic Party; but there is no expectation that the votes of all Blacks, all Hispanic Americans, or all Native Americans can be harnessed and shifted as a bloc.

Degree of societal elitism   Although constitutionally and politically committed to a democratic and even rather egalitarian ideal, Indian society is in many ways more elitist than American society. This is most strongly reflected in the hierarchical structure of Hindu castes. But both India's major religions (Hinduism and Islam) are fundamentally more elitist than those of the US (Protestantism and Catholicism); the authority of the Brahman and the Mullah is much greater than that of the Protestant minister and even the Catholic priest.[16] Moreover, British rule brought forth a new axis of elitism that is highly relevant for contemporary (more secular) India. Good command of the English language is the single most important qualification for entry into the Indian educated elite; yet good training in English (as a second language for almost all Indians) is available only to those whose families can afford to send them to the best educational institutions, most of which are private and costly. Differential access to good schooling is also an important class divider in the US; but for most Americans there is no single barrier to the under-represented as important as command of English in India, and both the economic and the educational gaps between the lower and upper classes are much wider in India. One noteworthy indicator of the greater degree of elitism in India is that rising from humble origins to achieve success is much less a matter of pride in the Indian cultural context than in it is the US.

Job prospects for educated youths   In a densely populated and relatively poor country like India, it is to be expected that labor markets in general are significantly less favorable to job-seekers than in a rich country like the US. Thus Indian labor markets are characterized not only by much lower wages but also by much higher unemployment or under-employment. For educated youths in India, this differential has been aggravated by the rapid expansion of the higher educational system (which contrasts sharply with the slow growth of the primary educational system). As a consequence, high-quality and well-paying jobs are available only to a relatively small fraction of India's college and university graduates − mainly those who go to the best of the nation's higher educational institutions. In the US the best positions also go largely to graduates of the top educational institutions; but the proportion of all college and university graduates who are likely to find reasonably good jobs is far higher.

Overall PD displacement impact   In India the fraction of the population eligible for positive discrimination on an ethnic basis has always been higher than in the US. Long before affirmative action policies were introduced into American workplaces and educational institutions, seats and positions were being reserved for members of various non-Hindu religions and of various non-Brahman Hindu castes and outcastes. In the early 1950s, when reservations for SCs and STs were established in independent India, these two groups alone accounted for almost one-quarter of the Indian population. In the early 1970s, when affirmative action policies were implemented for Hispanic and Native Americans as well as Blacks in the US, these three UREGs accounted for about one-fifth of the US population. By the turn of the century, rapid growth in the Hispanic-American population had increased this fraction to about one-quarter.[17] By the same time in India, however, widening reservations for members of OBCs had increased the fraction of the Indian population eligible for reservations to somewhere between one-quarter and a half (depending on the region and on the type of reservations).[18]

The overall proportion of positions displaced by PD policies in the US and in India depends not only on the fraction of the population eligible for positive discrimination, but also on the scope and magnitude of the policies. Empirical estimates of the number of positions in which positive discrimination has caused a UREG member to displace a non-UREG member are very hard to come by.[19] However, the fact that in India UREG members constitute

Table 5.1 **Differences in primary factor characteristics between US and Indian UREGs**

Primary factor characteristics	US UREGs			Indian UREGs		
Characteristics of the UREG	**B**	**N**	**H**	**D**	**A**	**O**
Degree of homogeneity	3	2	2	1	0	0
Degree of recognizability	3	2	2	1	2	0
Extent of socio-economic disadvantage	1	1	0	3	3	2
Extent of mistreatment	2	2	0	3	1	0
Extent of stigmatization	2	1	1	3	1	0
Extent of segregation	2	2	1	2	3	0
Characteristics of the PD policy	**B**	**N**	**H**	**D**	**A**	**O**
Magnitude of the preference	0	0	0	2	2	0
Sensitivity of the selection process★	2	2	2	0	0	0
Identifiability of the PD beneficiaries	0	0	0	2	2	2
Extent of support for PD beneficiaries★	2	2	2	0	0	0
Characteristics of the societal environment	**B**	**N**	**H**	**D**	**A**	**O**
Societal salience of ethnicity	0	0	0	2	2	2
Degree of societal elitism	0	0	0	2	2	2
Job prospects for educated youths★	2	2	2	0	0	0
Overall PD displacement impact	0	0	0	2	2	2

Notes:

★ Characteristics dependent on the society's level of economic development.

B = Blacks; N = Native Americans; H = Hispanic Americans; D = Dalits; A = Adivasis; O = OBC members.

a significantly higher fraction of the population than in the US, and the fact that India's PD policies are on the whole greater in terms of the magnitude of preferences extended to PD beneficiaries, together suggest that in all probability the overall displacement impact of PD policies is considerably greater in India than in the US. Moreover, in many contexts what most matters is not the actual but the perceived magnitude of the overall displacement impact; the latter is likely to be based largely on the fraction of the population eligible for positive discrimination, which is indeed considerably greater in India.

Summary comparison of the context for PD in the US and India

The analysis of the preceding sections is summarized in Table 5.1, which displays differences in primary factor characteristics as between all six UREGS favored by positive discrimination in the US and India. As in Table 4.1, the characteristics are listed in the first column, under the appropriate primary factor heading. Each of the six UREGs of the two countries is represented by a separate column in the table. The entry for any given characteristic under any given column indicates the extent to which that particular characteristic applies to the UREG at issue – not in absolute terms, but relative to its applicability to the other UREGs. I have used a scale from 0 to 3 to represent differences in the extent to which each relevant UREG characteristic applies to each UREG. In the cases of characteristics of a PD policy and of a societal environment, I have used only the numbers 0 and 2 on the scale, because on these characteristics there are significant differences mainly between the two countries and not among the UREGs within either country.

In reading Table 5.1, one should bear in mind that the numerical values are designed only to indicate rankings on a single characteristic. The numerical values themselves are arbitrary; a higher number on any given characteristic only indicates more of that characteristic than a lower number, not how much more. As well, the numerical values cannot be used to compare the significance of differences across characteristics. Even though the numbers for "homogeneity" range from 0 to 3, and the numbers for "magnitude of the preference" vary between 0 and 2, the difference in the amount of homogeneity characterizing a UREG with a 0 score and one with a 3 score is not necessarily greater (by any measure) than the difference in the amount of the preference characterizing a UREG with a 0 score and one with a 2 score.

Those characteristics of the PD policy and the societal environment that are most likely to be related (positively) to the level of economic development are indicated in Table 5.1 with an asterisk. The US is, of course, very much richer than India. This is an important reason as to why the US UREGs score higher on each of these three characteristics than the Indian UREGs.

6 A comparative analysis of the likely consequences of positive discrimination in the US and India

In Chapter 4 I analyzed how the context under which positive discrimination (PD) is undertaken can affect the extent to which PD policies are likely to "work well" or not – i.e. whether they can be expected to achieve their desired benefits without excessive costs. My analysis is summarized in Table 4.1. In that table the key characteristics that form the context for positive discrimination are listed in three groups, according to whether they involve the PD policy itself, the under-represented ethnic group (UREG), or the societal environment. The way in which each of the fourteen listed characteristics affects the outcome of a PD policy is also shown in Table 4.1, in the form of signs indicating the expected direction and strength of its effect on potential net benefits – indirectly via the quality of performance of PD beneficiaries, indirectly via the need for an ethnicity focus, or directly.

In Chapter 5 I compared the context for positive discrimination in the US and India. My comparison is summarized in Table 5.1, which displays differences between the US and India (and their respective UREGs) in each of the fourteen contextual characteristics. My objective in this chapter is to use the analytical framework of Chapter 4 to determine how differences in these characteristics as between the US and India are likely to result in differences in the benefits and costs generated by positive discrimination in each country.

To compare the likely consequences of positive discrimination in the US and India, we need in effect to enter the information from Table 5.1 – on inter-country differences in each contextual characteristic – into the analytical framework of Table 4.1, so as to determine the impact of these differences on the net benefits to be expected from each country's PD policies. Since many of the relevant characteristics differ not only between the US and India, but also among different UREGs in each country, we need to track the impact of these differences on PD net benefits separately for each UREG within each country. In the next section I undertake this analysis sequentially for the three types of contextual characteristics that influence PD net benefits; I then summarize the results of the analysis in Table 6.1.

Comparative effects of differences in the contexts for PD in the US and India

I begin by considering the characteristics of the UREGs favored by PD policies in each country, since the UREG is the relevant unit for comparative analysis of the consequences of positive discrimination.

Differences in UREGs

Degree of homogeneity   African Americans are clearly the most ethnically homogeneous of the UREGs favored by positive discrimination in the US and India. There are, to be sure, some differences among African Americans – depending on their region of origin and the circumstances of their arrival in the US, as well as on the extent of intermarriage in their family history – but virtually all of them share the powerful common social experience of being recognized and treated as Black in the US. Hispanic Americans, and even more so Native Americans, are differentiated into distinct sub-groups by their region of origin and their language or dialect, if not by their appearance. Each of the three Indian UREGs favored by positive discrimination is more heterogeneous than any of the US UREGs. The Dalits are divided vertically as well as horizontally into a great many different sub-groups; they do all share the burden of past untouchability, but the scope of that untouchability varies greatly from one Dalit sub-caste to another. India's "Other Backward Classes" (OBCs) are in the same way highly differentiated from one another; and they do not even share a common historical experience like untouchability. India's Adivasis are also extremely heterogeneous, being largely isolated from one another as well as from mainstream Indian society.

Homogeneity in a UREG has a strong positive influence on the net benefits from a PD policy, both directly and indirectly. It heightens the benefits from integrating society's elite, it reduces the costs associated with adverse redistributional effects, and it strengthens the need for an ethnicity focus. Because of the relatively high degree of homogeneity of US Blacks, PD policies favoring Blacks can be expected (other things being equal) to generate greater net benefits than PD policies favoring Hispanic Americans or Native Americans, and much greater net benefits than PD policies favoring members of India's highly heterogeneous UREGs.

Degree of recognizability   Just as they are the most ethnically homogeneous UREG in the US and India, Blacks are also the most recognizable on the basis of their physical features. Among the other UREGs, Dalits and OBC members in India are the least recognizable from their physical – as opposed to cultural – characteristics. Recognizability has a rather small impact on PD net benefits, in that it reduces the likelihood of costs associated with deceitful efforts to claim UREG status. With respect to this UREG characteristic, PD policies in favor of US Blacks are most likely to limit costs, and PD polices favoring India's Dalits and OBC members are least likely to do so.

Extent of socio-economic disadvantage   In both the US and India there are very substantial differences between the average well-being of UREG members and the average well-being of their fellow citizens; these differences are somewhat greater in India than in the US. Within the US the relative extent of socio-economic disadvantage is greatest in the cases of Blacks and Native Americans; within India it is greatest in the cases of Dalits and Adivasis. It follows that among the UREGs in both countries, the Adivasis and – to a slightly lesser extent – the Dalits are the most socio-economically disadvantaged, while Hispanic Americans are the least disadvantaged.

The extent of a UREG's socio-economic disadvantage has a negative effect on PD net benefits, because it tends to weaken the quality of performance of PD beneficiaries. With respect to this characteristic, Hispanic American PD beneficiaries are in a relatively strong position to generate net benefits, while Adivasi and Dalit beneficiaries tend to face the greatest difficulties.

Extent of mistreatment   Of the six groups targeted for positive discrimination in the US and India, it is the Dalits of India who are currently exposed to the highest degree of mistreatment, while African Americans and Native Americans have suffered from a comparable degree of past victimization. Both in the present and in the past, Hispanic Americans and India's OBC members have been somewhat less exposed to mistreatment than members of the other UREGs at issue.

The extent of mistreatment is arguably the most important characteristic contributing to the need for an ethnicity focus, which in turn has a positive influence on a variety of potential PD benefits and a negative influence on several potential PD costs. On this score, PD policies favoring Dalits (and, to a lesser extent, those favoring Blacks and Native Americans) are likely to generate the greatest net benefits, whereas PD policies favoring Hispanic Americans and OBCs are likely to generate the least net benefits.

Extent of stigmatization   The under-represented groups that face the most widespread negative stereotypes are Dalits in India and African Americans in the US. Stigmatization is more powerful and pervasive in the case of India's Dalits; the notion of Black inferiority has become, over time, less acceptable in the US, whereas such a trend is considerably less perceptible in the case of Dalits in India. Native Americans, "Mestizos" among Hispanic Americans, and Adivasis are subject to less stigmatization, because their lower (on average) position in society is at least as likely to be attributed to adverse environmental circumstances as to inferior innate abilities. Most OBC members are exposed to disparagement by members of the upper Hindu castes, but they are subject to far weaker stigmatization than the Dalits.

The extent of stigmatization is a characteristic contributing significantly to the need for an ethnicity focus and modestly to the expected quality of performance of PD beneficiaries – due to the way in which "stereotype threat" can hide the true capabilities of a UREG member. With respect to this characteristic, the greatest net benefits are to be expected from PD policies favoring Dalits (and, to a lesser extent, those favoring African Americans), whereas the least net benefits are to be expected from PD policies favoring OBCs.

Extent of segregation   Regional residential segregation is the norm for India's Adivasis and, to a somewhat lesser extent, for Native Americans. Local residential segregation characterizes a substantial part of the Dalit population in India and the Black population in the US. Segregation of either kind is somewhat less pronounced for Hispanic Americans and considerably less pronounced for OBC members in India.

The extent of segregation has a modest influence on the need for an ethnicity focus, and it has a modest direct influence on PD net benefits because of its effect on the prospective gains accruing to PD beneficiaries from enhanced social capital. Insofar as the degree of segregation matters, Adivasis should benefit most from a PD policy; following them would be Native Americans, Dalits and Blacks, Hispanic Americans, and – last – OBC members.

Differences in policy characteristics

Magnitude of the preference   Indian reservation policies overall extend more substantial preferences to UREG applicants than do US affirmative action policies. Among the six UREGs favored by PD policies in the US and India, Adivasis and Dalits receive the most sizeable preferences – a reflection of the fact that they tend to be the least well prepared for the positions at issue. The sizes of the preferences extended to Blacks, Native Americans, and Hispanic Americans under US affirmative action policies are quite similar to one another. Furthermore, they are not clearly different from those provided to members of OBCs favored by India's reservation policies.

The magnitude of the preference of a PD policy is a characteristic with a strong negative impact on the average quality of performance to be expected from PD beneficiaries, so it thereby indirectly reduces anticipated net benefits from the PD policy. It also has a significant direct negative impact on PD net benefits, because it increases the costs associated with resentment at PD beneficiaries and exacerbated consciousness of ethnic distinctions. The fact that Adivasis and Dalits receive substantially larger preferences than other UREGs means that PD policies favoring these two groups are that much less likely to generate net benefits than policies favoring the other UREGs.

Sensitivity of the selection process   In the US, affirmative action preferences are generally applied in a considerably more sensitive and nuanced manner than are reservation policies in India. This kind of sensitivity contributes positively to the expected average quality of performance from PD beneficiaries, and thereby indirectly to PD net benefits. It also contributes directly to PD net benefits by reducing the likelihood that PD beneficiaries come predominantly from privileged backgrounds, thereby limiting costs associated with favoring a "creamy layer" of UREG members.

Identifiability of the PD beneficiaries   A PD beneficiary is much more likely to be made identifiable as such in India than in the US. Such identifiability can reduce the expected quality of performance of PD beneficiaries because of enhanced pressure and anxiety to perform well.

Extent of support for the PD beneficiaries   Because of the huge gap in wealth between the two countries, US organizations and institutions are typically much better endowed than their Indian counterparts. It follows that significant post-selection support for PD beneficiaries is more likely to be provided in the US than in India. Such support can make a significant positive contribution to the average quality of performance by PD beneficiaries; and it can also contribute directly to PD net benefits by increasing the gains from ethnic diversity of personnel and by increasing the prospective gains accruing to PD beneficiaries from enhanced social capital.

Differences in the above three characteristics of PD policies, as between the US and India, all have the same comparative implication for the consequences of those policies: the net benefits to be anticipated from positive discrimination are greater for African Americans, Native Americans, and Hispanic Americans in the US than for Adivasis, Dalits, and OBC members in India.

Differences in societal characteristics

Societal salience of ethnicity   Consciousness of ethnic group identity – in the sense that membership in such a group is a strong part of the personal identity of individuals in the group, both in the minds of the individuals and in the minds of others – is considerably greater in India than in the US. Indeed, ethnicity has played a considerably larger role in Indian than in American politics. The salience of ethnicity, however, has two conflicting effects on the net benefits anticipated from PD policies. On the one hand, greater salience has an indirect positive effect because it strengthens the need for a focus on ethnicity in efforts to overcome inequalities. On the other hand, it has a direct negative effect because it is likely to heighten costs associated with provoking inter-ethnic tensions. The first effect tends to make PD policies more productive in India than in the US; the second effect does just the opposite.

Degree of societal elitism   Indian society is in fundamental ways more elitist than that of the US. The greater is the degree of a society's elitism, the greater are the benefits to be derived from integrating that society's elite. It follows that the inter-country differences in elitism portend greater benefits from PD policies in India than in the US.

Job prospects for educated youths   The labor market for educated youths is much stronger in the US than in India. The strength of job prospects has a significant direct effect on PD net benefits, because the greater is the demand for educated labor, the less will the additional competition resulting from positive discrimination in favor of PD beneficiaries be resented by others, and the smaller will be the costs associated with exacerbated consciousness of ethnic distinctions. It follows that PD policies will entail fewer such costs in the US than in India.

Overall PD displacement impact   Including OBCs as well as Scheduled Castes and Scheduled Tribes, the proportionate displacement impact of India's PD policies is in all likelihood considerably greater than is the case in the US. In any event, the displacement impact is certainly perceived as greater; for the fraction of the Indian population eligible for positive discrimination is much higher in India than in the US. The size of the (actual and/or perceived) displacement impact has a strongly negative direct impact on PD net benefits, because greater displacement of applicants ineligible for positive discrimination is bound to heighten their resentment of PD beneficiaries and exacerbate inter-ethnic strife. In this respect, one must expect significantly greater costs from PD policies in India than in the US.

Results of the comparative analysis

The results of my comparative analysis are summarized in Table 6.1, which displays how differences in contextual characteristics can be expected to lead to differences in the net benefits of PD policies applied to each UREG in the US and India. The table is divided horizontally into three sections, reflecting the different routes by which the characteristics can influence PD outcomes – (indirectly) via the quality of performance of PD beneficiaries (QP), (indirectly) via the need for an ethnicity focus (NEF), and directly. In each section, those characteristics that influence QP, NEF, and (directly) PD outcomes are listed in the order of the significance of their influence – according to the analysis in Chapter 4. In cases where more of a characteristic leads to less, rather than more, PD net benefits, a minus sign appears next to the name of the characteristic. A few characteristics are listed more than once, because they influence PD net benefits through more than one causal path.

Each of the six UREGs of the two countries is represented by a separate column, and the numerical entry for any given characteristic under any given column indicates the extent to which that particular characteristic applies to

Table 6.1 Comparative effects on PD net benefits of differing
characteristics in the US and India

Effects	US UREGs			Indian UREGs		
Via QP	**B**	**N**	**H**	**D**	**A**	**O**
Magnitude of the preference (-)	2	2	2	0	0	2
Extent of support for PD beneficiaries	2	2	2	0	0	0
Sensitivity of the selection process	2	2	2	0	0	0
Extent of socio-economic disadvantage (-)	2	2	3	0	0	1
Identifiability of the PD beneficiaries (-)	2	2	2	0	0	0
Extent of stigmatization	2	1	1	3	1	0
Overall ranking	*2*	*2*	*2*	*0*	*0*	*1*
Via NEF	**B**	**N**	**H**	**D**	**A**	**O**
Extent of mistreatment	2	2	0	3	1	0
Extent of stigmatization	2	1	1	3	1	0
Degree of homogeneity	3	2	2	1	0	0
Societal salience of ethnicity	0	0	0	2	2	2
Extent of segregation	2	2	1	2	3	0
Overall ranking	*2*	*2*	*1*	*3*	*1*	*0*
Direct	**B**	**N**	**H**	**D**	**A**	**O**
Degree of homogeneity	3	2	2	1	0	0
Overall PD displacement impact (-)	2	2	2	0	0	0
Magnitude of the preference (-)	2	2	2	0	0	2
Job prospects for educated youths	2	2	2	0	0	0
Degree of societal elitism	0	0	0	2	2	2
Extent of support for the PD beneficiaries	2	2	2	0	0	0
Societal salience of ethnicity (-)	2	2	2	0	0	0
Sensitivity of the selection process	2	2	2	0	0	0
Extent of segregation	2	2	1	2	3	0
Degree of recognizability	3	2	2	1	2	0
Overall ranking	*2*	*2*	*2*	*1*	*0*	*0*

Notes:

B = Blacks; N = Native Americans; H = Hispanic Americans; D = Dalits; A = Adivasis; O = OBC members.

the UREG at issue. In most cases, the entries in Table 6.1 are taken directly from Table 5.1. In cases where a characteristic is negatively related to PD net benefits, however, I have reversed the numbers; therefore all the numerical entries in Table 6.1 are such that a higher number represents a greater contribution to PD net benefits. This makes it easy to determine the comparative extent to which each UREG is likely to benefit from a PD policy, in light of the amount of the particular characteristic that it (or its country) possesses.

The reader should bear in mind that the numbers in Table 6.1, as in Table 5.1, are only indicators of the rank ordering of UREGs with respect to a single characteristic; thus, strictly speaking, the numbers should not be compared across characteristics. It is nonetheless permissible, however, to generalize across a set of characteristics for which the rank orderings are fairly consistent. Indeed, an overview of the entries in Table 6.1 suggests that within each of the three sections of the table, the rank orderings are indeed rather consistent. This is even more the case if one, in effect, gives more weight to the characteristics near the top of each section and less weight to those at the bottom – as one should, because the characteristics are listed in descending order of expected significance in influencing net PD benefits. Utilizing the above procedure, I have provided at the bottom of each section of Table 4 a numerical entry for each UREG; these entries represent roughly determined overall UREG rankings with respect to each of the three routes by which PD characteristics can influence PD outcomes.

The following comparative inferences can be drawn from the overall rankings displayed in Table 6.1:

- PD beneficiaries from the three US UREGs are better placed than PD beneficiaries from the three Indian UREGs to perform well enough to generate net benefits from positive discrimination, insofar as these benefits depend on the quality of beneficiary performance. In this respect one should not anticipate significant differences between the US UREGs; however, one can expect better results from India's OBC members than from India's Dalits and Adivasis.
- To the extent that PD net benefits depend upon the strength of the need for an ethnicity focus, one should expect the greatest net benefits in the case of India's Dalits – followed by African Americans and Native Americans. In this respect Hispanic Americans and India's Adivasis come in at the third rank, and India's OBC members are the least likely to generate net benefits.
- PD beneficiaries from the three US UREGs are better placed than PD beneficiaries from the three Indian UREGs to generate net benefits from positive discrimination, insofar as these are associated with the direct impact of contextual characteristics on net benefits. Among the Indian UREGs, however, Dalits are more likely than the others to realize PD net benefits in this way.

The above inferences, taken together, suggest that the net benefits from positive discrimination are most likely to be positive in the case of African Americans and Native Americans and least likely to be so in the case of India's OBC members. Hispanic Americans appear to rank a little below the other two US UREGs in terms of their likelihood of attaining positive PD net benefits; and Dalits appear to rank somewhat above the other two Indian UREGs in this respect. It is difficult to rank Dalits relative to Hispanic Americans in a rank ordering of expected PD net benefits, because there is little consistency in their overall rankings in the three sets of influences shown in Table 6.1. The need for an ethnicity focus is certainly much stronger in the case of Dalits; but Hispanic Americans rank higher in expected quality of performance and in direct positive effects on PD net benefits.

In concluding my analysis of the likely consequences of positive discrimination in the US and India, I must reiterate that the results of the analysis are strictly comparative. All that can be inferred is that the prospects for net PD benefits are greater under some particular circumstances than under others. This kind of analysis can rank different PD policy cases according to the likelihood of achieving positive net benefits; but it cannot determine in which cases those net benefits will be positive and in which cases they will be negative – much less the magnitude of the benefits and the costs to be expected in any particular case. To answer such questions requires detailed empirical investigation, of the kind to be discussed in Part II of this book.

Concluding observations on PD in the US and India

The main conclusions that I have reached on the basis of the foregoing analysis are the following:

1   Comparative analysis of the outcomes of PD policies can usefully be grounded in a theoretical framework that defines the context for such policies in terms of characteristics of the policies themselves, characteristics of the UREGs favored by positive discrimination, and certain characteristics of the societal environment in which the policies are carried out. In modeling the way in which these characteristics influence the prospects for net benefits from a PD policy, it is helpful to take account both of direct effects of these characteristics and of indirect effects that operate through two key intermediate variables: the need for a focus on ethnicity – as distinct from socio-economic status – in social welfare policies, and the ability of PD beneficiaries to perform well in the positions to which the policy provides them with preferred access.

2   In both the US and India the need for a focus on ethnicity in social policy is stronger in the case of some UREGs than in the case of others. The need is most compelling for India's Dalits (as victims of untouchability), African Americans (as victims of slavery), and Native Americans (as victims of population decimation and land deprivation). The need is

somewhat less strong for India's Adivasis and Hispanic Americans, and it is relatively weakest for India's OBCs.

3   The success of a PD policy depends significantly on the ability of PD beneficiaries to perform well, once selected to a desired position. An inherent obstacle to the success of PD policies is that the likelihood of good performance by PD beneficiaries tends to vary inversely with the need for giving preference to a particular UREG – since most members of groups with a strong case for positive discrimination will *ipso facto* be poorly prepared to compete with and perform as well as members of more advantaged groups.[1] This puts a premium on the capacity of PD policies to identify the most promising applicants among members of under-represented groups and to ensure support for PD beneficiaries in the positions that they are enabled to attain.

4   Affirmative action policies in the US have generally been less ambitious in the magnitude of the preference given to UREG applicants, more sensitive and nuanced in their process of selection, and more generous in the resources made available to support PD beneficiaries than has been the case with reservation policies in India. This is no doubt attributable in large part to the fact that India is much the poorer country. But the consequence is that beneficiaries of affirmative action in the US have been in a better position to perform well, and hence to generate positive net benefits from positive discrimination, than beneficiaries of reservation policies in India.

5   Not only the characteristics of PD policies themselves, but also some key characteristics of the societal environment in which positive discrimination is functioning, have been more favorable for the success of PD policies in the US than in India. In this respect, the most important characteristics differentiating the US from India have been a smaller overall PD displacement impact, better job prospects for educated youths, and lesser societal salience of ethnicity. The capacity of the US to offer better job prospects (as well as more sensitive selection processes and more resources to support PD beneficiaries) is rooted in another important societal difference between the two countries, namely the much greater wealth of the US.

6   Differences in the characteristics of UREGs in the US and India are important in the analysis of PD outcomes mainly insofar as they have differential impacts on the need for an ethnicity focus in social policy. Some UREG characteristics, however, have significant direct effects on PD outcomes; and differences in these characteristics across UREGs can account for substantial differences in the expected net benefits generated by a PD policy. In the case of US and Indian UREGs, the most important such characteristic is the degree of homogeneity of the UREG. Greater homogeneity contributes unambiguously to greater net PD benefits. In this respect, too, PD preferences for US UREGs – especially African Americans – promise greater net benefits than PD preferences for Indian UREGs.

7   From the above observations we can conclude that the context for positive discrimination is significantly more favorable in the US than in India,
so that US affirmative action policies are more likely to generate positive
net benefits than India's reservation policies. The one quite possible
exception to this general conclusion is that there could well be better
results from PD policies in the case of India's Dalits than in the case of
Hispanic Americans. Because the Dalits have a stronger case for an
ethnicity focus, while Hispanic Americans are likely to perform better as
PD beneficiaries, the comparative net benefits to be expected in these
two cases cannot be resolved by a priori analysis.

The above conclusions are comparative as between the two countries of
the US and India and across the UREGs in each country that are favored by
PD policies. Before bringing this part of the book to an end, I would like to
address briefly the way in which the passage of time may be altering the
context and the consequences of positive discrimination in the two countries.
Since the contemporary policies of positive discrimination were first
introduced (in the 1950s in independent India and in the 1960s in the US),
increasing numbers of members of the under-represented groups in each
country have experienced upward mobility – and some have joined the
society's elite. There can be little doubt that PD policies have contributed to
these developments, although the extent to which they are attributable to
positive discrimination – as distinct from more general policies of economic
and social development – is quite debatable. At the same time, there is no
doubt that a very substantial majority of the members of each favored group
remain highly under-represented vis-à-vis their fellow citizens in most
spheres of life; and members of these historically victimized groups
continue to experience discrimination of various kinds. Thus the strength
of the case for an ethnicity focus in social policy on behalf of each of these
groups has diminished somewhat over time; but it has certainly not disappeared altogether.
The passage of time has also led to a change in the quality of performance
to be expected from PD beneficiaries. For one thing, several decades of experience with positive discrimination have enabled institutions and
organizations in each country to improve the effectiveness of their PD policies – in selecting applicants capable of succeeding and in developing
programs to support those applicants. As well, with each passing decade there
has been improvement in the average level of qualification and preparedness
of UREG members, relative to that of others, in the pool of applicants likely
to attain positions in institutions and organizations where PD policies are
applied. These developments mean that the gap between the average quality
of performance of PD beneficiaries and that of other selectees is diminishing.
This increases the overall net benefits to be expected from PD policies, just as
the diminishing case for an ethnicity focus tends to reduce the overall net
benefits of PD policies.

In both the US and India, PD policies were initially applied primarily to under-represented groups that were relatively strongly deserving of ethnicity-based social assistance – African Americans in the US and the Scheduled Castes and Scheduled Tribes in India. Subsequently, however, PD benefits were increasingly extended to groups that were not so obviously deserving – notably Hispanic Americans in the US and OBCs in India. The extension of reservation policies to (many more) OBCs has resulted in considerably more serious problems for positive discrimination in India than has the extension of affirmative action policies to Hispanic Americans in the US. Both of these extensions have been problematical in bringing PD benefits to members of groups with a weaker need for ethnicity-based assistance than the earlier beneficiaries. But in India this extension (by various state governments in the 1970s and 1980s, and then most notably by central government adoption of key Mandal Commission recommendations in the 1990s) generated far more serious challenges to the legitimacy of the whole policy of positive discrimination. This is partly because it resulted in a much higher fraction of the whole population becoming eligible for reservations, thereby causing a much sharper conflict with conventional considerations of merit and efficiency and stirring much stronger resentment among those ineligible for PD. The challenge to PD was also greater in India because of India's history (and current reality) of sharper social tension and political contestation around issues of ethnic identity, and the greater difficulty (and consequently greater perceived arbitrariness) of demarcating groups as eligible for the benefits of positive discrimination.

The theoretical analysis of this part of the book has taken us some distance in assessing the likelihood that the benefits and costs envisaged in consequentialist arguments for and against positive discrimination in admissions to higher educational institutions will actually be realized in the US and in India. To reach firmer conclusions about the positive and negative consequences of positive discrimination, one must bring to bear empirical analysis of the impact of PD policies carried out in the two countries in recent decades. That is my objective in the second part of the book.

Part II

An empirical analysis of positive discrimination in admissions to higher educational institutions in the US and India

In the second part of this book I focus attention on one of the most important arenas in which affirmative action and reservation policies have been implemented: admissions to higher educational institutions. Preferential admission of students from under-represented ethnic groups[1] into colleges and universities, like positive discrimination (PD) policies in other spheres, has become an increasingly controversial issue in both the US and India. It is an issue that elicits high passion among both proponents and opponents, and it has given rise to at least as much polemical as scholarly writing, plenty of lively public debates, many demonstrations, and myriad lawsuits.[2] These are contexts in which a good deal more heat than light tends to be generated. My objective in this part of the book is to show how careful empirical analysis of the consequences of PD policies in higher education can lead to more reasoned evaluation of the overall impact of such policies.

Empirical analysis of any given PD policy must begin with an understanding of the various possible benefits or costs of such a policy. My first task is therefore to adapt the list of claims of beneficial or costly consequences of positive discrimination, generated in Part I and displayed in Tables 3.1 and 3.2, to the sphere of admissions to higher educational institutions. My second – and far more difficult – task is to compile and analyze empirical evidence that will shed light on the magnitudes of the potential positive and negative consequences of PD policies carried out in the concrete historical circumstances of the US and India. I propose to review relevant evidence on the consequences of positive discrimination in admissions to US and Indian universities[3] as practiced over most of the past four decades in each country.

Until the 1990s there was relatively little empirical evidence available in the US on the consequences of affirmative action in admissions to higher educational institutions. Within the last decade, however, the number and scope of relevant studies has grown significantly. As one would expect from a much wealthier nation, the volume of empirical evidence on positive discrimination in the US is now much larger – and more comprehensive in scope – than in India. Yet over the last three decades in India there has been a slow accretion of evidence on the consequences of reservation policies in admissions to higher educational institutions. I believe that a review of the available literature in each country can now shed a good deal of light on the consequences of PD policies in higher educational admissions in two important and contrasting contexts.

I begin in Chapter 7 by adapting the arguments and claims for and against PD policies in general to the specific context of university admissions. Then, in Chapter 8, I discuss the kinds of empirical evidence that are in principle required to assess the benefits and costs claimed by each of the consequentialist arguments for and against positive discrimination in higher education. Such ideal evidence is rarely available in the social sciences; but the interpretation of actually available evidence should be informed by an understanding of what is required in principle.

In Chapters 9 through 14 I examine different kinds of relevant evidence available from the US and India. Chapter 9 (on the US) and Chapter 10 (on India) are devoted to data on students enrolled in higher educational institutions; such data shed light on the impact of PD admission policies on the composition of enrolled students as well as on some of the benefits and costs claimed to result from positive discrimination. In Chapters 11 (on the US) and 12 (on India) I examine evidence relating to student academic performance in universities: how well do PD beneficiaries do in their studies? Such evidence is important for assessing the validity of many of the claims made by proponents and opponents of PD.

Chapter 13 focuses on the long-term consequences of positive discrimination in the US: how well do PD beneficiaries do in their post-university careers? Because very little information on this question is available from India, I address the Indian evidence in the last section of Chapter 12. In Chapter 14 I go on to consider other kinds of evidence from the US bearing on several specific benefits, and one important cost, claimed to result from positive discrimination. Finally, I conclude in Chapter 15 by reviewing the available evidence and summarizing what can be learned from the US and Indian experiences about the benefits and costs of positive discrimination in admissions to higher educational institutions.

7   Positive discrimination in admissions to higher educational institutions

In shifting the focus of my analysis of positive discrimination (PD) to the specific context of university admissions, I need first to adapt the arguments and claims made about PD policies in general (introduced in Chapter 3) to this new context. I begin by examining the impact that PD policies can be expected to have on the composition of students enrolled at the university level. Then I discuss how some of the arguments and claims formulated in Chapter 3 need to be modified to fit the higher educational context. Finally, I explore in some depth several of the arguments for and against PD policies in university admissions, in cases where considerable light can be shed on the validity of the arguments by a priori reasoning.

The impact of PD policies on university enrollments

To understand the consequences of PD policies in the sphere of higher education, it is essential to begin with a clear understanding of what impact such policies have on the composition of students enrolled in universities. Different PD policies will of course have different impacts. My purpose here is simply to discuss the way in which any PD admission policy is likely to affect the composition of students enrolled in universities.

The application of a PD policy by a selective[1] university may in some cases result in an expansion of the overall number of students admitted, so that additional applicants from under-represented ethnic groups (UREGs) can be admitted without reducing correspondingly the number of non-UREG students enrolled. Most often, however, it results in an increase in the number of UREG applicants admitted to the university, and a similar decrease in the number of non-UREG applicants admitted, as compared with what would have happened in the absence of positive discrimination. Thus, one can speak of the admission of "retrospectively rejected" students (those who would have been rejected in the absence of PD) and the rejection of "retrospectively admitted" students (those who would have been admitted in the absence of PD).[2]

These effects of a PD policy practiced by one selective university on the size and composition of its student body should be distinguished from the effects of the widespread application of PD policies across the higher educational system of a whole country. In this latter context, PD policies will have their greatest impact on the most highly selective and prestigious institutions.[3] It is in these institutions that UREG members would be most under-represented in the absence of PD (and were in fact most under-represented prior to the introduction of PD policies), because of the combination of circumstances that render them on average less qualified by conventional measures of achievement. As one goes further down the spectrum of university selectivity and prestige, the effect of PD policies will be less and less to increase the number of UREG students actually enrolled at the expense of the number of non-UREG students. Instead, the effect will be more and more to change the nature of the students enrolled: by conventional admissions criteria, UREG students will on average be less qualified and non-UREG students will be on average more qualified. When one reaches the lower tiers of the university spectrum, the numbers of UREG students enrolled will likely diminish and the numbers of non-UREG students will likely rise – unless the practice of positive discrimination encourages and enables a significant number of UREG members, who would otherwise not even consider higher education, to apply for admission to a higher educational institution.

Thus the primary overall effect of the general practice of positive discrimination in admissions to higher educational institutions is to change the distribution of UREG and non-UREG students across differing kinds of institutions. Specifically, positive discrimination redistributes some UREG students upward into more selective and presumably higher-quality institutions than they would otherwise attend; and it redistributes non-UREG students correspondingly downward. A secondary effect of positive discrimination is to increase the number of UREG university students, partly at the expense of the number of non-UREG students. The effect of positive discrimination is likely to be mainly redistributive at the level of undergraduate programs of study. At the graduate level there will be a similar tendency, but there is likely to be less redistribution of non-UREG students downward – especially to lower-level institutions – and more of a tendency for such students to forgo advanced studies altogether and instead go right into the job market. Thus positive discrimination at the graduate level may result in a significant increase in the overall number of UREG students enrolled as well as a significant upward redistribution of UREG students to higher-quality institutions.

Adapting PD arguments and claims to the context of higher education

In this section I review the arguments and claims for and against PD compiled in Chapter 3 (and listed in Tables 3.1 and 3.2), with a view to determining what modifications are needed to adapt them to the context of admissions to higher educational institutions.

The arguments for PD that involve overall societal well-being (arguments 1, 2, 7, and 8) apply in much the same way, whether the PD policy at issue is focused on educational admissions or on any other process of selection to a desirable position. Further consideration is needed only in the case of *claim 2.5* to the effect that *PD generates greater contributions of community-oriented service*. This is one of a variety of claims of benefits expected from the contribution of PD policies to the integration of society's elite; it rests on the premise that members of a UREG's elite are especially likely to contribute leadership and voluntary services both to their own communities and to the wider society.

Claim 2.5 focuses on the service that an educated university graduate may contribute to society, over and above his/her immediate job responsibilities, and with little or no compensation. Such service may take the form of playing a leadership role in a community organization, serving as a mentor to young people, or working as a volunteer in activities benefiting members of the local community or the broader society. This kind of service is most often – though not always – offered for the benefit of those who are relatively disadvantaged in socio-economic terms. Because successful UREG members themselves come from relatively disadvantaged communities, it does seem that they would be more likely to engage in service contributions to their own communities – and arguably, by extension, to other communities as well.

To the extent that PD increases the proportion of UREG members among university graduates, it is likely to increase the proportion of university graduates who will contribute service after graduation. To the extent that PD redistributes UREG students somewhat higher in the overall spectrum of university quality, it might also lead to more – or at least better – contributions of service. It could result in more such contributions if higher-quality universities instill or sustain more of a service ethic in their students. And it could result in better service if such universities enable their graduates, when they choose to contribute service, to do so more effectively. Such service contributions can be expected not only to increase the availability of services, opportunities, and resources to people at the lower end of the socio-economic ladder – including many UREG members. The improvement and expansion of service-oriented organizations can be expected also to strengthen institutions of civil society that are central to a successful democracy.

The arguments in Chapter 3 that involve the effectiveness of organizational performance (arguments 3, 4, and 9) translate in the higher educational context into arguments involving the educational mission of universities. *Argument 3* in favor of PD can be adapted in a very straightforward manner by minor rewording: *PD improves accuracy in the appraisal of academic qualifications of applicants to selective universities*, in a context in which conventional admissions criteria fail to credit the full potential of UREG students for success in their academic studies and related subsequent careers.[4] PD policies in university admissions redistribute upwards (in the quality spectrum of universities) UREG students whose academic potential is likely to be understated by conventional credentials, and they redistribute downwards non-UREG students whose academic potential is likely to be overstated by such credentials.

Claim 3.1 can be reworded as follows: *PD better serves the educational mission of universities by increasing the average academic quality of students enrolled in selective universities.* PD policies raise the average academic quality of incoming student cohorts at selective universities because they enable admissions offices to admit highly capable UREG applicants (who would otherwise be rejected) in favor of less capable non-UREG students (who would otherwise be admitted). This claim has the following implied corollary: that PD promotes higher academic standards at selective universities, which contributes in turn to higher-quality education and research at those institutions. Claim 3.2 remains as before.

Argument 9 against PD, and its associated claims, are precise counterparts to argument 3 and its claims; so these require corresponding changes in the context of higher education. Thus *argument 9* now reads: *PD injects inaccuracy into the appraisal of academic qualifications of applicants to selective universities*, by giving extra credit to UREG applicants for personal characteristics that have nothing to do with their actual or potential academic ability. By arbitrarily redistributing downwards (in the quality spectrum of universities) non-UREG students with stronger academic credentials and redistributing upwards UREG students with weaker academic credentials, PD is claimed to have the following three adverse consequences.

Claim 9.1 is that *PD impairs the educational mission of universities by reducing the average academic quality of students enrolled in selective universities.* PD policies reduce the average academic quality of incoming student cohorts because they result in the admission of under-qualified UREG applicants (who would otherwise be rejected) in favor of better-qualified non-UREG students (who would otherwise be admitted). This claim has the corollary that PD lowers academic standards at the more selective universities, which contributes in turn to lower-quality education and research at those institutions. Claim 9.2 needs no modification.

The remaining argument involving the educational mission of universities, *argument 4*, can be recast as follows: *PD, by assuring a more diverse student body, enables universities to provide a better educational experience for all students.* This has been the primary argument advanced by US university administrators over the last several decades to justify PD, because it addresses the one rationale for PD in university admissions that was deemed constitutional by the US Supreme Court in its landmark Bakke decision of 1978 – i.e. that a modest degree of race-based preference for members of under-represented minority groups is acceptable, provided that this is only one of many factors weighed in the admissions process, and provided that the resultant greater diversity in the student body contributes to the achievement of the overall educational mission of the university. The new landmark ruling issued by the Supreme Court in 2003 in the University of Michigan Law School decision reinforced this rationale (and indeed added a new rationale reflecting the argument that affirmative action generates benefits associated with the integration of society's elite).[5]

In Chapter 3, only one general claim was associated with argument 4. In the educational context, however, it is useful to distinguish between two different specific claims. *Claim 4.1* is that: *PD, by increasing diversity among students, improves their learning of academic subjects.* By introducing into the educational arena a greater variety of perspectives, ethnic diversity contributes to the ability of students of all backgrounds to learn in depth the academic subjects they are studying. This implies that university resources are being utilized more efficiently to enhance student acquisition of knowledge and skills. *Claim 4.2* is that: *PD, by increasing diversity among students, improves their ability to function in a multicultural society.* By increasing the number and the range of multicultural interactions in the university community, greater ethnic diversity of the student body enables students to learn how to function better as workers and citizens in a multicultural society. Gains in this kind of cultural understanding not only increase worker efficiency but also enhance people's ability to play a constructive role as citizens in a democracy.

The arguments in Chapter 3 that involve the welfare of UREG members (arguments 5, 6, 10, 11, and 12) translate in the higher educational context into arguments involving the welfare of UREG students. Arguments 5 and 11 and their associated claims, involving motivation and complacency on the part of UREG youths, are easily restated in terms of UREG students. The remaining arguments and claims, however, require some modification to fit PD policies applied to university admissions.

Argument 6 takes on more significance in the educational context, since educational institutions – especially at the university level – are critical sources of social capital in the form of access to job-related contacts and networks. This argument can be reworded as follows: *PD improves the spread of university-generated social capital.*

There is every reason to believe that the social capital endowments of UREG students will be enhanced to a greater extent by attendance at a good university than will those of their non-UREG peers. UREG members have on average considerably less in the way of useful contacts and networks at their disposal than do non-UREG members. They lack this kind of social capital because members of their own communities are under-represented in high-status jobs and positions of responsibility, a fact which in turn is linked to the history of past injustice done to UREG members.[6] By the same token, non-UREG members are much more likely to have access – through their family, friends, clubs, etc. – to people who can smooth their way to good career opportunities. Thus attendance at a more selective university is likely to do more to enhance the future career opportunities of UREG students than corresponding attendance at a less selective university would do to diminish those opportunities for non-UREG students.[7]

This reasoning leads to two distinct claims, of which the first is simply a rewording of the corresponding claim in Chapter 3 and the second is entirely new. *Claim 6.1* is that: *PD helps to offset UREG student deficits in social capital.* *Claim 6.2* is that: *PD increases the overall benefits from university-generated social capital*. The latter claim implies that PD is not simply a zero-sum game that redistributes social capital benefits from non-UREG to UREG students. Instead, PD is seen as a positive-sum game that provides net benefits to society as a whole – in the form of greater efficiency in the use of higher educational resources and a greater supply of candidates qualified and available to take on demanding jobs.[8]

Argument 10 and its claims also require some revision in the context of PD policies applied to university admissions decisions. The argument can be restated as: *PD results in a mismatch between its direct beneficiaries and the universities to which they gain access*, by placing them in an environment in which they are likely to do very poorly. The mismatch between their academic abilities and the academic expectations to which they are exposed by preferential admission to selective universities is seen as leading to three harmful consequences. The first and third involve only minor rewording of the more general claims; but the second is an entirely new claim.

Claim 10.1 is that: *UREG students generally display poor academic performance and often fail to graduate from universities to which they have gained access by virtue of PD*. Some critics of PD in the sphere of education go on to make an even stronger claim. They argue that PD beneficiaries are likely to end up worse off than they would have been if they had attended a less demanding university, from which they could have graduated with a strong rather than a weak academic record, or from which they could have graduated rather than dropped out – in either case going on to a more successful post-university career. They argue further that even those PD beneficiaries who would not have pursued their higher education at any university, in the absence of PD preferences, might well have gone on to a more successful career if PD had not assured their admission to a university. The new claim, *claim 10.2*, is thus as follows: *PD beneficiaries are made worse off when they gain admission to a university via a PD preference*. Both claims 10.1 and 10.2 involve costs in efficiency (via wasted educational resources) and costs in equity (via the losses experienced by PD beneficiaries).

Claim 10.3 is that *PD exacerbates negative stereotypes of UREG students as innately inferior*, because it creates a situation in which the academic performance of most UREG students is significantly below that of most of their non-UREG peers. By pushing UREG beneficiaries into university settings where they are unprepared to compete effectively with their non-UREG peers, PD causes UREG students to be very highly and disproportionately represented among the worst performers in many courses, among dropouts, and among low-ranking graduates. The noticeable crowding of UREG students into the lower academic ranks of selective universities can be expected, in turn, to strengthen already existing predilections to view UREG members as cognitively inferior. Indeed, it may well increase the tendency not only of non-UREG members but also of some UREG members themselves to hold this view.

Finally, *argument 12* and its claims can be adapted to the educational context with only minor modifications. The argument here is that: *PD results in devalu-*

ation of the academic accomplishments of UREG students, because these accomplishments are attributed at least in part to PD preferences rather than to the innate abilities and efforts of the students themselves – whether or not the students have actually benefited from PD.[9] When PD is applied to UREG applicants participating in a selective admissions process, successful UREG applicants will indeed, on average, have lower academic qualifications than successful non-UREG applicants (of whom the majority, it is safe to assume, will not have received equivalent preferences). Moreover, if observers cannot easily determine which of the admitted UREG students actually owe their admission to a PD preference,[10] it is rational to infer that any given UREG student is more likely than any non-UREG student to owe his/her admission to PD – and therefore more likely to have been admitted with lower academic qualifications. This inference will happen to be correct in the case of UREG students who were admitted by virtue of PD; and it will happen to be erroneous in the case of UREG students who would have been admitted in any case.[11]

In the educational context *claim 12.1* becomes the following: that *PD results in under-appreciation of the true capabilities and achievements of some UREG students*, since those UREG applicants who would have been admitted without any PD preference will sometimes be erroneously presumed to have lower academic qualifications than they really do. *Claim 12.2* is now that: *PD results in the stigmatization of UREG students as not really belonging on the university campus*. Because many UREG students will have been admitted into the university by virtue of PD preferences (and even more UREG students may be perceived to have done so), other members of the campus community will be likely to conclude that most UREG students attending the university are not as academically capable as their non-UREG counterparts. Any evidence of poorer academic performance (on average) by UREG students relative to non-UREG students will only reinforce this conclusion, which may lead to the view that most UREG students do not belong on campus. Whether this view is justified is quite another matter.[12]

Claim 12.3 is that: *PD results in low faculty expectations for UREG students*, which is likely to diminish their gains from a university education. Faculty may fail to notice strong academic potential on the part of some UREG students, and they may in turn fail to encourage these students to develop and realize that potential. Even faculty who are favorably disposed to UREG students may, because they hope to see them succeed, tend to patronize some of those students by holding them to levels of academic performance that are lower than those expected of their peers.[13] Either of these behaviors on the part of faculty with low expectations of UREG students will tend to discourage those students from developing the skills necessary for true academic competence. To what extent PD can be held responsible for such behaviors is an open question.[14]

Tables 7.1 and 7.2 list all of the arguments and claims for and against positive discrimination in higher educational admissions, in precisely the same format as the corresponding Tables 3.1 and 3.2 in Chapter 3.

Table 7.1 Arguments for positive discrimination in educational admissions,
related claims of benefits, and societal goals linked to each claim

Argument and related benefits	Societal goal
Involving overall societal well-being	
1 Compensation for historical injustice	
1.1 Affirmation of society's commitment to reduce UREG disadvantages	Harmony
2 Integration of society's elite	
2.1 Greater legitimacy of society's leadership	Democracy
2.2 More UREG decision-makers offering opportunities to UREG members	Equity
2.3 More UREG role models and mentors	Efficiency
2.4 Better performance of jobs if job-holder is of UREG status	Efficiency
2.5 Greater contributions of community-oriented service	Equity, democracy
2.6 More dispelling of negative stereotypes of UREG members	Harmony
Involving the educational mission of universities	
3 Accuracy in appraising academic qualifications	
3.1 Increase in average academic quality of students enrolled	Efficiency
3.2 Decrease in UREG cynicism about unfairness of selection processes	Harmony
4 Contribution of diversity to the educational process	
4.1 Better student learning of academic subjects	Efficiency
4.2 Better student ability to function in a multicultural society	Efficiency, democracy
Involving the welfare of UREG students	
5 Motivation of UREG students	
5.1 More development of human capital by UREG students	Efficiency, equity
6 Spread of social capital	
6.1 Greater offsetting of UREG student deficits in social capital	Equity
6.2 Greater overall benefits from social capital	Efficiency

Table 7.2 Arguments against positive discrimination in educational admissions, related claims of costs, and societal goals linked to each claim

Argument and related costs	Societal goal
Involving overall societal well-being	
7 *Poor tailoring to help the most disadvantaged*	
7.1 Exacerbation of inequalities among UREG members	Equity
7.2 Redistribution from non-UREG to better-off UREG members	Equity, harmony
8 *Exacerbation of ethnic group consciousness*	
8.1 More divisive identity group politics	Democracy, harmony
8.2 Deceitful efforts to claim UREG status to gain resulting benefits	Harmony
8.3 Snowballing demands for group preferences	Harmony, democracy
Involving the educational mission of universities	
9 *Inaccuracy in appraising academic qualifications*	
9.1 Decrease in average academic quality of students enrolled	Efficiency
9.2 Increase in non-UREG resentment about unfair admissions processes	Harmony
Involving the welfare of UREG students	
10 *Mismatch of PD beneficiaries with their universities*	
10.1 Poor academic performance and frequent failure by PD beneficiaries	Equity, efficiency
10.2 PD beneficiaries worse off when they gain admission via a preference	Equity, efficiency
10.3 Exacerbation of negative stereotypes of UREG students	Harmony
11 *Complacency of UREG students*	
11.1 Less development of human capital by UREG students	Efficiency, equity
12 *Devaluation of the accomplishments of UREG students*	
12.1 Under-appreciation of true capabilities of some UREG students	Equity, efficiency
12.2 Stigmatization of UREG students as not belonging on campus	Harmony
12.3 Low faculty expectations of UREG students	Equity, efficiency

Exploring the impact of PD policies on the accuracy of appraisal of applicants' academic qualifications

The opposing arguments 3 for PD and 9 against PD in higher education share the same objective: to assure that the applicants who are academically most qualified for university study are admitted to selective universities. This can be expected to result in the best match of students to universities, the highest academic standards, and the least resentment against – or cynicism about – admissions procedures. On the other hand, the two arguments are diametrically opposed in their judgment about the contribution of PD to achieving the desired objective. Proponents of the pro-PD argument believe that PD serves as a helpful corrective to a biased set of conventional admissions criteria; whereas proponents of the anti-PD argument believe that it serves only to distort an otherwise appropriate set of admissions criteria.

For many observers it seems obvious that an applicant's academic qualifications for admission to a university should be based on the realized level of the applicant's pre-university academic achievement – whether measured by scores on standardized examinations or more refined indicators that take into account other evidence of realized academic achievement, such as high-school grades and indicators of the difficulty of courses taken. Such measures are reasonably good indicators of how well prepared an applicant is for university-level studies.[15] Moreover, students who come to a university with the best preparation are arguably likely to be best able to further enhance their level of education and skills through a university education;[16] and they are certainly likely to contribute most to the education of their fellow students and to the research efforts of faculty. Rewarding greater realized achievement prior to university entry with admission to more selective (and higher-quality) universities will also maintain a strong incentive for students to achieve in their pre-university education. It is therefore not unreasonable to begin with the presumption that university admissions decisions designed to admit the most academically qualified students into a university should be based largely on indicators of past realized academic achievement – which is indeed the practice of admissions officers at most universities.

It is unreasonable, however, to leave matters there. Indicators of realized academic achievement must be distinguished from indicators of potential academic achievement. One's potential academic achievement is reflected in one's realized academic achievement *relative* to what might be expected given initial situational conditions, which generally differ from one applicant to the next. For example, the attainment of a given standardized test score by an applicant with poor secondary school preparation, and without the benefit of test-coaching classes, indicates a significantly higher level of potential academic achievement than the attainment of the same score by an applicant from an excellent high school who had the opportunity to enroll in a test-coaching class.

Given the enormous range of situational advantage and disadvantage that characterizes most every society, and therefore characterizes applicants for admission to universities,[17] there must be many applicants whose past realized achievements are not good indicators of either their innate ability or the effort they have put into their pre-university education. And, once a student is admitted to a university, high levels of innate ability and/or of individual effort are likely to be at least as important as situational advantage in contributing to the achievement of the goals listed above. It follows that admissions officers seeking to admit applicants with the strongest academic potential ought to give extra weight to that part of an applicant's realized achievement that does not result from situational advantage. If PD is to be justified as improving the accuracy of appraisal of applicants' academic qualifications, this must be grounded in the notion that preferences in favor of UREG applicants serve as a way of bringing consideration of potential academic achievement into an admissions decision-making process that would otherwise rely too heavily on realized academic achievement.

There can be no doubt that UREG members face a variety of forms of discrimination, exclusion, or stereotyping (whether overt, covert, structural, or incidental) that constitute elements of situational disadvantage. Arguably, all UREG members face some such obstacles linked to their UREG status, independently of any other forms of situational disadvantage they may experience. To overcome these obstacles and achieve any given level of conventionally measured achievement, a typical UREG applicant must therefore display resourcefulness and perseverance to an extent not required of a typical non-UREG applicant. These very qualities of resourcefulness and perseverance are likely to contribute to success in university studies and/or in one's later career. It would seem appropriate, therefore, to treat UREG status as an indicator of a relevant dimension of an applicant's qualification for admission to a university.

Before crediting the use of this kind of PD in admissions as a way of offsetting situational disadvantages confronted by UREG applicants, however, one must ask whether or not it is a good way of taking into account their potential achievement. Not every UREG member faces the same degree of situational disadvantage because of his/her UREG status. If PD were applied in a uniform way to all UREG applicants – e.g. in the form of lowered minimal qualifying levels for admission, or extra points in an admissibility index – this would fail to distinguish differing degrees of potential achievement on the part of different individual UREG members. There are, however, some alternative approaches that appear likely to be more accurate in this respect.

One alternative approach is to apply PD in admissions in a more sensitive and nuanced manner.[18] Instead of the quantitative kind of procedures described in the previous paragraph, admissions officers could implement a qualitative procedure that begins with the presumption that UREG applicants have had to overcome more obstacles than non-UREG applicants, but goes on to assess the degree to which this is true of any given UREG applicant by probing that applicant's background and life experiences. This nuanced approach requires more information from applicants and more attention by admissions officers to each individual applicant, including possibly a personal interview.

Another possible procedure, less dependent on the investment of additional resources in the admissions process, would make use of the same standardized tests that are commonly used to measure an applicant's realized academic achievement. Via a multivariate analysis that links test scores to a variety of background characteristics of the test-takers, one could establish group means for test-takers with different socio-economic and ascriptive group statuses. A test-taker's potential academic achievement could then be calculated as the difference between the person's actual test score and the mean test score of all the test-takers with the same background characteristics.[19] This approach has the advantage of enabling admissions officers to credit applicants with over-coming a variety of different kinds of disadvantages – not only those that are associated with UREG status. But its reliance on standardized test scores as measures of realized academic achievement makes it vulnerable to criticism based on the shortcomings of such tests.

A final logical extension of the above, more nuanced procedures for imple-menting PD in university admissions would be to identify a series of indicators of potential achievement that credit disadvantaged applicants with characteristics like resourcefulness and perseverance – without having to refer to their group status at all. Suppose that such indicators could indeed be iden-tified and measured, in such a way as to reflect academic potential that is obscured by the kinds of situational disadvantages facing UREG members and possibly, to some extent, non-UREG members as well. If these indicators were included in the assessment of the admissions qualifications of all appli-cants, then the playing field could be leveled for UREG applicants as well as for other applicants who may have faced similar situational disadvantages. Most importantly, the level playing field would be achieved in a manner that would lay to rest concerns about arbitrary identity-based distortion of admis-sions credentials raised by opponents of the use of PD as a way of assuring admission of the most qualified students.

Refinement of university admissions criteria along these lines – as an alter-native to using a PD policy – is surely a worthwhile task, for it would enable some important prospective benefits of PD to be achieved without incurring some of the main prospective costs. The difficulty (or the expense) of accom-plishing this task in a satisfactory manner, however, may prevent success from being achieved in the foreseeable future. In that case one must face head-on the question of whether the application of some form of PD is likely to help or to hinder the identification of applicants best qualified to enter a selective university. From the foregoing discussion we may conclude that only a highly nuanced form of PD, or a well-crafted multivariate regression analysis (including UREG status as one of several background variables) to determine potential academic achievement, could conceivably generate the benefits ensuing from improvement in the accuracy with which applicant qualifications are appraised.

The kinds of PD policies most often practiced are not likely to meet the above criteria. They are therefore unlikely to be successful in crediting academic potential ignored by conventional achievement indicators. Thus PD in university admissions will typically generate costs of the kind envisaged by argument 9, not benefits as envisaged by argument 3 – unless the PD policy is unusually sensitive.

Exploring the impact of PD policies on UREG student motivation

The opposing arguments 5 for PD and 11 against PD in higher education share the same primary concern with the structure of incentives facing young UREG members in educational institutions at all levels. Advocates of each argument want to assure that UREG youths are motivated to work hard rather than to become complacent in their studies. But the two sides hold diametrically opposed views on the effect of PD on the incentive structure. Proponents of PD believe that, by providing more opportunities for UREG students at selective universities, it encourages more effort and hard work on the part of UREG youths. Opponents of PD believe that, by providing young UREG members with an easier path into and through selective universities, it fosters complacency on their part – and perhaps a tendency to depend on help from others rather than on their own effort.

Let us consider first the incentives facing young UREG members seeking admission to a selective university. There is no question that a UREG youth who expends a given amount of effort on his/her studies will be more likely to gain admission when PD is being practiced than when it is not. This fact, however, does not resolve the debate, for PD improves the educational prospects both of UREG youths who work hard and of UREG youths who do not. What is relevant to the incentive structure facing young UREG members is the effect that PD has on the payoff to *marginal* effort on their part: is an additional unit of effort likely to improve prospects of admission to a desired university more when PD is in place or when it is not? This clearly depends on the circumstances under which the PD policy is applied.

If the PD policy is such as to guarantee admission to a UREG applicant, then there is no payoff to additional effort. This would be the case if there were a quota of seats reserved for applicants from a particular UREG, if the minimum qualifications required for admission were easily achievable, and if there were enough seats available to accommodate all potential applicants from that UREG group. If, however, the number of UREG admits were less than the corresponding number of applicants, and/or if admission of UREG applicants were dependent on qualifications including prior academic performance, then additional effort in pre-university studies on the part of a UREG applicant would clearly have some payoff. The greater the degree of competition for entry into a given selective university – as measured, for example, by the ratio of admits to applicants (in the relevant category) – the greater the payoff to additional effort on the part of any given applicant is likely to be. This logic holds up to the point where competition is so keen that an applicant has virtually no chance of being admitted, no matter how much effort he/she puts in.

This analysis indicates that there is no simple link between PD and the incentive for a young UREG member to work hard in the hope of gaining admission to a selective university. What can be concluded is that PD is likely to increase that incentive when it converts the competition for admission to a desired university (or one of a set of desirable universities) from one in which the UREG applicant has little hope of gaining admission to one in which the prospects of admission are real but uncertain. By the same token, PD will decrease the work incentive when it converts competition for admission to a desired university (or one of a set of desirable universities) into something close to a guarantee.

The same logic applies to incentives for UREG students to study hard at a university after gaining admission. If PD has the effect of virtually guaranteeing to UREG students favorable outcomes – graduation, good marks, good subsequent career opportunities – then it removes the payoff to hard work. But if PD increases the range of possible career outcomes open to UREG students, and if the particular outcome attained by any given UREG student depends on how well that student does in his/her university studies, then the payoff to hard work is likely to be enhanced rather than diminished.

As with other arguments for or against PD, an assessment of which side of the argument with respect to incentives is valid cannot be rendered without considering the circumstances under which PD is applied. On the basis of a priori reasoning, however, one can say that cases in which PD dampens incentives for UREG youths to do well in their studies are bound to be relatively rare. Unless UREG applicants are virtually guaranteed access to their first choice of university, and unless their graduation with a creditable degree is virtually assured once they enter university, their future opportunities will still depend to a significant degree on how much they achieve in their secondary and higher education. Only in the case of reserved-seat quotas, and then only if the quotas typically go unfilled, will UREG applicants be insulated from competition with other UREG applicants as well as non-UREG applicants for admission to selective universities. Competition for graduation from such universities may be less stiff than competition for entry; but it will still make some difference whether a student graduates with a strong or a weak record, unless there is such a strong form of PD in the sphere of employment that UREG students are guaranteed a good job by virtue of university graduation alone.[20]

Exploring the impact of ethnic diversity on educational quality

Argument 4 in favor of PD policies in higher education entails claims of two kinds of benefits from greater ethnic diversity in a university's student body: better student learning of academic subjects and better student ability to function in a multicultural society.

The theoretical case for the first of these benefits can be summarized in two sentences, as follows.[21] Diversity among students in a class promotes the challenging of assumptions, presumptions, and stereotypes; and it leads to sympathetic engagement with arguments from many different perspectives. The more diverse the student body is, the livelier is the educational process, the more students learn from one another; indeed, faculty research may also benefit from diversity among students. These assertions are plausible in the humanities and in the social sciences, as well as in pre-professional fields like law, health, and business, where human behavior and interaction is an essential element of the field of study. It is harder, however, to see how learning and research in mathematics and the natural sciences could be advanced by the exchange of different perspectives from a diverse set of students. The case for the second of the anticipated benefits of student diversity seems a good deal stronger: the more the ethnic composition of the student body reflects that of the larger society, the better are students likely to learn how to function well in a diverse larger society.

An important question remains, however, in both cases: why focus on ethnicity as the key dimension of diversity? The benefits of diversity for learning academic subjects stem from exposure to a diversity of views and perspectives; this kind of diversity would be at least as well – if not better – served by a policy that sought to promote diversity in student socio-economic backgrounds, experiences, and views rather than simply diversity in ethnicity. Critics of PD as a means of improving students' educational experience argue that the focus on ethnic diversity as a means of expanding the range of viewpoints among students reflects a perniciously stereotypical view that one's ethnicity determines one's viewpoint. Advocates of PD on these kinds of grounds reply that ethnicity is a reasonable proxy for certain kinds of common experiences, but certainly not for particular views. To the contrary, the actual diversity of views among people of a given ethnicity is important in defusing stereotypes about the tight link between ethnicity and views.

This last argument is a good one, but it lends more support to the case for student ethnic diversity not as a means of improving the academic learning process but as a means of enabling students to function well in a multicultural society. Indeed, universities are particularly well placed to achieve this goal because of their unique role within the larger society.[22] For one thing, university students are at a formative age and thus especially open to new ideas and new behavioral patterns. Secondly, the university setting is likely to offer many students their first opportunity to live and study in a multicultural environment, since primary and secondary educational institutions tend to reflect patterns of residential segregation that isolate different ethnic groups from one another.[23] Finally, a university campus is a relatively open-minded, protective environment, where ideas can more easily be tested and boundaries more easily crossed. Thus universities are especially well placed to break down ethnic barriers.[24]

For PD to be justified as a means of improving the academic learning process, it is not enough to show that this process can benefit from greater ethnic diversity among students. It must be shown also that there is no good way to achieve the same end without some kind of ethnically based discrimination. In principle, an admission policy designed to generate more viewpoint diversity would seem to be a better way to achieve the desired end than an admission policy designed to generate more ethnic diversity. In practice, however, it would be more difficult to ascertain an applicant's viewpoint than his/her ethnicity. Moreover, any effort to reward certain viewpoints in the admissions process could distort incentives and/or lead to misrepresentation; and, in any case, the viewpoint of an entering university student is surely much more changeable than his/her ethnicity. Thus there may not in fact be a good alternative to focusing attention on ethnicity if the objective is to ensure a diversity of viewpoints among students admitted to a university.[25]

In the case of professional schools in fields like law, health, and business, ethnic diversity is probably especially important for the learning process. This is because it is arguably very important for students to gain an understanding of the perspectives of members of UREGs (as opposed to members of non-UREGs who happen to hold different views), because students will tend to be more lacking in their understanding of cultural differences than in their understanding of viewpoint differences – and because they will need to acquire sensitivity to the cultural differences that characterize many UREG members with whom they will be interacting in their professional activities.

I conclude that the argument from diversity in support of PD is probably stronger in claim 4.2 – that it will help students function in a multicultural society – than in claim 4.1 – that it will improve academic learning. If one wants to learn to live and work more constructively in a larger society that is ethnically diverse, one would certainly ask for a university environment that reflects the ethnic diversity of the population as a whole. The second claim is also plausible, however, in fields like the humanities and (at least some) social sciences, as well as in many of the professions for which students are prepared in professional schools. By redistributing UREG students upward in the university spectrum, PD unquestionably brings greater ethnic diversity to the student body of the more selective universities – very probably without reducing correspondingly the diversity of the student body at the less selective universities.[26]

8 Toward an empirical assessment of claims of benefits and costs from positive discrimination

Before examining empirical evidence on positive discrimination (PD) policies available from the US and India, one needs to understand how such evidence can and should be used to test the validity of claims made about the consequences of such policies. In this chapter I begin by discussing briefly the larger benefit-cost framework of my approach to the empirical evidence, and then I consider what kind of evidence is required to assess the benefits and costs claimed by each of the consequentialist arguments for and against positive discrimination in higher educational admissions.

Evaluating the benefits and costs of PD policies in university admissions

In order to evaluate the net benefits – and hence the overall worth – of any given PD policy, we should in principle undertake a comprehensive benefit-cost analysis. Such an analysis would involve the following steps:

1   identify which of the possible beneficial and costly consequences of the PD policy are actually realized;
2   measure the extent to which each such consequence is realized;
3   identify which valued societal goals are affected, positively or negatively, by each consequence of the PD policy;
4   determine how much each consequence contributes, positively or negatively, to each relevant societal goal; and
5   decide on the relative importance of each societal goal, so that positive and negative contributions of the PD policy to the various goals can be aggregated together into a single overall measure of net societal benefits.

In the next section of this chapter I will discuss how steps (1) and (2) can in principle best be achieved. Step (2) is considerably more difficult than step (1), because many of the consequences of a PD policy cannot easily be quantified. In Chapter 3, pp. 56–8, I addressed step (3) by identifying a set of four valued societal goals potentially served or disserved by policies of positive discrimination: social harmony, democracy, productive efficiency, and distributive equity. The fact that these goals are broadly qualitative in nature makes it very difficult to carry out step (4) in a systematic quantitative manner. Step (5) is a matter of making one's values explicit; different people are bound to differ on the relative importance of different societal goals. The difficulties and complexities of these last two steps make it impossible to carry out a complete comprehensive benefit-cost analysis of any given PD policy in university admissions. However, by pursuing as systematically as possible the positive empirical investigation implied by the first two steps, while keeping in mind the normative framework implied by the last three steps, one can nonetheless gain much understanding about the desirability of given PD policies.

Because PD policies are highly controversial, and because debates about positive discrimination all too often proceed in a polemical fashion undisturbed by facts, it is especially important to bring relevant and well-grounded empirical evidence to bear on the discussion. As it happens, a considerable amount of empirical research has in fact been carried out on questions that bear on the consequences of PD policies in university admissions both in the US and in India. This kind of research not only documents the extent of implementation of PD admission policies and the performance of under-represented ethnic group (UREG) students at various higher educational institutions; it also includes some systematic studies of the long-term career trajectories of UREG students. Not surprisingly, considerably more work of this kind has been done in the US than in India. Nonetheless, enough has been done in each country so as to permit at least tentative conclusions about some of the successes and the failures of PD admission policies in the two countries.

Testing the claims of benefits and costs from PD policies in university admissions

To determine whether or not a PD policy generates a benefit or cost that is claimed for it, one would ideally like to compare the actual situation observed under the PD policy with the counterfactual situation that would have been observed in the absence of the policy. By definition, such a counterfactual situation cannot actually be observed. Assessment of the impact of a PD policy must therefore be based on comparison of the actually observed outcomes with some kind of estimate of the relevant counterfactual outcomes – based on reasonable inferences drawn from actual observations in comparable situations.

In pursuing this line of empirical enquiry, the first question one must answer is what impact a given PD policy has on the composition of the student bodies of the institutions affected by the policy (including both those institutions where PD is practiced and other institutions whose admissions are indirectly affected by the practice of PD in the former institutions). This will depend both on the precise nature of the PD policy and on the conditions under which it is applied – including both the characteristics of actual and potential applicants for admission to the institutions and the set of alternatives available to them in the event that they are denied admission. I will focus the next two chapters on evidence relating to the likely effects of PD policies in the US and India on the composition of the student body in higher educational institutions affected by those policies.

The following four chapters will then be devoted to an empirical analysis of the consequences of positive discrimination. For this purpose I need to consider the range of possible benefits and costs that are claimed by proponents and opponents of positive discrimination and listed, respectively, in Tables 7.1 and 7.2. These claims clearly cover a very wide range of possible consequences – from broad societal developments to changes in the functioning of educational institutions to gains or losses for individual UREG students. Moreover, the anticipated benefits and costs are quite varied in nature. Some have to do with inter-ethnic harmony or disharmony; some have to do with the functioning of a democratic system; some involve the efficiency or inefficiency of use of educational and other resources; and some involve considerations of equity or inequity between individuals or groups.

In the rest of this chapter I consider how claims of various benefits and costs resulting from positive discrimination should in principle be assessed empirically – and to what extent this is likely to be feasible. My focus is on methodological issues, but I consider also the kinds of data needed for empirical analysis. I will address all of the potential benefits and costs of positive discrimination identified in Tables 7.1 and 7.2, grouping related claims of benefits and/or costs together; and I will start with claims that are relatively easy to test empirically and then move on to claims that are increasingly difficult to test.

Costs from snowballing demands for group preferences (claim 8.3).

The first and most obvious step in assessing the validity of this claim is to study the political history of the country in question to determine whether or not the granting of PD admissions preferences to some ethnic group(s) was in fact followed by demands by other groups for similar preferences. This is not hard to ascertain. If such demands have been rare or insignificant, one can confidently reject the claim. If there have been significant demands for the extension of PD admissions preferences to new groups, the claim can be validated by showing that these demands are attributable in some degree to the presence of the existing PD admission policies. One can be reasonably certain that this is the case if the snowballing demands for PD preferences include demands for PD in university admissions.

Costs from poor academic performance and frequent failure of PD beneficiaries to graduate with a degree (claim 10.1)

To assess the presence and the significance of such mismatch costs, one needs to determine the extent to which PD beneficiaries actually do perform poorly and fail to graduate from the degree program in which they are enrolled. Information on graduation rates and academic performance is regularly collected and recorded by higher educational institutions; so empirical assessment of this claim should not pose much of a problem.

Benefits/costs from an increase/decrease in the average academic quality of students enrolled in selective universities (claim 3.1 vs. claim 9.1)

For benefits from greater accuracy in the appraisal of applicant qualifications to be realized, it is necessary that the academic performance of PD beneficiaries (the "retrospectively rejected" students) be on average at least as strong as that of the students displaced by PD beneficiaries (the "retrospectively admitted" students). Otherwise, the claim of costs from greater inaccuracy will be validated, to an extent that varies with the degree to which the standard is not met. Since it is not always possible to identify the specific UREG students who owe their admission to PD, much less those non-UREG students who would only have been admitted in the absence of PD, one may have to estimate the relevant characteristics of the retrospectively rejected and retrospectively admitted students on the basis of averages for the UREG and non-UREG student population as a whole – or (much better) for subsets of those populations that can be presumed to be similar to those on the margin of admission/rejection. Conventional measures of academic performance – such as graduation rates, grade-point averages (GPAs), and achievement of academic honors – will suffice here. Information on these measures is regularly collected and recorded by higher educational institutions; so such data for enrolled students are certainly available – although they may be difficult to obtain.

A somewhat more demanding way of testing the validity of the claims that the use of PD improves the accuracy of applicant appraisal is to calculate whether or not conventional indicators of applicant academic qualifications (e.g. standardized test scores) under-predict academic performance in universities by the PD beneficiaries among UREG students – as would be the case if the true potential of PD beneficiaries for good academic performance is undervalued by the conventional indicators. This could be determined by including UREG status as an additional explanatory variable in multivariate regression equations in which indicators of academic performance are analyzed as a function of various student academic qualifications upon entry into a university; the more significantly positive/negative the sign of the regression coefficient on the UREG status variable, the more the claims of benefits/costs would be supported.

One should, however, consider carefully whether the kinds of empirical tests suggested above are likely to be definitive. There is in fact some reason for doubt on that score. First of all, conventional indicators of academic performance (e.g. the GPA) are known to be imperfect measures of the quality of students' academic achievements – in ways, and for reasons, similar to those for which conventional indicators of pre-university academic achievement are deficient. Moreover, even if conventional academic performance indicators do a reasonably good job of measuring academic achievement at the university, they surely do not capture the full range of education acquired at a university that a graduate will be able to deploy after graduating from the university. The ultimate test of the potential and accomplishments of PD beneficiaries may well come after graduation. To address these concerns, it would be desirable to look not only at evidence of students' academic achievements at the university itself but also at evidence of their achievements in subsequent careers.

Costs from exacerbation of inequalities among UREG members and redistribution of opportunities from less well-off non-UREG to better-off UREG members (claims 7.1 and 7.2)

To determine the extent to which these claims of poor tailoring are valid, one must in principle compare the average socio-economic class background of the PD beneficiaries among UREG students with (1) the average socio-economic class background of all the UREG members and (2) the average socio-economic class background of the non-UREG students displaced by PD. If one cannot identify precisely the PD beneficiaries, it may again be necessary to approximate them with an appropriate subset of UREG students. And since it is likely to be difficult to identify the non-UREG students who were denied admission because of PD, one will probably have to approximate their characteristics with those of an appropriate subset of admitted non-UREG students. Information on the socio-economic class background of students is somewhat harder to obtain than information about academic performance, so the claims at issue here are somewhat more difficult to test than the ones discussed above.

Costs from PD beneficiaries being worse off when gaining admission via a preference (claim 10.2)

To assess the validity of this strong mismatch claim, one needs to compare the career achievements of retrospectively rejected UREG students with the career achievements that the same UREG students would have realized had they attended the kind of less selective universities to which they would have been admitted in the absence of PD. The latter achievements cannot of course be directly ascertained. They can, however, be estimated by examining the actual career achievements of UREG students with similar entry credentials in alternative, less selective, universities. It is not easy to measure career achievements, much less to quantify them in a readily comparable way. A relevant measure might be an indicator of the socio-economic status of the job one has attained a certain number of year after graduation, or one's annual earnings from that job. Clearly, the empirical task of comparing career achievements poses significantly greater challenges than the empirical task of comparing academic performance records.

Benefits from spreading social capital: greater offsetting of UREG student deficits in social capital; and greater overall benefits from social capital (claims 6.1 and 6.2)

The value to students of the social capital generated by a higher educational institution is strongly correlated with the prestige of that institution; indeed, significant social capital is likely to be generated only in relatively elite institutions. The primary way in which PD policies affect the spread of social capital is therefore by placing more UREG students and fewer non-UREG students in selective universities. For UREG students attending these universities actually to benefit from the additional social capital to which they gain access, they must of course perform well enough to complete their programs and graduate with a degree. Evidence that PD beneficiaries do so at a reasonable rate, and one which is not much inferior to that of non-UREG students displaced by PD, is therefore a minimum requirement for the above claims to be validated.

To explore further the validity of the claims, one must estimate the size of the career boosts derived from attendance at a more highly selective university by the typical UREG student and by the typical non-UREG student. The greater the boost derived by the former relative to the latter, the more likely it is that UREG students' initial endowments of social capital are deficient and that society as a whole gains from some reallocation of social capital from (otherwise similar) non-UREG students who need it less to UREG students who need it more. This would provide further support for both claims. To sustain the claims, however, one must also determine to what extent such career boosts are due to the additional social capital made available in selective universities, as opposed to the presumably better education that students receive in such universities. To the extent that social capital plays a significant role in the career boosts, the benefits associated with the claims will be greater.

To compare UREG and non-UREG career boosts, one needs to compile evidence on the post-university career paths of UREG and non-UREG students in selective universities and compare it with evidence on the post-university career paths of otherwise similar UREG and non-UREG students attending less selective universities. These are challenging empirical demands, but they are by no means impossible to meet. To determine the extent to which social capital is responsible for the career boosts is much more difficult, for it is inherently difficult to disentangle the effects of greater social capital from those of greater human capital. Here one may have to rely on the reasonable presumption, buttressed perhaps by anecdotal evidence, that access to job-related contacts and networks makes a significant difference to students' post-university careers.

Benefits from integrating society's elite: more opportunities for UREG members offered by UREG decision-makers; more inspiration of UREG youth by UREG role models and mentors; better performance of multiculturally sensitive jobs; and greater contributions of community-oriented service (claims 2.2, 2.3, 2.4, and 2.5)

To subject these claims to empirical testing, one must first of all gather evidence on measures of career success or failure on the part of PD beneficiaries among UREG students (or a similar subset of UREG students). To support the claims, it is necessary – though not sufficient – to show that a significant proportion of PD beneficiaries do in fact take jobs of high status and responsibility, thereby helping to increase UREG representation in society's elite.

More complex tests are needed, however, to determine if PD policies have really contributed to the benefits associated with the claims at issue here. If the anticipated benefits are to be credited to PD, it must be because the PD beneficiaries were able to achieve more in their careers by virtue of attending the selective university to which they were admitted than they would have been able to achieve by attending the kind of less selective universities to which they would have been admitted in the absence of PD (or by not attending a university at all, if that is the relevant alternative). Thus the same kind of comparison of actual and hypothetical career achievements of retrospectively rejected UREG students is needed here as in the case of the previous set of claims. Measuring actual career achievements poses an empirical challenge; measuring hypothetical career achievements, on the basis of the actual achievements of a comparable set of students in different circumstances, poses a somewhat greater challenge.

The task of testing empirically the extent of the claims of benefits from the integration of society's elite does not end with a determination of whether or not PD has enabled retrospectively rejected UREG students to achieve more successful careers. To validate the claims, one should in principle also find a way to determine whether or not PD beneficiaries, as a result of their more successful career paths, have been able to provide more of the specific benefits anticipated in each claim – i.e. more job-related opportunities for UREG members in general, better quality of performance of jobs in which UREG status matters, greater contributions of community service, and more role-model inspiration for UREG youths – than would have been provided had the beneficiaries not been aided in their career outcomes by PD. To measure with any precision the amount of additional benefits of these kinds generated by PD would be virtually impossible; but it may at least be feasible to determine whether they do or do not exist at all – which is sufficient for testing the validity of the claims, if not the magnitude of the associated benefits.

Benefits from greater student diversity: better learning of academic subjects and better ability to function in a multicultural society (claims 4.1 and 4.2)

A necessary – but of course not sufficient – condition for these claims to be realized is that PD admission policies do in fact serve to increase significantly the ethnic diversity of students enrolled in higher educational institutions. This is highly likely a priori, and it is easy to verify empirically. Far more challenging is the task of determining whether increased ethnic diversity generates significant learning benefits among university students.

In principle one would like to assess the validity of the above claims by relating measures of the extent of learning of academic subjects, as well as the extent of learning how to function in a multicultural society, with indicators of the extent to which students have been exposed to ethnic diversity in their classrooms, residence halls, and campus activities – controlling for other characteristics of their universities that might be expected to affect the relevant kinds of learning. Analytically, this calls for careful construction of a multivariate causal model that enables one to isolate the effect of student ethnic diversity from the effects of many other factors that are likely to affect learning of various kinds. Empirically, it requires the gathering of evidence not only on the extent of student learning, but also on relevant indicators of ethnic diversity and on a host of other factors likely to influence learning. Measuring the extent of learning of any kind is notoriously difficult; and even constructing a relevant measure of diversity is no easy matter. Thus empirical testing of the validity of the claims and the size of the benefits at issue here is bound to pose significant challenges both of measurement and of statistical analysis.

Costs from the devaluation of UREG student accomplishments: under-appreciation of true capabilities and achievements of some UREG students; stigmatization of UREG students as not belonging on campus; and low faculty expectations for UREG students (claims 12.1, 12.2, and 12.3)

In Chapter 4, p. 53, I noted that costs associated with the devaluation of the accomplishments of UREG members could be avoided only if PD beneficiaries perform at least as well as those displaced by PD would have done. This is the same demanding criterion that must be satisfied in order to achieve the benefits of greater accuracy in the appraisal of applicants' academic qualifications (claim 3.1) and to avoid the costs of greater inaccuracy (claim 9.1). If PD beneficiaries are in fact enabled to enter universities with lower academic qualifications (on average) than most other students, then the latter claim is validated, PD beneficiaries will not perform as well (on average) as most other students, and some degree of devaluation of the accomplishments of UREG students is unavoidable. The validity of the claims at issue here can therefore be tested in the same way as suggested above for validating claim 9.1.

If the claims do prove valid, assessment of the magnitude of the associated costs would raise very difficult research challenges. It would require investigation of the extent of the under-appreciation of the accomplishments of those UREG students who do not happen to be PD beneficiaries, the degree to which UREG students in general are stigmatized, and the extent to which faculty hold low expectations for them. It would require also enquiry into the multiple causes of these phenomena. One would need to develop a model, to gather evidence on relevant variables, and to undertake statistical analysis to determine the extent to which each phenomenon can be attributed to PD.

The magnitude of the costs associated with a devaluation of UREG student accomplishments at any given university will likely depend on the average academic performance of UREG students at that university. This is because the extent to which PD – as opposed to ability, effort, and potential achievement – is deemed to account for the success of UREG students in getting admitted to the university will probably vary with the extent to which they do not perform as well as other students. The costs associated with the devaluation argument are thus likely to be more significant the more strongly the mismatch claim of poor academic performance by PD beneficiaries (claim 10.1) is supported.[1]

Costs from deceitful efforts to claim UREG status in order to gain resulting benefits (claim 8.2)

Because this claim involves deceit that perpetrators are bound to make every effort to hide, it is inherently difficult to validate or to reject the claim on the basis of systematic study. Anecdotal evidence, however, should suffice to indicate whether or not the phenomenon exists; and it may be all that one can expect to have as a basis for estimating how widespread the phenomenon really is. Should such evidence suggest that it is indeed widespread, then this might warrant the launching of some kind of systematic investigation to estimate its overall magnitude. Clearly this would require investigative powers beyond the reach of conventional social science research.

Benefits or costs linked to UREG student motivation or complacency: more/less development of human capital by UREG students (claim 5.1 vs. claim 11.1)

To determine which – if either – of these claims is empirically valid, one would first need to develop indicators of student motivation (from highly motivated to utterly complacent) and to find ways of determining the extent to which any given UREG student was motivated to pursue his/her education. This would in all likelihood require the use of survey techniques. Next, one would have to develop a model for explaining different degrees of such motivation in terms of variables reflecting relevant aspects of the context in which a UREG student finds him/herself – including, in particular, the presence or absence of PD policies in the educational institutions to which he/she can legitimately aspire. Then one would need to gather evidence on the dependent and independent variables of such a model, across time periods or locations in which PD admission policies are sometimes present and sometimes absent; and finally one would need to undertake the appropriate statistical analysis. This kind of project is certainly a difficult one, but it does not exceed the capabilities of empirical social science.

Benefits or costs linked to perceptions of the fairness of admissions processes: decreasing UREG cynicism about the unfairness of selection processes; or increasing non-UREG resentment because of perceived unfairness in admissions (claim 3.2 vs. claim 9.2)

The empirical challenge of determining which – if either – of these sets of claims is empirically valid is similar to the one involved in assessing whether PD policies stimulate UREG student motivation or complacency.[2] One needs to develop indicators of people's perceptions about fairness in admissions processes and conduct surveys among the relevant population, across times and places where PD admission policies sometimes obtain and sometimes do not. One needs also to develop a model explaining such perceptions and to gather data on the relevant independent variables, so that a multivariate statistical analysis can be carried out. Again, this is a difficult but not impossible task.

Benefits from integrating society's elite: more dispelling of negative stereotypes of UREG members (claim 2.6); and costs of mismatching UREG students and academic institutions: exacerbation of negative stereotypes of UREG members (claim 10.3)

One can reject the claim that PD will help to dispel negative stereotypes about UREG members if there is evidence that attendance at a more selective university does not enable PD beneficiaries to go on to a more successful career than they would have been able to go on to without PD. Evidence to the contrary would be necessary, but not sufficient, to validate the claim. Even if PD does give UREG students a significant career boost, it does not necessarily follow that having greater numbers of UREG members among society's elite will actually reduce negative stereotyping. One would also have to show somehow that the extent of negative stereotyping of UREG members is less than it would have been in the absence of the greater career successes achieved by beneficiaries of PD admission policies. Since many different factors can affect the extent of negative stereotyping of UREG members in a society, it is bound to be very hard to isolate the effect of PD admission policies in particular.

Similarly, one can reject the claim that poor academic performance by PD beneficiaries will reinforce negative stereotypes about UREG members if there is evidence that UREG students are not disproportionately represented in the lower academic ranks of selective universities. But even if the evidence shows that there is such disproportional representation of UREG members among poor academic performers, it does not necessarily follow that the claim is validated. One would also have to show somehow that the extent of negative stereotyping of UREG members is greater than it would have been had no UREG students benefited from PD admission policies. This is by no means a foregone conclusion, for negative stereotyping may also be reinforced simply by under-representation of UREG members at selective universities.[3]

Benefits from affirming society's commitment to reduce continuing disadvantages of UREG members (claim 1.1); benefits from strengthening the legitimacy of society's leadership (claim 2.1); and costs from more divisive identity group politics (claim 8.1)

These three claims involve anticipated benefits or costs primarily with respect to the basic societal goals of social harmony and democracy. This poses two formidable challenges to any kind of empirical assessment of the validity of the claims, not to mention assessment of the magnitude of the associated costs. First of all, it is very difficult to formulate a satisfactory indicator with which to measure the direction, much less the quantitative magnitude, of any change with respect to achievement of the goals in question – because of their very broad and qualitative nature. Secondly, it is even more difficult to estimate the relevant counterfactual: to what extent would these broad and qualitative goals have been achieved in the absence of any particular PD policy – or even in the absence of the whole complex of PD policies that may have been in effect in a given country (or region) during any given period of time.

The best hope for meaningful empirical evidence in this area would be to undertake inter-temporal and/or cross-sectional studies in which significant variation in PD policies can be observed and correlated with changes in variables associated with achievement of the goals in question. Such studies, however, would have to contend with the thorny problems of omitted variables and auto-correlation, as well as a paucity of observations in relation to the number of relevant explanatory variables. For all these reasons, systematic evidence on these kinds of benefits and costs has simply not been generated up to now and is highly unlikely to be generated in the future. As a result, assertions about the validity and significance of most of the claims in question have had to be grounded essentially in informed speculation.

Having established how – in principle – empirical evidence can best be utilized to shed light on the significance of claims of PD policy benefits and costs, I turn now to the actually available evidence from the US and India bearing on the consequences of PD policies in admissions to higher educational institutions.

9 Affirmative action and enrollments in US universities

I begin this chapter by compiling evidence on the enrollment of members of under-represented ethnic groups (UREGs) in US higher educational institutions. Next I address the impact of affirmative action (AA) policies on higher educational enrollments. I then go on to consider the consequences of AA for the academic qualifications of UREG students relative to those of their White student peers. Finally, I examine evidence on the socio-economic impact of AA policies: do AA beneficiaries constitute a "creamy layer" of UREG students, and are they socio-economically better off than the non-UREG students whom they displace?

UREG enrollments in higher education

Data on the growth of higher educational enrollments for each of the UREGs in the US are presented in Table 9.1. Detailed data for each group, and by different types of institutions, became available only as of 1976. These data show significant growth in the Hispanic-American proportion and modest growth in the Native-American proportion of higher educational enrollments (at both the undergraduate and the graduate level) over a twenty-one-year period. The African-American proportion of enrollments dipped slightly from 1976 to 1990 but then increased sharply from 1990 to 1997. Prior to 1976 there are data available only for African Americans in all higher educational programs; these data show that the African-American proportion of higher educational enrollments more than doubled between 1960 and 1976.

More illuminating as a measure of the progress made by UREG members in acquiring higher education at any given level is the "representation ratio" – i.e. the UREG proportion of enrollments relative to the UREG proportion of the total US population. By 1997 the representation ratio for African Americans in all undergraduate programs (including both two- and four-year colleges) was close to 1. The representation ratio is significantly lower – about 0.6 – at the graduate level (including professional as well as graduate schools). The data in Table 9.1 indicate that, as of 1997, Hispanic Americans lagged behind African Americans in their representation ratios at all levels of higher education; but Native Americans had actually attained representation ratios that were higher than those of either of the other two groups.

Higher educational enrollments (%) of under-represented groups in the US

Group	% of population*	1960	1976	1980	1990	1997
Undergraduate programs						
African Americans	11–12		10.2	9.9	9.8	11.5
Hispanic Americans	7–11		3.8	4.2	6.2	9.2
Native Americans	0.6–0.7		0.8	0.8	0.8	1.1
All three groups	19–25		14.8	14.9	16.8	21.8
Graduate and professional programs						
African Americans	11–12		5.7	5.4	5.4	7.5
Hispanic Americans	7–11		2.0	2.4	3.1	4.5
Native Americans	0.6–0.7		0.4	0.4	0.4	0.6
All three groups	19–25		8.1	8.2	8.9	12.6
All higher educational programs						
African Americans	11–12	4.1**	9.6	9.4	9.3	11.0
Hispanic Americans	7–11		3.6	4.0	5.8	8.6
Native Americans	0.6–0.7		0.7	0.7	0.8	1.0
All three groups	19–25		13.9	14.1	15.9	20.6

Source: All figures from US Department of Education, National Center for Education Statist ics, *Digest of Education Statistics*, Table 208 (available on the Internet), except for 1960 African - American enrollments in all programs, which is from Thernstrom and Thernstrom (1997: 389, Table 1).

Notes:

* The first and second percentages listed are s hares of the under-represented group in the total population of the US in 1980 and 1997, from US Census Bureau, *2001 Statistical Abstract of the US*, Table 15.

** 2.3% of the listed 4.1% are in historically Black colleges (HBCs); the % in HBCs falls slowly over time to 1.7% by the 1990s (Thernstrom and Thernstrom 1997: 389).

Alternative sources of evidence allow us to describe from a different perspective some of the gains in higher education made by members of under-represented groups in the US since AA admission policies were first introduced by many higher educational institutions. From 1967 to 1999 the proportion of Black 18–24-year-olds enrolled in degree-granting institutions increased from 13 per cent to 30.4 per cent, as compared with an increase from 26.9 per cent to 39.4 per cent for Whites; from 1972 to 1999 the proportion of Hispanic 18–24-year-olds enrolled in degree-granting institutions increased from 13.4 per cent to 18.7 per cent, as compared with an increase from 27.2 per cent to 39.4 per cent for Whites.[1] Over the period from the early 1960s to the mid-1990s, the proportion of Blacks aged 25–29 who had graduated from college rose from 5.4 per cent to 15.4 per cent; over the same period, the proportion who had graduated from law school rose from 1 per cent to 7.5 per cent, and the proportion who had graduated from medical school rose from 2.2 per cent to 8.1 per cent.[2] From 1970 – when AA admission policies began to be extended to Hispanic and Native Americans as well – to 1995, the proportion of Hispanic Americans aged 25 or older who had graduated from college rose from 4.5 per cent to 9.3 per cent, and the (much smaller) proportion with professional and doctoral degrees nearly doubled.

The impact of AA on UREG enrollments

The evidence presented in the previous section shows that there have been significant increases in the enrollment of under-represented groups in US higher educational institutions over recent decades. During this period, AA policies giving some degree of preference to UREG members have been widely instituted and practiced by educational institutions in both the US and India. No doubt such AA policies have had a positive effect on UREG enrollments in higher education; but simple time-series trends in UREG enrollments surely overstate the independent effects of AA. What can the available evidence tell us about the difference that AA policies themselves have made in the enrollment of UREGs?

It is essential to distinguish between student enrollments in undergraduate programs and enrollments in graduate or professional schools. I will characterize the former as "colleges" (though many undergraduate programs are offered at universities) and address them first.

AA preferences for UREG applicants are given by only a minority of four-year colleges – the most selective ones. Junior (two-year) colleges admit any student with a high-school degree; and a majority of four-year colleges admit any student who meets certain minimum criteria, irrespective of UREG status. Kane (1998: 433–40) has estimated that only the top 20 per cent of four-year colleges – the "elite" colleges – actually give significant preferences to UREG students in the admissions process. On the basis of an analysis of a nationwide representative sample of 1982 high-school graduates, he found (controlling for scores on the standardized national college-entrance test (the SAT[3]), high-school grades, and personal characteristics) that admission rates for Black and Hispanic applicants are significantly higher than for White applicants in the case of the top 20 per cent of US colleges,[4] but only modestly higher in the case of the next quintile of colleges, and no higher at all in the case of the bottom three quintiles of four-year colleges. Although AA is not practiced in the great majority of US colleges, AA in admissions to the elite colleges clearly affects the student bodies of the non-elite colleges – because it has the effect of redistributing admissions from some non-UREG applicants (who would otherwise have gone to an elite college) to some UREG applicants (who would otherwise have gone to non-elite colleges).

Many scholars have shown that AA preferences have a very significant effect on UREG enrollments in highly selective schools. Cross and Slater (1997) have calculated that, in 1997, Blacks held roughly 3,000 out of 50,000 seats (6 per cent) in the entering classes of the top twenty-five US colleges; but that, if scores on the SAT alone had served as the criterion for admission, less than 1,000 Blacks (2 per cent) would have been admitted. Of course, test scores are not the sole criteria used for admissions decisions; and Blacks are likely to be disproportionately favored by some of the other criteria often applied, such as low socio-economic status (SES), evidence of community involvement or civic leadership, demonstrated ability in athletics, music, art, etc. Thus it is fair to conclude that at least 1,000 Blacks would have been admitted without AA preferences; but that still implies that 2,000 Blacks – about 4 per cent of the total enrollment – were likely beneficiaries of AA as practiced by the most highly selective colleges in the country.

The most comprehensive study ever carried out on the consequences of AA in US colleges and universities is Bowen and Bok (1998), who focused on undergraduate students in a sample of twenty-eight highly regarded US colleges. The Bowen and Bok research team made use of a massive database compiled by the Andrew W. Mellon Foundation, "College and Beyond" (C&B), which includes detailed records of the characteristics, college academic performance, and graduate degrees of a total of roughly 45,000 students – including about 3,500 Blacks – in the class cohorts beginning their undergraduate studies in 1976 and 1989. They supplemented the C&B database with even more detailed data related to admission of the 1989 entry cohort in five of the twenty-eight colleges and with a lengthy questionnaire survey on post-college experiences and reflections of the entire 1976 entering cohort and a large sub-sample of the 1989 entering cohort of students in the C&B database. For analytical purposes, Bowen and Bok further divided their twenty-eight colleges into three groups, according to degree of selectivity. The top group included only private colleges, such as Princeton, Stanford, and Swarthmore; the second group also included only private colleges, such as Columbia, Northwestern, and Oberlin; and the third group was dominated by colleges in large public universities, such as the Universities of Michigan and North Carolina.

The first quantitative task that Bowen and Bok took on was to estimate the impact of AA preferences in 1989 on the admission of Black students into elite colleges at the three different levels of selectivity (Bowen and Bok 1998: Ch. 2 and App. A). The overall national enrollment of students entering college at each of these selectivity levels was roughly 16,000 at level 1, 39,000 at level 2, and 250,000 at level 3 – a total of roughly 300,000, as compared to an overall total of roughly 1 million full-time students entering all four-year colleges for the first time.[5] This means that the colleges at Bowen and Bok's first two selectivity levels comprise roughly the same colleges as the earlier-cited top twenty-five colleges, plus perhaps a half dozen more; all of them are private institutions. Bowen and Bok arrived at the following estimates of the impact of AA in 1989: in the most highly selective group, AA preferences increased the proportion of African Americans from 2.1 to 7.8 per cent; in the second group, the preferences increased that proportion from 2.8 to 5.8 per cent; and in the third group, the preferences increased the proportion from 4.5 to 6.6 per cent. The figures for the top two levels of selectivity are quite similar to those cited in the previous paragraph (roughly 2 to 6.3 per cent).

Applying Bowen and Bok's estimates to the total numbers of students entering college at each level of selectivity, we can estimate roughly that AA policies increased the number of Black students admitted to selectivity level-1 colleges from a hypothetical 300 to an actual 1,200; to selectivity level-2 colleges from a hypothetical 1,100 to an actual 2,300; and to selectivity level-3 colleges from a hypothetical 11,300 to an actual 16,500. This implies that the overall impact of AA was to increase Black entrants into selective four-year colleges from a hypothetical level of roughly 13,000 to an actual level of 20,000 (or from a little over 4 per cent to a little under 7 per cent of the total selective-college entering enrollment of roughly 300,000). Other scholars addressing this issue believe that these figures understate the effect of AA preferences on admission of Black students to the most selective colleges.[6] One may therefore reasonably conclude that only about 10,000 Black students (a little over 3 per cent of the total) would have been admitted without AA, and that AA preferences doubled the number of Black entrants to about 20,000.

Black students constituted roughly two-thirds of the UREG students enrolled in US four-year colleges in 1990.[7] This implies that roughly 10,000 Hispanic- and Native-American students entered selective four-year colleges in 1989. Most of these students are Hispanic Americans, who tend to have somewhat better academic credentials than African American applicants to college. It is therefore reasonable to assume that two-thirds of them (as opposed to one-half of the first-year Black students) would have been admitted without AA. This means that, out of a total of 30,000 UREG students admitted to selective colleges in 1989 (about 10 per cent of the total), roughly 13,000 (a little over 4 per cent) owed their admission to AA. Assuming that total student enrollment in selective four-year colleges is four times the size of the entering class,[8] and taking into account the fact that graduation rates were about 10 per cent lower for UREG students than for non-UREG students in Bowen and Bok's sample of selective colleges,[9] we reach a final very rough estimate that AA increased overall UREG enrollment in the selective colleges at issue by about 50,000 in 1989 – raising the UREG proportion by about 4 per cent, from close to 6 per cent to a little less than 10 per cent of the total selective-college enrollment.

The consequences of AA for the ethnic composition of the cohorts of students entering colleges further down the selectivity spectrum are less clear.

Since students who are minimally qualified and motivated to go to college will be accepted at the majority of (less selective) institutions, there is no reason to suspect that AA has a significant impact on the number of UREG members or non-UREG members who go to college overall. Some UREG students are probably more likely to choose to go to college insofar as AA increases the selectivity of colleges they can expect to enter, and some non-UREG students may be discouraged about going to college insofar as AA has the opposite effect on their expectations. Thus AA may have a slight positive effect on the number of UREG students entering college and a corresponding negative effect on the number of non-UREG students doing so. The most important effect of AA, however, is to redistribute UREG students upward and non-UREG students downward across the selectivity spectrum of colleges. It stands to reason that this redistributive effect of AA on student enrollments will cascade down the spectrum of college selectivity, with diminishing impact, all the way to two-year colleges.

It is much harder to estimate the impact of AA on enrollment in graduate and professional schools, since there have been only a few studies that shed light on this question – and they have been carried out only for professional schools in highly competitive fields. The best-known such empirical study was by Wightman (1997), who showed that if a "race-blind" admissions process – based solely on undergraduate grade-point average (GPA) and scores on the national Law School Admissions Test – had been applied to the group of persons entering law schools in 1991, approximately 90 per cent of Black applicants and 70 per cent of all UREG applicants would not have been admitted to the best of the law schools to which they applied. Wightman also estimates that 77 per cent of Black applicants and 43 per cent of UREG applicants would not have been admitted to any of the 173 law schools approved by the American Bar Association (which constituted her sample). Her findings imply that the proportion of Blacks admitted to US law schools would have fallen from 6.8 to 1.6 per cent, and the proportion of Hispanic Americans from 4.6 to 2.4 per cent, were it not for AA preferences. These estimates might be biased toward overstating the effects of AA because, even in the absence of AA, graduate and professional programs would not rely exclusively on grades and test scores to make their admissions decisions; and by other criteria UREG applicants might well do better. On the other hand, the estimates are likely to be biased in the opposite direction by the fact that a significant number of UREG applicants might choose not to begin graduate study at all if they could be admitted only to less selective and presumably lower quality institutions. All things considered, the findings suggest that AA is probably responsible for as many as three-quarters of Black enrollments and at least one-half of overall UREG enrollments in all law schools taken together. There is every reason to believe that similar estimates apply to other highly competitive professional schools as well – such as schools of medicine and of business.

As part of a comprehensive analysis of the consequences of AA in admissions to the highly selective University of Michigan (UM) Law School,

Lempert *et al.* (2000a) devised a procedure to approximate the number of UREG students who would have been admitted to the Law School from 1970 through 1996 under a completely "color-blind" process. Their estimate was that a little over 90 per cent of all the UREG students actually admitted owed their admission to some preference based on their UREG status.[10] The proportion of UREG students who benefited from AA admission preferences was higher in the earlier years and somewhat lower in the later years, because from the 1970s to the 1990s the number of UREG applicants with strong conventional admissions credentials gradually increased.

Because the UM Law School is one of the top ten law schools in the country, the enormous impact of AA on its UREG student enrollment can be taken as indicative of the impact of AA only at the most elite of professional programs. At less elite programs one would expect the impact of AA to be correspondingly smaller. Unlike in the case of undergraduate programs, however, the overall effect of AA at the graduate level is not predominantly a redistributive one. Had AA not given potential UREG students access to graduate and professional programs of a quality higher than those they would otherwise have been able to enter, some would have entered lower-quality programs; but many others would have been obliged – or would have chosen – to forgo graduate training altogether. By the same token, AA not only redistributes non-UREG students downward across the selectivity spectrum of institutions; it also results in fewer non-UREG students entering graduate or professional programs at all.

According to figures compiled by the US Department of Education, the total number of students enrolled in professional and graduate schools in 1990 was roughly 1.8 million, of which 165,000 (9 per cent) were African, Hispanic or Native American.[11] The studies cited in the preceding paragraphs suggest that as many as half of the UREG students enrolled in highly competitive professional schools and in highly competitive graduate school programs owe their admissions to AA. If we estimate very roughly that 20 per cent of the graduate-level programs are highly competitive, these figures imply that in 1990, AA was responsible for roughly 15,000 UREG students enrolling in such schools. Moreover, AA surely encouraged many UREG students to pursue graduate-level studies at other schools, rather than forgo higher education at the graduate level; but there is no way of estimating their numbers.

AA and the academic qualifications of enrolled UREG students

The whole point of AA in admissions is to admit more UREG applicants and fewer non-UREG applicants than would be admitted by "conventional" admissions criteria – i.e. by those criteria that have generally been used prior to the implementation of an AA policy, or that are being used by institutions not practicing AA. It follows as an inevitable consequence that the conventional qualifications of those UREG applicants admitted by virtue of some

AA preference will be lower than those of applicants admitted without any such preference. If AA beneficiaries constitute a large fraction of all UREG students admitted to a particular institution, then it follows as well that the average level of conventional qualifications of all entering UREG students will be lower than those of the entering non-UREG students.

The relevant conventional admissions criteria typically include scores on standardized tests, and they often also include GPAs; these are the major academic criteria employed in admissions decisions.[12] There are also non-academic admissions criteria that can play a role in admissions decisions, especially in the US and at the undergraduate level: these include musical, artistic, or athletic ability; low socio-economic status; public or community service; residence in a remote area; and family connections to the institution (e.g. as prior graduates). Because academic criteria are always important and often decisive in admissions decisions, the academic qualifications of entering students are subject to the most scrutiny. For the reasons noted above, AA beneficiaries – and, more generally, UREG students – typically have lower academic qualifications than their student peers, especially with respect to the most visible and comparable of such qualifications: one's score on the relevant standardized test. Discrepancies between the average standardized test scores registered by UREG students and by non-UREG students have thus become a major source of tension between advocates and critics of positive discrimination (PD) in admissions to higher educational institutions.

Before I examine data on the test scores of UREG and non-UREG students, of the kind that have entered prominently into debates about the desirability of PD in both the US and India, one caveat is in order. Comparisons of average test scores between groups can be highly misleading, because such simple comparisons necessarily fail to reflect potentially important characteristics of the distribution of observations from which an average is computed.

This point is germane to the present discussion because it is often assumed that, in the absence of PD, the average test scores of admitted UREG students and admitted non-UREG students would tend to be the same. Differences in these average test scores are then taken as an indicator of the extent to which a PD policy has altered the pattern of admissions that would otherwise have prevailed. As many analysts have pointed out, however, this inference is false when applied to differences between the average scores of UREG and non-UREG students on standardized tests.[13] This is because UREG students – for reasons associated with the typically disadvantaged circumstances in which they have grown up and been educated – are highly under-represented in the upper reaches of the frequency distribution of standardized test scores. Even if a PD-free policy of admitting all applicants above a certain cut-off point in exam scores were implemented, the average test score of admitted UREGs would be well below that of admitted non-UREGs. It follows that PD policies are not responsible for the extent of the average test-score differentials observed between UREG and non-UREG admitted students; what they do is to increase to some extent the size of the differential that would in any case be observed.

A substantial amount of evidence on test-score differentials between UREG and non-UREG entrants into US four-year colleges has been compiled over the last decade or so. For example, Bunzel (1996) reports the following average overall SAT scores for students entering the University of California at Berkeley (UC-Berkeley) in 1988: Asian American, 1,269; White, 1,267; Hispanic, 1,053; and African American, 979 (the maximum possible score is 1,600). Cherry (2001: 213) reports that at the University of Michigan, the average SAT score of UREGs accepted for admission to the first year of undergraduate study in 1994 was about 200 points lower than that of the White students accepted. Cherry (2001: 215, Table 10.1) also presents information on the significantly higher admission rates for UREG students in 1994 than for White students in the same test-score and high-school GPA ranges.

Differential group average test scores are even larger for entrants into graduate and professional schools. Bunzel (1996) reports that the UCLA School of Law offered admission to all ten Black applicants and two of fifteen Hispanic applicants with undergraduate GPAs of 2.75 to 3 and Law School Admissions Test (LSAT) percentile scores of 75 to 80, but to none of the twenty-nine White and thirteen Asian-American applicants in the same GPA and LSAT range; while the UCLA School of Medicine offered admission to 30 out of 522 Black, Hispanic-American, and Native-American applicants who had pre-med GPAs of 3.24 or below and Medical College Admission Test (MCAT) biology and chemistry percentile scores below 90, but to none of the 1,200 White or Asian applicants in the same GPA and MCAT range.

In an analysis highly critical of AA in admissions, Thernstrom and Thernstrom (1997: 398, Table 3) provided comprehensive evidence on Black/White differentials in the average test scores of college entrants over the 20-year period from 1976 to 1995. They found that throughout the period, the overall Black/White gap in SAT scores remained in excess of 200 points, which is close to the figures reported earlier for UC-Berkeley and UM. Their evidence also showed a gradual decline in the gap from 258 points in 1976 to 202 points in 1995.

In assessing the import of these SAT score gaps, it is important to bear in mind several considerations that operate to reduce their significance. First, as noted above, there would be some gap even in the absence of any AA policies because of the under-representation of Black students in the uppermost range of SAT scores. Secondly, as Dickens and Kane (1999) have pointed out, among many indicators of college-success test scores are the ones on which Blacks fare relatively worst – so test scores exaggerate the academic differences between Blacks and Whites even when the same standards are being used.[14] Thirdly, test scores for Hispanic-American students run somewhat higher than those of Blacks (although still well below those of Whites). Taking all these considerations into account, it is clear that AA policies account for only a fraction – and perhaps a very small fraction – of the oft-cited differentials between average SAT scores of UREG and non-UREG undergraduate students in the US.

A direct way to assess the effect that AA policies have on the differential between UREG and non-UREG test scores would be to compare the average SAT score of the AA beneficiaries among the UREG students with the average score of the non-UREG applicants who are displaced by AA. This cannot be done at all precisely, since it is impossible to identify the particular students who were admitted or rejected by virtue of AA. One can, however, estimate the average characteristics of these two groups of students by assuming that in the absence of AA, colleges would have admitted the same percentage of Black and White applicants from each 100-point SAT bracket. Applying this methodology to five of the selective schools – the only ones for which they had sufficient data – Bowen and Bok (1998: 42) found that the estimated average SAT score of the retrospectively rejected students (the UREG beneficiaries of AA) was 1,145 and the average score of the retrospectively admitted students (the non-UREG applicants displaced by AA) was 1,181. This is a very small difference indeed! It should be noted, however, that the five colleges on which these estimates are based are all in the top two selectivity groups of Bowen and Bok's sample;[15] as they themselves note, the difference is probably greater in the case of their selectivity level-3 colleges, which admit the great majority of Black students in their sample.

According to data compiled by Thernstrom and Thernstrom (1997: 398, Table 3), there has been some narrowing of the Black/White test-score gap among college-goers from the mid-1970s to the mid-1990s.[16] Bowen and Bok (1998: 20–3) also report a narrowing between 1976 and 1989 of the Black/White test-score gap for students entering a subset of four of the selective colleges in their sample (those with enough data to permit analysis of the time trend). Such a narrowing could be explained by a decline in the SAT gap in the test-taking population as a whole or by more effective recruitment and admissions practices by selective colleges (so that the extent of the preferences given to Black applicants is reduced); most probably both of these trends have been occurring.

At the graduate level, relevant data are again relatively scanty. The previously mentioned studies by Wightman (1997) and Lempert *et al.* (2000a) leave no room for doubt, however, that UREG AA beneficiaries enter law schools with, on average, considerably lower undergraduate GPAs and LSAT scores. There is every reason to believe that the same is true in other professional schools and graduate programs where AA policies are carried out and have a significant impact on the composition of student enrollments.

AA and the "creamy layer"

Critics of AA admission policies have claimed that they are inequitable in terms of distributive justice, because they make available valuable educational opportunities to well-to-do UREG applicants – the creamy layer – rather than to more needy UREG members, and in so doing they may also be reducing such opportunities for less well-off non-UREG applicants. Such claims are well illustrated by Thernstrom and Thernstrom, who wrote that:

> Although [Bowen and Bok] pass over the information hastily, it is startling to find that fully 64 per cent of the African Americans in their 1989 sample had at least one parent who had graduated from college, nearly six times the proportion among all black college-age youths. Perhaps even more striking, a mere 14 per cent of the blacks attending elite colleges were from families of low socioeconomic status, defined as those earning less than $22,000 annually and in which neither parent had a college degree.
>
> (Thernstrom and Thernstrom 1999b: 1603)

These figures establish the fact that the typical Black AA beneficiary at a highly selective college is very much better off than most other Blacks. The figures do not, however, address the question of whether well-off Blacks are thus benefiting at the expense of less well-off Whites.

Bowen and Bok (1998: 49, Fig. 2.12) do present more evidence on the SES of the families of students in their sample – evidence that is quite relevant to the question at hand. As compared to the 14 per cent of Black students in the 1989 entering cohort whose families were classified as low SES, only 2 per cent of the White students came from low-SES families. At the other end of the spectrum, 15 per cent of the White students, but only 3 per cent of the Black students, came from families classified as high SES.[17] This is not precisely the right comparison, for we are interested in the backgrounds of the retrospectively rejected among Black students and the retrospectively admitted among White applicants. It is well known that socio-economic background is highly correlated with educational preparation and academic qualifications.[18] Since both the retrospectively rejected Black students and the retrospectively admitted White applicants can be expected to be located predominantly at the lower ends of the academic qualification distributions of all Blacks and Whites enrolled in the selective colleges, the socio-economic class backgrounds applying to both of the relevant AA-affected groups will tend to be lower than those reflected in the figures just cited. But there is no reason to expect that differences in the extent of the lowering would be so great as to alter the basic inference to be drawn: that admitting more Blacks and fewer White applicants to selective schools redistributes educational opportunities from better-off to less well-off students rather than the other way round.

This conclusion gains even greater strength when we recognize that socio-economic status classifications based solely on income and education, like those used by Bowen and Bok, are quite misleading when applied in the same way to White and Black families. For any given level of income and education, Black parents are likely to have accumulated far less financial wealth and far less social capital than White families; and they are also likely to have poorer access to public facilities and more restricted opportunities of many kinds.[19] Thus Black beneficiaries of AA are all the more likely to be less well off than the Whites displaced by AA than is indicated even by the substantial differentials in the SES indicators cited above.

10 Reservation policies and enrollments in Indian universities

In this chapter I review evidence available from India pertaining to the impact of its reservation policies (RP) on the student body of higher educational institutions. First I compile data on enrollments in higher education of members of the two primary under-represented ethnic groups (UREGs) – Scheduled Castes (SCs) and Scheduled Tribes (STs).[1] Then I consider the impact of reservation policies on SC and ST enrollment as well as the reasons for the low representation of SC and ST students, despite their access to reserved seats. I go on to explore how reservation policies have affected the relationship between the academic qualifications of reserved-seat and other students. Finally, I examine the oft-raised issue of whether RP beneficiaries represent a socio-economically privileged "creamy layer" of UREG members.

SC and ST enrollments in higher education

Total student enrollment in higher educational institutions in India has been increasing rapidly over the past half-century, from less than 200,000 in 1950 to almost 7 million by the year 2000.[2] During this time the proportionate representation of SC and ST students in total higher educational enrollment has been slowly rising. From the late 1970s to the late 1990s, the SC proportion rose from 7 to 7.8 per cent and the ST proportion rose from 1.6 to 2.7 per cent.[3] These percentage figures should be compared to the corresponding SC and ST shares of the total population of India: roughly 16 and 8 per cent, respectively.[4] Thus, by the end of the century, SC and ST student representation in higher educational institutions had reached roughly one-half and one-third of their representation in the population as a whole.

SC and ST students are distributed quite unevenly across the various degree programs offered at Indian colleges and universities.[5] "Arts" programs (encompassing the humanities and most social sciences) have the lowest prestige, and a Bachelor of Arts degree offers the least favorable job prospects, as compared with degrees in programs such as commerce, science, engineering, law, and medicine. Roughly 40 per cent of all higher education students in India are enrolled in arts programs, but the corresponding figure for SC students is over 60 per cent and for ST students roughly 75 per cent.

Correspondingly, the percentages of SC and ST students enrolled in the most prestigious programs – engineering, law, and medicine – are much lower than for students from the rest of the population. Not surprisingly, SC and ST students tend to be more under-represented in Master's and Ph.D. programs than at the Bachelor's degree level.

One further point about SC and ST enrollments in Indian higher educational institutions is worth noting. It is often claimed by critics of reservation policies that undeserving individuals are motivated deceitfully to claim SC and ST status in order to enter an institution into which they would otherwise not be admitted. Several scholars of reservation policies in educational admissions suggest that this is indeed not an uncommon practice. Thus Velaskar (1986: 600–1) has noted that

> evidence of the lackadaisical approach to implementation [of RP] came in the form of discovery of misappropriation of reserved seats in the "SC" and [other] categories...optimal utilization is constrained by the inability to check dishonest elements – [non-backward class] students gain admission on a false claim to backward status.

Similarly, Patwardhan and Palshikar (1992: 24) have observed that:

> We often hear of cases where admissions are taken in medical colleges with the help of false caste/community certificates. One wonders whether [non-SC] Kolis and Rajputs are passing themselves off as [SC] Mahadev-Kolis and Rajput-Bhumyas.

There is hardly enough evidence on which to base an estimate of the quantitative importance of this kind of practice; but it is clearly a real and not just an imagined phenomenon.

There is a limited amount of evidence available on the number of Dalits and Adivasis who have graduated from higher educational institutions. I have calculated from census data[6] that the SC proportion of all graduates of Indian higher educational institutions rose from 0.9 per cent in 1961 to 3.3 per cent in 1981, and the corresponding ST proportion rose from 0.1 per cent in 1961 to 0.8 per cent in 1981. No doubt the SC and ST proportions have increased further since then. But SC and ST graduates represented in 1981 only about 3 and 1 per cent of all Indian graduates – far below their shares of the total Indian population (roughly 16 and 8 per cent).

The impact of RP on SC and ST enrollments

There can be no doubt that a substantial share of SC and ST student enrollment in Indian higher educational institutions is attributable to India's reservation policies. It is very difficult, however, to estimate just how much difference these policies have made. The difficulty of such estimation is due not only to the scarcity of detailed data on the composition of higher educational enrollments in India. It is also due to the complexity of the way in which India's reservation policies in the educational sphere are structured and administered. First of all, the policies apply only to public institutions. The vast majority of Indian higher educational institutions are indeed public, under central or state-level government control; but the number of private institutions has been growing rapidly since the early 1990s.

In virtually all centrally controlled higher educational institutions in India, 15 per cent of the seats are reserved for SC members and 7.5 per cent for ST members; these ratios were established to reflect the corresponding shares of Dalits and Adivasis in the national population.[7] In the case of higher educational institutions controlled at the state level, the percentages of SC and ST reserved seats are determined by the (approximate) proportions of these groups in the state population. Some states also have a percentage of seats reserved for OBCs. Admission generally requires completion of the relevant prior degree program; admissions decisions are made separately for "general entry" students and for students eligible for each category of reserved seats. These decisions are usually based on scores registered on high-school completion or university-level entrance examinations; in each category students are admitted in descending order of their scores, until the available seats are filled. To qualify for any category of reserved seats, applicants must show documentation of their caste or tribal status, certified by an administrative official from their locality of origin. Although the reservation of seats at higher educational institutions for SC and ST students was established as a national policy in the early 1950s, its actual implementation was delayed by a decade or two in various regions and institutions, and even now it is not fully established everywhere in India.

General entry seats are filled first, with applicants ranging from those with the highest scores to those with scores at the relevant cut-off point. Where OBC seats are reserved, these too are almost always filled – using a somewhat lower cut-off point score. In the case of the SC and ST reserved seats, minimum qualifying scores are set well below the cut-off point for general entry applicants, and some schools do not require any minimum exam score; age limits are also often waived for SC and ST students. Even so, SC and ST reserved seats often go unfilled – especially at the more selective schools – because there are not enough applicants from these groups who have completed secondary education and otherwise meet the requirements for admission. The unfilled seats are then made available to general-entry applicants, and OBC applicants where applicable, in descending order of their exam scores below the general-entry cut-off point.

In principle, SC and ST (as well as OBC) applicants who score well enough to be admitted as general-entry students are supposed to be included in that category rather than be counted toward the corresponding quota of reserved seats. In practice, however, such high-scoring UREG applicants are often placed in seats reserved for their category of applicant. (Among other things, such placement makes it easier for SC and ST students to take advantage of government aid in the form of grants, loans, and special facilities – notably hostels reserved for SC and/or ST students.) Figures compiled on the number of SC and ST students attending a given higher educational institution therefore may or may not include those admitted via the general-entry list. Indeed, some of the latter may not reveal their SC or ST identity in any formal way – though informally such identity is hard to disguise.

One piece of hard evidence on the impact of reservation policies comes from Patwardhan and Palshikar's (1992) study of a respected regional medical college in Pune, Maharashtra. They found that roughly one-sixth of a sample of SC and ST students who were admitted to reserved seats scored high enough on the qualifying entrance examination to have been admitted as general-entry students. In the case of OBC students in reserved seats, the corresponding figure was roughly five-sixths (Patwardhan and Palshikar 1992: 44).

What does all of the above imply for estimation of the overall impact of reservation policies on the representation of SC and ST students in Indian higher educational institutions? First of all, one can be quite confident that virtually all SC and ST students at the most elite Indian universities and institutions for professional and technical training (most of which are centrally controlled) would not have been admitted in the absence of reserved seats. Very few SC and ST students can succeed in open competition for general-entry seats at prestigious institutions because they rarely have access to high-quality secondary education, or to privately funded preparatory workshops and tutorials, all of which contribute to the substantial competitive edge enjoyed by students from relatively well-to-do families. Even with lower cut-off points for admission, SC and ST students typically do not come close to filling the available reserved seats at such institutions. Thus almost all SC and ST students in the highly coveted elite schools, whose graduates are virtually guaranteed a good job and career, owe their presence there to reservation policies.

It is much harder to estimate the number of SC and ST enrollments attributable to reservation policies in the vast majority of Indian higher educational institutions, where admissions requirements are much less demanding than at the elite schools. A considerable number of SC and ST applicants score high enough on the relevant examinations to qualify for general-entry admission to some non-elite institutions. In many cases the effect of reservation policies, as in the case of affirmative action in the US, is simply to redistribute UREG students upward in the hierarchy of institutional selectivity and quality. Without reserved seats, however, the appeal of a higher educational institution for SC and ST potential students is likely to be substantially diminished. For one thing, the availability of reserved seats improves the quality of the school that an SC or ST student can enter – and hence the value of a higher educational degree in the job market. Secondly, admission to a reserved seat enhances the ability of an SC or ST student to gain access to financial and other forms of government aid, without which staying in school may prove very difficult. Government provision of scholarships, special hostels, meals, supplies, and book loans have enabled many SC and ST students to enter and persist in higher education; even though such support is usually inadequate to meet all the economic and social needs of such students, it often makes the difference as to whether such a student decides to continue his/her education.[8]

In order to get a sense of the overall quantitative significance of India's reservation policies in higher education, I will estimate how many SC and ST students have been enabled by reservation policies to enroll in "desirable" higher educational programs. As a rough approximation, one may consider all programs other than the low-prestige arts programs to be (relatively) desirable. In the previous section I presented data showing that an overall total of 512,000 SC students and 180,000 ST students were enrolled in Indian universities in 1996–7; and I cited estimates that roughly 60 per cent of SC students and 75 per cent of ST students were enrolled in arts programs. These figures imply that roughly 200,000 SC students and 45,000 ST students were enrolled in the remaining programs – commerce, science, engineering, etc. A non-negligible fraction of these students would surely have qualified for admission to some – the relatively less demanding – of these programs; so a very rough estimate of the total number of SC and ST students enabled by reservation policies to attend desirable programs is 200,000.

In sum, it seems reasonable to conclude that about one-third of the SC and ST students enrolled in Indian higher educational institutions in the late 1990s were pursuing higher education in a relatively desirable program because of the existence of India's reservation policies in admissions.[9] Taking into account also the likelihood that a significant number of SC and ST students were encouraged by reservation policies to pursue higher education in less desirable programs, one may conclude that these policies have made a difference in the case of about half of the roughly 700,000 SC and ST students enrolled in higher education in the late 1990s. Still, the data adduced in the previous section indicate that, even fifty years after independence, at least half of the seats reserved in Indian higher educational institutions for SC students, and at least two-thirds of the seats reserved for ST students, go unfilled.

There are a multitude of reasons why SC and ST students remain so under-represented in Indian institutions of higher education, in spite of strong reservation policies (and related government programs) designed to ameliorate the situation. The most immediate reason is that the pool of potential SC and ST applicants to colleges and universities is severely limited by "wastage" (dropping out) as well as "stagnation" (repeating courses, because of failure or attendance gaps) at prior levels of education. By the 1990s, Dalit and Adivasi children were going to primary school at about the same rate as all Indian children. In 1994–5, SC and ST pupils constituted 16.2 and 8.2 per cent of all primary school pupils – almost exactly their shares of the Indian population.[10]

At each subsequent level of education, however, the proportion of SC and ST students was lower. The corresponding 1994–5 figures for middle school are 14 and 5.5 per cent, and for secondary school they are 12 and 4.3 per cent.

In the late 1980s only about one-quarter of Indian children were completing ten years of school; but the figures for Dalit and Adivasi children were even lower (18 and 12 per cent, respectively). Even fewer students complete the additional two years of "higher secondary" school required for admission to a higher educational institution. Numerous studies have documented the fact that access to education – and especially good-quality education – is strongly and inversely related to caste status in India. For example, in an analysis of schools in Andhra Pradesh, Parmaji (1985: Section 2) found that the proportion of all children attending school falls steadily from the primary to the higher secondary level, but that the rate at which it falls is considerably greater as one moves from "forward castes" to "backward castes" to Dalits and Adivasis. Furthermore, he found the vast majority of students attending private (fee-charging) schools, which are typically of superior quality, are from "forward castes."

The reasons as to why relatively few Dalit and Adivasi children make it through primary and secondary schooling and become eligible for higher education are many and varied.[11] First, Dalit and Adivasi children come predominantly from families at the lowest rungs of the Indian socio-economic ladder. Their parents are typically very poor, being engaged in agricultural labor or menial industrial and service activities; they often need their children at home or at work to help eke out a minimal standard of living. Most Adivasi families, and also a disproportionate number of Dalit families, live in rural and relatively remote geographical areas, where access to schooling is distinctly inferior to the access in urban areas. Even when Dalit and Adivasi children do manage to stay in school, the quality of the schools to which they have access is likely to be of very poor quality. Finally, SC and ST students remain likely to face discriminatory treatment at the hands of school officials and teachers, who come disproportionately from the higher castes and the more privileged sectors of society.

RP and the academic qualifications of enrolled UREG students

The evidence presented at the beginning of the chapter shows that there have been significant increases in the enrollment of SC and ST students in Indian higher educational institutions over recent decades, even though SC and ST representation in such institutions remains proportionately well below that of the general population. Indian reservation policies have no doubt played a major role in increasing the opportunities for SC and ST students to continue their education at the college and university level. Indeed, the reserved-seat policies (and related government aid programs) account in much larger measure for the growth in overall UREG enrollments in Indian higher education than do affirmative action policies in US higher education.

They have done so, however, in large part by requiring of SC and ST students significantly lower minimum exam scores to enter universities – as compared with the scores required of general-entry applicants. While entrance-qualifying exam scores cannot be considered a good predictor of performance in higher education, the lower scores characteristic of most SC and ST students – especially at elite institutions – do reflect less adequate academic preparation for the demands of a university-level education. Both the lower scores and the less adequate academic preparation are also, of course, correlated with socio-economic disadvantage, which further heightens the challenge faced by the typical SC or ST student embarking on a higher educational experience.

The situation of SC and ST students at elite Indian institutions is well illustrated by their experience at the Indian Institutes of Technology (IITs), whose programs attract many of the best students in India. The five main IITs[12] began implementing reservation policies in admissions in the early 1970s, admitting SC and ST students with entrance exam scores well below the cut-off score for general-entry students. After an initial period during which many SC and ST students admitted via reservations were found to be poorly prepared and dropped out, these IITs established a year-long preparatory program for students whose entrance exam scores are less than two-thirds of the general-entry cut-off score; these students gain admission to reserved seats only if they successfully complete that preparatory program. Yet by the mid-1990s, after reservation policies and related programs had been underway for two decades and the process was well established, many of the seats reserved for SC and ST students continued to go unfilled. Admissions data for 1994–5 indicate that only about half of the seats reserved for SC students were filled, while the corresponding figure for ST students was less than one-sixth.[13]

In non-elite higher educational institutions, reserved seats for SC and ST members have also often gone unfilled. According to Aikara (1980), medical schools in Gujarat filled less than 5 per cent of their reserved seats in the 1970s. Velaskar (1986) conducted very useful research on medical colleges in Bombay, generating the following findings. In 1969, SC students filled much less than half of the 11 per cent of seats reserved for them. Minimum qualifying standards for Bombay medical colleges were subsequently lowered; but in 1979–80 and 1980–1, still only one-third of them filled their SC and ST quotas – while some had no SC and ST students at all. In more recent times, Bombay medical colleges have most often been filling SC reserved seats (sometimes, as noted earlier, with students whose claims to SC status are questionable); but medical schools across the country have continued to lag in this respect. Those SC students who do enroll in medical schools tend increasingly to come from a few dominant Dalit castes and from relatively well-off Dalit families living in urban areas, which enables some of them to attend private secondary schools. This trend toward larger numbers of SC applicants with relatively privileged backgrounds suggests that the average level of academic qualifications of incoming SC students may be rising.

There is indeed some evidence of a decline over time in the gap between the average entering exam scores of SC and ST reserved-seat students and those of general-entry students – at least in the better schools. The best evidence of this comes from an unusually thorough and detailed study by Patwardhan and Palshikar (1992), who compiled and analyzed a rich set of data on students who attended a prominent regional medical college – the B.J. Medical College in Pune, affiliated with the University of Pune. This college admits students in five separate categories, consisting of general-entry seats and seats reserved for members of OBCs, SCs, STs, and "Vimukta tribes" (a regional group of tribal communities). Comparing the entrance exam scores of students in each category admitted in 1970, 1980, and 1985, the study found – not surprisingly – that the cut-off scores for admission were highest in the general-entry category and successively lower in the OBC, SC, and tribal categories. Significantly, however, the study also documented a general upward trend in the cut-off scores for admission in each category as well as a general reduction in the gaps in admitted student scores as between the different categories. The authors suggest that the significant rise in the cut-off marks for admission in the case of the reserved groups may be due in part to a second-generation effect, in which a growing proportion of OBC, SC, and ST applicants are the children of parents who have been able to improve their educational and socio-economic status by virtue of their own access to reserved seats in educational institutions.

The issue of the "creamy layer"

As in the US, critics of positive discrimination (PD) in admission policies in India have claimed that it is inequitable because it makes available valuable educational opportunities mainly to well-to-do UREG applicants – the creamy layer – rather than to more needy UREG members. Thus it is argued that reservations for SC and ST applicants increase inequalities within these groups and reduce educational opportunities for general-entry UREG applicants who may be worse off than the SC and ST beneficiaries.

Whether reservation policies in university admissions have increased overall inequalities, by benefiting well-off Dalits and Adivasis at the expense of less-well-off university applicants from the rest of the population, is very hard to verify. To determine the existence and possible significance of such inequitable redistributive effects, one would have to compare the socio-economic class backgrounds of SC and ST beneficiaries with the class backgrounds of those general-entry applicants displaced from university admissions by the reservation policies. On this question there is little reliable empirical evidence. On the redistributive effects of reservation policies within SC and ST groups, however, there is indeed much evidence.

There can hardly be any doubt that it is indeed a creamy layer of Dalits and Adivasis who constitute the vast majority of the beneficiaries of India's reservation policies in university admissions. With few exceptions, only children from the better-off Dalit and Adivasi families are able to stay in school through a full secondary education and thus even be in a position to apply to a college or university. In a case study of wastage and stagnation in Maharashtrian primary and middle schools, Henriques and Wankhede (1985) show that those SC and ST students who do finish their secondary education are more likely to be boys than girls, and that they are most likely to come from the uppermost socio-economic strata of the Dalit and Adivasi populations. The fact that higher education represents potential earnings forgone and calls for expenditures on school supplies, housing, and possibly transportation, which are rarely covered in full by government aid programs, means that it is mainly the best-off students who can afford to spend several post-secondary years in an educational institution.

As Velaskar (1986: 604) observes, "it is clear that the [reservation] policy is steadily serving as a channel of access to mediocre performers of the relatively privileged sections of the Dalit population." She goes on to note that there is a small segment of SC students that performs on a par with general-entry students; these high performers typically come from well-off families and English-medium high schools. Patwardhan and Palshikar (1992) conclude that reservations favor urban and male students, and that they disproportionately benefit a small number of sub-castes within the SC group and particular tribes within the ST group. They suggest, further, that the beneficiaries of reserved seats are increasingly second-generation students from the favored groups, whose families have benefited from positive discrimination to become middle to upper-middle class; while children from more backward sub-castes and tribes find it difficult to compete. This proposition receives clear empirical support in the experience of the elite IITs: Kirpal and Gupta (1999: 148) found that 40 per cent of the SC and ST students in their sample of IIT B.Tech. students admitted from 1989 through 1992 were second-generation beneficiaries – undoubtedly a much higher percentage than when reserved-seat admissions were first begun in the early 1970s.

Rao corroborated the above observations in writing that "the schemes of reservation tend to reproduce within the beneficiary class the same kind of clustering the reservation is meant to remedy…those among the beneficiaries who already enjoy the greatest advantages obtain disproportionately large shares of the benefits" (Rao 2001: 51). This process operates across sub-castes and tribes, as well as across socio-economic strata, within the SC and ST groups. This has led to calls for more finely subdivided categories for reserved seats, so that the least-well-off sub-castes and tribes (who typically capture few reserved seats) would be entitled to their own separate reservation category.[14]

The evidence clearly supports the contention that reservation policies in university admissions have, at least in their direct effect, increased inequalities among Dalits and Adivasis by providing benefits primarily to the best-off individuals and sub-groups within the Dalit and Adivasi populations. According to pro-PD argument 2, however, PD policies may indirectly benefit less well-off members of the beneficiary groups, insofar as the direct beneficiaries are thereby enabled more effectively and more extensively to hire, support, and otherwise come to the aid of their less well-off kinsfolk and community members. The empirical significance of such indirect benefits in India is hotly disputed.

Sachchidananda's (1977) work on the "Harijan elite" tends to support the common view that reservation policies have created a privileged Dalit elite devoted to its own petty advancement and uncaring about the wider Dalit community. Such criticism has grown also among some Dalits themselves, who have also expressed concern about the stigmatization of SC occupants of reserved positions as inferior. But Mendelsohn and Vicziany (1998: Ch. 8), in reporting on interviews with Dalit members of parliament, suggest that – far from conveying the impression of being any kind of elite – they themselves are often struggling with personal material and social deprivation and against a hostile power structure. Mendelsohn and Vicziany find little evidence that reservation policies have created a particularly selfish and uncaring Dalit community of politicians; indeed, they are inclined to turn Sachchidananda's conclusion on its head, opining that "the creation of a more privileged group among Untouchables could well be of benefit to the general Untouchable population" (1998: 255) – by enabling them to play a stronger and more independent role as leaders of their own communities.

11 Affirmative action and academic performance in US universities

In this chapter I discuss evidence, first, on graduation rates and, next, on grade-point averages (GPAs) for under-represented ethnic group (UREG) and non-UREG students in US universities. I then go on to review and analyze studies of an issue with important implications for claims made by critics of affirmative action (AA) in admissions to US higher educational institutions: the effect of college/university selectivity on student academic performance.

UREG and non-UREG graduation rates

There is much more evidence available on graduation rates at the undergraduate level than at the graduate level, and the evidence is more plentiful for African Americans than for members of other under-represented groups. Bunzel (1988) was one of the first to draw attention to the relatively low graduation rates of UREG students at major US universities. Bunzel cited figures for the University of California at Berkeley (UC–Berkeley) in the 1980s, according to which 66 per cent of White students could be expected to graduate within five years, whereas the corresponding figure for Hispanic Americans is 41 per cent and for Blacks 27 per cent.

Thernstrom and Thernstrom (1997: 391, Table 2) have provided more comprehensive data on time trends of college attendance as well as graduation rates by Blacks and Whites in the US. During the three decades from 1965 to 1995 – years in which preferential admissions via AA to Black students became widespread – the percentage of Blacks attending colleges rose from 15 per cent to 45 per cent, as the percentage of Whites increased from 26 per cent to 55 per cent. The percentage of Black students actually completing four years of college rose only from 7 per cent to 15 per cent, as compared to an increase from 13 per cent to 26 per cent for Whites. This implies that the fraction of undergraduate students actually completing four years of college fell from 45 per cent to 34 per cent for Blacks, while remaining close to 50 per cent for Whites.[1]

Another body of evidence highlighted by Thernstrom and Thernstrom addresses differential performance by Blacks and Whites on the Scholastic Aptitude (or Assessment) Test (SAT), the standardized test widely utilized by admissions offices as an important indicator of the academic qualifications of college applicants.[2] That Blacks (and Hispanics), on average, score less highly on the SAT than Whites (or Asians) has been a well-known and persistent fact since such data were first collected.[3] There is also considerable evidence that graduation rates among students at any given college or university are positively correlated with the students' SAT scores – especially at relatively competitive universities.[4] Thernstrom and Thernstrom (1997: 406–9, esp. Table 9) focus attention on the relationship between the mean SAT-score gap and the graduation-rate gap between Blacks and Whites accepted into thirteen four-year colleges at elite universities where AA is practiced. The mean SAT-score gaps vary from 95 at Harvard to 288 at UC-Berkeley; the corresponding graduation-rate gaps vary from 2 per cent at Harvard to 26 per cent at UC-Berkeley.[5] As Thernstrom and Thernstrom emphasize, there is a clear positive correlation between the size of the mean SAT gap and the size of the graduation-rate gap between Black and White students.

The mean SAT score of entering first-year undergraduates serves as a rough proxy for the degree of selectivity – as well as the degree of competitiveness – of US universities. Thernstrom and Thernstrom's data reveal also a significant positive correlation between the degree of selectivity of an elite university and the average rate of graduation for both Black and White students. This suggests that the greater success of more elite universities in graduating Black students may have something to do with their quality as well as with the smaller mean SAT gaps of their entering classes – a point that I will pursue below (see pp. 163–7).

Further evidence on the relationship between SAT scores, college selectivity, and academic performance has been compiled and analyzed by Datcher Loury and Garman (1995). They utilized a rich database of college-goers from a representative nationwide sample of male high-school graduates of 1972, whose college choices span a much broader range than the elite ones highlighted by Thernstrom and Thernstrom. Table 11.1 summarizes Datcher Loury and Garman's findings for graduation rates as a function of student SAT scores and college selectivity, controlling for family background as well as gender.

Table 11.1 **Graduation rates related to own SAT scores and college median SAT scores**

Students' own SATs	900	1,000	College median SAT	900	1,000
	White males		Graduation rates (%)	Black males	
700 or less	42	59		38	26
701–850	47	60		56	39
851–1,000	54	59	Over 850	77	52
Over 1,000	54	57			

Source: Datcher Loury and Garman (1995: 304, Table 4).

Table 11.2 GPAs related to own SAT scores and college median SAT scores

Students' own SATs	900	1,000	College median SAT	900	1,000
	White males		*GPAs*	*Black males*	
700 or less	2.66	2.66		2.58	2.24
701–850	2.67	2.73		3.05	2.73
851–1,000	2.75	2.81	Over 850	2.87	2.65
Over 1,000	3.07	3.10			

Source: Datcher Loury and Garman (1995: 304, Table 4).

If one uses the median SAT score again as a proxy for college selectivity and competitiveness, Table 11.1 suggests that Black male students – in each SAT bracket – have a significantly lower probability of graduating at a more competitive college (with a median SAT of 1,000 rather than 900). By contrast, the probability of graduation for White male students in each SAT bracket is actually higher at a more competitive college. (I will return to this anomaly below; see pp. 163–7.) Thernstrom and Thernstrom (1997: 410) note that the average White student in this sample had an SAT score of 1,011 and went to a college with a median SAT of 1,019; while the average Black student had an SAT score of 768 and went to a college with a median SAT of 936.[6] They take this as evidence that White students are typically well matched to their college, but that Black students are lifted by AA into excessively competitive colleges – from which they graduate at lower rates than they would have if properly matched. This inference is also drawn by Datcher Loury and Garman, who conclude that "The principal cost of attending more selective schools for 'mismatched' Blacks is the lower probability of graduation and the subsequently lower earnings for those who fail to complete college" (Datcher Loury and Garman 1995: 306–7). This conclusion, however, is not easy to reconcile with the evidence in the above table that the extent of the reduction in graduation rates for Blacks at more selective colleges rises with their SAT bracket, i.e. the graduation reduction is greater for Black students who are less mismatched.

An alternative perspective is provided by Bowen and Bok's findings on graduation rates of students who entered selective colleges in 1976 and 1989. These findings, for various ethnic groups of students and for the three different selectivity groups of colleges in their sample of twenty-eight, are presented in Table 11.3. The figures in the table show the percentage of students who graduated within six years from the college they entered.[7] Graduation rates from each selectivity group of colleges in the Bowen and Bok sample increased significantly from the 1976 to the 1989 cohort.

Table 11.3 Graduation rates, by student ethnic group and college selectivity, 1976 and 1989

Bowen and Bok's selectivity group	Year	All (%)	White (%)	Black (%)	Hispanic-American (%)	Native-American (%)
1	1976	86	87	81	77	70
2	1976	78	80	67	67	64
3	1976	72	74	56	55	46
1	1989	94	95	85	92	79
2	1989	85	86	76	79	89
3	1989	81	82	68	71	72
All four-year colleges★	1989	58	59	40		

Source: Bowen and Bok (1998: 57; 376–9, Tables D.3.1 and D.3.2).

Note:

★ A representative sample of four-year colleges.

Differences among ethnic groups are evident for both the 1976 and 1989 cohorts. Among students in the latter cohort, UREG members (Blacks, Hispanics, and Native Americans) graduated from the Bowen and Bok colleges at a somewhat lower rate than Whites; but in both cases these rates were much higher than the corresponding graduation rates from a representative sample of all US colleges.

Table 11.3 indicates also that in Bowen and Bok's sample, graduation rates for both Whites and UREGs rose with the selectivity of the college. Bowen and Bok's findings about the positive relationship between graduation rates and the degree of selectivity of a college remain robust even when they undertake multivariate regression analysis to control for a variety of entry qualifications – including scores on the nationwide standardized college entry test (the SAT), secondary-school grades, gender, and socio-economic status.[8] These findings stand in sharp contrast to those of Thernstrom and Thernstrom (1997) and Datcher Loury and Garman (1995), which suggest a negative relationship between college selectivity and graduation rates; I will return to this controversy below (see pp. 163–7).

Evidence on graduation rates from graduate and professional schools, separately for different ethnic groups, is rather scarce. Once again, law schools have been the object of the most systematic studies of differences among students from different ethnic groups. In her comprehensive study of

1990–91 applicants to American Bar Association-approved law schools, Wightman (1997) found that Black and Hispanic-American students who enrolled in these schools had somewhat lower graduation rates than White students. This is hardly surprising; the reasons as to why students do not complete law school are as likely to be economic as academic, and UREG students are typically much more heavily burdened by financial problems. What is more relevant to the issue of the impact of AA on differential ethnic graduation rates is that Wightman's analysis showed that there was no significant difference between the graduation rates of those UREG students who would have been accepted to law schools in the absence of AA and the graduation rates of those who owed their admission to AA.

In their study of the consequences of AA at the elite University of Michigan (UM) Law School, Lempert *et al.* (2000a) found that underrepresented minority students, although admitted with quantitative entry credentials that (on average) were considerably lower than those of White students, did just about as well in their law-school studies. They report that "96 per cent of the minority students and 98.5 per cent of the white students who entered the UM Law School between 1983[9] and 1992 graduated from Michigan with the J.D. [Doctor of Laws] degree" (Lempert *et al.* 2000a: 422). Of those White and minority students who entered but did not graduate, most left in academic good-standing to attend other schools or to pursue other careers.

UREG and non–UREG grade performance

As in the case of graduation rates, much of the available data on differential grade performance by UREG and non–UREG students in the US has been compiled for Blacks and Whites. Moreover, the first reports on such differentials came from critics of affirmative action. Thus Bunzel (1988) provided information on group-wise GPAs at UC-Berkeley in 1986, according to which 93 per cent of White and Asian-American students had GPAs of 2.0 or better, whereas the corresponding figure for Chicanos was 76 per cent and for Blacks 72 per cent.

The first systematic and statistically sophisticated investigation of differences in GPAs between Blacks and Whites was carried out by Datcher Loury and Garman (1995), utilizing their database of college-goers from a representative nationwide sample of male high-school graduates of 1972. Among these college-goers the mean cumulative GPA was 2.91 for Whites and 2.69 for Blacks (on a scale running from 0 to 4).[10] Datcher Loury and Garman analyzed Black and White student GPAs as a function of student SAT scores and college selectivity, controlling for family background as well as gender, in the same way as they analyzed graduation rates. Their findings are summarized in Table 11.2.

The evidence in Table 11.2 indicates that Black male students – in each SAT bracket – achieve on average a significantly lower GPA when they attend a more competitive college (with a median SAT of 1,000 rather than 900); whereas for White male students, college median SAT makes little difference. These findings suggest that Black students would do better attending less selective colleges. In this case, the figures on comparative GPA reductions for Black males attending more selective colleges indicate that the extent of GPA reduction is positively correlated with the extent of the mismatch between the student's SAT score and the median college SAT (though the GPAs for Black males in the middle SAT bracket seem anomalously high).

Data compiled by Bowen and Bok (1998: 72–8) for the cohort of students entering their "College and Beyond" (C&B) sample of selective colleges in 1989 show that there is a significant difference between Blacks and Whites in grade performance: the average GPA is 2.61 for Blacks and 3.15 for Whites. The lower average GPA for Black students is not explainable simply in terms of lower entry test scores. Bowen and Bok find that the average Black GPA of 2.61 is in fact less than would be predicted on the basis of their average SAT score; this reflects what has been characterized as "underperformance."[11] In Bowen and Bok's sample the average Black graduate ranks in the twenty-third percentile (from the bottom) of the graduating class; whereas the average White ranks in the fifty-third percentile. Even controlling for SAT scores and other available college-entry characteristics, Bowen and Bok find that Blacks graduate on average with a significantly lower class rank than Whites. As one would expect, Bowen and Bok also find (1998: 383, Table D.3.6) that, controlling for college-entry characteristics, both Blacks and Whites are likely to graduate at a lower class rank from a more selective college. This implies that they are likely to graduate from a more selective college with a lower GPA as well – unless the overall distribution of grades in that college is significantly higher than in the alternative, less selective school.

That under-represented minority students compile lower cumulative GPAs than Whites is a finding that applies to the graduate as well as the undergraduate level of post-secondary education. In the case of law schools, many studies have shown: (1) that Black, Hispanic-, and Native-American students enter with considerably lower average cumulative undergraduate GPAs and considerably lower average scores on the nationwide standardized Law School Admissions Test (the LSAT) than do White and Asian-American students; (2) that an index based on these two indicators is a statistically significant predictor of grades earned by students in their first year of study; and (3) that UREG students on average earn lower grades and graduate at lower class ranks than do non-UREG students.[12] Lempert *et al.* (2000a: 459–68), in the context of their analysis of affirmative action at the UM Law School from the late 1960s to the mid-1990s, confirmed these findings and found also that an index combining the two pre-law-school quantitative indicators has a significant effect on the cumulative as well as the first-year law-school GPAs of UM Law School students.

Bowen and Bok assert that the phenomenon of underperformance characterizes Black students (on average) at the graduate as well as at the undergraduate level.[13] Their own findings at the undergraduate level are corroborated and extended by Vars and Bowen (1998), who made use of data on students who entered in 1989 a subset of eleven colleges in the same C&B database. They found that student GPAs are correlated with student SATs (although less so for Blacks than for Whites), and that in every SAT bracket, Blacks earn lower grades than Whites, even after controlling for other variables like high-school grades and family socio-economic status. Interestingly, the performance gap is greatest for those Blacks with the highest SATs. As they note, "for reasons not well understood, many gifted Blacks are not reaching their full academic potential at selective institutions" (Vars and Bowen 1998: 458).

The fact that the average level of academic performance of Black students remains lower than that of White students, even controlling for standardized test scores (and often other entry characteristics as well), has been a source of much concern and discussion. The evidence for this kind of underperformance on the part of African Americans is especially strong at selective US colleges and universities. What could account for such findings?

There are two possible reasons for findings of underperformance, each of which encompasses a variety of possible explanations. On the one hand, the studies may fail to control for certain characteristics of entering students that are both difficult to measure and on the whole less favorable for Blacks than for Whites. For example, Blacks entering college typically come from home, community, and school environments that are less conducive to good study habits and learning practices – in ways that are not necessarily reflected in test scores or other readily measured entry characteristics.[14] On the other hand, it may be the case that higher educational institutions tend not to be as successful in educating Black students as they are in educating otherwise similar White students. For this there are several different possible explanations, each with very different implications.[15]

One such explanation for this difference in educational effectiveness is that predominantly White faculty members may not have the cultural awareness to teach Black students as well as they do White students. Another possibility is that Black students may tend to find their in-college experience more difficult than do White students, facing, for example, greater problems adjusting to a new (and White-dominated) college campus environment, greater vulnerability to race-related social tensions, and possibly subtle (if not overt) forms of racial discrimination. Yet another possibility is that many Black students are characterized by a form of "stereotype bias" that inhibits them from performing well on examinations and in other competitive academic activities.[16] Finally, it is possible that a considerable number of Black students in a predominantly White environment may develop an alternative subculture that disparages academic achievement as "White"; peer pressure along these lines could inhibit even highly capable students from doing as well as they otherwise might.[17]

Over the last thirty years, selective US colleges and universities have made increasingly well-informed efforts to assist Black students in overcoming some

– if not all – of the above obstacles to academic success. The more prestigious and well-endowed institutions have been able to do more along these lines. Few can credibly claim, however, that they have fully equalized the learning environment for Black and White students.

Analysis of the relationship between college selectivity and student academic performance

In the previous two sections I have presented evidence mainly on the comparative academic performance of UREG and non-UREG students attending the same higher educational institutions. In discussing such evidence, however, I noted how several studies sought to estimate the way in which the academic performance of a given student would likely vary across institutions of differing selectivity and quality. As noted in Chapter 8, the relationship between the selectivity of a higher educational institution and the academic performance of given students is critical to the assessment of several of the claims made by proponents or opponents of AA in higher education – especially claims related to the argument that AA results in a mismatch between AA beneficiaries and their universities. In this chapter, therefore, I will discuss in more detail the nature and implications of studies that have addressed this relationship. (Thus far such studies have been done only in the US.)

Some of the studies on differential academic performance of Whites and Blacks, which I discussed in the preceding sections, also addressed the claim that Black students who enter selective colleges by virtue of AA tend to perform poorly or drop out of those colleges because they are academically mismatched. This is the implication of Thernstrom and Thernstom's (1997) comparison of the Black-White SAT gap with the corresponding graduation gap at elite colleges; and this is also the implication of Datcher Loury and Garman's (1995) findings on the relationship between selectivity and both graduation rates and GPAs. Yet the Bowen and Bok (1998) study points to the opposite conclusion with respect to graduation rates. And there remains an unresolved anomaly in Datcher Loury and Garman's finding that the probability of graduation for Whites increases with college selectivity whereas for Blacks it decreases. In order to reconcile the apparent inconsistencies in the above findings with respect to the effect of selectivity, it will be helpful to consider more generally how to analyze the determinants of a given student's academic performance.

What are the factors that one might expect to influence a student's academic performance at college – beyond the natural-born ability and readiness to apply effort that the student brings to college? The following factors are surely relevant:

- *Family socio-economic background*   This is important for at least two distinct reasons. First, a better-off family can provide more economic security –

making it less likely that a student will be troubled in school by economic concerns, or burdened at school by having to take on a paying job, or obliged to quit school to work full-time at a paying job. Secondly, a better-off family can provide a student with a home and community environment more conducive to the development of good studying and learning habits.

- *Prior academic achievement* A student who enters college with better academic qualifications – as measured by indicators such as his/her high-school SAT score, class rank, or GPA, and the competitiveness of the high school attended – will tend to do better in his/her college studies.
- *Quality of the college* Higher-quality colleges (as measured, e.g., by the median SAT of students attending) have higher-quality students and faculties, and tend to have more resources; they are likely to do a better job of educating students because students will have better-prepared class-mates, better teachers, more and/or better support programs and facilities, and probably also more favorable social-educational norms.
- *Match to the academic environment* To the extent that a student's own academic qualifications match those of his/her peers, it is more likely that the student will thrive rather than suffer in the college's educational environment.[18]
- *Match to the social environment* The more that a student's own social/cultural background matches that of his/her college campus environment, the more likely the student is to adjust to and prosper (academically as well as socially) at the college.

AA policies lead to changes in the ethnic composition of college student bodies in such a way as to increase the salience of the last three of the above factors. By redistributing UREG students upward and non-UREG students downward in the selectivity/quality spectrum of colleges, they put the typical UREG student into a higher-quality college. If the upward redistribution of UREG students has the effect of putting the typical UREG student into a college where his/her typical non-UREG peer has stronger academic qualifications – which is amply confirmed by the evidence reviewed in Chapter 9, pp. 140–3, and above, pp. 160–3 – then AA policies simultaneously increase the extent of the academic mismatch between the typical UREG student and his/her college. AA policies also increase the extent of the social mismatch for the typical UREG student, insofar as they lead some students away from predominantly UREG colleges (like the historically Black colleges (HBCs)) and into predominantly non-UREG colleges (like the selective colleges that practice AA in admissions).

Critics of AA claim that the negative effect on academic performance from increasing the academic mismatch faced by the typical UREG student will outweigh any positive effect derived from the correspondingly increased quality of the college attended. Proponents of AA claim just the opposite. The fact that these claims are simultaneously and directly opposed to one another should facilitate empirical testing of their validity – by means of an analysis of the effect of increased college selectivity on the academic performance of AA beneficiaries. For such an analysis to be statistically legitimate and for its findings to be compelling, however, it must control as effectively as possible for influences on student academic performance other than selectivity itself. In particular, it must control for the other three factors in the list above – family socio-economic background, prior academic achievement, and match to the social environment – so that differences in academic performance due to variation in these factors are not confused with differences of college quality and academic mismatch due to variance in college selectivity. With this in mind, let us examine the available empirical evidence.

Thernstrom and Thernstrom's (1997) implicit correlation of the size of the Black-White SAT gap with the size of the Black-White graduation gap across highly selective colleges (where a large percentage of the Black students can be assumed to be AA beneficiaries) does not prove that an AA-induced SAT mismatch between Black students and their college peers is the cause of their lower graduation rates. This is because the correlation fails to control for differences in the socio-economic background and the prior academic achievement of Black students at different colleges. Those Black students in the Thernstrom and Thernstrom sample who were more SAT-mismatched and more likely to drop out of college might have dropped out for reasons that would have applied wherever they had attended college – e.g. because of economic insecurity associated with a low socio-economic status family background,[19] or because of inadequate prior educational preparation.

Datcher Loury and Garman (1995), utilizing a much richer database on students going to a much broader variety of colleges, address the major limitations of the Thernstrom and Thernstrom findings by introducing into their analysis of student academic performance (as a function of college selectivity) variables for student family background and prior academic achievement. These variables control reasonably well, though far from perfectly, for differences in relevant characteristics of students attending colleges of varying selectivity. But Datcher Loury and Garman included HBCs in their sample, without controlling for the resultant differences in the matching of Black students and White students to the social environments of HBCs as distinct from White-dominated colleges.

Bowen and Bok (1998) did control for social match or mismatch, by the simple expedient of confining their sample to elite (highly selective) colleges and thus excluding all HBCs. They tabulated many of their findings on differential Black and White student academic performance as averages, for their full sample of colleges and for three sub-groups distinguished according to level of selectivity. From such tabulations they found a positive relationship between graduation rates and college selectivity; but those findings are subject to the same criticism levied above against the Thernstrom and Thernstrom findings. Bowen and Bok went on, however, to undertake multivariate regression analyses of various measures of student performance, in

which they were able to control to a considerable extent for family background and prior academic achievement; and they found that the positive
relationship between graduation rates and college selectivity, while somewhat
weakened, remained robust.

In a sophisticated effort to address these issues, Kane (1998: 440–8) made
use of a longitudinal database for a nationwide representative sample of high-
school graduates of 1982 – similar to Datcher Loury and Garman's database,
but from observations ten years later. Kane was able to distinguish observations on Hispanic Americans from observations on (non-Hispanic) Blacks and
non-Hispanic others; in the research discussed below, he combined Hispanic-
American and Black students into a single under-represented minority
category, and the remaining "White" category includes Asian Americans. He
sought to predict student academic performance – both probability of graduation and cumulative GPA – as a function of family background (family
income and parental education), prior academic achievement (measured by
individual SAT and high-school GPA), and quality/selectivity of college
(college median SAT). Holding the family background and prior academic
achievement indicators constant, Kane found that greater college selectivity is
associated with a higher probability of graduating and with a slightly lower
GPA.[20] His findings support Bowen and Bok's rejection of the academic
mismatch claim for graduation rates, and they are consistent also with Bowen
and Bok's confirmation of the mismatch claim with respect to class rank.

Kane's initial results were also fairly consistent with those of Datcher Loury
and Garman's, in that greater college selectivity was associated with a higher
probability of graduation for Whites but much less so for Blacks and Hispanic
Americans (Kane did not find the negative relationship for Blacks highlighted
by Datcher Loury and Garman). When he controlled for HBCs, however, he
found that this difference disappeared – greater selectivity is associated with
higher probability of graduation for both under-represented minority and
White students. Evidently the difference found by Datcher Loury and
Garman was due to the fact that Black students attending HBCs have relatively low SAT scores but relatively high graduation rates. Kane's findings on
college selectivity lend strong support to those who reject the academic
mismatch claim; and they also explain the seemingly anomalous Datcher
Loury and Garman result about the favorable effect of college selectivity on
White graduation rates. Kane is hesitant to claim a positive effect of college
selectivity on graduation rates because of the possibility that the omission of
variables on student academic competence (other than SAT scores and high-
school grades) may have biased upwards his estimates of the selectivity effect;
but he sees no reason that an upward bias would differ by race, and he
unequivocally rejects a negative selectivity effect.[21]

The evidence I have reviewed here, in its totality, appears to reject very
convincingly the academic mismatch hypothesis as applied to the probability
of graduation from college of UREG students. The evidence indicates that
students of any ethnic group are no less likely to graduate from a more selec-

tive college, though they will graduate with a lower class rank from a more selective college. Since more selective colleges can be expected on the whole to impart higher-quality educational services to their students, one can draw the conclusion that it is generally in the academic interest of any given student to attend the most selective college to which he/she can gain access. This implies, of course, that AA action policies do serve the best academic interests of the UREG students whom they affect; by the same token, they harm the academic interests of the non-UREG students whom they affect.

There is one respect, however, in which the evidence is not sufficient to support the contention that UREG students are well served academically by AA policies. It is not clear that Black students generally have just as high a probability of graduating from highly selective predominantly White colleges as they do from less selective HBCs. Bowen and Bok's findings do not speak to this issue at all, since they excluded HBCs from their sample.[22] When Datcher Loury and Garman and Kane include observations from HBCs in their analysis, their findings are at best ambiguous with respect to the contention that increased college selectivity does not have a negative effect on the probability of graduation of Black students.

Thus it may be true that Black students who seize an opportunity (of the kind afforded by AA) to go to a more selective, predominantly White college pay an academic price, in terms of a probability of graduation that is lower than the one they would have had at an HBC. This would constitute a cost attributable to mismatch. It would have to be attributed, however, to a social rather than an academic mismatch; for the evidence suggests that academic mismatch alone – holding the social environment constant – does not result in a lower probability of student graduation. Moreover, even if there is an expected cost in lower probability of graduation to be paid by a Black student shifting from an HBC to a more selective, predominantly White college, that cost may be more than offset by a higher expected economic return to graduation from an elite college. To determine whether or not it is in the economic interest of Black students to make such a shift requires evidence on the way in which college selectivity affects post-college career prospects – an issue to which I will turn in Chapter 13.

12 Reservation policies and academic performance in Indian universities

In this chapter I review evidence available from India pertaining to the academic performance of the primary beneficiaries of reservation policies (RP) in higher education – Scheduled Caste (SC) and Scheduled Tribe (ST) students. Their academic performance tends to be relatively poor, for reasons that I explore. Finally, I discuss the available evidence on the post-university accomplishments of the beneficiaries of reservation policies.

Academic performance of RP beneficiaries

The availability of data on the performance of SC and ST students in higher education is unfortunately rather limited. In most cases these data apply strictly to SC and ST students who occupy reserved seats. Even when they include also some other SC and ST students, however, these others are usually few in number; so the overall data are very likely to reflect the experience of those who have benefited from reservation policies. In the following paragraphs I report on the most relevant studies and findings, in chronological order.

The earliest systematic studies of SC and ST student academic performance in higher educational institutions are based on data collected in the late 1960s and early 1970s. Karlekar (1975) reports on a survey by the University Grants Commission (UGC) of fifteen universities in the academic year 1965/6, which found that only 36 per cent of 4,100 SC students (in a variety of undergraduate and postgraduate fields) had passed their examinations. Galanter (1984: 63) cites a Maharashtra Department of Social Welfare study of 1969, which found that only 8 per cent of SC and ST students earned their college degrees in the prescribed four years and altogether only 15 per cent ultimately received their degree. Even those who did so tended on average to receive rather low grades. Chitnis (1972) surveyed arts and science colleges in Bombay in the late 1960s and found that most of the SC students were enrolled in colleges the students of which tended to be the least successful in the University of Bombay examinations taken by most of the local college students. In any given college, the average academic performance of SC students was distinctly worse than that of non-SC students; and rates of wastage (dropping out) and stagnation (repeating courses) were very high among SC students.

In a major research project sponsored by the Indian Council of Social Science Research (ICSSR), systematic surveys of SC and ST high-school and college students were carried out in fifteen Indian states in 1972–3. Reporting on the findings of this study, Chitnis (1981) indicated that most of the student respondents were progressing satisfactorily in their studies. She noted, however, that the surveys did not throw any light on the performance of SC students compared to that of other students, and she cautioned that the SC students faced many challenging obstacles in their efforts to pursue a successful educational career. Karlekar (1975) made use of data from some of the ICSSR surveys, as well as from the UGC study cited above and annual reports of the commissioner for SCs and STs, to conclude that SC students in higher educational institutions experienced high drop-out rates (mainly because of economic pressures) as well as relatively low academic marks.

A very informative study of SC student academic performance at the university level was carried out by Aikara (1980), on the basis of data from the early 1970s collected from ten Bombay colleges. The study included colleges spanning a variety of fields (arts, science, commerce, law, medicine, and engineering), and it included private as well as government colleges. Of all the students enrolled in these colleges (at all four year-levels of a college education) during the period of the study, a little over 10 per cent were SC students. Most of the SC students were enrolled in the (less prestigious and less demanding) private colleges, and a majority of them were clustered in one single college catering primarily to SC students. Very few SC students were enrolled in the (more prestigious and more demanding) government colleges and/or in the (highly coveted) medical and engineering programs.

Comparing the performance of SC students and (a stratified sample of) non-SC students enrolled at all levels in the ten colleges over the three academic years from 1970 to 1973, Aikara found that only 23 per cent of SC students passed their year-end examinations, whereas 52 per cent of non-SC students did so. Of those who did not pass, a majority in both cases took but did not pass the exams – thus stagnating; the rest did not even appear for them – thus dropping out. A substantial majority of SC student drop-outs left college while enrolled in the first-year class, but many of these SC drop-outs were already in their second or third year of study at that year-level. Roughly 60 per cent of SC students who initially enrolled in 1970 were gone within three years; not having data beyond 1973, Aikara did not have precise figures on the percentage of those students who ultimately graduated, but it seems reasonable to infer that it must have been below 20 per cent.

In all ten colleges the academic performance of SC students was lower than that of non-SC students. Interestingly, those (few) SC students enrolled in the more challenging government and/or medical and engineering colleges were considerably more likely to pass their examinations than those (many) SC students enrolled in the remaining colleges. The former appear to have been exceptionally well motivated, considerably more skilled, and better prepared and supported than the great majority of SC students who enrolled in low-prestige colleges. Without reserved seats, there would no doubt have been even fewer such SC students enrolled in the more challenging colleges and fields. Aikara concludes from his study of Bombay colleges that, with the exception of a high-performing minority, the great majority of SC students suffered from high rates of wastage and stagnation and registered lower rates of performance and progress as compared to their non-SC peers.

In her research on medical colleges in Bombay in the 1970s, cited in Chapter 10, Velaskar (1986) found that roughly one-quarter of SC students finished their degree program on time – as compared to roughly three-quarters of non-SC students. Vakil (1985: 138) reported a similar finding with respect to the few SC students who entered Nehru Medical College in Raipur in the late 1960s and early 1970s: of forty-two entering students, only four completed college within the standard four and a half years; twenty-three did so within eight years. Velaskar found that a majority of the SC students do eventually manage to graduate from Bombay's medical colleges, typically requiring some extra years of study; virtually all non-SC students graduate, most often on time. She noted also that SC students generally enter medical school with an academic background significantly poorer than that of non-SC students, and – with a few exceptions – they perform more poorly than "Other Backward Class" (OBC) students as well as general-entry students. However, she found that they are considerably more likely to persist in and graduate from Bombay's medical colleges than from engineering colleges – probably because the former have a social environment that is more local in flavor and thus more congenial to SC students, who are less comfortable with the national culture in general and the English language in particular.[1]

More recent evidence on the academic performance of SC and ST students is available from two very well designed and executed studies published in the 1990s. The first of these is the study by Patwardhan and Palshikar (1992), first cited in Chapter 10, based on a rich set of data on students admitted to the B.J. Medical College in Pune – a well-established and well-respected government-run college. The authors not only compiled academic records (at entry into as well as in each year of college) for reserved-seat students and a control group of general-entry students over a period stretching from the 1970s to the 1980s; they also sent out questionnaires to a substantial number of reserved-seat and general-entry graduates, and conducted personal interviews with each respondent. Outlined here are their principal findings with respect to the in-college performance of reserved-seat students (which they address in Part II of their long and detailed paper). I will review their findings with respect to post-college career performance later in this chapter (see below, pp. 175–78).

As expected, the rank ordering of average exam marks by student category runs from general-entry students (at the top) to OBC students to SC students to ST students.[2] By and large the same ordering applies – inversely, of course

– to the number of attempts needed to pass a given exam, to the number of years taken to complete the degree program, and to the proportion of students who sooner or later drop out of the program. But an impressive proportion of SC and ST students do ultimately graduate: among students entering in 1972–6 (and graduating by 1984), the graduation rate for SCs was 92 per cent and for STs 87 per cent.

Overall, Patwardhan and Palshikar found that SC and ST students are behind other students academically at the time of their admission to the B.J. Medical College, and that they tend to fall further behind academically during the course of their studies. But of the admitted SC and ST students, they find that only about 25–30 per cent perform in a less than satisfactory manner – either by dropping out, by requiring more than eight years to complete their degree program, or by graduating with barely more than the minimum passing score on their final examinations. Moreover, the authors speculate that the success rate for SC and ST students has likely increased since the period of their study – because the cut-off marks for admission of students to the SC and ST reserved seats have been rising over the years.

The most recent systematic study of the performance of SC and ST students in higher educational institutions was carried out by Kirpal and Gupta (1999), who focused their attention on the prestigious Indian Institutes of Technology (IITs). It is safe to assume that virtually all the SC and ST students enrolling in an IIT are doing so via the SC and ST reserved-seat categories, since the competition for general-entry seats at these most elite of Indian national higher educational institutions is ferocious.[3] Following several earlier studies of SC and ST students at IIT-Bombay in the 1970s,[4] the two scholars compiled a rich data set on the reserved-seat students entering the B.Tech. programs of all five of the main IIT campuses – Bombay (Mumbai), Delhi, Kanpur, Kharagpur, and Madras (Chennai) – between 1981 and 1992.

Kirpal and Gupta found, first of all, that the consolidated average graduation rate for all SC and ST students was 84 per cent, as compared with 94 per cent for general-entry students.[5] The average drop-out rate of 16 per cent for reserved-seat students entering in the 1980s compares very favorably with the much higher rates of wastage found among such students in the 1970s by Kirpal *et al.* (1985) and Chitnis (1986). As a result of those higher earlier rates, the IITs instituted significantly improved recruitment, preparation, and retention programs – including a year-long remedial program for many SC and ST applicants. Kirpal and Gupta's principal findings with respect to student academic performance at the IITs can be summarized in terms of the "Mean Cumulative Performance Index" (MCPI) of a roughly 10 per cent sample of general-entry, SC, and ST students who enrolled during the years 1989–92. The MCPI figures were 7.88 for 436 general-entry students, 6.23 for 115 SC students, and 5.93 for 21 ST students. Clearly, and not surprisingly, SC and ST students lag well behind general-entry students in their performance on IIT examinations. Moreover, those who graduate as a rule take more years to do so than their general-entry peers. Still, the fact that graduation rates for SC and ST students are now over 80 per cent at the elite IITs suggests that these beneficiaries of reserved seats – and the institutions that are admitting them – are achieving important successes.

Reasons for the relatively poor academic performance of RP beneficiaries

Scholars who have studied the experience of SC and ST students in higher education report widely varying rates of graduation, depending on the institution, the circumstances, and the time period. They are unanimous, however, in concluding that, on average, the academic performance of SC and ST students is well below that of their peers. SC and ST students typically attend less prestigious universities, tend to follow less promising fields of study, take longer to complete their degree, drop out at higher rates, and score lower in their exams. There is no lack of plausible explanations for the relatively poor performance of these students, most of whom benefit in some way from India's reservation policies.

First of all, SC and ST students – with relatively few exceptions – come from socio-economic backgrounds distinctly less privileged than those of their peers. All of the scholars whose work was cited in the previous section provide evidence of the relatively low socio-economic status (SES) of SC and ST students. For example, Aikara (1980: Table 4.2) found that only 5 per cent of the SC students in his sample had at least one college-educated parent, as compared with 32 per cent of non-SC students; 34 per cent of the SC students had two illiterate parents, as compared with 11 per cent in the case of non-SC students. Furthermore, 88 per cent of SC students had at least partial "freeships" (scholarships) to support them in their studies, and only 4 per cent of them relied largely or fully on parents or relatives for financial support; the corresponding figures for non-SC students, by contrast, were 14 and 64 per cent. Aikara (1980: Table 3) also noted that the primary reason as to why SC students dropped out of college was failure at exams; but almost as significant was a need to find employment in order to provide financial support for oneself and one's family. He concluded that considerably higher levels of financial aid would be necessary in order to reduce the high incidence of SC student wastage and stagnation.

In their study of students at the B.J. Medical College in Pune, Patwardhan and Palshikar (1992: Part II) found that 40 per cent of the parents or guardians of general-entry students were professionals, while only 1 per cent were laborers; they also discovered that 53 per cent of the general-entry students came from Brahman families. In the case of both SC and ST students, only 9 per cent of their parents or guardians were professionals; 21 per cent and 17 per cent, respectively, were laborers.

In the elite IITs, the family backgrounds of SC and ST students were relatively higher in socio-economic terms, though still on average well below those of the general-entry students. Kirpal and Gupta (1999: Tables 2.3 and

2.4) reported that 54 per cent of the general-entry IIT students in their sample had fathers who were high-ranking executives and 22 per cent had fathers who were educators; 66 per cent of the fathers had postgraduate or professional degrees. The corresponding figures for SC students were 27, 21, and 34 per cent; and for ST students they were 29, 10, and 24 per cent. Kirpal and Gupta (1999: Table 2.7) also reported that 84 per cent of the general-entry students attended English-medium secondary schools, while 63 per cent of the SC students and 38 per cent of the ST students did so.

Velaskar (1986), in her study of medical colleges in Bombay, confirmed that SC students typically enter college with poorer socio-economic and academic backgrounds, which helps to explain why they perform more poorly than either OBC students or general-entry students. SC students tend to go to lower-quality primary and secondary schools than other students; and very few of them can afford the kinds of special tutoring or coaching classes that enable so many other students to prepare themselves well for exams. Like several other scholars, however, Velaskar did note the existence of a small minority of SC students who perform on a par with other students. These latter students, with a few heroic exceptions, typically come from well-off families and have attended English-medium high schools.

Velaskar argues that the relatively poor academic performance of most SC students can be explained more fully in terms of differences in their *socio-cultural* backgrounds than in terms of differences in their socio-economic backgrounds. The families of SC students are certainly not well off, but – in spite of frequent financial problems – they were by the 1980s comparable in SES to the families of a significant fraction of (the less well-off) general-entry students. The most significant disadvantage that SC students must contend with vis-à-vis their general-entry peers is a lack of "cultural capital." The cultural capital deprivation of SC students is evidenced by lower levels of education among family members, lower levels of participation in edifying cultural activities, and in general a home environment less conducive to learning. Most critically, SC students typically lack the most important source of cultural capital in modern India – a good command of the English language.[6] General-entry students who are at the same socio-economic level as SC students are much more likely to have greater cultural capital, including significantly better English language capabilities. The importance of a strong socio-cultural background, as distinct from high socio-economic status per se, is suggested also by the over-representation of Brahmans among general-entry students. Many Brahman families are of low SES; but even low SES Brahman families are likely to be much richer than Dalit families in cultural capital.

As Velaskar points out, SC students are generally not accepted by others as equals – as much because of their inferior socio-cultural backgrounds as because of their inferior academic backgrounds and performance. Kirpal and Gupta (1999: Chs. 4 and 5) provide much evidence of the same phenomenon in the IITs. The more privileged general-entry students have usually benefited not only from a home environment more conducive to educational success but also from a secondary education at schools with better non-academic facilities as well as a better academic environment. All of this contributes to their relatively confident disposition and their linguistic competence, both of which go a long way in interviews and oral examinations. SC students experience considerable social distancing because of disdain from non-SC students, which tends to be compounded by their own feelings of inferiority. Social discrimination against SC students in colleges and universities is a fact of Indian life; what is not so clear is if it is based primarily on caste identity per se or on cultural differences. To overcome this kind of handicap requires great motivation and effort on the part of the SC student, as well as a facilitating environment – including friendship and help from other students.

Parmaji (1985) reports on a series of survey-based research studies he undertook (with others) in the 1970s and early 1980s at a number of higher educational institutions in Andhra Pradesh. Distinguishing between "forward castes," "backward castes," and SCs and STs, he found that performance on various examinations was positively and significantly correlated with caste status. He attributed the relatively poorer performance of the lower castes more to cultural deprivation than to low socio-economic status, for he found that among students from castes with a similar SES, those from "Sanskritized" castes did better than others. By "Sanskritization" he meant, following Srinivas (1962), the imitation by lower castes of Brahmanical culture, which in turn implies the acquisition of superior linguistic abilities and cultural levels. Interestingly, Parmaji also found some evidence to suggest that among students pursuing higher education in a residential college or university, the extent to which examination performance improves from admission to graduation is inversely correlated with caste status (unlike the absolute level of performance at any given stage). He concludes that a stimulating milieu at a later stage of education can help overcome the prior cultural deprivation of lower castes.

All the scholars who have examined the relationship between socio-economic status and academic performance confirm that high SES is correlated with good academic performance in higher educational institutions. This is true within each major category of student (general-entry, SC, ST, etc.) as well as across the student body as a whole. Patwardhan and Palshikar (1992), however, have noted an interesting twist on this correlation. In their sample of students at a prominent medical college in Pune, they found that students from families at the very lowest socio-economic level (illiterate and/or laborers) did better on their exams than students from families at an intermediate socio-economic level (e.g. lower-level government service, schoolteaching). In a parallel fashion, students from the most favored Dalit sub-caste (Mahars) did not do as well as students from other Dalit sub-castes. The authors speculate that students from families that have made it up from the lowest rungs of the socio-economic and caste ladder may have become somewhat complacent, as compared with those who are still struggling to make it out of the nether ranks (Patwardhan and Palshikar 1992: 33–4).

Limited evidence on the post–university career paths of RP beneficiaries

In any effort to assess the extent to which positive discrimination policies are achieving their objectives, it is critically important to consider evidence on the long-run career paths of the beneficiaries. Systematic evidence of this kind is difficult to obtain, since it calls for information to be gathered on the trajectories of representative samples of former students long after they have graduated from – or dropped out of – college and/or university degree programs. It is therefore not surprising, but nonetheless regrettable, that very little such systematic evidence is available in the case of SC and ST beneficiaries of India's reservation policies. In this section I report on the findings of four studies that have addressed in one way or another the career paths of Dalit and Adivasi students following their higher educational experiences at particular institutions.[7]

Wankhede (1978) carried out the first such study on a sample of students at the Milind College of Arts (MCA) at Aurangabad, Maharashtra. MCA is the first higher educational institution in India set up specifically for Dalits. It was founded by Dr. B.R. Ambedkar and run by his People's Education Society, which subsequently established several high schools and several more colleges (of law, commerce, science) in Aurangabad along the same lines. In these institutions most students and many faculty are Dalits, and students receive scholarships, special facilities, and extra attention more readily than in most government high schools and colleges in India. The Dalit students at MCA are obviously not beneficiaries of reserved seats under India's reservation policies in higher education. Their experiences are nonetheless relevant to a study of such policies, because they are representative of the kind of Dalit students who would be likely to qualify for reserved seats at more prestigious government-run institutions of higher education. They can thus serve as a kind of control group against which to consider the experiences of actual beneficiaries of higher educational reservation policies.

Wankhede focused his research on those MCA students who completed their BAs in 1972. Most of these students were from the Mahar sub-caste of Dalits, and most were male, unmarried, and neo-Buddhist (a designation given to Dalits who converted to Buddhism in the wake of Dr. Ambedkar's conversion in 1956).[8] Data are not available on how many students in the same cohort dropped out before completing their BAs; but the graduation record of the MCA is good, and it is probable that most of the students who enroll do ultimately graduate.

Questionnaires were mailed in the mid-1970s to all of the 170 MCA graduates of 1972 and Wankhede received responses from roughly three-quarters of them. He found that about half of the respondents had gone on to pursue further education at the Master's level; of those, about 40 per cent actually completed their program and attained the degree. At the time of the survey, roughly one-third of the MCA graduates were unemployed and one-sixth were pursuing further studies. The remaining half were working in low-paid jobs for which the minimum qualification was only a completed secondary-school education. None of the graduates had secured a Class I or II (administrative, as opposed to clerical or menial) government job, in spite of the fact that there are SC reservations for these jobs. However, most of the graduates found better jobs than their fathers – e.g. involving service rather than manual labor – and their earnings were on average three times as high.

Wankhede was disappointed by his findings, because of the limited degree of social mobility that they reflected. In spite of a favorable post-secondary educational environment, the career trajectories of the predominantly Dalit students appeared to involve mainly moves from a traditionally poor back-ground only as far as what he termed the "disadvantaged educated class." This is no doubt due in large part to the generally poor prospects for Indian college graduates, in an economy that suffers from a substantial excess supply of educated job-seekers vis-à-vis the number of vacancies in positions requiring a high level of education. But it does suggest that if reservations for SC and ST students are to have a major positive impact, they will probably have to involve reserved seats at institutions whose graduates are unusually well positioned to move into good jobs.

Among such institutions are the Bombay medical colleges studied by Velaskar (1986), which are considered quite good by national standards.[9] As previously noted, Velaskar found that most SC students who enrolled (via reserved seats) at these colleges did graduate – although they typically required more years to do so than non-SC students. She did not conduct a systematic post-graduation survey, but she was able to ascertain that the SC graduates by and large did end up in responsible and well-paying medical positions.

Velaskar also discovered some interesting differences between SC students and their non-SC counterparts in their choice of fields of special-ization and in the nature of their postgraduate careers. SC students were relatively more oriented to – and did better at – clinical, as opposed to theoretical, courses and training. SC graduates were most likely to become general practitioners, while non-SC graduates more often became (often consulting) specialists. Evidently, SC graduates placed a higher value on developing a good rapport with patients than did non-SC graduates. In general, Velaskar found that SC medical students (as well as general-entry students of a comparably low SES) were more motivated to render service and to reach out to help communities in need, while general-entry students of a higher SES (often the product of medical/professional families) were more materialistic in their career aspirations.

By far the best and most systematic effort to trace the post-graduation career paths of beneficiaries of India's reservation policies in higher education is the study carried out by Patwardhan and Palshikar (1992: Part III). These scholars first sent questionnaires to a large stratified sample of doctors who had graduated from the B.J. Medical College in Pune between 1971 and

1982. They received 100 responses, which they found fairly representative of the full sample (by comparison of basic characteristics of the respondents with those of the larger group). Their respondents were distributed across the main admissions categories as follows: general entry, 26; OBCs, 34; SCs, 30; STs, 3; and Vimukta Tribes (VTs), 7. The latter four (much more heavily sampled) categories constitute the reserved-seat group to which 74 respondents belonged.

The general-entry and reserved-seat respondents – especially those from the last three categories – were quite typically differentiated by family background. Only about one-eighth of the SC, ST, and VT doctors were from high SES families, while very few general-entry doctors were from low SES families. Most of the SC, ST, and VT doctors found their medical program of study very tough (especially the viva voce exams); and they felt that their academic performance was often aggravated by non-academic factors such as teacher aloofness and sometimes even contempt. Of the entire group of 100 respondents, four were in the process of completing a postgraduate medical degree program; of the remainder, about one-third were employed in government medical service and two-thirds were engaged in private practice. The SC, ST, and VT doctors were disproportionately likely to be involved in government service – a more secure, but much less lucrative, position than is usually found in private practice. This appears to be attributable to a combination of lack of self-confidence, lack of capital and resources, aversion to risk – and in some cases a sense on the part of the SC, ST, and VT doctors that they are likely to be more fairly treated in the public sector (whether or not they benefit directly from its employment reservations).

On the whole, the respondent doctors from the three most under-represented groups were doing quite well: about half of them were in private practice and half in government service, in almost all cases having attained a level of earnings and overall socio-economic status much higher than that of their parents – if less than that of their general-entry and OBC peers. It might be assumed that most SC, ST, and VT doctors in private practice end up in remote rural areas or impoverished urban areas, serving a clientele consisting primarily of members of their own community. However, among the questionnaire respondents this was not at all the case. While the location and clientele of the SC, ST, and VT doctors tended not to be as high-class as that of the general-entry and OBC doctors, and upper-caste patients do come less frequently to the former than to the latter, SC, ST, and VT doctors typically serve a broad variety of communities and groups.

Patwardhan and Palshikar (1992: Part IV) also arranged for personal interviews with 42 of the 100 respondents to their questionnaire, from which they were able to provide detailed accounts of the lifestyles and views of a reasonably representative sample of doctors from each of their five admissions categories. These interviews reinforced their conclusions that reserved-seat graduates – especially the SC, ST, and VT doctors – have successfully achieved a significant upward movement on the socio-economic scale, and that virtually all reserved-seat graduates are unquestionably competent as doctors. Indeed, the study's authors sharply reject the widespread belief that the more disadvantaged of the reserved-seat students are unable to qualify as competent doctors and set up private practices. The interview evidence also shows clearly how high–SES family backgrounds provide critical benefits to most general-entry and some OBC students, in the form of capital, contacts, and other kinds of support that facilitate advancement and success in one's professional career. On the other hand, there is evidence to suggest that the few most successful of the SC, ST, and VT doctors – those who have completed postgraduate programs in medical education and have attained highly prestigious positions, comparable to those of the top general-entry doctors – are likely to join the affluent professional elite and to limit their contact with and forgo potential leadership of their own disadvantaged caste or tribal community.

Kirpal and Gupta (1999), in their study of reservation policies at the five main IITs, did not gather any evidence from graduates of those institutions. They did, however, ask current SC and ST students in their sample about their future plans and career goals. The authors found that 60 per cent of their respondents indicated that they planned to avail themselves of reservations in the future, either in the context of admissions to postgraduate educational programs or in applying for government employment (including jobs in public sector enterprises as well as administrative services).[10] In a rank ordering of career goals, the most commonly cited – each by about 20 per cent of the respondents – were employment in a public sector enterprise and in administrative service; roughly 15 per cent cited private sector jobs, 5 per cent cited setting up their own business, and about half the rest focused on the attainment of a higher degree (usually overseas). Kirpal and Gupta concluded from the responses they received from their overall survey of reservation policy beneficiaries that

> it was obvious that reservations were helping the beneficiaries chiefly by improving their SES [as] reflected in better financial conditions and better career options. But…it was equally obvious that internal growth in terms of self-confidence, acceptance, integration with mainstream students and the ability to stand on their own feet, was generally lacking.
>
> (Kirpal and Gupta 1999: 156–7)

13 Affirmative action and career accomplishments in the US

An ultimate judgment about the consequences of affirmative action (AA) in higher education cannot be rendered without consideration of the long-run effects of AA on the careers of its beneficiaries. Evidence on career accomplishments is thus critical; but it is also the hardest to gather. In this chapter I first compile what evidence is available from the US on the accomplishments of under-represented ethnic group (UREG) and non–UREG students after their undergraduate or graduate studies. Next I focus on evidence regarding the effect of college/university selectivity on student long-term career success. Then I address a number of questions that have been raised about the validity of research findings suggesting that US AA beneficiaries have on the whole been successful in their studies and in their careers.

UREG and non–UREG career accomplishments

Studies designed explicitly to shed light on the long-term consequences of AA in higher educational admissions are of relatively recent vintage. For a long time, however, researchers have addressed the issue of the long-run economic returns to education. Some of these studies shed light on an issue of importance to the debate over AA: the comparative returns to education for Blacks and Whites.

One of the earliest studies directed at precisely this issue was that of Hoffman (1984), who concluded that the relative income returns to a Bachelor's degree for Black men were significantly higher than those for White men in the 1970s. Duncan and Hoffman (1984) and Smith and Welch (1986) reached similar conclusions. In a more recent and widely cited study utilizing data from the 1980s, Bound and Freeman (1992) found evidence of generally higher returns to education for Blacks than for Whites. Pascarella and Terenzini (1991: 506–8) summarize the consensus as follows:

> [I]t would appear that in terms of occupational status, nonwhite or black men derive somewhat greater relative benefits from a bachelor's degree than do white men. The evidence on earnings is less consistent but suggests that since about 1970 nonwhite or black men may also be

receiving somewhat greater relative benefits from a bachelor's degree than are their white counterparts.

Very few studies have been carried out on the comparative economic returns to graduate education. There is some evidence, however, on the differences in returns to medical and law degrees by race. After reviewing the evidence produced by the relevant studies, Conrad and Sharpe (1996) reported that the monetary returns to being a doctor or lawyer do not appear to differ systematically by race. However, they noted that the monetary returns associated with being a doctor or lawyer constitute a very narrow measure of career success – since not all graduates aspire to lucrative practices in medicine and law, and there is likely to be an inverse relationship between earnings and psychic income.

Turning now to evidence from studies designed specifically to address the long-run consequences of AA, one finds again that the work of Bowen and Bok looms large. Bowen and Bok (1998: Ch. 4) first considered the extent to which the college-goers in their sample had gone on to obtain advanced degrees. They found that the proportion of Blacks earning a graduate-level degree was virtually the same as the proportion of Whites. Blacks were a little more likely to get professional degrees in medicine, law, or business, while Whites were somewhat more likely to get Ph.D.s. The average rate at which advanced degrees were obtained rose appreciably with the degree of selectivity of the undergraduate college from which students graduated. But even the rates at which advanced degrees were earned by students from the least selective group of colleges were much higher than the average rates for all US colleges.

Bowen and Bok also found that, in contrast to their "underperformance" in cumulative grade-point average (GPA) and class rank while at college, Blacks actually "over-perform" in earning advanced degrees – i.e. they obtain advanced degrees in greater numbers than would be predicted by their Scholastic Aptitude (or Assessment) Test (SAT) scores and other college-entry characteristics. Why might this be so? Bowen and Bok allow that it might be partly attributable to affirmative action at the graduate level (though AA preferences would presumably affect admission to graduate programs much more than successful completion of them). They suggest that it could also be due to a relatively greater desire of African Americans to get advanced degrees. Blacks tend to have less access than Whites to informal contacts and networks that can help pave the way to a good job;[1] so they may well have a greater need for degree credentials, and the pay-off to their obtaining an advanced degree is likely to be greater.

Earnings are clearly an important indicator – though by no means the only indicator – of long-run career success. Bowen and Bok's (1998) findings on the average earnings in 1996 of White and Black students of the college-entering cohort of 1976 are presented in Table 13.1, along with corresponding figures for a national sample of college entrants.[2] It is evident

Table 13.1 **Average full-time worker earnings (US$) in 1995, for the 1976 entering cohort**

Bowen and Bok's selectivity group	*Men*		*Women*	
	White	*Black*	*White*	*Black*
1	111,000	88,000	74,000	72,000
2	107,000	77,000	63,000	66,000
3	87,000	68,000	56,000	48,000
Nationwide	63,000	47,000	43,000	38,000

Source: Bowen and Bok (1998: 124, Fig. 5.2; 139, Fig. 6).

from the figures in the table that Black students from selective colleges have done very well, by comparison with the nationwide average earnings of Black college students. It is also evident that Black males lag well behind White males in earnings of full-time workers; but the earnings gap between Black and White females is considerably more modest. There is clearly a significant gender gap in earnings for both Blacks and Whites.

The gross earnings premiums for college selectivity that can be derived from Table 13.1 overstate the actual boost in pay resulting from attendance at a more selective college, because they reflect to some extent the fact that the individual students going to the more selective colleges are on average more qualified than those going to less selective ones. I will address the question of the true vs. the apparent size of the college selectivity effect in the next section. It might also be the case that the earnings figures in the table overstate the earnings of AA beneficiaries among the Black students at selective colleges, because the AA beneficiaries are typically not as highly qualified upon entry into college – by conventional measures of academic credentials – as their Black classmates who would have been admitted in any case. Bowen and Bok (1998: 395–402, Tables D.5.2–D.5.5) carried out multivariate regressions of the earnings of college graduates in their sample in order to estimate the effect of various factors known at the time of college entry. From the regression results, they concluded that higher SAT scores are associated with higher earnings; but that this effect is due mainly to the fact that SAT scores are correlated with the selectivity of the college attended (which has a very significant effect on earnings). It follows that differences in SAT scores – and, very probably, other conventional entry credentials – among Black students entering a given college make little difference to their ultimate earnings; and the figures in the above table are reasonably representative of the earnings of the AA beneficiaries among Black students.

From the Bowen and Bok evidence already reviewed, one can conclude that Black students from selective colleges have typically gone on to very promising careers and well-paid jobs. I estimated in Chapter 9, pp. 136–40, that AA was responsible for the admission of 13,000 UREG students in 1989 to selective colleges (at all three levels of selectivity defined by Bowen and Bok). Bowen and Bok's figures on graduation rates (1998: Ch. 15, Section A) suggest that a little over three-quarters of those students went on to graduate. This implies that in 1989, AA was responsible for the graduation of roughly 10,000 UREG students who went on to the kinds of jobs and earnings suggested by Bowen and Bok's findings.

At the graduate level there have been a number of studies undertaken to assess the career paths of AA beneficiaries. Once again, the published research has focused on medical and law schools.

The most widely cited study concerning the long-run consequences of AA in medical schools is that of Davidson and Lewis (1987). These scholars had access to detailed information on students attending the University of California at Davis (UC-Davis) Medical School – all those who were admitted over a twenty-year period from 1968 to 1997. They could not separate out the AA beneficiaries, nor all the UREG students; but they were able to separate all the "special admits" from the "regular admits." Special admits constituted about 20 per cent of the whole sample of students; and UREGs accounted for a little less than half of them. No details were available on the reasons for admission of the other special admits; presumably these students had conventional entry qualifications insufficient to gain them admission, but were distinguished by special characteristics such as low family socio-economic status, remote area of residence, unusual talents, and/or legacy status.

Davidson and Lewis found that the special admits received lower grades (but were no more likely to fail core courses); had slightly lower graduation rates (94 per cent instead of 97 per cent); and scored significantly lower on the certification examinations of the National Board of Medical Examiners (NBME) (and were more likely to have to repeat exams in order to pass them). Following graduation, however, the experiences of special admits became similar to those of regular admits: there was no difference in completion of residency training or evaluation of performance by residency directors, and the practice characteristics of the two groups were quite similar. Davidson and Lewis concluded that the admissions process at the UC-Davis Medical School succeeded well in identifying students who could become successful medical practitioners, even though their conventional entry credentials were below levels that would alone have gained them admission. They concluded a fortiori that AA preferences in the admissions process achieved greater cultural diversity, without any perceptible diminution of the quantity or quality of the school's graduates – for they observed a gradual convergence of the special admit and the regular admit populations from the time they entered medical school to the time they established themselves in their careers.

Findings such as those of Davidson and Lewis have led to criticism, geared in particular to the differential pass rates of NBME certification exams. For example, Thernstrom and Thernstrom (1999) have noted that large ethnic disparities show up in NBME examinations; and they cite evidence that under-represented minority student scores on such exams depend significantly on their (conventionally measured) academic qualifications prior to entry into medical school. As Cook (1995) observes, there is no question that a smaller percentage of Black, Hispanic- and Native-American students pass NBME certification exams on their first try. Drake (1994) has compiled evidence, however, showing that the percentages ultimately passing such exams are quite similar.

Wightman's (1997) comprehensive study of law-school students admitted in the year 1991 did not trace their career paths beyond the bar examination. But she did find that, in terms of the probability of each group passing the bar examination, there was virtually no difference between those law students who would and those who would not have been admitted to a law school on the basis of their conventional academic qualifications for entry – i.e. their score on the Law School Admissions Test (LSAT) and undergraduate GPA. This may imply that students admitted to law school by virtue of AA (with inadequate conventional academic qualifications) were not significantly handicapped, by the time they finished law school, in their ability to pass the bar exam.

There is considerable evidence, however, that UREG students are more likely to have to take this examination more than once in order to pass it. Conrad and Sharpe (1996) report that in 1994, 97 per cent of White and 83 per cent of minority graduates of the University of California law schools passed the California bar exam upon taking it for the first time. Thernstrom and Thernstrom (1999) report that in 1997, the corresponding figures were 77 per cent for Whites and 43 per cent for Blacks. Thernstrom and Thernstrom also note that Wightman's study revealed that 27 per cent of those Black graduates who were likely AA beneficiaries were unable to pass a bar examination within three years of graduation, whereas the corresponding failure rate for likely non-AA beneficiaries was only about 10 per cent. These differences presumably become much smaller as one extends the period of time for passing the bar exam.

The above-cited evidence on the success of AA beneficiaries upon leaving law school is somewhat mixed. One recent and very systematic study, however, yielded strikingly positive conclusions about the post-law-school career paths and achievements of under-represented minority students – most of whom were clearly AA beneficiaries.[3] In their study of students admitted to the University of Michigan (UM) Law School over three decades, Lempert *et al.* (2000a) found that these students entered career paths that were generally quite comparable to those of their White peers. Minority graduates (96 per cent of all the minority students who entered the UM Law School, as noted in Chapter 11, p. 160) were only slightly less successful than White graduates in passing a bar examination. On average, White graduates from the 1970s and the 1980s earned significantly more income in 1996 than minority graduates; but White and minority graduates from the 1990s had virtually the same average earnings.[4] By any standard, the average minority graduate from the UM Law School – no matter what the year of graduation – was doing very well.

Apart from documenting differences between minority and White graduates in terms of various aspects of career success, Lempert *et al.* also carried out multivariate regression analysis in an effort to determine what factors were most important in predicting career success for UM Law School graduates during the whole period under consideration. Their most noteworthy finding was that LSAT scores and undergraduate GPAs, which figure prominently in law-school admissions decisions and correlate strongly with cumulative law-school GPAs, had no relationship to the post-law-school earned income of UM students. Yet law-school GPAs themselves did have some independent effect on earned income. Evidently, something involved in the achievement of high law-school grades, but not associated with the kind of previous achievement reflected in a high undergraduate GPA or a high LSAT, has a positive effect on subsequent earnings. This may well be a behavioral characteristic, involving a student's ability to make a success of his/her law-school experience whatever the level of past achievement – such as the determination to do well in law school, or the ability to relate well to others in the law-school community. Whatever the reason, these findings do indicate that UM Law School admissions officers did a good job in carrying out their AA policies – in identifying candidates with good prospects for successful law-school performance and successful law careers among applicants whose conventional academic qualifications were not as impressive as those of the typical law-school admit.[5]

Analysis of the relationship between college selectivity and student career accomplishments

In Chapter 11, pp. 163–7, I reviewed evidence on the relationship between the selectivity of US colleges and the academic performance of given students, because this is critical to the assessment of several of the claims made by proponents or opponents of affirmative action in higher education. The most important of such claims is that AA beneficiaries are likely to be mismatched at the colleges to which they gain access, so that AA really does a disservice to those whom it claims to help. In this section I will consider the available evidence on the relationship between college selectivity and student career accomplishments. Even if AA beneficiaries struggle with their studies in college, it does not necessarily harm them to be placed in highly competitive academic environments if they succeed in going on to successful careers.

A considerable amount of research by sociologists and economists suggests that college selectivity does have a positive effect on career outcomes, including earnings; see, for example, Wales (1972), Hearn (1984), James (1989), and Pascarella and Terenzini (1991). Several of the studies discussed in previous chapters of this book have also addressed this issue.

Utilizing their representative nationwide sample of male high-school graduates of 1972, Datcher Loury and Garman (1995) analyzed weekly earnings in 1986 for White and Black male students as a function of student SAT scores and college selectivity, controlling for family background (in the same way that they analyzed graduation rates and GPAs, as reported in Chapter 11, pp. 156–63). They summarized their findings, for Whites and for Blacks, as follows: "The earnings results show that overall there were only small, statistically insignificant differences between those with similar individual SAT scores who attended more selective colleges compared to those who attended less elective schools" (Datcher Loury and Garman 1995: 305). For Blacks, this implies that the lower probability of graduation and lower GPA level that Datcher Loury and Garman found to be associated with their attendance at a more selective college is essentially offset by the earnings advantage of attending such a college.[6] As noted earlier, these authors included in their sample students attending historically Black colleges (HBCs), which – in the case of graduation rates – led to a conclusion that is not valid for predominantly White colleges. In the case of earnings, however, the inclusion of HBC students would not appear to bias the results. That is because HBC students, who have relatively low SAT scores and relatively high graduation rates, do not have relatively high earnings.

Bowen and Bok (1998) found that attending a highly selective educational institution gives a significant boost to the career prospects of both Black and White students. They showed that, holding constant initial test scores and grades, college students are not only more likely to graduate but also more likely to earn advanced degrees and more likely to receive high salaries, the more selective is the college they attended – even though they are also more likely to receive lower grades and end up in a lower class rank than they would have done at a less selective college. Bowen and Bok found that SAT scores have relatively little independent effect on college students' earnings later in life; the degree of selectivity of the college they attended is a far more important determinant of earnings.

It is clear from Table 13.1 that for Blacks and Whites, and for males and females, there is a substantial earnings premium associated with attendance at a higher-selectivity college. Moreover, this evidence suggests that attendance at and graduation from an elite institution is especially beneficial for UREG members; though Black college-goers do not end up earning as much on average as White college-goers, the earnings premiums associated with going to a more selective college are generally higher (in percentage terms) for African Americans than for Whites.

As noted earlier, these gross earnings premiums overstate the actual boost in pay due to greater college selectivity, because they do not control for the qualifications of students going to colleges of differing selectivity. Bowen and Bok (1998) attempt to calculate the extent of this kind of selection bias in two ways. First, they compare the earnings of graduates of the colleges in their own sample with a nationwide sample of college graduates with similar talents and abilities. Secondly, they carry out a set of multivariate regressions of the earnings of students in their sample, in order to estimate the effect of college selectivity on higher earnings while controlling for various measures of student ability (Bowen and Bok 1998: 395–402, Tables D.5.2–D.5.5).[7] They conclude from these analyses that the gross earnings premiums shown in Table 13.1 are attributable in considerably greater part to the nature of the college attended than to the qualifications of the individual students attending them.

Bowen and Bok (1998: 128) also cite evidence to support the claim that "the strictly economic payoff from attending a selective college has been even greater for Blacks than for Whites"; they refer to Behrman *et al.* (1996) and Daniel *et al.* (1997), who find that the return on college quality for Black men is several times that for White men. In further research, Daniel *et al.* (2001) find that the return on college quality is roughly three times greater both for Black women and for Black men than it is for their White counterparts. This lends further credence to the proposition that academic credentials are relatively more important for Blacks, if not all UREGs, than for Whites. This differential in pay-offs may well be attributable to the fact that a selective college provides access to networks of contacts with highly placed job-holders, which UREG students are especially likely to be lacking. It may also be that a degree from a selective college helps to overcome stereotypical presumptions that Blacks are likely to be less competent than Whites.

Kane (1998: 445–6) also found a significant positive effect of college selectivity on earnings, which contrasts sharply with his caution about whether there is any positive selectivity effect on graduation rates. For his nationwide representative sample of high-school graduates of 1982, a 100-point increase in college median SAT is associated with a 6 per cent increase in students' earnings in 1991[8] – controlling for student characteristics including family income and parental education, individual SAT score, and high-school GPA. Kane did not find a significant difference between the pay-off to college selectivity for Blacks and Whites. Moreover, unlike the case of graduation rates, he found that in the case of earnings the pay-off to college selectivity is not affected by whether or not HBCs are included in the analysis.

Two more recent studies reached somewhat different conclusions about the positive impact of college selectivity on earnings. Hoxby (1998) made use of several different data sources to estimate the pay-off to a male student from moving up an eight-step ladder of college selectivity categories, for students entering college in four different years from 1960 to 1996. She controlled extensively for differing levels of aptitude and preparation on the part of students attending colleges of differing selectivity, in order to isolate the selectivity effect as fully as possible. She found that across the full spectrum of colleges, there was a significant monetary return to investing in a college of greater selectivity, even taking into account the higher costs of attending more selective colleges, and that the return has been increasing since 1972. The size of the pay-off was especially big for students moving into (or higher up within) the top three ranks of colleges by selectivity and competitiveness.[9]

In an analysis of the 1995 earnings of college students, Dale and Krueger (1999) were able to control more thoroughly than prior researchers for unmeasured differences between students in colleges of differing selectivity. They were able to do so by making use of data on students accepted by elite colleges who chose to attend less selective institutions. They found that, in general, the earnings of these students did not differ significantly from the earnings of those students who chose to attend the elite colleges that had accepted them. Dale and Krueger did find, however, that one group of students – those from low-income families – benefited financially by attending highly selective institutions. This is consistent with studies that have found a larger return to selectivity for UREG students than for White students, because the former are proportionately much likelier to come from low-income families. Indeed, referring to the low-income students who he found benefited from greater selectivity, Krueger observed that "These are the students who come to school really needing the network the most...If you're a Kennedy, your family has access to a network of opportunities that a student from the inner city most likely would not have" (quoted by Gose 2000: A52).

There is no systematic comparative evidence from graduate or professional schools on the effects of institutional selectivity on earnings or other career accomplishments. However, the research on UM Law School graduates done by Lempert *et al.* (2000a), as reported above, pp. 183–4, does suggest that UREG students benefit a great deal from attending that highly elite school. Moreover, the authors report that the UM minority graduates value the prestige of their degree considerably more than do White graduates. This leads them to comment: "It appears that those with reason to feel that their demographic status is likely to hamper their career chances place a special value on the way in which a high-prestige law degree can open up career opportunities" (Lempert *et al.* 2000a: 419).

There are a number of plausible explanations for the boost in pay conferred by attendance at a higher-selectivity college. The most straightforward explanation is that it is due to the higher quality of education that a college with more resources, a more prestigious faculty, and a more highly qualified student body can provide.[10] Yet there is good reason to believe that it is due in considerable part to the fact that higher-selectivity colleges provide students with more social capital – in the form of access to key contacts and networks enabling them to enter better graduate degree programs and/or better jobs. The evidence reviewed here cannot directly distinguish between these competing explanations. Findings that the pay-off to college selectivity is greatest for UREG students, however, suggest that the social capital explanation is an important part of the story. Either way, it seems abundantly clear that there is a significant pay-off to both Black and White students in being able to go to a highly selective and prestigious college.

Questions about the evidence for good performance by AA beneficiaries

The evidence presented in this chapter and the previous one suggests that, on the whole, the beneficiaries of AA have done reasonably well in their academic studies and have done quite well in their subsequent careers. This evidence appears to refute some of the key assertions of critics of affirmative action in admissions – especially the claim that AA harms rather than helps its beneficiaries, because they are mismatched to their academic environment, with the implication that these AA beneficiaries would have been better off going to less competitive academic institutions. Critics of AA, however, have raised a variety of reasons for questioning whether the evidence can really be interpreted as refuting this claim. I will consider each such reason in turn, casting each reason in the form of a skeptical question.

1   *Don't figures on the average performance of UREG students overstate the perfor-mance of AA beneficiaries, since these figures include the performance of academically well-qualified UREG students who would have been admitted without any AA preferences?*

It is true that some of the available data on the academic and the career performance of UREG students are for populations not restricted to AA beneficiaries – for example, much of the data adduced by Bowen and Bok (1998) and all of the data adduced by Lempert *et al.* (2000a) and by Davidson and Lewis (1997). As Thernstrom and Thernstrom wrote in a critical review of Bowen and Bok's work, their figures on the academic performance of Black students are

> deceptively rosy, because [they include] many students who met the regular academic requirements for admission and received no racial pref-erence – about half of the black undergraduates at C&B schools, the authors estimate. If Bowen and Bok had examined the classroom perfor-mance of the half of the black student population that had been preferentially admitted, the picture would doubtless have looked worse.
> (Thernstrom and Thernstrom 1999b: 1605–6)[11]

Sandalow (1999) raised the same kind of objection to Bowen and Bok's work.

In the case of AA policies in the US, there is no way to identify precisely the individual students whose admission hinged on AA preferences; so it is impossible to distinguish these students and compile data for them only. But some researchers – e.g. Bowen and Bok, and Lempert *et al.* – have tried to estimate roughly the numbers of UREG students that would have been admitted to the various degree programs without any AA preferences. The numbers estimated by the latter for the UM Law School are so small that their impact on the overall findings for UREG students is surely negligible.[12]

In the case of the selective colleges in Bowen and Bok's sample, however, the authors estimated (as noted in Chapter 9, pp. 137–8) that the percentage of Black students who would have been admitted without AA preferences is 27 per cent, 48 per cent, and 68 per cent in colleges of the first, second, and third levels of selectivity, respectively.

In an effort to address this concern, Bowen and Bok (1998: 17–23, 42–4) made use of detailed data available from five of the twenty-eight colleges in their sample – all at the first two levels of selectivity[13] – to distinguish between the average entry characteristics of UREG students who would likely have been accepted without AA preferences and those who would likely have been rejected. As a result, they found that the average SAT score of the "retrospectively rejected" group was only a little bit lower than that of the "survivor" group. If they had had the requisite data on colleges at the third level of selectivity, they would in all likelihood have found a greater SAT score differential.[14] But Bowen and Bok (1998: 281, 359; 1999: 1920–21) also undertook to estimate, in a reasonable but fairly rough manner, differentials in the academic and career performance of the retrospectively rejected and the survivor groups for all the colleges in their sample. Remarkably, they found that the accomplishments of the former were not significantly different to those of the latter. This suggests that the failure to focus solely on the AA beneficiaries among Black students did not seriously bias Bowen and Bok's findings.

Yet there is another reason to question the salience of this line of criticism. There is good evidence for the hypothesis that the academic performance of UREG students, in an educational setting dominated by White students, improves when there are more UREG students present.[15] It stands to reason that a single UREG student in an otherwise White classroom or cohort will feel extra stress when he/she is the only representative of the UREG group. The greater the number of UREG students in a given class or cohort, the more this stress will be relieved. If indeed the performance of UREG students does tend to improve when there is a larger proportion of them in the student body, then it would not be that misleading to attribute good performance by students admitted without AA preference to the AA admission policy.[16]

2 *Doesn't the evidence suggest that AA beneficiaries are actually not doing very well in terms of academic performance?*

It is true that the evidence is a good deal more positive for UREG career accomplishments than it is for academic performance. Many of the studies show that UREGs on average get considerably lower grades and graduate at considerably lower class ranks than other students – to an extent that may be underestimated by conflating AA beneficiaries with other UREG students – even where graduation rates are more nearly similar. Thus Bowen and Bok (1998: Ch. 3 and Appendix) found that the academic mismatch claim is

confirmed for class rank and GPA, while it is disconfirmed for college graduation rates as well as for post-college attainment of advanced degrees, annual
earnings, and retrospective satisfaction. Likewise, the available evidence on
medical board exams and bar exams shows that UREG performance is below
average. But should one really expect catch-up by graduation (or very soon
thereafter)? Surely the ultimate proof of the pudding is in long-term career
trajectories.

3   *Isn't the academic performance of AA beneficiaries exaggerated by lenient grading
    or generalized grade inflation?*

Some critics[17] have charged that the academic achievements of minority
students in selective universities, celebrated by Bowen and Bok and others,
overstate the true achievements of these students because many professors and
administrators bend over backwards to help UREG students and to be lenient
toward them in enforcing requirements. It is argued that university administrators responsible for AA preferences in admissions have a strong stake in the
success of the UREG students consequently admitted, and that they therefore
do what they can to ensure that these students remain enrolled and go on to
graduate. It is argued also that many professors are reluctant to fail struggling
UREG students, and that they are therefore more accommodating and/or
more helpful to these students.

There may be some truth to these charges. Before concluding that they imply
overestimation of UREG student academic performance, however, one must
distinguish carefully between two very different kinds of leniency that might be
extended to UREG students. On the one hand, administrators and/or professors
might choose to invest, on average, more time and resources in the education of
UREG students than in that of White students. This can be seen as a laudable
effort to level an otherwise unequal academic terrain. On the other hand,
administrators and/or professors might choose to hold UREG students to
academic standards that are lower than those to which they hold White students.
Such efforts, linked to low expectations for UREG students, are indeed potentially damaging. No doubt there are instances of such behavior on the part of
some administrators and faculty; but here the evidence is at best anecdotal.

What seems more plausible is that academic standards might be lowered to
some degree for all students, not just for UREG students, in a context in
which AA preferences result in the admission of students with – on average –
lower scores on standardized entry examinations. There is in fact considerable
evidence of a trend toward overall grade inflation in US universities.[18] This
does not compromise the comparative evidence on UREG and White
student performance amassed by Bowen and Bok and others. To the extent
that it results from an effort to offset possible failures by students admitted
with lower quantitative academic credentials, however, it would represent a
real cost of policies of AA preferences in admissions – to be weighed against
the various benefits highlighted by the studies under review.

4   *Isn't the post-graduation performance of AA beneficiaries exaggerated by further AA preferences?*

The achievements of UREG students after they have graduated from a college or university will indeed be over-stated to the extent that they benefit from AA preferences at subsequent stages of their careers. But this critique of the evidence of post-graduation UREG student success would appear to be considerably more potent with respect to their entry into graduate and professional schools than with respect to their long-term career achievements.

US graduate and professional schools experience motivations and/or pressures to diversify their student bodies that are similar to those experienced by selective undergraduate colleges. The numbers of UREG students admitted to graduate degree programs – especially highly selective ones like those at the UM Law School – are therefore certainly raised by AA preferences in admissions. Employers in large organizations or firms may also experience motivations and/or pressures to diversify their personnel, though these are surely weaker than those operating in the case of higher educational institutions – both because the legal basis for AA preferences is weaker in employment and because profitability considerations will limit the extent to which firms will take the risk of hiring a UREG candidate with conventional credentials that are lower than those of a non-UREG competitor.

Even when AA preferences have influenced the decisions of a graduate degree program admissions officer or those of an employer, however, such preferences are most unlikely to continue forward throughout a student's progress toward a degree or throughout an employee's long-term employment. In most academic institutions, UREG students are expected to meet the same standards for attaining advanced degrees as their non-UREG peers. And employers are unlikely to retain for long any UREG employees who are not meeting their expectations of performance on the job. With respect to UREG graduates from the UM Law School, Lempert *et al.* (2000a), do cite evidence that large law firms hiring new personnel have sought to increase the ethnic diversity of their ranks. However, they find no evidence that UREG students have had more trouble than Whites in retaining their positions in such firms.

5   *Isn't the apparent positive effect of college selectivity on a given student's academic and career performance due to a failure to include certain important unobservable student characteristics in the analysis?*

As discussed in Chapter 11, pp. 163–7, and above, pp. 184–7, scholars carrying out research on the effect of college selectivity on various indicators of student academic and career performance have been quite sensitive to this concern. They have tried, as far as their data sources have permitted, to hold student characteristics constant in an effort to isolate the selectivity effect. Yet, as Kane (1998: 447) points out, it remains the case that higher educational institutions – especially the more selective ones – ask applicants for more information than is available from sources of systematic quantitative data, and this additional information tends to improve the ability of admissions officers to predict how applicants are likely to perform. One must therefore assume that they admit students who are more competitive in ways not reflected in the entry characteristics – like SAT scores and high-school records – that are typically available to researchers. This means that some part of the effect attributed by most of the research findings to college selectivity is probably due to applicant characteristics; and so the estimated effects of college selectivity have an upward bias.[19] Yet it stretches credibility to assert that this kind of selection bias is likely to account for all of the evidence found by researchers for a positive effect of college selectivity on student performance. If this were the case, it would be hard to explain the intensity with which students (backed by their parents) are determined to get into the most prestigious school they possibly can!

6   *Don't AA beneficiaries derive benefits from going to a more selective university only if that university is a highly elite institution?*

The most comprehensive evidence on the benefits of selectivity for UREG students is provided by Bowen and Bok's (1998) mammoth study of undergraduate students in twenty-eight colleges. They found that Black students within every SAT bracket do better in terms of graduation rates and career achievements (though not in terms of class rank and GPA) by attending more elite colleges. Their C&B sample of colleges is divided into three different selectivity levels, but all of the included colleges are drawn from the most selective and prestigious colleges in the US – surely among the top 10 per cent. These colleges are also among the best endowed, in terms of both their resource base and their faculty quality. This suggests that the positive selectivity effect found by Bowen and Bok may apply mainly to elite colleges and not so much (if at all) to the great majority of colleges further down along the quality spectrum.

There is, however, much evidence that the positive selectivity effect does apply to UREG students throughout the college quality spectrum. First of all, Bowen and Bok themselves provide evidence that graduation rates for Black students even at the lowest-selectivity colleges in the C&B sample are higher than those of White as well as Black students at a representative sample of all four-year colleges (see Table 11.3). Although these figures do not control for students' academic entry qualifications, they are still telling – for one can reasonably presume that White students in the representative sample of colleges are similar in terms of their qualifications to Black students in the lowest-selectivity C&B colleges.[20] Secondly, Kane's (1998) study of a representative sample of high-school graduates of 1982 does suggest that there is a general positive effect – for both UREG and White students – of attending a more selective college. And thirdly, Hoxby's (1998) study of the return to male students of attending a more selective college found a significant pay-off to higher selectivity at all selectivity levels; she also found that the pay-off was higher at the uppermost levels of selectivity.

All of the above evidence applies to undergraduate programs. In the case of graduate and professional schools, there is no systematic evidence (across a broad quality spectrum) that has any bearing on the benefits to UREG students of attending more selective institutions. There is, to be sure, a strong presumption – and at least anecdotal evidence – that attending a highly selective and elite professional school provides UREG graduates with a considerable career boost.[21] But the jury is still out on whether such a positive selectivity effect applies also to less elite institutions.

14 Further evidence on the effects of affirmative action in US universities

The evidence from the US that I have discussed in Chapters 9, 11, and 13 is relevant to claims made by many of the consequentialist arguments for and against positive discrimination in admission policies, but there is yet more evidence to be considered. In this chapter I examine additional evidence relevant to several specific claims about the benefits or costs of affirmative action (AA) in US universities. First I consider evidence on whether certain jobs are better performed when the job-holder is of under-represented ethnic group (UREG) status (claim 2.4). Then I look at evidence on the contributions of unremunerated service to deserving communities on the part of UREG graduates (claim 2.5). I go on to examine whether the available evidence supports the argument (argument 4) that greater ethnic diversity in the composition of students has a positive impact on educational outcomes. Finally, I address evidence bearing on the argument (argument 12) that a system of AA preferences can cause the achievements of UREG students and graduates to be devalued.

UREG status and job performance

There are two circumstances in which it is plausible to suggest that a job is likely to be done better if, other things being equal, it is done by someone belonging to a particular ethnic group. First, if the job involves providing a service to a clientele that is predominantly of a certain ethnicity, then a service provider of the same ethnicity may well be able to deliver more service, or better quality service, than an otherwise similar person because he/she is more oriented to and familiar with the cultural environment of his/her clients; or, at least, he/she is perceived as being more sensitive to their needs. Secondly, if the job involves working with a multicultural set of co-workers, and/or serving a multicultural clientele, then a job-holder from a UREG might work more effectively than an otherwise similar person from the majority group because he/she is much more likely to have had the experience of operating in a culturally heterogeneous environment.

There is little evidence on the second of the above claims, but a considerable variety of evidence supports the first claim. Many educators concerned with the educational progress of UREG children have observed that there are significant educational benefits to be had from the presence in a classroom of a teacher of the same ethnicity as the students.[1] In many US cities, police departments have been striving to hire more UREG officers in order to deal more effectively with predominantly UREG communities. And such personal services as haircuts, manicures, etc., are provided almost exclusively by and to members of the same ethnic community.

A substantial body of research has documented a link between the training of UREG doctors and both the quantity and the quality of health care services delivered to the corresponding UREG communities.[2] Penn (1986) found that doctors who had entered the University of California at San Diego Medical School as "special admits" see more patients per day and are more likely to have a poor clientele than are their classmates. Keith *et al.* (1987) found that UREG (and mostly preferential) admits were more likely to provide medical services to UREG communities. Komaromy *et al.* (1997) found that all physicians tend to care primarily for patients of their own race and ethnicity, but that this is especially true for Black and Hispanic-American physicians. According to the Association of American Medical Colleges (1995), under-represented minority physicians are more likely than White physicians to practice in deprived areas and to serve patients who are Medicaid recipients (who are disproportionately of UREG "race" or ethnicity themselves). Holzer and Neumark concluded in a survey article that

> Research on medical education finds evidence that minority students…perform less well in school, and are less likely to achieve high levels of expertise. At the same time, this research also suggests that these students are ultimately more likely to serve minority patients, which may provide a positive externality that helps offset the lower qualifications or skill levels that these students attain.
>
> (Holzer and Neumark 2000: 553)

Considerably less empirical research has been done on the social benefits of educating UREG lawyers as compared to the research done on UREG doctors. However, Lempert *et al.* (2000a: 435–40) did document among University of Michigan (UM) Law School graduates a clear tendency for under-represented minority lawyers to serve more low-income clients than White lawyers, and an even more pronounced tendency for minority lawyers to serve clients of the same ethnicity. As they observe:

> From one point of view, the strong relationship between the ethnicity of minority lawyers and the ethnicity of their clients is an aspect of the success of Michigan's commitment to train more minority lawyers…From another point of view, the implications of the race-linked pattern of client relationships are a discouraging reminder of the continuing deep significance of race in personal and professional relationships in American society.
>
> (Lempert *et al.* 2000a: 439–40)

Voluntary service contributions to deserving communities

It is often claimed that AA generates benefits in the form of greater service, in quantitative and/or qualitative terms, to communities most in need. For the same reason that professionals are disproportionately likely to provide their professional services to clients of their own ethnicity, it is also likely that they will disproportionately make voluntary service contributions to communities of their own ethnicity. Since the most needy communities are most often communities populated predominantly by UREG members, it stands to reason that professionals of the ethnicities targeted by AA policies will be the most likely to make voluntary service contributions to such communities.

This expectation is also confirmed by the somewhat limited evidence available. The Association of American Medical Colleges (1996) reported that under-represented minority students were more likely to participate in public health screening clinics, to deliver medical services to under-served populations outside of clinical rotations, and to volunteer to educate high-school and college students about science and medicine. Lempert *et al.* (2000a: 453–8) found that minority graduates of the UM Law School were somewhat more likely than White graduates to engage in such community-oriented service activities as pro bono legal work on behalf of the poor, service (without pay) on the board of non-profit organizations, and the mentoring of younger attorneys.

Bowen and Bok (1998: Ch. 6) included in their survey instrument questions about various kinds of contributions to community and public life that go beyond fulfilling one's immediate job responsibilities – such as participating in volunteer civic and social-service activities, assuming leadership roles in public and community organizations, and serving as mentors and/or role models for less advantaged community members. In general they found that the African Americans in their sample were significantly more likely to get involved in these kinds of activities and efforts than the Whites – possibly because, as members of a UREG, they are more conscious of their own relatively privileged position and have a correspondingly greater sense of responsibility toward those who remain less fortunate.

The kind of comparative evidence on UREG and White job performance and service contributions reviewed in this and the preceding section does not directly address the most relevant question, which is: how much more (in quantity and quality) did UREG graduates contribute in the way of relevant services than they would have if they had not benefited from AA?[3] In the absence of AA, undergraduate UREG students would have been redistributed downward in the selectivity hierarchy of universities. One can get a sense of what this would imply for service contributions by looking at data on such contributions that Bowen and Bok (1998: 156–60) present separately for their sample of colleges and for a nationwide control group. This evidence shows that Black graduates from selective colleges do not have much higher rates of service contributions than Black graduates from other colleges. One might still make a case, however, that the effectiveness of service contributions by UREG graduates is greater the more selective is the college they attended, on the grounds that in more selective colleges they will receive better training and better credentials with which to make their contributions.[4] Certainly this case can be made for the quality of job performance by AA beneficiaries.

At the graduate level, AA significantly increases the numbers of UREG students in addition to redistributing them upward. Comparisons of job performance and voluntary service contributions, as between UREG and White graduates, are therefore much more indicative of differences between what would happen with AA and without AA than is the case at the under-graduate level.

Some critics have argued that voluntary service contributions, however laudable they may be, are at best irrelevant to professional accomplishment and at worst a form of compensation for inadequacy in one's main line of work.[5] This perspective seems a bit too cynical. Even to the extent that it is true, it does not preclude a positive evaluation of contributions made by AA beneficiaries beyond their main job. The fact that UREG members do contribute significant unremunerated services to their communities indicates that – contrary to the jaundiced view of some critics – they are redistributing some of the benefits of their access to higher education rather than allowing the lure of personal gain to remove any sense of obligation to others.

Ethnic diversity and educational outcomes

College and university administrators in the US have often articulated the view that greater ethnic diversity of the student body enriches the educational environment and thereby enhances the educational experience of all students, both at the undergraduate and at the graduate level. Professional school educators have stressed, in particular, the way in which UREG students can improve the competence of their White classmates to work with people of UREG status. Until recently, however, there was very little empirical evidence to support or to reject the hypothesis that ethnic diversity has positive educational consequences.

In one of the earliest studies to address the effects of student ethnic diversity, Deppe (1989) investigated the relationship between the percentage of non-white students in the student body on different campuses and the average degree of "social concern" of all students. Social concern was defined as the importance placed by students on a series of possible goals or values – namely influencing political structure, influencing social values, helping others who are in difficulty, developing a meaningful philosophy of life, participating in community action, and helping to promote inter-racial understanding. Deppe did not find evidence of a significant relationship between ethnic diversity and the importance students placed on these goals. Astin (1993) also found no significant cross-campus relationship between the ethnic diversity of the student body and a variety of educational and value outcomes. However, Astin did find that socializing with students from different ethnic groups has a strong positive effect on "cultural awareness" and commitment to promoting inter-ethnic understanding. In a longitudinal study using nationwide student survey data, Chang (2001) found that greater inter-racial student interaction is positively related to several elements of a good educational experience, such as social and intellectual self-confidence.

None of the above studies addressed directly the extent to which student diversity affects the learning of academic subjects, as distinct from the development of broader cultural awareness, greater social concern, or more self-confidence as a student. This is not surprising, for it is inherently a very difficult task. Simply measuring academic learning outcomes is a challenge; quantitative indicators such as grades and standardized tests have well-known weaknesses as measures of what, or how well, a student has learned. It is even more challenging to isolate in a systematic way the impact of any one factor – such as ethnic diversity – on the learning process. Two of the studies cited frequently in the preceding chapters for their relevant evidence on the consequences of AA did not attempt to assess comprehensively the contribution of ethnic diversity to learning; they did, however, analyze survey responses to several questions relating to inter-ethnic interactions.[6]

Bowen and Bok (1998: Ch. 8) reported that 57 per cent of the Blacks and 46 per cent of the Whites in their cohort of selective college students entering in 1976 felt that their college experience contributed significantly to their "ability to work effectively and get along with people from different races." These percentages rose to 70 per cent of Blacks and 63 per cent of Whites in the entering cohort of 1989, who were in college when UREGs were somewhat better represented in the student body. Bowen and Bok also reported that 56 per cent of the White students in the 1989 entering cohort knew well two or more African-American students (though the latter constitute only 7 per cent of the overall student population), and that 88 per cent of the African-American students in this cohort knew well two or more White students (80 per cent of the student population). Interestingly, these percentages are higher the higher the level of selectivity of the college. Finally, Bowen and Bok reported the views of students themselves on the value of ethnic diversity on campus. Most of the student respondents – both Black and White – applauded their college's emphasis on diversity; some thought that even more such emphasis was needed.

Lempert *et al.* (2000a: 413–14, 494) also relied on self-reported reflections from the graduates in their UM Law School survey sample for evidence on the benefits of ethnic diversity. They reported that about 60 per cent of the under-represented minority students and about 35 per cent of the White students believed that their learning experience in law-school classrooms benefited significantly from the ethnic diversity of their peers. Although the percentage of the former sharing this view remained about the same over all three decades, the percentage of Whites holding this view increased from decade to decade – starting at 25 per cent in the 1970s and rising to 50 per cent in the 1990s. During this time the proportion of under-represented minority students in law-school cohorts also increased significantly, from roughly 7.5 per cent in the 1970s to roughly 15 per cent in the 1990s.

The evidence reported by Bowen and Bok and Lempert *et al.* has obvious limitations. First, it does not address the effect of greater ethnic diversity on the learning process in a narrowly construed academic and intellectual sense. The Bowen and Bok study does provide some evidence that the enrollment of greater numbers of UREG students has increased the quantity and quality of inter-ethnic interactions; and both studies present evidence that greater diversity has improved learning in a broader civic sense. Yet these findings are somewhat suspect, because they are based solely on reports by the respondents themselves. Moreover, it is far from clear that the respondents' views would have been any different in the absence of AA-generated diversity on campus. Still, the increase over time in the percentage of UREG students on elite university campuses, and the high and growing percentage of all students who believe that such diversity has a positive effect, is suggestive. It provides some modest support for the hypothesis that greater ethnic diversity leads to better inter-cultural relations, as distinct from educational performance as conventionally understood. The evidence that Bowen and Bok and Lempert *et al.* provide is not sufficient to establish a clear causal link (positive or negative) from diversity to other outcomes. However, their evidence does serve at least to diminish the import of a frequently voiced criticism of AA preferences, to the effect that they result in a high degree of UREG self-segregation on university campuses and thereby exacerbate rather than alleviate inter-ethnic tensions.

The state of the evidence on the educational effects of ethnic diversity in higher education has recently been much enhanced by the work of Patricia Gurin, together with some of her colleagues at the University of Michigan, published in various forms between 1999 and 2002.[7] Gurin's research on the way in which ethnic diversity has affected educational outcomes, primarily among UM undergraduates, constitutes by far the most systematic and thoroughgoing scholarly work on this subject.

The University of Michigan has pursued for several decades a policy of granting substantial admission preferences to members of UREGs; for that reason it has achieved one of the most ethnically diverse student populations among major public universities in the country. This is no doubt also the reason that its admission policies were targeted by two prominent lawsuits, filed in 1997 and ruled on by the US Supreme Court in 2003.[8] Gurin's research was first presented as an expert witness report in favor of AA in the context of the lawsuits. As such, it drew sharp criticism in two lengthy reports sponsored by organizations opposed to AA, which were in turn rebutted by Gurin and others. The critical reports as well the rebuttals (all of which will be addressed below) have formed the basis of further contributions to the court cases. The most accessible and up-to-date presentation of Gurin's research methods and findings is in the article by Gurin *et al.* (2002).

Gurin made use of three different sources of data: the UCLA-based Cooperative Institutional Research Program (CIRP) national database on college students and educational outcomes, for the years 1985–9, as well as two UM databases – one from a study of UM undergraduate students and the other from a study of the UM Intergroup Relations, Community, and Conflict Program. She developed a two-stage model of the impact of ethnic diversity on educational outcomes. In the first stage, "structural diversity" – defined as the degree to which students of color are represented in the student body – is seen as influencing the extent of student "campus diversity experiences"; in the second stage these diversity experiences are seen as influencing educational outcomes. She identifies four types of diversity experience: taking an ethnic studies course (where classes are most likely to be highly diverse); "informal interactional diversity" (outside the classroom); the amount of inter-ethnic socializing; and the quality of campus inter-ethnic interactions. And she is concerned with three kinds of educational outcomes: "learning outcomes"; "democracy outcomes"; and "living and working in a diverse society." The latter two outcomes involve the broader kind of learning associated with better inter-cultural understanding and social concern. The first outcome involves various abilities and skills related to growth in active thinking processes, engagement in and motivation for learning, and general intellectual and academic accomplishment.

In her empirical analysis, Gurin found first, utilizing cross-college CIRP data, that the structural diversity of campuses (excluding historically Black and junior colleges) does have a statistically significant effect on each of the four kinds of "campus diversity experience" she identified. She then made use of data from the UM databases as well as CIRP to analyze the impact of each kind of diversity experience on each kind of educational outcome. The three kinds of outcomes were measured by student gains with respect to a set of indicators of learning, commitment to democracy, and ability to live and work in a diverse society, respectively. These gains were self-assessed and self-reported by students (distinguished by ethnic group) responding to survey questions. In the case of questions addressed to learning outcomes, the indicators involved various abilities and skills related to growth in active thinking processes, engagement in and motivation for learning, and general intellectual and academic accomplishment. Carrying out regressions to test the validity of the various second-stage relationships between diversity experiences and educational outcomes, Gurin found that many were indeed positive and significant – more so for White students than for Blacks or Hispanic Americans.

Gurin's research was subject to sharp critiques by Wood and Sherman (2001) and by Lerner and Nagai (2001), on grounds of both methodology and data. The most important methodological point of criticism was aimed at Gurin's separate testing of each stage of her two-stage model. The critics argued that she should have directly tested the relationship between ethnic diversity and educational outcomes across different colleges. They expressed confidence that if she had done so, she would have found no significant cross-college association between campus diversity and educational outcomes – as did Astin (1993), who also made use of the CIRP database. Among a variety of objections to Gurin's data, the critics complained that her indicators of educational outcomes were inadequate. They were skeptical of the importance of two of Gurin's three categories of desirable outcomes – commitment to democracy, and ability to live and work in a diverse society – and they also felt that some of the indicators of these outcomes reflected a politically liberal perspective rather than an objective capability. With respect to the third educational outcome – learning – they objected to the fact that Gurin's indicators included only one "hard" variable, namely grade-point average (GPA), and that that variable was available only for tests using the CIRP database.

Gurin's (2001a, 2001b) response to the methodological criticism was compelling; and it was supported also by other scholars of higher education – e.g. Thomas and Shavelson (2001). As Gurin pointed out, structural diversity per se is necessary, but not sufficient, to generate educational outcome benefits. To achieve such benefits, educational institutions must make good use of the structural diversity by fostering inter-group interactions in appropriate settings – both inside and outside the classroom. The relevant inter-group interactions are precisely what Gurin sought to measure by her "campus diversity experience" variables, which are the essential intermediate variables in her model between structural diversity and the various educational outcomes. One would not expect to find a simple cross-college correlation between the degree of ethnic diversity and the extent of desirable educational outcomes, for those outcomes would not be achievable even on a highly diverse campus if the appropriate inter-group interactions were not fostered.

Gurin rejected the charge that two of her three categories of educational outcome variables were questionable as goals of a higher educational institution. She noted, as have countless higher educational administrators, that the democracy and multicultural ability outcomes are legitimate and desirable objectives of a university – especially a public one like the University of Michigan – which should and does have the civic mission of graduating students who will become well-educated leaders and active participants in an increasingly diverse democratic nation. In response to the charge of using "soft" measures of learning outcomes, she asserted that one must distinguish real learning from "knowledge stuffing." She argued that soft variables – such as self-reported "active thinking," "intellectual engagement," and "perspective taking" – are the best kind of indicators of the extent of a student's true learning. Grades, on the other hand, are highly problematic as measures of learning because they do not measure the amount that a student has actually learned from a course (as opposed to the student's absolute level of knowledge at the end of the course), and they are not standardized across courses, majors, or institutions.

Gurin's insistence on the relevance of the educational goals of developing in students a commitment to democracy and an ability to work effectively in a diverse society is probably widely shared, though some believe that a higher educational institution should focus exclusively on academic goals. Measurement of progress toward achievement of these broader educational goals, however, is very difficult because of their highly qualitative nature; so the results of any research in this area are bound to be contested. Gurin's concentration on "soft" measures of learning outcomes will probably not meet with widespread approval, if only because so much research on educational outcomes has focused on quantitative measures like the GPA. Even those who believe that she is right in her identification of what is important in true learning may find reason to question her measures of progress in this direction, for one is dealing here again with qualitative concepts that are very difficult to pin down.

In sum, Gurin's research represents a major step forward in the attempt to analyze the way in which ethnic diversity affects various educational outcomes; and it can successfully withstand the kind of methodological criticism levied at it by its critics. Because of the great difficulty of measuring (undoubtedly important) qualitative phenomena, however, her findings can at most be considered highly suggestive; more work will need to be done in this area before results of this kind can be expected to gain broad acceptance.

Just before the US Supreme Court heard oral arguments in the UM admissions lawsuits (in April 2003), a new study of the effects of racial/ethnic diversity on educational outcomes was published and – because of the timing – gained much media attention. In a journal article as well as in a more popular form, Rothman *et al.* (2003a, 2003b) reported on survey research that appeared to show that greater diversity on college campuses was associated with lower levels of educational quality and higher levels of inter-racial tension. Rothman *et al.* surveyed administrators, professors, and students at 140 US colleges regarding their perceptions of the quality of the educational experience offered by their college and of the racial climate on campus. They found that perceptions of educational quality tended to be lower, and (to a less significant extent) perceptions of ethnic tensions tended to be higher, the greater was the proportion of Blacks in the college's student body – controlling for some other potential causal factors that could have generated these correlations. The lead author of the study, Stanley Rothman, did not claim that it presented evidence strong enough to support the contention that greater ethnic diversity actually worsened educational quality or heightened inter-racial conflict; but he did suggest that it called into serious question claims that greater ethnic diversity improves the education and racial milieu at US colleges and universities.

The research of Rothman *et al.* is itself, of course, not beyond challenge. Among other things, it is vulnerable to the methodological point stressed by Gurin (in response to the earlier criticism of her work) that "structural diversity" – as measured simply by the ethnic composition of the student body – is by itself insufficient to generate positive outcomes from ethnic diversity. Moreover, Rothman *et al.* did not address educational benefits in the form of positive "democracy outcomes" and greater capacity for "living and working in a diverse society," which for Gurin (and others) are just as important as positive "learning outcomes."

Responding to a charge by Lerner and Nagai (2001) that AA policies tend to aggravate inter-ethnic hostility on campus, Gurin (2001c) drew on a good deal of counter-evidence from her research utilizing the two UM databases. Survey results from the UM student study showed that only a very small proportion of students from all ethnic groups reported having had a significant number of "tense, somewhat hostile interactions" or "guarded, cautious interactions" with students of differing race or ethnicity. Moreover, the UM student study revealed that the students who had had the most experience with diverse peers – through classes, informal relationships, multicultural events, and inter-group dialogues – expressed the strongest sense of commonality and understanding with students of diverse backgrounds. Finally, from her analysis of the UM Intergroup Relations, Community, and Conflict Program, Gurin confirmed the social-psychological hypothesis that inter-group interactions in a context of small groups and close personal relations promote a sense of commonality and greater understanding of diverse others. These findings lend strong support to the contention that one cannot safely generalize about the impact of greater ethnic diversity on inter-ethnic relations; whether these are likely to be positive or negative depends at least as much on the campus context ("diversity experiences") as it does on the composition of the student body ("structural diversity").

Devaluation of the achievements of UREG students

There is plenty of anecdotal evidence – notably in the writings of African-American intellectuals opposed to or ambivalent about AA[9] – that AA results in the devaluation of achievements of UREG members, because people are likely to assume that these achievements are due at least in part to AA preferences rather than solely to true ability and competence. Since it is often impossible to know precisely who has actually benefited from AA preferences, this assumption can easily taint the achievements of UREG members whether or not they were in fact AA beneficiaries. The resulting stigmatization of those who are successful makes it all the more difficult to overcome damaging negative stereotypes about all members of UREGs targeted for AA preferences.

Non-UREG students – and some faculty as well – at relatively selective US universities have been heard from time to time to complain that UREG students, presumed to be AA beneficiaries, "do not belong on campus." Likewise, one hears complaints that faculty in such institutions tend to hold low expectations for such students and do not challenge them to do their best work.[10] Anecdotal evidence and hearsay along similar lines is not uncommon with respect to UREG students at Indian higher educational institutions.

There is only a limited amount of systematic evidence – all from the US – in support of the above claims. Studies by Heilman *et al.* (1992), in the context of employment, and Garcia *et al.* (1981), in a university setting, confirm that AA programs can stigmatize their perceived beneficiaries by devaluing their accomplishments. Nickens and Cohen (1996: 572–4), discussing the way in which AA can thus be a double-edged sword, note that "[A]ccounts of early minority pioneers…make it clear that they suffered from the hostility of some of their classmates and teachers, and all too often suffered alone." But they go on to opine that

> most of those pioneers, and their contemporary counterparts, would regard questions about their legitimacy to be there as a small price to pay for increasing opportunities available to UREG students, and for increasing the number of young Americans who are educated on campuses that are racially and ethnically diverse.

Bowen and Bok (1998: 193–201) touched on the concern about how AA might devalue the achievements of UREG students in the context of a discussion of how graduates in their survey sample look back at their college experiences. They found that a substantial majority of African-American respondents were very satisfied with their college experience (the percentage was higher the more selective the college). Although the levels of satisfaction reported by Blacks were not quite as high as those reported by Whites, Blacks were more inclined than Whites to credit their undergraduate experience with helping them learn skills crucial for their subsequent careers. Bowen and Bok concluded that the vast majority of Black college-goers do not think that they have been harmed by stigmatization at college and would certainly not give up preferences in admissions to selective colleges in order to reduce the degree of stigmatization they might experience in college or thereafter. But this conclusion, while plausible, is not well grounded in the survey evidence gathered. As Thernstrom and Thernstrom (1999b: 1609) point out in their critique of Bowen and Bok's work, "none of the items in the C&B survey was designed to tap personal feelings of stigmatization…Students can say, 'Yes, we are pleased we had the opportunity to attend Kenyon College,' while at the same time harboring doubts about their own academic abilities."

Hard evidence on how significant is the devaluation of the achievements of UREG students, in an environment of AA preferences, remains to be collected. What one can say with some assurance is that the phenomenon is a real one, and that it does impose a cost on its victims. At the same time, it seems unlikely that many AA beneficiaries would be prepared to give up the advantages they gain from AA in order to avoid this kind of cost.

15 Review of the findings on the consequences of positive discrimination policies in university admissions

In the preceding six chapters I have reviewed much of the evidence available in the US and India that has a bearing on the consequences of positive discrimination (PD) policies in admissions to higher educational institutions. In this chapter I summarize this evidence, organizing it so as to shed light on the extent to which the various claims of PD benefits and costs have actually been validated in the experience of the US and India with PD policies. Then I draw on the summarized evidence, as well as a priori reasoning, to draw conclusions about the consequences of PD policies in admissions to higher educational institutions.

Summary of the evidence

I begin with estimates of the overall number and the average academic qualifications of PD beneficiaries in each country. Then I go on to summarize the evidence that has a bearing on each of the claims of benefits and costs made by proponents and critics of PD policies in higher educational admissions, starting with claims for which the evidence is relatively abundant and then moving on to claims for which evidence is increasingly difficult to obtain.[1] At the end of each relevant paragraph – or section thereof – in which evidence is summarized, I note (in parentheses) in which chapters and pages of this book a detailed discussion of the evidence can be found.

Estimates of the total number of PD beneficiaries

In the US, the most important effect of affirmative action (AA) policies in university admissions at the undergraduate/college level is to redistribute under-represented ethnic group (UREG) students upward and non-UREG students downward across the selectivity spectrum of universities, thereby increasing UREG enrollments in the more selective and higher-quality colleges. At the graduate and professional level, AA policies not only redistribute students in this way; they also add significantly to the total number of UREG students enrolling in degree programs. In the late 1990s, UREG members – i.e. African Americans, Hispanic Americans, and Native

Americans – constituted roughly 25 per cent of the total US population. By 1997, UREG student enrollment at the undergraduate level had reached about 80 per cent of their population share, while UREG student enrollment at the graduate and professional level had reached about 50 per cent of this population share; these representation rates were highest for Native Americans, followed by African Americans, and then by Hispanic Americans. I estimate that US AA policies in the 1990s increased overall UREG enroll-ment in selective colleges by roughly 50,000 – raising the UREG proportion from about 6 per cent to about 10 per cent of total selective college enroll-ment.[2] I estimate, very roughly, that AA policies also increased overall UREG enrollment in highly competitive graduate and professional schools by about 15,000. (See Chapter 9, pp. 134–40.)

In the Indian case, reservation policies at all levels of higher education both redistribute UREG students upward in the university quality hierarchy and attract into universities significant numbers of UREG students who would not otherwise pursue higher education. By the late 1990s, Scheduled Caste (SC) and Scheduled Tribe (ST) students together accounted for roughly 10 per cent of higher educational enrollment; SC students were represented at a rate of about one-half of their population share of 16 per cent and ST students at a rate of about one-third of their population share 8 per cent. My very rough estimate is that reservation policies enabled about one-half of the 700,000 SC and ST students attending Indian universities in the late 1990s either to gain access to a relatively desirable institution or program, rather than settle for a relatively mediocre one, or to enroll in a university at all, rather than abandon any possibility of pursuing higher education. (See Chapter 10, pp. 146–51.)

Academic qualifications of PD beneficiaries

An inevitable consequence of the application of a PD policy in university admissions is that conventional measures of the academic qualifications of incoming students (like standardized test scores) will be lower for PD benefi-ciaries than for other admitted students – and indeed lower than those of the non-UREG applicants displaced by PD. Where PD policies are applied, entry test scores are also almost certain to be lower for all UREG students than for all non-UREG students. But PD policies are by no means the only factors responsible for the full extent of the differentials observed on average between UREG and non-UREG students; even in the absence of PD, one would expect there to be some such differentials because UREG students – if only for socio-economic reasons – are vastly under-represented in the uppermost reaches of test-score frequency distributions.

In the US case, the evidence at the undergraduate level suggests that AA policies account for a relatively small fraction of the widely discussed differen-tials between average entry test scores of UREG and non-UREG students.[3] Much of the magnitude of these differentials can be attributed not only to differences in the shape of the respective frequency distributions but also to the fact that test scores are only one of many admissions criteria, and some of the other relevant criteria are not highly correlated with test scores. At the graduate level, however, AA policies appear likely to have contributed more to the differentials between average entry test scores of UREG and non-UREG students.

In the Indian case, reservation policies clearly account for a large fraction of the magnitude of average test-score differentials, because they are designed explicitly to admit UREG students whose entry test scores are not high enough for them to gain admission in a general competition with other applicants. Moreover, Indian PD beneficiaries tend to enter university programs with a greater handicap in lower academic qualifications – and correspondingly poorer preparation for university studies – than is the case in the US. There is evidence in both the US and India, however, that the entry test-score gap between UREG and non-UREG students has been narrowing over the past few decades. In each country this may well be due to the fact that a growing proportion of PD beneficiaries are the children of parents who have been able to improve their own educational and socio-economic status by virtue of PD policies in education and/or employment. (See Chapter 9, pp. 140–3, and Chapter 10, pp. 151–3.)

Costs from snowballing demands for group preferences (claim 8.3)

The comparative history of the development of PD policies makes clear that demands for group preferences have had a strong tendency to snowball in independent India, since such preferences for "backward" groups were given a constitutional basis in 1950. SC and ST students were granted reservations in higher educational institutions at both the national and the state levels from the early 1950s, and in subsequent decades SC and ST reserved seats were in fact implemented in most such institutions. Reserved seats for students from certain "Other Backward Classes" (OBCs) were also established by some states in the early 1950s. Since then, in response to growing demands from other OBC groups, the scope of reserved seats for OBC students at educational institutions at the state level has been increasing – although the Mandal Commission recommendations for OBC reservations at the national level are being implemented only in the employment sphere. (See Chapter 1.)

By comparison with India, the snowballing of demands for preferences has been remarkably limited in the US, in higher educational admissions as well as in other spheres. It is true that the introduction of AA admission policies favoring African Americans, by many colleges and universities in the 1960s, was followed by the implementation of similar policies favoring Hispanic Americans and Native Americans in the early 1970s – in response to political pressure from the latter groups. Since then, however, there has hardly been a call from any other under-represented or disadvantaged ethnic group for a further widening of the boundaries of eligibility for affirmative action. (See Chapter 1.)

Costs from poor academic performance and frequent failure of PD beneficiaries to graduate with a degree (claim 10.1)

There is a great deal of evidence from the US that UREG students do not do as well (on average) as non-UREG students in terms of conventional measures of academic performance at higher educational institutions – both at the undergraduate and at the graduate levels. Since AA beneficiaries among the UREG students have entering academic credentials that are lower than those of other UREG students, their academic performance is almost certainly inferior (on average) to that of the non-beneficiary UREG students. It follows that the gap in academic performance between AA beneficiaries and AA non-beneficiaries is greater than that between UREG and non-UREG students.

The fact that AA beneficiaries perform relatively poorly, however, does not necessarily mean that they fail to meet acceptable absolute standards of academic performance. Indeed, the evidence suggests that PD beneficiaries, while tending to cluster in the lower ranks of their class cohorts according to grade-point average (GPA), nonetheless most often successfully complete their degree programs. Graduation rates of UREG students in US selective colleges are about 10 per cent lower than those of their non-UREG peers; and graduation rates of PD beneficiaries among the UREG students are no doubt somewhat lower still. But a clear majority of both categories of UREG students at selective colleges do graduate – and at rates much higher than those of UREG students at non-selective colleges. The graduation rates of UREG students at US professional schools are only slightly lower than those of their non-UREG peers; and there is evidence that, among UREG students, graduation rates for AA beneficiaries are no different than they are for non-beneficiaries. (See Chapter 11, pp. 156–63.)

The evidence available from India shows that the average academic performance of SC and ST students (almost all of whom are beneficiaries of reserved seats) is distinctly worse than that of other students, and that their graduation rates too are considerably lower than those of other students. In both these respects, Indian PD beneficiaries do not do as well as US beneficiaries. This is hardly surprising, in view of the fact that the gaps in entering test scores and academic preparation – as well as the obstacles to pursuing a degree program to completion – are significantly greater for SC and ST students in India than for UREG students in the US. It appears, however, that the differential between the graduation rates of SC/ST students and those of other students is not so great in India's elite higher educational institutions – mainly because SC and ST students in these institutions are more likely to remain in school for an extra year or more in order ultimately to meet the requirements for earning a degree. There is also some evidence from relatively selective institutions that graduation rates for SC and ST students have been improving over time, as the entering qualifications of these students have risen and as the institutions themselves have found ways to improve the students' learning environment. (See Chapter 12, pp. 168–72.)

We may conclude that the claim of poor academic performance by PD beneficiaries is validated a good deal more strongly in India than in the US. In both countries the performance of PD beneficiaries is clearly poorer than that of non-beneficiaries; but it is not so clear that it is poor by absolute standards. The graduation rates of PD beneficiaries in selective US universities and in elite Indian institutions do not lag much behind those of other students; and there is evidence that the differential has been declining over time.

Benefits/costs from an increase/decrease in the average academic quality of students enrolled in selective universities (claim 3.1 vs. claim 9.1)

For a PD policy to have succeeded in improving the accuracy with which applicant qualifications are assessed, PD beneficiaries must perform at least as well as – indeed slightly better than – those applicants displaced by PD would have done. The fact that UREG students do significantly worse in terms of conventional academic performance indicators than non-UREG students (as shown by the evidence discussed under the previous heading) suggests that neither in the US nor in India has this demanding "catch-up" level of academic performance been achieved by PD beneficiaries. It is true that performance comparisons between all UREG students and all non-UREG students may not accurately reflect the performance gap between "retrospectively rejected" and "retrospectively admitted" students, because the latter sub-groups are likely to be concentrated at the lower end of their respective groups in terms of academic performance. However, there is good reason to believe that even the latter gap remains significant in both countries.

In the US, studies of undergraduate academic performance indicate that lower GPAs for Black students (on average) are not explainable simply in terms of their lower average entry test scores; Black students tend to "underperform" academically not only relative to other students but also relative to what would be predicted on the basis of their own average Scholastic Aptitude (or Assessment) Test (SAT) scores. This suggests that the true potential of PD beneficiaries for good academic performance is not undervalued by the conventional qualification indicators, and that UREG students admitted retrospectively with lower SAT scores than the non-UREG applicants they displace will on average perform less well. (See Chapter 11, pp. 160–3.) No such evidence is available from India; but the fact that SC and ST beneficiaries of reserved seats displace other applicants with significantly higher entering test scores – and evidence shows that academic performance does correlate somewhat with entering test scores – suggests that the academic performance of PD beneficiaries is generally lower than that of the retrospectively admitted applicants as well as that of all non-UREG students. (See Chapter 12, pp. 168–72.)

The gap in performance between UREG and non-UREG students is considerably less in post-university career achievements than in within-university conventionally measured academic performance; and the same is almost surely true as between the retrospectively rejected and retrospectively admitted subsets of these students. (See Chapter 12, pp. 175–8, and Chapter 13, pp. 179–84.) This suggests either that UREG catch-up progresses further after university studies or that conventional within-university performance measures understate what UREG students are actually gaining from higher education. One should therefore be cautious in relying on conventional performance indicators. It seems safe to conclude, nonetheless, that the evidence from both the US and India rejects claim 3.1 and supports claim 9.1 – to the effect that PD policies lower the average academic quality of students admitted to selective universities.

Costs from exacerbation of inequalities among UREG members and redistribution of opportunities from less well-off to better-off UREG members (claims 7.1 and 7.2)

There is plenty of evidence that the typical Black beneficiary of affirmative action at a highly selective US college is much better off than most other Blacks; and the same is no doubt true of Hispanic Americans and Native Americans. There is also some evidence from selective schools suggesting that the marginal Black applicants admitted tend to be less well-off than the marginal White applicants rejected. (See Chapter 9, pp. 143–45.) Evidence from India leaves little doubt that the vast majority of SC and ST beneficiaries of India's reservation policies in university admissions do indeed come from a "creamy layer" of the Dalit and Adivasi population; it could hardly be otherwise, given the immense obstacles faced by the poor in any effort to persist in school through higher education. There is also much evidence that PD beneficiaries in India tend to come disproportionately from the better-off castes and tribes within the SC and ST categories. But there is very little evidence on the basis of which to determine whether reservation policies have benefited well-off Dalits and Adivasis at the expense of less-well-off university applicants from the rest of the population. (See Chapter 10, pp. 153–5.)

We can conclude that PD policies in both the US and India have, at least in terms of their direct impact,[4] increased inequalities within the UREG population (claim 7.1). In the US they do not appear to have increased overall inequalities; and in India the jury is still out on this question (claim 7.2).

Costs from PD beneficiaries being worse off when gaining admission via a preference (claim 10.2)

To determine whether or not there is empirical support for this strong mismatch claim, one must in principle compare the actual career achievements of PD beneficiaries with the career achievements that the same UREG students would have realized had they not benefited from a PD policy – in which case either they would have attended a less selective university or they would not have pursued their higher education at all. In the US, a number of studies have addressed this issue, using sophisticated analytical methods to estimate the counterfactual situation. The studies point to the following conclusions. AA beneficiaries at selective US colleges do attain GPAs and class ranks that are lower than those they would have attained at less selective colleges (their most likely alternative); but they tend to graduate at higher rates, they are more likely to attain advanced degrees, and their earnings as well as their retrospective satisfaction with their career paths are greater.[5] The evidence suggests that it is in the long-run interest of any student to attend the most selective college to which he/she can gain access, and that this is even more true for UREG than for non-UREG students. UREG students in professional schools, many of whom are AA beneficiaries, also perform less well in their studies than do non-UREG students; but the great majority do graduate, most go on to successful careers, and there can be little doubt that their prospects are greater the more prestigious is the school from which they receive their degree. (See Chapter 11, pp. 163–7, and Chapter 13, pp. 179–87.)

There have been no comparably sophisticated studies of the way in which the career achievements of Indian PD beneficiaries compare with what might have been expected in the absence of PD policies. However, the limited available evidence does suggest that SC and ST students are graduating at reasonable rates from the more elite higher educational institutions (even though their academic performance tends to be inferior to that of their peers), and that for the most part the SC and ST graduates from these institutions are going on to successful careers. This evidence, and the undeniable fact that a degree from an elite institution carries much greater promise of a good career than a degree from a run-of-the-mill school, suggests that it is very unlikely that Indian beneficiaries of reservation policies at the more elite schools would have been better off without access to reserved seats at such institutions. The jury remains out, however, with respect to those SC and ST students whom reservation policies have enabled to pursue higher education at the great majority of Indian higher educational institutions that are rather mediocre. In India as in the US, it is those PD policies that provide access to educational institutions of relatively good quality that are most unambiguously favorable to PD beneficiaries.[6] (See Chapter 12, pp. 168–72 and 175–8.)

Benefits from spreading social capital: greater offsetting of UREG student deficits in social capital; and greater overall benefits from social capital (claims 6.1 and 6.2)

Some of the evidence already discussed above bears directly on the claim that PD policies generate benefits by spreading social capital, which is likely to be provided on a significant scale only by relatively selective educational institutions.

First, there is evidence that PD beneficiaries graduate from selective institutions in both the US and India at rates that are not far below those of non-UREG students. This suggests that, by and large, PD beneficiaries are not squandering but making good use of whatever social capital is extended to them by those institutions. Furthermore, there is little doubt that most students do get some career boost from attending a relatively selective higher educational institution. It seems eminently plausible that UREG students tend to receive a greater career boost than non-UREG students, and that this is due in significant part to the social capital provided by selective schools. Empirical evidence on these latter two points, however, is hard to come by; and the most relevant studies have thus far been carried out in the US.

A number of careful quantitative studies have been done to determine the effects of the selectivity of US educational institutions on various measures of career success. Several such studies have concluded that the economic pay-off to attending a more selective college is significantly greater for Blacks than for Whites; one concluded that there is a larger return to selectivity for low-income than for high-income students. Studies of comparable sophistication have not been carried out for graduate or professional schools; but one study of an elite law school found evidence that UREG students benefit greatly from attending such schools and, indeed, value the prestige of their degree more than do their non-UREG peers. There is as yet no systematic research that has been able to shed light on the extent to which social capital, as distinct from human capital, accounts for the pay-off to higher selectivity. However, the fact that the pay-off to college selectivity is greater for UREG than for non-UREG students suggests that social capital is indeed an important part of the story. (See Chapter 13, pp. 184–7.)

Benefits from integrating society's elite: more opportunities for UREG members offered by UREG decision-makers; more inspiration of UREG youth by UREG role models and mentors; better performance of multiculturally sensitive jobs; and greater contributions of community-oriented service (claims 2.2, 2.3, 2.4, and 2.5)

PD policies in higher education can generate benefits associated with the integration of society's elite insofar as they enable greater numbers of UREG members to join that elite; so it is those PD policies affecting admissions to the more elite (and very selective) higher educational institutions that are at issue here. I have already adduced evidence that PD policies have substantially increased admissions of UREG applicants to such institutions both in the US and India, and that the UREG beneficiaries of PD policies in elite institutions have – for the most part – done well enough in their degree programs to graduate. Validation of the claims of benefits ensuing from greater integration of society's elite calls for evidence that large numbers of these PD beneficiaries have indeed joined the elite, and evidence that they have been instrumental in generating more of the specific types of benefits than would otherwise have been possible.

There is much evidence from the US that UREG students in general, and PD beneficiaries in particular, have gone on from selective colleges to pursue successful careers in esteemed positions. Studies have shown that Blacks go on to earn advanced degrees at about the same rate as Whites – in both cases at much higher rates than their counterparts at less selective colleges (or than they themselves would likely have done at less selective colleges). Black students entering selective colleges do not end up earning as much as their White peers, but they earn far more than the average Black student who enters college (and, again, a good deal more than they themselves would likely have done at less selective colleges). Evidence from graduate and professional schools is somewhat scantier, but it points to very similar conclusions. (See Chapter 13, pp. 179–87.)

As usual, there is much less evidence from India, for there have been very few studies attempting to trace the post-university careers of entering cohorts of students at Indian higher educational institutions. The few studies that have actually been done suggest that UREG students who graduate from relatively elite institutions tend to end up in responsible and well-paying positions, typically attaining a much higher socio-economic status than their parents – albeit not as high as that of their non-UREG peers. (See Chapter 12, pp. 175–8.) Although the evidence that PD beneficiaries have entered society's elite in large numbers is more plentiful and considerably stronger in the US than in India, there can hardly be any question that PD policies have significantly increased the representation of UREG members in the upper socio-economic echelons of both countries.

There is not much hard evidence from either country that speaks directly to the extent to which UREG members of society's elite have enhanced opportunities for less-well-placed UREG members, served as role models and mentors for UREG youth, performed better in multiculturally sensitive jobs, or contributed more community service. It stands to reason that all these kinds of benefits will be a positive function of the number of UREG members who succeed in joining the elite; but it is not clear how much difference that makes. A number of studies in the US suggest that UREG graduates do better than non-UREG graduates in certain jobs that involve working with multicultural co-workers or serving a multicultural clientele, where knowing how best to relate to members of different communities is important. Other studies provide evidence that UREG graduates make more community service contributions than non-UREG graduates, both to their own community and to society in general. Comparative evidence on Black graduates from selective schools and from non-selective schools suggests that the former do not contribute service at significantly higher rates than the latter; but it does seem likely that the effectiveness of the contributions rises with the degree of selectivity of the school. (See Chapter 14, pp. 197–7.)

For India there is scattered evidence that SC and ST students are more likely than other students to make service contributions, less likely to pursue purely materialistic goals, and more likely to pursue careers in ways in which they can be helpful to members of communities in need. (See Chapter 12, pp. 175–8.) The evidence that UREG members in both the US and India do contribute significant unremunerated services to their communities indicates that – contrary to the jaundiced view of some critics – they are indeed redistributing some of the benefits of their preferential access to a good higher education rather than allowing the lure of personal gain to remove any sense of obligation to others.

Benefits from greater student diversity: better learning of academic subjects and better ability to function in a multicultural society (claims 4.1 and 4.2)

There is plenty of evidence that AA policies in admissions have significantly increased racial/ethnic diversity among students in selective colleges and in graduate and professional schools in the US. In the case of non-selective institutions, these policies have mainly affected which UREG students enroll – not their overall number. (See Chapter 9, pp. 136–40.) In India, there is strong evidence that reservation policies in admissions have significantly increased enrollment of SC and ST students in selective higher educational institutions; indeed, there would otherwise hardly have been any SC and ST students attending the most elite institutions. Although there is less direct evidence in the case of non-selective institutions, it is quite clear that PD polices have encouraged larger numbers of SC and ST students to enroll than would otherwise have been the case. (See Chapter 10, pp. 147–51.)

Studies of the impact of greater racial/ethnic diversity on educational outcomes have only been carried out in the US, and most of the studies are of fairly recent vintage. The findings from this research remain preliminary; more research will need to be done before definitive conclusions can be reached. There is, however, some highly suggestive – if contested – evidence that students' academic learning and their ability to function well in a multicultural society are indeed improved by greater student diversity. Such positive outcomes appear to require informal inter-ethnic student interactions, inside and outside of the classroom, of a kind that are more likely to take place in US than in Indian university settings. (See Chapter 14, pp. 197–203.)

Costs from the devaluation of UREG student accomplishments: under-appreciation of true capabilities and achievements of some UREG students; stigmatization of UREG students as not belonging on campus; and low faculty expectations for UREG students (claims 12.1, 12.2, and 12.3)

There can be no doubt that, in both the US and India, many UREG students are stigmatized by the presumption that their enrollment at a higher educational institution is due to preferential admission policies rather than solely to their own capabilities. This presumption is in fact true of the PD beneficiaries among UREG students, except to the extent that PD policies improve the accuracy of appraisal of applicant qualifications; but it is not true of other UREG students, whose true capabilities are therefore liable to being under-appreciated. The evidence adduced above in the context of claims 3.1 and 9.1 showed that both in the US and in India, PD beneficiaries do not perform as well on average as the non-UREG students displaced by PD students would likely have done. This means that under-appreciation of the true capabilities of non-PD-beneficiary UREG students is virtually inevitable, so long as these students cannot readily be distinguished from PD beneficiaries. Neither in the US nor in India is this distinction readily apparent,[7] so in both countries non-PD beneficiaries among UREG students are quite likely to have their capabilities under-appreciated.

There is very little systematic evidence on how widespread are the related phenomena of stigmatization of UREG students as not belonging on campus and low faculty expectations for UREG students. But at selective higher educational institutions in both the US and India, one often hears complaints (usually from non-UREG students) that UREG students, presumed to be PD beneficiaries, do not really belong on campus. At least in the US, one also hears charges that faculty in such institutions disserve UREG students by holding low expectations for them and thus by patronizing them. (See Chapter 14, pp. 203–4.) In neither of these cases, however, is there evidence to determine the extent to which these views are attributable to PD policies rather than to a general predilection toward negative stereotyping of UREG students.

Costs from deceitful efforts to claim UREG status in order to gain resulting benefits (claim 8.2)

In India, there is widespread suspicion, and some anecdotal evidence, that many students from groups ineligible for reserved seats in educational institutions have succeeded in acquiring documents attesting to their membership of an eligible group. There is no hard evidence on the basis of which to determine how significant this phenomenon really is; but there can be little doubt that it exists. (See Chapter 10, pp. 146–7.). In the US, applicants for admission simply declare their own racial/ethnic status, so it is quite possible to succeed in falsifying that status if one's appearance does not make it obvious. This means that such deceit is most likely to occur when an applicant is light-skinned but claims some Hispanic or Native American heritage. There is some anecdotal evidence of false claims of this sort, but the phenomenon does not appear to be widespread and is surely less significant than in India.

With respect to the remaining claims of benefits or costs from PD policies, to be addressed below, pertinent direct evidence from the US and Indian experiences with positive discrimination in admissions to higher educational institutions does not yet exist. In the case of some claims, relevant direct evidence may yet become available as a result of new research efforts; in other cases, the challenges confronting systematic research into the validity of the claims (as detailed in Chapter 8, pp. 131–3) may be too formidable to overcome. One can, nonetheless, draw a few very tentative conclusions about the validity of some of the remaining claims of costs and benefits on the basis of partial or indirect evidence – as in the following paragraphs.

Benefits or costs linked to UREG student motivation or complacency: more/less development of human capital by UREG students (claim 5.1 vs. claim 11.1)

A minimum condition for young UREG students to be positively motivated by PD policies is that the actual beneficiaries of such policies in higher educational institutions do well enough in their studies so as to encourage the young UREG students to believe that they can be successful when given preferential access to such opportunities. The evidence discussed above with respect to the claim (claim 10.1) of poor academic performance and frequent failure of PD beneficiaries suggests that, at least in the case of the more selective institutions in both the US and India, PD beneficiaries do well enough to meet this condition. There is no systematic evidence either from the US or India that bears directly on how PD policies affect the motivation of UREG youths to develop their human capital.

Benefits or costs linked to perceptions of the fairness of admissions processes: decreasing UREG cynicism about the unfairness of selection processes; or increasing non-UREG resentment because of perceived unfairness in admissions (claim 3.2 vs. claim 9.2)

The evidence discussed above with respect to the claims (claim 3.1 vs. claim 9.1) relating to whether PD policies increase or decrease the average academic quality of the student body (by increasing or decreasing the accuracy with which applicant qualifications are appraised) strongly suggests that PD policies decrease academic quality and appraisal accuracy both in the US and in India. It follows that the claim of costs from increasing non-UREG resentment is considerably more likely to be validated in each country than the claim of benefits from decreasing UREG cynicism. It should be noted, however, that both of these latter claims could hold simultaneously – unlike the directly conflicting claims to which they are related.

***Benefits from integrating society's elite: more dispelling of negative
stereotypes of UREG members (claim 2.6); and costs of mismatching
UREG students and academic institutions: exacerbation of negative
stereotypes of UREG members (claim 10.3).***

The validity of these claims can be partially and indirectly tested by considering evidence on related claims associated with the arguments on which each claim is based. In exploring claims 2.2–2.5 based on the integration of society's elite, I cited evidence that PD policies have indeed enabled substantial numbers of UREG members to enter esteemed occupations and thereby expand UREG representation among the elite both in the US and in India. This provides some indirect support for the claim that negative stereotyping of UREG members has been reduced to some extent, for it is quite plausible that greater UREG representation among the elite would have that effect. In the US, there is indeed scattered evidence from public opinion surveys of reduced negative stereotyping of minorities of color; but the extent to which this is attributable to AA policies remains to be established.

In examining the evidence for claim 10.1 regarding poor academic performance by PD beneficiaries at the institutions to which PD provides them access, I found much evidence that PD beneficiaries perform less well than their peers. This prevents one from invalidating the claim that PD exacerbates negative stereotyping of UREG members. To validate the claim, however, it is necessary to show that the extent of negative stereotyping is greater than it would have been had no UREG students benefited from PD admission policies. In that case, UREG students would have constituted smaller minorities in selective higher educational institutions, and much smaller minorities in the most elite ones. This no-PD situation might easily precipitate as much negative stereotyping as the PD alternative; so, absent systematic research on this issue, there is nothing one can conclude – even very tentatively – about the validity of claim 10.3 either in the US or in India.

***Benefits from affirming society's commitment to reduce continuing
disadvantages of UREG members (claim 1.1); benefits from
strengthening the legitimacy of society's leadership (claim 2.1); and
costs from more divisive identity group politics (claim 8.1)***

These last three claims are by far the most difficult to subject to systematic and persuasive empirical testing, because it is extremely difficult to design and execute data-based research that will enable one to draw convincing inferences about the extent to which PD policies (whether in higher educational admissions alone or more generally) affect such qualitative concerns. One hears many statements asserting the existence and the importance of the benefits or costs associated with the above claims, but there is no systematic evidence from either the US or India about the extent to which they can be attributed to PD policies.

Table 15.1 **Evidence from the US and India on each claim of benefits from positive discrimination in higher educational admissions**

Benefit (societal goal)		US	India
1	*Compensation for historical injustice*		
1.1	Affirmation of commitment to reduce UREG disadvantages (harmony)	★★★	★★★
2	*Integration of society's elite*		
2.1	Greater legitimacy of society's leadership (democracy)	–	–
2.2	More UREG decision-makers offering opportunities (equity)	(yes)	(yes)
2.3	More UREG role models and mentors (efficiency)	(yes)	(yes)
2.4	Better performance of jobs if job-holder is of UREG status (efficiency)	YES	yes
2.5	Greater contributions of community-oriented service (equity, democracy)	YES	yes
2.6	More dispelling of negative stereotypes of UREG members (harmony)	(yes)	(yes)
3	*Accuracy in appraising qualifications*		
3.1	Increase in average academic quality of students (efficiency)	NO	NO
3.2	Decrease in UREG cynicism about unfairness (harmony)	–	–
4	*Contribution of diversity to education*		
4.1	Better learning of academic subjects (efficiency)	yes	–
4.2	Better ability to function in a multicultural society (efficiency, democracy)	yes	–
5	*Motivation of UREG students*		
5.1	More development of human capital (efficiency, equity)	(yes)	(yes)
6	*Spread of social capital*		
6.1	Greater offsetting of UREG student deficits in social capital (equity)	YES[a]	yes[a]
6.2	Greater overall benefits from social capital (efficiency)	YES[a]	–

Notes:

[a] For PD beneficiaries in relatively selective/elite institutions.

★★★ Highly plausible on the basis of a priori reasoning.

Table 15.2 **Evidence from the US and India on each claim of costs from positive discrimination in higher educational admissions**

Cost (societal goal)	US	India
7 *Poor tailoring to help most disadvantaged*		
7.1 Exacerbation of inequalities among UREG members (equity)	YES	YES
7.2 Redistribution from non-UREG to UREG members (equity, harmony)	NO	–
8 *Exacerbation of ethnic group consciousness*		
8.1 More divisive identity group politics (democracy, harmony)	★★★	★★★
8.2 Deceitful efforts to claim UREG status (harmony)	–	yes
8.3 Snowballing demands for group preferences (harmony, democracy)	NO	YES
9 *Inaccuracy in appraising qualifications*		
9.1 Decrease in average academic quality of students (efficiency)	YES	YES
9.2 Increase in non-UREG resentment of unfairness (harmony)	(yes)	(yes)
10 *Mismatch of UREG students with universities*		
10.1 Poor academic performance and frequent failure (equity, efficiency)	YES[a]	YES[a]
10.2 PD beneficiaries worse off (equity, efficiency)	NO	NO[b]
10.3 Exacerbation of negative stereotypes of UREG students (harmony)	–	–
11 *Complacency of UREG students*		
11.1 Less development of human capital (efficiency, equity)	–	–
12 *Devaluation of UREG student accomplishments*		
12.1 Under-appreciation of capabilities of some students (equity, efficiency)	YES	YES
12.2 Stigmatization of UREG students as not belonging (harmony)	(yes)	(yes)
12.3 Low faculty expectations of UREG students (equity, efficiency)	(yes)	(yes)

Notes:

[a] *But*: PD beneficiaries are considerably more likely to graduate from relatively selective/elite institutions than not.

[b] At least for PD beneficiaries in relatively selective/elite institutions.

★★★ Highly plausible on the basis of a priori reasoning.

Tables 15.1 and 15.2 display in abbreviated form all of the summarized evidence from the US and India on each of the claims both for and against positive discrimination in admissions to higher educational institutions. "Yes" or "no" indicates whether or not the evidence supports the claim. If the word is capitalized, the evidence is relatively strong; otherwise, the evidence is weaker and more disputable. Parentheses indicate that the evidence is incomplete or indirect, so that the claim is only very tentatively supported or rejected.

Supplementary insights into the consequences of PD policies in university admissions

Empirical evidence on the consequences of PD policies in higher education can usefully be supplemented by a priori reasoning. Such reasoning enables us to draw some conclusions about the validity of some of the claims of benefits and costs from PD policies, if not about their magnitude.

Consider, for example, the last three (highly qualitative) claims addressed in the preceding section, for which no useful empirical evidence is available either in the US or in India. Common sense suggests that one of the claims of PD benefits plus the claim of PD costs are eminently plausible and, indeed, almost certainly true to some degree. Policies of positive discrimination surely do represent an effort to ameliorate the position of UREG members in society, whatever their tangible consequences may be; there can be even less doubt that the abolition of PD policies would be taken as a major affront by many UREG members, unless it were accompanied by significant alternative measures to ameliorate their position. And there can hardly be any question that PD policies, by focusing attention on ethnicity, exacerbate consciousness of a person's ethnic group identity and thereby contribute in some measure to identity group politics that are potentially divisive. In Tables 15.1 and 15.2, I have entered the symbol "★★★" to indicate that these two of the qualitative claims are almost certainly valid, although we cannot say anything about the magnitude of the associated benefits and costs either in the US or in India.

What about the third qualitative claim? One might presuppose that in a multicultural society in which ethnic differences are salient, greater representation of UREGs among society's leaders would strengthen the legitimacy of society's leadership. This is indisputably so, in the eyes of most members of the affected UREGs. It is also possible, however, that PD policies could tend to erode the legitimacy of society's leadership in the eyes of non-UREG members. Whether the overall impact of PD in this case is favorable or unfavorable is therefore indeterminate on theoretical grounds.

A priori reasoning developed in Chapter 7 can provide some further insights into the validity and significance of some of the claims for which empirical evidence is available. Thus, on the basis of the available evidence, I concluded earlier that one should reject both in the US and in India the claim (claim 3.1) that PD policies – by improving the accuracy with which applicant qualifications are appraised – increase the average academic quality of enrolled students. But theoretical considerations suggest that this claim could be validated under certain circumstances. In particular, a highly sensitive and nuanced PD policy, or a well-crafted multivariate regression analysis, could possibly identify high potential in conventionally under-qualified UREG applicants and thereby generate benefits from improving the accuracy of applicant appraisal. (See Chapter 7, pp. 115–19.)

The available empirical evidence from the US and India provides only very limited support for the claim (claim 5.1) that PD policies generate benefits by motivating UREG students to develop more assiduously their human capital; and it does not enable one to reject the alternative claim (claim 11.1) that PD policies actually foster complacency in this respect. Theoretical analysis of the pay-off to academic effort by UREG students shows, however, that PD policies are far more likely to cause potential UREG applicants for admission – as well as enrolled UREG students – to become more highly motivated for academic effort than to become complacent about their studies. Such complacency is likely to result among UREG university applicants only in situations where there are quotas of reserved seats, and then only if there are no meaningful minimum criteria for admission and if the quota is not likely to be filled; complacency is likely to result among UREG university students only in situations where they are essentially guaranteed passing grades, whatever their academic accomplishments (or lack thereof). This implies that claim 5.1, not claim 11.1, is most likely to be true in the US; and that it is also most likely to be true in India, except where PD policies insulate UREG applicants or students from any meaningful competition. (See Chapter 7 pp. 119–20.)

On the contribution of diversity to educational outcomes, there is useful evidence only from the US, on the basis of which I concluded earlier that claims of benefits from better student academic learning and better student ability to function in a multicultural society are at least weakly supported. Theoretical reasoning suggests that ethnic diversity is rather more likely to generate benefits of the second type. It stands to reason that the experience of ethnic diversity in a higher educational setting will contribute to some extent to one's ability to live and work constructively in an ethnically diverse society. It is harder to see why ethnic diversity should improve a student's ability to learn academic subjects, except in fields in which multicultural awareness is an important element of one's understanding of the subject matter. This would seem to be the case mainly in the humanities and in some social sciences, as well as in professional schools preparing students for occupations involving frequent contact with fellow citizens of multiple ethnicities. (See Chapter 7, pp. 119–20.)

One final way in which a priori reasoning can supplement the available evidence on the consequences of PD policies in higher education is by shedding light on the relative success of those policies with respect to different UREGs. The available empirical evidence is quite uneven in its coverage of the different UREGs favored by positive discrimination in the US and in India. In the US, considerably more evidence is available for Blacks than for

Hispanic Americans or for Native Americans. In India, very little quantitative evidence is available for OBCs as a group. Indeed, because PD policies applied to OBCs – like the OBCs themselves – vary enormously from one state to another, it is often not meaningful to analyze in general terms the consequences of such policies. In stark contrast, policies with respect to SCs and STs are similar throughout India, and these two UREGs are recognized officially at the national and state levels as groups for which statistical information is regularly collected.[8] The available empirical evidence on PD policy consequences in India is more plentiful with respect to SCs than STs, and it does not always distinguish clearly between the two groups. However, from the qualitative comparative analysis in Part I of this book – summarized in Table 6.1 – we can derive some insights into the way in which conclusions about PD policy consequences drawn from the available evidence differ across the different UREGs within the US and within India.

In the US, there is little a priori reason to expect significant differences among UREGs in the quality of academic performance. The strength of the need for a focus on ethnicity – associated especially with extent of mistreatment, extent of stigmatization, and degree of homogeneity – is greater in the case of African Americans and Native Americans than in the case of Hispanic Americans. This implies that the benefits derived from integration of society's elite and from the spread of social capital can be expected to be greater for the former two groups than for the latter.[9] In India, costs hinging on relatively weak academic performance – such as those associated with inaccuracy in appraising applicant qualifications and devaluation of UREG accomplishments – are surely less serious for OBC students than for SC or ST students. On the other hand, the need for a focus on ethnicity is strongest in the case of SC students and weakest in the case of OBC students; so benefits associated with integration and social capital will be greater for SC students than for ST students and greater for ST students than for OBC students.

Conclusions

From the evidence summarized in Tables 15.1 and 15.2, supplemented by the a priori reasoning noted in the preceding section, we can arrive at a series of findings about the consequences of PD policies in admissions to higher educational institutions. Of these, the findings that are most solidly grounded are the following:

• PD policies in both the US and India have generated a variety of benefits from greater ethnic integration of society's elite, contributing to greater efficiency and equity – and probably also to greater inter-ethnic social harmony and greater democratic vitality. Moreover, PD policies in selective higher educational institutions in both the US and India have helped to spread social capital to members of under-represented ethnic groups, contributing to greater equity and – at least in the case of the US –

greater efficiency. These kinds of benefits have been more significant for African and Native Americans than for Hispanic Americans within the US, and more significant for Dalits and (to a lesser extent) Adivasis than for OBC members within India.

- PD policies in both the US and India have resulted in a situation in which the academic performance of PD beneficiaries is on average inferior to that of their peers and where the failure rate is higher; within India, this is more true of SC and ST students than of OBC students. There is considerable evidence, however, to reject the strong mismatch hypothesis that PD beneficiaries would have been better off attending a less selective and prestigious school than PD policies made possible. Graduation rates for PD beneficiaries in both countries rise with the degree of selectivity of the institution, and there is no doubt that – on average – PD beneficiaries enrolled in relatively selective institutions go on to have careers that are more successful than those they would have had in the absence of PD.
- Neither in the US nor in India have PD policies served, on the whole, to improve the accuracy with which applicant qualifications are appraised in the admissions process. On the contrary, they have contributed to a decrease in the average academic quality of enrolled students, with resulting efficiency costs. They have also led to increased resentment by non-PD beneficiaries over unfairness in admissions processes – with some resulting costs in social harmony.
- PD policies in both the US and India have exacerbated ethnic group consciousness, with consequent costs in social harmony and democratic vitality. India's PD policies have generated more divisive identity politics, deceitful efforts to claim preferred status, and snowballing demands for group preferences. US PD policies have generated mainly the first of these problems – and almost surely to a lesser extent than in India.

The following conclusions are somewhat less solidly grounded – or less significant in their likely magnitude – than those mentioned above:

- PD policies in the US have most probably generated benefits from greater racial/ethnic diversity in selective higher educational institutions, at least in the form of greater student ability to function in a multicultural society – with consequent gains in efficiency and democratic vitality. It is unlikely that any such benefits have been significant in India.
- PD policies in both the US and India (at least in terms of their direct impact) have clearly been poorly tailored to help the most disadvantaged members of their societies. These policies have therefore resulted in equity costs associated with the exacerbation of inequalities among members of under-represented ethnic groups. However, they do not

appear to have led to equity costs by exacerbating overall inequalities – at least in the US.

- PD policies both in the US and in India have most probably generated benefits associated with the motivation of students from under-represented ethnic groups to acquire more education and work to develop their skills, with consequent gains in efficiency as well as equity. It does not seem likely that PD policies have caused much complacency on the part of such students, except in India in (relatively unusual) situations where SC and ST students are virtually guaranteed access to reserved seats, irrespective of their conventional qualifications.

- PD policies in both the US and India have clearly had the effect of devaluing the accomplishments of students from under-represented ethnic groups who do not happen to be PD beneficiaries, leading to efficiency and equity costs at least because of the under-appreciation of the capabilities of those students. The resulting costs are greater in the US than in India, because the number of such students – relative to the number of PD beneficiaries – is considerably higher in the US than in India. It is likely that PD policies have also exacerbated the stigmatization of students from under-represented ethnic groups as not belonging on campus and contributed to low faculty expectations for such students; but these phenomena are by no means solely attributable to such policies.

- PD policies in both the US and India have served to affirm the commitment of their societies to reduce the continuing disadvantages faced by members of under-represented ethnic groups. How much this has contributed to greater social harmony is debatable; but there is no doubt that ending PD policies would have a significantly adverse effect on social harmony, unless they were replaced by significant alternative policies with similar objectives.

From these findings it is clear that PD policies in admissions to higher educational institutions in both the US and India have resulted in a complex mixture of benefits and costs. The evidence is not broad and deep enough to permit us to measure the relative magnitudes of the various kinds of positive and negative consequences of PD policies in either country, nor is there a single widely accepted set of value weights that we could use to evaluate the relative importance of contributions to harmony, democracy, efficiency, or equity. What we can conclude, with a reasonable degree of confidence, is the following:

1   The most significant and most varied benefits from PD policies in higher educational admissions in the US and in India have been generated by the ethnic integration of society's elite; and significant equity benefits have probably also arisen from the spread of social capital to UREG students. These kinds of benefits have been strongest for African Americans and Native Americans in the US and for Dalits in India.

Other possibly significant sources of benefits include the positive motivation of UREG students, and – in the US – the contribution of diversity in the composition of enrolled students to their ability to function in a multicultural society; but it seems unlikely that either one of these sources of benefits could have as much impact as the integration of society's elite.

2   The most significant costs of PD policies in higher educational admissions in the US and in India stem from two sources: exacerbation of ethnic group consciousness, with costs in social harmony and democratic vitality, and the failure to select the academically most qualified applicants, with costs in efficiency and probably also in social harmony. Other sources of costs from PD policies include the devaluation of UREG student accomplishments and the exacerbation of inequalities among UREG members; but it is hard to believe that these kinds of costs could have as much impact as the first two sources mentioned.

3   PD-induced costs arising from the exacerbation of ethnic group consciousness, and the degree to which PD results in failure to select the academically most qualified applicants, have both been more significant in India than in the US. Furthermore, PD-induced benefits from student ethnic diversity have probably been realized in the US but not in India. It follows that the overall net benefits of PD policies in higher education have in all probability been greater in the US than in India.[10]

But have the benefits of PD policies in higher educational admissions over the past several decades exceeded the costs, either in the US or in India, for some or all of their officially recognized under-represented ethnic groups? We simply cannot answer this question in a definitive fashion. What we can say is that the answer almost certainly hinges on the comparative importance of integration and social capital benefits as compared with ethnic consciousness and academic quality costs. The overall net benefits of a PD policy are more likely to be positive the more evidence one finds for – and the more value one assigns to – the various kinds of benefits arising from the ethnic integration of society's elite and the equity benefits from the spread of social capital to UREG students. PD net benefits are more likely to be negative the more evidence one finds for – and the more value one assigns to – social harmony and democracy costs arising from the exacerbation of ethnic group consciousness and efficiency costs from the failure to select the academically most qualified applicants. Furthermore, we can say with some confidence that the net benefits are more likely to have been positive in the US than in India; within the US, PD policies favoring African Americans and Native Americans are most likely to have generated positive net benefits; and within India, policies favoring Dalits are most likely to have generated positive net benefits.[11]

Both the uncertainty and the complexity of these conclusions point to the need for more empirical research on the consequences of PD policies in higher educational admissions – especially in India, where the evidence is particularly scant. To reiterate a quotation from the front of the book: "The absence of empirical studies of the achievements of reservation, and changes resulting from these in the larger social situation, is one of the many reasons why it becomes difficult to conduct an informed debate" (Patwardhan and Palshikar 1992: 4).[12] These two Indian scholars are themselves the authors of one of the very few studies in India that tracks the post-university careers of PD beneficiaries and their classmates. Such studies are critical for arriving at an understanding of some of the key consequences of PD policies; and one hopes that many more will be undertaken in the future.[13]

Part III
Conclusion

16 Concluding observations on policies of positive discrimination

In this final chapter of the book I draw on the preceding theoretical and empirical comparative analysis of positive discrimination in the US and India to present concluding observations on the rationale for positive discrimination policies, the optimal design of such policies, and the consequences of the policies actually implemented in the two countries.

On the rationale for policies of positive discrimination in favor of ethnic identity groups

Positive discrimination (PD), as I have defined the term, means preferential selection of members of a group to positions in the larger society in which that group is under-represented. In this book I have addressed PD policies favoring members of ethnic groups (defining ethnicity broadly to include race, caste, and tribe), whose shared ethnic identity is involuntary and rarely alterable. The under-representation of such groups in positions commanding respect and authority is not necessarily but almost always associated with members of these groups being of a low average socio-economic status, as compared to that of the rest of their society's population. Positive discrimination in favor of under-represented ethnic groups (UREGs) is one of many possible kinds of social policy intended to enable people of relatively low socio-economic status to gain greater opportunities for social, political, and economic advancement.

The actual or prospective use of ethnicity-oriented PD policies thus raises two fundamental questions. First, why should a social policy be oriented to ethnic identity rather than to socio-economic class, with ethnicity rather than socio-economic disadvantage serving as the criterion for eligibility for benefits? Secondly, why should preferential selection policies be utilized rather than other kinds of social policies designed to improve access to opportunities for advancement on the part of people whose opportunities have been limited in the past? The possible alternative policies include redistributive transfers of income or wealth in favor of such people and development programs that increase their capacity to participate in the life of the society – e.g. programs that improve their health, education, or living environment.

Ethnic identity vs. socio-economic class

There are several good reasons for having some social policies focus on ethnic identity groups. Because ethnicity is frequently (if wrongly) perceived to be defined in genetic terms, members of ethnic groups are especially vulnerable to being stigmatized as innately inferior in terms of their capabilities. Needless to say, such stigmatization is deeply contemptuous and highly debilitating, making it particularly difficult for those concerned to overcome inequalities. Furthermore, disparities among ethnic groups in average socio-economic status and representation in esteemed positions are especially likely to give rise to the suspicion that they have been caused by mistreatment of members of the under-represented groups – a suspicion that often contains much truth. Whatever the case, it serves as a source of much social tension. Indeed, the historical record shows that inter-ethnic conflicts have been a source of much greater conflict and brutality than, for example, inter-class inequalities.[1]

Some critics of ethnicity-oriented PD policies make the point that ethnic categories have mostly been used by members of groups over-represented in society's esteemed positions in order to limit access by others, rather than by members of under-represented groups to increase their access. This is certainly true as a matter of historical fact. It is not relevant, however, to the case for or against the use of ethnic group identity in PD policies, for positive discrimination is designed explicitly to include more members of previously under-represented groups. As Dworkin (1998: 100–1) has argued, one must distinguish between malign and benign uses of ethnic criteria. It is malign when such criteria are used to limit the access of UREG members to esteemed positions – especially so when this limitation or exclusion is linked (as is usually the case) to invidious stereotypes about the alleged inferiority of such groups. It is benign when such criteria are used to increase the access of UREG members to esteemed positions. In the latter case, ethnic distinctions do not inflict on members of the over-represented groups whose access is limited any injury that is at all comparable in its fundamental derision to that suffered by under-represented group members when their access is limited.

Another frequent criticism leveled at ethnicity-oriented PD policies is that they benefit only a fraction of all the disadvantaged members of a society, and that it is quite arbitrary to help people who happen to be of the right ethnicity but not similarly disadvantaged people who happen to be of the wrong ethnicity. These critics often propose that PD policies be altered so as to target not members of under-represented ethnic groups but people who are worst off in terms of socio-economic class. For example, Kahlenberg (1995) argues that because US affirmative action policies fail to reach the most needy, they should be reoriented to provide class-based rather than ethnicity-based preferences; in that way the beneficiaries would be the poor, and the burden would fall on the middle- or upper-income classes. This line of reasoning is linked to the argument against positive discrimination that PD is poorly tailored to help the most disadvantaged and, in fact, makes inequalities worse.

There are several reasons not to reorient PD policies strictly to socio-economically disadvantaged individuals rather than to members of under-represented ethnic groups, some of whom are likely not to be so disadvantaged. For one thing, this might well lead to poorer performance by the beneficiaries in the educational or job settings to which they gain greater access – since beneficiaries who are more disadvantaged socio-economically can be expected to be less well prepared for university studies or challenging job responsibilities. In the case of university admissions, at least, class-based preferences would be more costly than ethnicity-based preferences in terms of scholarship support required by needy students to take up an offer of admission. Furthermore, like a progressive income tax, class-based preferences could generate some disincentive for poorer families to increase their income. Because one's ethnic identity cannot be altered (except in rare cases, or by deceit), and because one's socio-economic class status can indeed be altered (most easily in a downward direction, and also by deceit), the incentive to become eligible for benefits will rarely lead those who are ethnically disadvantaged to change their ethnic identity, but that incentive will likely have some dampening effect on the effort that those who are socio-economically disadvantaged put into improving their class status.[2]

Most importantly, the argument in favor of class-based preferences misses the point. There are many good reasons and good policies for improving the lot of the most disadvantaged people in a society and for reducing socio-economic class inequalities among individuals. As I have argued throughout this book, however, ethnically based PD policies are designed to address those inequalities that are linked to (and in many ways attributable to) a person's ethnic-group identity – i.e. to reduce inter-group inequalities between ethnic groups of individuals. This is the reason that (in Chapter 4, pp. 59–61) I highlighted as an important intermediate factor influencing the success of a PD policy the strength of the need for a focus on ethnicity – as an alternative to a focus on socio-economic class. Among the key characteristics that strengthen the need for an ethnicity focus are the *extent of mistreatment* and the *extent of stigmatization* resulting from one's ethnic identity. The extent of socio-economic disadvantage, on the other hand, does not strengthen the need for an ethnicity focus; it is an ethnic group characteristic that contributes (negatively) to the other intermediate factor influencing the success of a PD policy – the quality of performance of PD beneficiaries.

In an ideal world, one would adopt some policies designed to address the ethnicity-group inequalities that ethnicity-based PD policies are intended to ameliorate, and some other policies to address socio-economic class inequalities. One set of policies need not compete with, much less exclude, the other. But these two kinds of policies could be seen as competitive in at least two important respects: the political energy needed to get them seriously addressed, and the resources needed to implement them. One must grant that two alternative social policies could be competitive politically, though this would not seem to be an overwhelming problem. Surely politicians are capable of focusing on more than one issue – if not simultaneously, then at least over a period of time. On the other hand, resource competition between the alternative policies could pose a more serious problem.

The main thing that the socio-economically disadvantaged lack is resources. A successful effort to reduce their disadvantage must therefore involve a significant investment of resources, whether in the form of a redistributive transfer or a development program. One of the key things that the ethnicity-disadvantaged lack is respect from members of other ethnic groups; many, but by no means all, also lack resources. This implies that a social policy unlinked to resource transfer does very little good for the socio-economically disadvantaged. (What good is it to get into Harvard if you are too poor to pay the tuition, or to get a good job in a distant locality, to which you would have to move your whole family? In both cases you will need some form of financial aid to take advantage of the opportunity to which you get access.) A social policy unlinked to resource transfer does, however, do some good for the ethnicity-disadvantaged (some of whom have the wherewithal to pay Harvard tuition, or to move a long distance to take a good job). It follows that resources made available for a social policy will stretch across greater numbers of the ethnicity-disadvantaged than of the socio-economically disadvantaged.

Socio-economic disadvantage therefore cannot and should not replace UREG identity as a basis for identifying appropriate beneficiaries of social policy. The characteristics of a UREG that strengthen the need for ethnicity-oriented social policy – mistreatment, stigmatization, etc., on account of ethnic identity – are likely to be correlated with socio-economic disadvantage; but where the correlation is not perfect, it is the ethnicity-related characteristics – not socio-economic class indicators – that matter.[3] Of course, the implementation of social policies on behalf of UREGs does not preclude the simultaneous implementation of social policies targeting the lower socio-economic classes. To the contrary, in multicultural societies it will generally be desirable to carry out policies that serve the socio-economically disadvantaged as well as policies that serve the ethnicity-disadvantaged.

Preferential selection vs. other kinds of social policy

PD policies are based on preferential selection to desirable positions of members of certain groups deemed to deserve assistance. Why should policies of preferential selection be utilized rather than other kinds of social policies, involving redistributive transfers or development programs in favor of members of deserving groups?

Like most public policies with a prospect of delivering aggregate net gains to a society, preferential policies bring losses to some people while bringing gains to others. If, as is often the case, there is no practical way to arrange for compensation of the losers, using some of the gains of the winners, then it is desirable at least to spread the costs widely and hence thinly among losers –

both in the interest of fairness and in the interest of warding off potentially damaging resentment on the part of substantial losers. From this perspective, preferential policies are problematical, because they concentrate losses on those applicants who were displaced by the selection of the beneficiaries. The problem is heightened by the fact that many of the applicants not selected are likely to attribute their failure to be selected to a preferential policy, even if they would not in fact have been selected in the absence of such a policy.

Such concerns lead some to reject policies of preferential selection and to support other kinds of social policies in support of would-be beneficiaries of preferential selection. No doubt there are redistributive and developmental policies that would share the costs much more widely among non-beneficiaries. One good example is an income-tax-financed program to improve primary and secondary education in residential areas with high concentrations of deserving beneficiaries. There is, however, a significant weakness to this line of reasoning. The social policies proposed as better alternatives to preferential selection tend to be significantly more expensive.[4]

A policy of preferential selection, though not without attendant resource costs, can be implemented at far less cost to the organization responsible than can redistributive or developmental policies of aid to the needy. Some of the costs of a preferential selection policy are imposed on those applicants who are displaced by the beneficiaries; they must settle for less attractive alternative options. (These costs are lower the smaller is the overall displacement impact of preferential selection policies; thus it is desirable to limit the proportion of positions subject to preferential selection.) Some of the costs are absorbed by the beneficiaries – e.g. in the form of tuition payments and related expenses and earnings foregone while enrolled in an educational institution, or in the form of extra living, transportation, and other expenses associated with holding a good job. What must be borne by the organization responsible for the preferential policy, or the government agency on which it may be financially dependent, are the resources it invests in the selection process and in developmental support for the beneficiaries. Moreover, in the case of educational institutions, an important additional expense is financial aid[5] to those beneficiaries who are unable to afford all of the tuition and related expenses associated with attending the institution – and whom the institution wants to include in its student body.

A preferential selection policy is thus far from being without cost to the organization responsible for determining and implementing it. Because a significant portion of its costs are generally deflected to others, however, it is likely to provide policy-makers with a way of providing a given amount of benefit to a given group of beneficiaries that is significantly less expensive than the alternative of redistributive transfers or developmental programs. Most often it is the government that is called upon to finance social policies (directly or indirectly), so funds must be raised from the general public. This almost always poses a political challenge. Preferential selection policies have the political virtue of being relatively inexpensive to taxpayers.

Everyone can agree that policies designed to increase the representation of UREG members in selective higher educational institutions and in high-status jobs, even if successful in generating the net benefits anticipated by proponents of PD policies, cannot by themselves overcome the huge overall inter-group disparities in average socio-economic status that do so much to motivate positive discrimination in the first place. Substantial progress with respect to the long-run goal of greater inter-group equity will surely require a much broader effort, including policies that target more directly the welfare of ordinary UREG members, as distinct from the opportunities open to highly educated UREG members. One cannot expect positive discrimination to accomplish this; but one can at least ask of PD policies that they do not have the effect of making it more difficult to mount the kinds of social policies that would most directly and substantially improve the lot of the ordinary members. Thus one must pose the following question: is the implementation of PD policies likely to help or to hinder the mobilization of a political movement strong enough to push successfully for other policies that will help to reduce inter-group socio-economic disparities?

As is so often the case, the answer could go either way – depending on the circumstances. PD policies might help initiate the needed political mobilization by increasing the representation of members of under-represented and socio-economically disadvantaged ethnic groups in politically powerful positions. It might also improve the implementation of redistributive and developmental policies benefiting ordinary UREG members by increasing the number of more privileged UREG members in important administrative positions. On the other hand, PD policies could hinder the needed political mobilization by deflecting resources and energy away from activities serving the interests of the broad mass of deserving UREG members into activities benefiting only a relatively privileged sub-group.

Toward optimal choice of PD policies

The underlying theme of this book is that policies of positive discrimination should be analyzed in terms of consequences that are likely to entail both benefits and costs, so one should pursue PD policies only insofar as they promise to generate net benefits. Viewing positive discrimination from this perspective suggests the possibility – indeed the desirability – of fine-tuning PD policies so as to maximize their potential for generating net benefits.

As we have seen, the consequences of any given PD policy depend on three kinds of characteristics of the context for PD: characteristics of the under-represented group favored by the PD policy; procedural characteristics of the PD policy itself; and certain characteristics of the overall societal environment. Of these three primary causal factors, only the procedural characteristics of a PD policy are obviously variable (though within limits set by the societal environment). The characteristics of any given UREG cannot be varied; but the set of UREGs to be targeted by a PD policy, and the precise definition of each of them, constitute important PD policy variables. After exploring choices with respect to these two kinds of PD policy variables, I go on to address several other elements of choice in the structuring of PD policies.

UREGs eligible for positive discrimination

The potential net benefits from positive discrimination in favor of an under-represented ethnic group depend on its characteristics; so the desirability of pursuing a PD policy will vary from one UREG to another. Indeed, the choice of UREG(s) to be favored by PD – the choice of what I will call "eligible" UREGs – is surely the most critical decision to be made in adopting policies of positive discrimination. In principle, one should try to estimate the net benefits associated with each distinct UREG for whom a case for PD seems plausible, in order to determine which ones should be made eligible. In practice, one may need to limit such an effort to those ethnic groups whose members have already demonstrated a strong sense of common ethnic identity by organizing ethnicity-based associations with a substantial membership base. If such a group is indeed clearly under-represented in society's esteemed positions, there is at least a presumption that it will be a plausible candidate for a PD policy.

Deciding which UREGs should be eligible for PD benefits is likely to be an especially challenging task when an actual or prospective UREG contains distinct sub-groups, for this gives rise to the following question: should all of these sub-groups or only some of them be eligible? In the US and Indian contexts, this question is especially salient with respect to the definition of Hispanic Americans and "Other Backward Class" (OBC) members. Neither of these two UREGs has as strong a case for positive discrimination as do the other two UREGs recognized in each country.[6] And each of these UREGs comprise an amalgamation of fairly distinct ethnic groups, which are especially numerous and heterogeneous in the case of OBCs. The expected net benefits from a PD policy might be significantly increased if some – rather than all – Hispanic-American or OBC sub-groups were identified as UREGs eligible for PD benefits.

A related question is whether different UREGs eligible for PD policies in any given country should be accorded the same amount and kind of benefits. Indeed, the net benefits of a PD policy in favor of any particular UREG are dependent on the magnitude of the preference given. This means that, in determining the PD-eligibility of a UREG, one should explore a range of possible preference magnitudes before deciding if the net benefits of a PD policy in favor of that UREG are likely to be positive. It means also that that the optimal magnitude of preference is likely to differ from one UREG to another, so one should in principle establish different preference magnitudes for different eligible UREGs. I will discuss this question further in addressing the procedural characteristics of a PD policy below.

The same logic would suggest that distinct sub-groups within an eligible UREG should each have their own preference magnitude. Calls for separate quotas for different caste sub-groups within India's Scheduled Caste and OBC UREGs express the desire for precisely such an approach, for they stem from fears that a uniform preference magnitude – implied by a single quota of reserved seats – will result in most benefits going to members of a small number of sub-groups within each UREG. There are good reasons, however, for maintaining a uniform magnitude of preference for all sub-groups within an eligible UREG. As a practical matter, it will be very difficult to estimate optimal preference magnitudes with any precision for different sub-groups. Moreover, the capture by a strong sub-group of the lion's share of PD benefits should not be a cause for concern, provided the UREG has been defined in a way that groups together people with a genuinely common ethnic identity. This is because most of the benefits anticipated from a PD policy have to do with better representation of a UREG in a set of esteemed positions; and from this perspective what matters is that those UREG members with the best chance of succeeding in such positions get that opportunity, and that other UREG members have a reason to identify with them. If members of one UREG sub-group do not in fact feel that they are well represented by members of another sub-group from the same UREG, then the net benefits from a PD policy favoring that UREG will be significantly diminished; and one should reconsider whether the two sub-groups belong in the same UREG – or, indeed, whether they belong in any eligible UREG.

Consideration of the eligibility of potentially PD-eligible UREGs and UREG sub-groups could lead to a narrowing, if not a complete elimination, of the scope of eligibility for PD within currently eligible UREGs; and it could conceivably lead to the extension of eligibility to a new group. For example, under-represented ethnic or religious minorities like Pacific Islanders in the US or Muslims in India have been mentioned as groups possibly deserving PD eligibility. In all such cases, research should focus on the prospect of significant net benefits from a PD policy favoring a given UREG; if these prospects are not clearly favorable, the UREG should be excluded from such eligibility. Note that exclusion from PD benefits does not mean that UREG members have no access to broader social welfare benefits. The point is that where there is not a strong rationale for such benefits to be targeted specifically on the basis of a person's ethnic identity, under-represented ethnic groups should not be favored by a PD policy. Instead, needy members of UREGs excluded from PD benefits should be able to benefit from more general policies in aid of people who are socio-economically disadvantaged.

Determining on a rational basis which under-represented ethnic groups should be eligible for positive discrimination is, to be sure, no simple task. It requires meticulous and dispassionate social scientific research, along lines only very roughly sketched out in my analysis in Chapters 4–6 of the varying degrees of strength of the rationale for an ethnicity focus in the case of the currently recognized UREGs in the US and India.[7] Given the political stakes involved in the outcome of such research, it is bound to be very difficult to keep politics from interfering with the process. The history of positive discrimination in both countries makes abundantly clear what a strong role politics has played in the identification of PD-eligible groups to date. India's Mandal Commission was mandated to undertake precisely the kind of research advocated here; the nature of its work and the process whereby many of its recommendations were adopted provide sobering reminders of how difficult it is to keep political considerations at bay when eligibility for PD is at issue.

In advocating reconsideration of the eligibility of UREGs currently favored by PD, one must recognize that there is an asymmetry between the adoption and the removal of a PD policy. The removal of PD eligibility from a UREG is a political blow of considerably greater magnitude than the failure to grant such eligibility in the first place. This is a political reality that cannot and should not be ignored. Thus removal of eligibility from some groups or sub-groups, while others continue to be eligible, must be limited to situations where the case for doing so is very strong and well supported by widely respected research findings. This criterion would probably be somewhat easier to meet in the case of OBCs and Hispanic Americans – or some sub-groups thereof – than in the case of any other currently favored UREGs.

Given all of the difficulties and complications associated with determining which under-represented ethnic groups should be eligible for PD, there is a very strong case for simplicity – in the following respects: first, in limiting the number of eligible UREGs to the most compelling cases; secondly, in defining UREGs by simple criteria that clearly distinguish those sub-groups and individuals who are members of the UREG from those who are not; and thirdly, in grouping together into one UREG sub-groups that might have an argument for being considered separate UREGs – unless that argument is extremely compelling.

One further question regarding the composition of PD-eligible UREGs warrants consideration, since it has often been raised where PD policies are practiced. The idea of using *means tests* to distinguish between deserving and undeserving members of an eligible UREG is on its face attractive, if only because much criticism of PD policies has focused on the way in which they tend to benefit primarily the better-off members of a UREG. (This is the gist of the claims of argument 7, that PD policies are poorly tailored to meet the needs of the disadvantaged.) In India, one often hears proposals to exclude from PD eligibility second-generation UREG applicants, whose parents have benefited from PD to move up the socio-economic ladder.[8] Indeed, when the Supreme Court of India in 1992 gave its approval to national-level public-sector job reservations in favor of OBCs (as recommended by the Mandal Commission), it imposed a "creamy layer test" of individual eligibility, in order to eliminate persons from affluent or professional families.[9]

The wisdom of such a test, however, is highly questionable. This is because it would remove from the ranks of PD beneficiaries precisely those UREG members who are likely to be best prepared to perform well in the positions to which PD helps them gain access. Many of the anticipated benefits of PD arise from better representation of under-represented ethnic groups, and they require good performance to be realized. A "creamy layer test" would almost certainly have an adverse effect on the quality of performance of PD beneficiaries, because it would remove from the pool of potential beneficiaries those applicants whose more favorable socio-economic backgrounds have enabled them to become better prepared for the demands of a selective educational institution or a challenging job.[10] Concern about socio-economic inequalities in a society can best be addressed by policies oriented directly to the disadvantaged, rather than by changing the scope of eligibility for positive discrimination.

Procedural characteristics of a PD policy

In designing a PD policy, choices need to be made with respect to each of its four key characteristics: the magnitude of the preference, the sensitivity of the selection process, the identifiability of individual PD beneficiaries, and the extent of support for PD beneficiaries. From my earlier analysis, there is little doubt about the kinds of PD characteristics that are most likely to maximize the beneficial and minimize the costly consequences of positive discrimination.

The *magnitude of the preference* given to UREG applicants is obviously a key choice variable for any PD policy. The smaller the preference, the fewer will be the number of UREG applicants selected, but the greater will be the proportion of them who are likely to perform as well as their non-UREG peers. The larger the preference, the greater will be the number of PD beneficiaries, but the smaller will be the proportion who perform as well as their peers. There are positive net benefits associated with each PD beneficiary who performs well, and there are negative net benefits associated with each PD beneficiary who performs poorly. As one increases the magnitude of the preference, one selects fewer of the former and more of the latter. Where one should best draw the line depends on the relative frequency of each type of selection and on the relationship between the net benefits associated with good and bad selection decisions.[11]

In principle, with full information about the consequences of different preference magnitudes, and with a common standard for evaluating the net benefits from a good and a bad selection decision, one could estimate both the number of PD beneficiaries and the overall net benefits associated with each preference magnitude. For any given UREG – other things being equal – the net benefits from PD would presumably rise initially, as the magnitude of the preference was raised from zero, because at low magnitudes PD beneficiaries could be expected to perform almost as well as other applicants. After a certain point, however, the additional net benefits from a higher preference magnitude would turn negative; this is because, at ever higher magnitudes, an ever smaller proportion of additional PD beneficiaries selected would be able to perform well.[12] The magnitude of the preference at that turning point could therefore be identified as the optimal one, which maximizes the expected net benefits from a PD policy favoring the given UREG. PD policies would then be judged worthy of adoption in favor of each UREG for which the maximum expected net benefits are in fact positive, with the magnitude of the PD preference set at the optimal level for each eligible UREG.

In reality, of course, decision-makers will never have access to sufficient information to determine in such a systematic and precise manner the optimal preference magnitudes and the corresponding expected net benefits for each UREG under consideration for PD eligibility. Instead, they will have to mix available information with educated guesses and rely on their own best judgment to determine which UREGs should best be made PD eligible and at what level the preference magnitude for each eligible UREG should be set. In the interests of simplicity (as advocated earlier), the preference magnitudes should be set at the same level unless there is a compelling reason to do otherwise for a particular UREG.

It is clearly desirable to make the PD *selection processes as sensitive and nuanced as possible*, so as to maximize the potential for determining which UREG applicants – who are under-qualified in terms of conventional indicators – have the greatest potential to be successful. This implies, first of all, that one should not try to fill quotas of reserved seats with UREG applicants, irrespective of their conventional qualifications; rather, one should give each such applicant the same magnitude of preference in competition with non-UREG applicants.[13] This implies, further, that one should make use of a variety of relevant qualification criteria, and that evaluation of the extent to which an individual applicant is qualified should be based as much as possible on the exercise of qualitative judgments by selection decision-makers rather than on the input of mechanistically determined scores into a quantitative composite overall index.[14]

The extent to which a PD selection process can be made sensitive does, of course, depend on the resources available to finance the process. Thus one cannot expect it to be applied as intensively in poor countries and organizations as in richer ones; and there is a difficult decision to be made as to how far to invest limited resources into processes of selection. It is a safe guess that such investment is usually not carried as far as it should be, since some of the benefits of better selection will not accrue to the organization doing the selection; subsidies may therefore be needed to achieve the desired end.

It is best that a PD policy *not render its beneficiaries easily identifiable* as such by others. A PD beneficiary's self-esteem, as well as the way he/she is treated by others, may well be adversely affected by knowledge that he/she would not have been selected in the absence of the PD policy. One of the most common ways in which PD beneficiaries are in practice rendered identifiable is by including them in remedial and developmental programs designed to facilitate their adjustment to the demands of the competitive environment to which they have gained access. The objective of such programs is certainly a worthy one (as I discuss just below). But to avoid the negative fallout of making PD beneficiaries easily identifiable, it is desirable – wherever possible – not to confine these programs exclusively to PD beneficiaries but to include in them also non-PD beneficiaries who are likely to benefit from them.

Finally, the success of a PD policy will clearly be a positive function of the extent to which it provides *support for under-prepared UREG selectees*. Other things being equal, such support increases the prospects for PD beneficiaries to overcome their disadvantage and perform well. Just as it takes resources to improve the sensitivity of selection processes, so it takes resources to provide this kind of developmental support. Decisions about how much to invest in support for PD beneficiaries will therefore have a significant impact on the overall net benefits of the PD policies. In the early years of affirmative action in the US and reservation policies in India, such investments tended to be ignored. Later, they began to be taken more seriously. Resources are always limited, and the pay-offs to this kind of investment are not always obvious – nor are they all captured by the investors. Once again, therefore, there may be need for subsidies to encourage organizations practicing PD to make sufficient investments of this kind.

I have argued above that the prospective success of a PD policy can be significantly enhanced by financial resource commitments to selection programs, which increase the ability to select promising beneficiaries, and to developmental programs, which improve the performance of beneficiaries. There is one further kind of financial resource commitment that can make a significant contribution to the success of a PD policy: *financial aid to needy beneficiaries*. Student PD beneficiaries may not be able to afford all of the (unsubsidized) expenses associated with attending an educational institution, so they may require financial aid just to enroll. Moreover, for some PD beneficiaries, economic insecurity is a potentially significant source of poor performance. Students from socio-economically disadvantaged families are much more likely to have to drop out of an educational program – temporarily or permanently – in order to help out their family by contributing their labor to work within the family or by earning additional income. Employees from socio-economically disadvantaged families are more likely to absent themselves from work – if not to quit their job – in order to address family crises. Financial aid to PD beneficiaries who are students, and loans to those who are employees, can help to prevent such problems from compromising the success of PD policies.

This latter context is one in which a means test is perfectly appropriate and wholly desirable. As noted above, excluding well-to-do PD beneficiaries from access to PD preferences would mean foregoing some important benefits of PD policies. It would be perfectly appropriate, however, to exclude well-to-do PD beneficiaries from financial aid programs designed to enable socio-economically disadvantaged PD beneficiaries to remain active in the positions to which PD has given them access.

Quotas vs. preferences

Comparisons of the differences in the procedural characteristics of PD policies in India and the US often focus on the best-known of these differences: the use of quotas as against the use of preferences, i.e. preferential boosts,[15] respectively. As I have argued in Chapter 4, pp. 62–3, however, this difference is not a fundamental one – unless one has in mind a "pure" quota system in which reserved seats are to be filled regardless of the conventional qualifications of the PD beneficiaries involved. In particular, if a quota system is constrained by a requirement that UREG applicants meet a minimum level of conventional qualifications in order to selected, then it has (formally) the same effect as a preferential boost system in which the size of the preferential boost is equal to the difference between the minimum conventional qualifications required of a successful UREG applicant and those of the last applicant admitted in the general competition.[16] In practice, constrained quota systems are far more common than pure quota systems – at least in the context of esteemed positions – because one would not want such positions filled by PD beneficiaries whose conventional qualifications were far below those of other selectees.

What really matters in comparing a quota system like India's and a preferential boost system like that of the US are the differences in the key preference-system characteristics that I have already discussed just above. One can, however, make a few generalizations about the relative desirability of quota and preferential boost systems, insofar as this choice has implications for those key characteristics. First of all, a pure quota system clearly makes no sense. To try to fill quotas of reserved seats with UREG applicants, irrespective of their conventional qualifications, is to invite poor performance by those selectees whose conventional qualifications are well below the qualifications required of applicants in a general competition. This is especially likely to be the case if the size of the quota is determined by the UREG fraction of the overall population, as opposed to the UREG fraction of a smaller population consisting of plausible recruits to the positions in question.

A quota system constrained by minimum qualifications requirements, on the other hand, is a possibly acceptable alternative to a preferential boost system, the size of whose boost is equal to the implicit boost given by the constrained quota system. In many situations, however, the constrained quota alternative will be less desirable than the corresponding preferential boost system, for several reasons. For one thing, a constrained quota system in which the quota is consistently unfilled may put pressure on the relevant authorities to increase the magnitude of the preference given to UREG applicants – beyond that which would otherwise (e.g. in a preferential boost system) be considered reasonable. Moreover, it is somewhat easier to introduce sensitivity into the selection process of a preferential boost system than into that of a constrained quota system. This is because the latter requires the explicit specification of minimum qualifications for selection, and such specification is

likely to be possible only in terms of categorical and quantitative indicators –
thus ruling out a more nuanced and holistic consideration of a potential PD
beneficiary's qualifications. It also tends to be somewhat easier in preferential
boost systems to avoid explicit identification of those UREG selectees who
are actually PD beneficiaries, as opposed to those who would have been
admitted without PD.

Other elements of choice in PD policies

One aspect of the structuring of PD policies that I have not yet discussed is
the optimal choice of the sphere of activity to which such policies should be
applied. This is closely related to the role of "developmental" – as opposed to
preferential – approaches to overcoming significant inter-ethnic-group disparities in representation in society's esteemed positions. I turn now to address
each of these issues.

Spheres of activity for positive discrimination

In this book I have focused attention on positive discrimination primarily in
the spheres of employment and education. These are indeed the spheres of
activity in which PD policies are currently most widely applied both in the
US and in India.[17] In education, PD is practiced in both countries primarily
in admissions to higher educational institutions. In employment, PD involves
selection into public sector jobs in India, whereas in the US it involves selection into a range of private sector jobs as well. The relative significance of PD
in employment is greater in India, however, because the labor market is much
less favorable to job-seekers in India, and because the long-term security and
fringe benefits of public sector jobs make them especially valuable in the
Indian context. Moreover, reserved seats are quantitatively as well as qualitatively more significant as a source of employment for members of
under-represented groups in India than are preferential policies in the US.

   For several reasons it would be desirable, in general, to focus PD policies
more on access to educational opportunities and less on access to jobs. First of
all, the difficulties that PD beneficiaries face in achieving good performance
in a challenging setting tend to be less daunting when PD beneficiaries are
younger and have not yet suffered so many of the cumulative effects of group
stigmatization and socio-economic disadvantage. The earlier in the life cycle
that PD beneficiaries are asked to catch up with their less disadvantaged peers,
the more important are their potential capabilities as opposed to their realized
capabilities, and the greater are their chances of success. This implies, too, that
it is better to apply PD in higher educational admissions at the undergraduate
level than at the graduate/post-graduate level (other things being equal).

   Secondly, the negative consequences of poor performance in educational
institutions are likely to be confined largely to the individual PD beneficiary;
whereas in job settings poor performance can hurt other parties as well. Thus,

to the extent that PD generates a conflict between justice/equity and merit/efficiency, this conflict is likely to be smaller in magnitude and easier to manage in an educational setting than in a job environment.[18] Indeed, PD in higher education provides a way of defusing the tension between representation and expertise in professional and responsible positions, because attending more selective universities enables UREG members to gain the skills necessary to qualify for – and fulfill the responsibilities of – such high-status positions. In this way the advantages of a more group-integrated professional elite can be gained without much loss in the competence of those filling the positions.

A third possible reason to prefer PD in education over PD in employment is that passions and resentments about the actual and/or perceived unfairness of the selection processes involved are likely to run higher in the employment than in the educational sphere. This is because the stakes for the individuals involved – whether they are preferred or displaced by PD – tend to be greater when it comes to jobs as against admissions to educational institutions (unless the latter serve as perfectly straightforward channels to good jobs). Thus the costs of positive discrimination associated with inter-group tension and conflict may be less serious in the case of educational admissions. Indeed, the greater degree of inter-group tension and conflict in India as compared to that in the US may be partly attributable to the relatively greater importance in India of employment as compared to educational reservations.

There is one consideration that could put a premium on PD preferences in the employment sphere. Some important prospective benefits of PD – e.g. the integration of the societal elite – require for their realization that UREG members occupy high-status positions. If there is any doubt that qualified UREG members will be hired into and/or promoted up to high-status positions, then PD policies may be needed at the employment stage of the life cycle.

Developmental vs. preferential approaches

Everyone can agree that it would be desirable to find ways to enable UREG members to increase their numbers in high-quality educational institutions and in esteemed occupations by becoming more successful in a fully competitive selection process, rather than by receiving PD preferences (of the sort that do not serve to improve accuracy in measuring applicant qualifications). This has led some observers to propose that policies of "preferential positive discrimination" – i.e. the kind of PD policies discussed in this book – be replaced by policies of "developmental positive discrimination."

Developmental PD would encompass programs to improve the primary and secondary education accessible to most UREG youths; programs to enable UREG applicants to perform better on standardized tests, whether for admission to educational institutions or for selection to jobs; and, more generally, programs to improve the physical and social environments of the relatively poor neighborhoods and regions in which UREG members typically live, so as to make these environments more conducive to their advancement. Certainly, developmental PD, as defined in this way, is much to be desired. It cannot, however, be considered an alternative to preferential PD. On the one hand, developmental PD involves the channeling of greater resources disproportionately to members of certain under-represented ethnic groups, so it has a significantly preferential character. On the other hand, preferential PD often enables its beneficiaries to attain positions where they are likely to be better able to develop their skills and abilities, so it becomes partly developmental in character.[19] Furthermore, as I have stressed earlier in this chapter, any kind of developmental program typically calls for a much greater commitment of resources than does a purely preferential PD policy. This is the reason why it has proven much more difficult to get developmental programs going on an adequate scale than to enact preferential policies.

In general, it is certainly desirable to ensure that PD policies will serve a developmental function, not merely one of preferential selection. Except in circumstances where the selection process identifies under-credentialed applicants who are actually better prepared to do the work, the PD beneficiary will face the challenge of catching up with peers selected without any preference. His/her chances of success will depend significantly on the extent to which the new position that PD has enabled the beneficiary to attain has a development component – one that will help the beneficiary to develop his/her capabilities and overcome the initial disadvantage that he/she faces. This seems more likely to be the case when PD is applied to the selection of applicants for an educational program rather than for employment. But within the latter sphere, PD policies can be expected to work better when the role of on-the-job training is more significant.

Concluding observations

I have concluded from the analysis in this book that ethnicity-based PD policies do not – and should not try to – redistribute resources or opportunities from those individuals most guilty of injustice to those most victimized by it, nor from the richest or most advantaged people to the poorest or most disadvantaged. The most important objective of such PD policies is to bring about greater ethnic integration of society's elite, on the reasonable premise that society functions more efficiently, more equitably, more democratically, and more harmoniously if its professional, managerial, academic, and political elite is ethnically well integrated. There is much evidence from the US and India that PD policies have succeeded in accomplishing this. There is also much evidence, however, that in so doing PD policies have exacerbated consciousness of ethnic differences, with some resulting costs in social harmony and (especially in India) democratic vitality.

I have concluded further that PD policies in admissions to higher educational institutions have had some adverse effect on the average academic quality of enrolled students, with resultant costs in efficiency if not also social harmony. However, evidence from both the US and India refutes the contention that PD beneficiary students have suffered by being placed in excessively competitive environments. To the contrary, they have most often benefited from enhancement of their social as well as human capital when gaining access to more selective and prestigious educational institutions. Moreover, there is evidence from the US that greater ethnic diversity in the student body has contributed positively to the educational experience of all students. At the same time, there can be no doubt that PD policies have also had the effect of devaluing the accomplishments of beneficiary group members by encouraging the presumption that these accomplishments are attributable in some degree to preferential selection.

Finally, I have concluded that PD policies in higher educational admissions have in all likelihood generated greater net benefits in the US than in India. This can be attributed to many factors, of which the most important are probably the following. PD policies in the US have tended to involve smaller preferential boosts than in India; and they have also generally involved greater sensitivity of admissions procedures and greater developmental support for PD beneficiaries – facilitated by the much greater wealth of the US. These factors have made the prospects for academic success of PD beneficiaries greater in the US than in India. Furthermore, PD policies in India have provided preferences to a larger proportion of the population, resulting in a greater overall displacement impact; and the beneficiary groups have been more heterogeneous than in the US. These factors have made the likelihood of social tensions and political divisiveness greater in India than in the US.

Whenever and wherever PD preferences have been applied, they have proved to be controversial. Such controversy is bound to surround a policy that engages a fundamental political tension – between the individual right to equal treatment and the societal goal of overcoming profound group inequalities – and that is capable of generating both significant benefits and significant costs. In this context, public confidence in the desirability of a PD policy becomes an important element in its success. Both policy-makers and the general public need to be assured that a given PD policy is working well, and that, if and when this is no longer the case, it will be restructured or terminated. There is therefore a clear need for mechanisms to monitor, review, and evaluate – on as factual a basis as possible – whether or not a given PD policy is generating the anticipated benefits without incurring too many of the possible costs.

To assess whether or not a given PD policy is on balance desirable in any given situation, as I have stressed throughout this book, one needs to undertake a kind of benefit-cost analysis based on empirical investigation of the consequences of that PD policy. In order to accomplish this task, evidence must be gathered with respect to the wide variety of possible benefits and costs that may be generated by the policy. It is particularly important to gather evidence on the performance of the (likely) beneficiaries of the PD policy; for the ability of PD beneficiaries to succeed in the educational institutions and job settings to which PD helps them gain access is critical to the success of any PD policy.

In evaluating the success of PD policies in admissions to higher educational institutions, it is not enough to compile evidence on the academic performance of (likely) PD beneficiaries in those institutions. It is critical also to collect evidence on the post-university careers of the beneficiaries. This is important not only because the career outcomes of the beneficiaries speak to the degree of success achieved with respect to the key PD objective of integrating the societal elite. It is also important because indicators of academic achievement do not capture the full range of education and skills, acquired at a university, which a graduate will be able to deploy after graduation. The ultimate test of the accomplishments of beneficiaries of PD policies in higher educational admissions is thus to be found in the career profiles of the beneficiaries. Because this kind of evidence is crucial to the evaluation of the overall success or failure of PD policies, both in education and in employment, it should be the focus of much more empirical research.

Notes

Introduction

1   The relevant literature includes books by Parikh (1997) and Nesiah (1997), conference proceedings edited by Cunningham (1997), and articles by Weiner (1983), Dubey (1991), Chandola (1992), and Jenkins (1998). Nesiah, Cunningham, and Jenkins address positive discrimination policies also in countries other than the US and India.

Part I: Introduction

1   President Kennedy first used the term "affirmative action" in Executive Order No. 10925, dated 6 March 1961 (see Mills 1994: 5).
2   I will use "affirmative action" and "reservation policies" when referring specifically to the corresponding policies implemented in the US and India, respectively. I will use the term "positive discrimination" to denote the general practice of preferential selection of members of under-represented identity groups – except that I have used "affirmative action" in the book title because this term is surely more familiar to most readers.
3   As many scholars have shown, the term "race," as used in the context of identity groups, does not correspond to any scientifically valid biological or genetic concept of race; membership in a "racial" group is socially determined. See, for example, American Anthropological Association (1998).
4   This list of characteristics that may define an identity group is not exhaustive; sexual orientation, native language, and family religious background could be added as well. Although not a physical or cultural characteristic, place of birth can also confer identity to a group because it, too, is involuntary and unalterable.
5   For studies of positive discrimination policies in favor of women, see Bergmann (1996) on the US and Jenkins (1999) on India.

1   On the origins and nature of positive discrimination policies in the US and India

1   My sources for this section include Dubey (1991), Nesiah (1997), Parikh (1997), and Jenkins (1998).
2   I will use the term "Black" interchangeably with the term "African American," reflecting common practice, unless the context calls for the latter, more official term. In the cases of Hispanic Americans, Native Americans, and Asian Americans, there are no widely utilized shorter terms that are identical in

meaning; so I use the longer terms – except when distinguishing "Mestizos" from Hispanic Americans in general.

3 For a listing and description of the key US Supreme Court cases affecting the nature and scope of AA policies, see Anderson (2003).

4 *Regents of the University of California v. Bakke*, 438 U.S. 265 (1978).

5 *Gratz et al. v. Bollinger et al.*, 529 U.S. (2003) and *Grutter et al. v. Bollinger et al.*, 539 U.S. (2003).

6 My sources for this section include Mukarji (1981), Galanter (1984), Chanana (1993), Nesiah (1997), Parikh (1997), Mendelsohn and Vicziany (1998), and Dirks (2001: esp. Ch. 13).

7 Nehru emphasized the need to provide help to people defined as disadvantaged in socio-economic rather than in religious or ethnic terms. He said: "I try to look upon the problem not in the sense of a religious minority, but rather in the sense of helping backward groups in the country" (quoted in Mendelsohn and Vicziany 1998: 132).

8 A very small number of parliamentary seats are also reserved for Anglo-Indians.

9 On this issue, see especially Chitnis (1997) and also Galanter (1984: Chs. 5–6).

10 The Kalelkar Commission (appointed by Jawaharlal Nehru's Congress Party Administration) issued a report in 1955 that recommended national-level reservations for OBCs in educational admissions but not in government service. When an effort to devise OBC socio-economic criteria other than caste failed, however, national-level reservations for OBCs were rejected by Kalelkar himself and by the Government of India – but they let states have discretion to choose their own criteria, encouraging the use of economic tests. For details, see Radhakrishnan (1990).

11 Government of India (1981). Although officially labeled the "Backward Classes Commission," it became known as the "Mandal Commission," after its chairman, B.P. Mandal. For a detailed and favorable account of the report, see Yadav (1994: esp. Ch. 3). For critical reviews, see Kumar (1992) and Radhakrishnan (1996).

12 The Mandal Commission was severely handicapped in its efforts to identify "other backward classes" by a lack of systematic and up-to-date information on the caste/sub-caste affiliations of the Indian population, for the latest census of India to collect comprehensive and detailed information about caste status had been the census of 1931. In subsequent censuses such data have been collected only for caste and tribal groups on the official SC and ST lists.

13 *Indra Sawhney v. Union of India* (*All India Reporter*, 1993, S.C. 477).

14 My sources for this section include Galanter (1984), Radhakrishnan (1996), Sivaramayya (1996), and Rao (2001).

15 In actual practice, SC and ST members are sometimes placed in the reserved category even when they have succeeded in gaining a position via open competition.

16 Even where they are mandated, numerous institutions (especially quasi-autonomous educational institutions) have failed to implement reservations for SC and ST members; it often takes action on the part of Dalit and Adivasi organizations and/or politicians to ensure that the reservation policies are fully implemented.

17 See Mendelsohn and Vicziany (1998: esp. Chs. 7–8) and Jaffrelot (2002) for insightful analyses of Dalit politics and Dalit politicians in the context of reservation policies in the political sphere.

18 Henceforth I will refer to the two groups as Dalits and Adivasis, except in contexts in which their official status as members of STs and SCs is at issue.

19 According to the 1991 census of India, SCs and STs accounted for 16.5 per cent and 8.1 per cent of the Indian population, respectively.

20 These figures are taken from US Census Bureau, *2001 Statistical Abstract of the US*, Table 15.

2 The debate over positive discrimination in the US and in India

1 See, for example, Parmaji (1985), who studied samples of students and faculty members at a number of higher educational institutions in Andhra Pradesh. Interestingly, he found that the main exceptions to his general finding – that caste status determines one's opinion on reservations – were to be found among high-caste members or supporters of left-wing parties, who tended to favor reservations.
2 It is noteworthy that in the two issues of the monthly periodical *Seminar* (widely read by the English-speaking elite) devoted to symposia on reservation policies (December 1981 and November 1990), only five out of twenty contributors were unambiguously in favor of reservations; these included all three of the politicians and only two of the seventeen academicians who wrote on the subject.
3 The most prominent example of a Reagan appointee opposed to affirmative action was Clarence Thomas, who was tapped by President Reagan to head the Equal Employment Opportunity Commission. Thomas was nominated in 1991 by Reagan's successor, George Bush, to be a Supreme Court justice; and he assumed that position in 1992 after a contentious confirmation battled in the US Senate.
4 Poll results on this issue, however, are notoriously volatile; much depends on the way questions are phrased. For a detailed analysis of polling on issues related to affirmative action, see Steeh and Krysan (1996).
5 Indeed, in the landmark 1978 Bakke decision, Supreme Court Justice Lewis Powell observed (in a largely forgotten footnote):

> Racial classifications in admissions conceivably could serve a fifth purpose, one which [the University of California] does not articulate: fair appraisal of each individual's academic promise in the light of some cultural bias in grading or testing procedures. To the extent that race and ethnic background were considered only to the extent of curing established inaccuracies in predicting academic performance, it might be argued that there is no "preference" at all.
> (*Regents of the University of California v. Bakke*, 438 U.S. 265 at 306 n43: opinion of Powell, J.)

6 This last argument has gained increasing currency in the context of empirical studies of the long-run career paths of minority students and their counterparts in elite US colleges and universities; see, for example, Bowen and Bok (1998) and Lempert *et al.* (2000a).
7 Parallel arguments can be made to support preferences in selection to jobs: see pp. 48–9.
8 The term "social capital" has come increasingly into use to denote contacts, associations, and networks that help society to function well (economically and politically) and that enable individuals to improve their own position in society. See Sobel (2002) for a review of the various ways social scientists have made use of the concept of social capital.
9 See Loury (1976, 1977) for a pioneering effort to analyze the relationship between differential access to social capital and racial inequalities in the US.
10 The survey was part of an extensive study carried out by Patwardhan and Palshikar (1992); see esp. pp. 48–9.

11 Ilaiah is the author of a widely read book (Ilaiah 1996) that eloquently rejects "Hindutva" – i.e. Hindu social and cultural hegemony.
12 Kumar (1990: 12), for example, makes this point.
13 For a detailed account of the situation of Dalit and Adivasi students in the prestigious Indian Institutes of Technology, see Kirpal and Gupta (1999: esp. Chs. 5–6).
14 See, for example, Kahlenberg (1995).
15 See, for example, Thernstrom and Thernstrom (1997: Ch. 14), as well as Sowell (1990).
16 McWhorter (2000) has also advanced this line of argument.
17 Shelby Steele (1990) and Stephen Carter (1991) are the most prominent exponents of this argument.
18 Thus critics have charged that the increased frequency of Indian railway accidents is attributable to reservation policies, because they result in a larger proportion of less competent railway officials and/or they lower overall staff morale. See, for example, "Job reservation in railways and accidents," *Indian Express*, 19 September 1990 (cited by Kumar 1992: 301). On the other hand, a supporter of reservations has written that

> The erosion in the level of competence in government and public sector enterprises is due to corruption, nepotism, connections, etc....and not reservations for SC and ST. It is well known that the relation between merit and selection is compounded by considerations of class, community and caste.
> (Sachchidananda 1990: 19)

19 I have heard many complaints from Indian students – and indeed faculty – about undeserving SC and ST students from well-to-do Dalit and Adivasi families who have benefited from higher educational reservations.
20 See, for example, Dreze and Sen (1995: 90ff.) and Ramachandran (1997).
21 This point is made, for example, by Andre Beteille (1981).
22 Myron Weiner has developed this point in considerable depth. He argues that

> preferential policies facilitate the mobilization of groups to demand their extension, creating political struggles over how the state should allocate benefits to ethnic groups, generating a backlash on the part of those ethnic groups excluded from benefits, intensifying the militancy of the beneficiaries and reinforcing the importance of ascription as the principle of choice in allocating social benefits and facilitating mobility.
> (Weiner 1983: 49)

23 See Patwardhan and Palshikar (1992: 71).
24 One prominent exception to this rule is the distinguished sociologist Andre Beteille. In his 1990 lecture entitled "Distributive justice and institutional well-being," he explicitly characterized Indian reservation policies as "reverse discrimination" (Beteille 1992: 53). It is probably not a coincidence that in this lecture he addresses the US experience with affirmative action as well as the Indian experience with reservation policies.

3 The potential benefits and costs of positive discrimination

1 The arguments and claims that I discuss here involve PD policies that provide some degree of preference to under-represented ethnic group members in admissions to educational institutions or in selections to desirable jobs, for these are the

spheres most often targeted by PD policies. Some of the arguments and claims, however, are relevant also to PD policies in other spheres – e.g. government contracting or political representation.

2   The kinds of capital relevant here include not only (conventional) physical and financial capital but also human, social, and cultural capital.

3   To be consistent in ruling out involuntary characteristics taken on by virtue of an applicant's family background, critics of PD should exclude not just UREG status but all such characteristics. Other characteristics in frequent use are place of residence and (in the sphere of higher education) legacy status, i.e. whether other members of the family have attended the same institution. Yet those who charge "reverse discrimination" on the basis of UREG status rarely seek to remove such other involuntary characteristics from selection decision-making processes.

4   Claim 1.1 does raise the following question: why should PD carry symbolic value independently of its practical value in generating benefits? If one were starting from scratch, the best way of affirming society's commitment to reduce the continuing disadvantages experienced by UREG members would be to implement policies that are most effective in bringing real benefits to the disadvantaged. The matter takes on a different salience, however, when the issue is whether or not to discontinue an already existing PD policy. In that case the dismantling of PD arguably does carry symbolic weight over and above whatever real losses (or gains) might result – the more so, the broader the scope of the dismantling. In other words, discontinuing a PD policy that has been in effect is very likely to be perceived by UREG groups as a much more significant and hostile act than failure to adopt a PD policy in the first place. If one is nonetheless inclined to reject PD on the grounds that there are better ways to affirm society's commitment to reduce the continuing disadvantages faced by UREG members, then one had best see to it that a better alternative is actually substituted for PD.

5   In considering the case for PD in order to integrate the societal elite, one must recognize that there is a significant difference between the political elite and the professional elite – as Beteille (1992) has most clearly shown. The desirability of proportionate group representation is considerably less controversial in the political arena than in professional fields. It is widely recognized that for a representative democracy to function well, people need to be assured that they are adequately represented not only as individuals but also as members of groups. To overcome the fact and the perception of group differences in opportunity to occupy political office, democratic electoral systems are often explicitly structured so as to ensure adequate representation for different groups defined in geographic or in ethnic terms. More controversial is the notion that adequate representation for different groups should characterize the occupants of other elite positions that are not essentially representational in nature – e.g. managers of enterprises and organizations, high-level civil servants, lawyers, doctors, and academics. Here there is potentially a real trade-off between representation and expertise.

6   In helping to offset UREG applicant deficits of social capital, PD provides a form of compensation for past injustice that goes mainly to those who most need it. This argument, argument 6, is thus related to argument 1 on compensation for injustice; but I have separated it because it focuses primarily on the welfare of individual UREG members, whereas the earlier one focuses on the welfare of society as a whole.

7   This argument is linked to a critique of the compensation-for-injustice argument in favor of PD, to the effect that PD does not achieve its compensatory objective because it does not benefit primarily those who have suffered most from past injustice, nor does it penalize primarily those who have gained from that injustice. From this critique it is a short step to the argument that PD has undesirable redistributive

consequences, because it provides benefits to people who are less needy than those on whom it imposes costs.

8 Sunita Parikh has expressed very well the inherently double-edged effects on democracy of a focus on ascribed group ethnicity:

> authentic democratic politics increases the controversy associated with ascriptive politics...This suggests a paradox: as groups become politically active, which is desirable in a democracy, ascriptive politics both spur them to participate and exacerbate separations between them and other groups that do not share these ascriptive characteristics.
>
> (Parikh 1997: 198)

9 This argument, argument 10, is closely related to the preceding one; it involves essentially a key implication of argument 9. I have separated it from argument 9, however, both because of its importance and because it focuses on the welfare of individual PD beneficiaries, as opposed to the functioning of the organizations or institutions to which they gain access.

10 I use this two-word term because efficiency per se is not a goal; it is a quality that may or may not characterize the process of achieving some specified goal. Thus a process is efficient if a given goal is achieved with minimum expenditure of effort or resources, or if a given amount of effort or resources is deployed so as to obtain the maximum benefit. By prefacing efficiency with "productive," I focus attention on the goal of achieving the maximum net product from a society's given resources.

11 By a "comprehensive" benefit-cost analysis I mean what is sometimes referred to as a "social" benefit-cost analysis; it is distinguished from a conventional benefit-cost analysis by the fact that the underlying criterion of value is not confined to societal wealth but takes into account broader elements of societal well-being (see Goodwin *et al.* 2003: Ch.1).

4   A theoretical analysis of the consequences of positive discrimination policies

1 The practice of excluding from a reserved quota those UREG applicants who are selected in open competition is not uncommon in India. This practice is, however, very hard to justify. Since the whole point of positive discrimination is to assure adequate representation of under-represented groups, why should one exclude from the count of UREG selectees those UREG members who happen to have been selected without the aid of a PD policy?

2 There is one minor exception to this rule. If the last applicant selected to fill a quota has qualifications equal to those of one or more of the top applicants who failed to be selected, then a preferential-boost system would have to either accept or reject all of the marginal applicants with equal qualifications.

3 If and when the preferential boost implied by a minimum qualifications requirement in a constrained quota system is not binding – i.e. if it alone would allow more applicants to be selected than the size of the quota – then there is of course a difference in outcome as between the constrained quota system and the corresponding preferential-boost system.

4 Note that the two alternative approaches to measuring the impact of a PD policy (the displacement impact and the magnitude of the preference) are analogous to the two alternative preference mechanisms (a pure quota system and a preferential-boost system).

5 Because of the overlap in distributions, the difference in scores between any individual low-scoring selected UREG applicant and any individual low-scoring

selected non-UREG applicant will vary widely depending on the pair of individuals chosen. Indeed, in the context of a qualitative PD selection process, a randomly chosen low-scoring UREG applicant might well have a higher score than a randomly chosen low-scoring non-UREG applicant.

6 The fundamental importance of stigmatization is argued forcefully by Loury (2002). As he defines the term, "stigmatization is not merely the drawing of a negative surmise about someone's productive attributes. It entails doubting the person's worthiness and consigning him or her to a social netherworld" (Loury 2002: 61).

7 Claude Steele has done the pioneering work on "stereotype threat"; see Steele (1992) and Steele and Aronson (1998). Steele first developed and tested his analysis in the context of poor academic performance by Black students in the US. He posited that the internalization of racial stereotypes of Black intellectual inferiority by Black students themselves threatens them with the prospect that their failures will be interpreted as reflecting badly on the whole African-American community. This has an adverse effect on their performance in most testing situations; and it can also lead to dis-identification with academic achievement as a strategy for coping with the "stereotype vulnerability" that threatens Black students' self-esteem.

8 This much-cited dictum is from US Supreme Court Justice Harry Blackmun's opinion in the 1978 Bakke decision (*Regents of the University of California v. Bakke*, 438 U.S. 265: opinion of Blackmun, H.).

9 The importance of social segregation in perpetuating group inequalities is convincingly argued by Anderson (2002) and Loury (2002).

10 There is actually one way in which a society's level of economic development could influence PD net benefits in an unfavorable direction. The relative desirability of focusing on ethnicity rather than on socio-economic disadvantage in determining eligibility for social welfare benefits depends in part on a practical consideration: the degree of difficulty in measuring socio-economic disadvantage. It is always harder to assess and to verify the extent to which a family is socio-economically disadvantaged than to determine its ethnic identity, for the determination of socio-economic class status requires more information to be gathered and analyzed. But the differential difficulty of measuring the socio-economic dimensions of inequality is greater in poor countries, because social and economic data are less likely to be available and tend to be less reliable when available. Thus the desirability of using simple ascriptive indicators, such as ethnic identity, as a basis of eligibility for social welfare benefits is greater in poorer societies. This chain of causation, however, is surely not strong enough to outweigh the favorable effects of greater wealth on PD net benefits; and its impact is likely to be too small to warrant further attention.

5 The differing contexts of positive discrimination in the US and India

1 My sources for this section are Takaki (1994), Cunningham and Madhava Menon (1999), and Loury (2002) for the US, and Berreman (1975), Mendelsohn and Vicziany (1998), Deliege (1999), and Gupta (2000) for India.

2 See the introduction to Part I, pp. 3–5.

3 In this context it is interesting to note that the Sanskrit term *varna*, which refers to the broadly defined caste ranks of Hindu society, also means "color" or "complexion."

4 The primary racial/ethnic minority groups in the US are each associated with a different non-white color: black for African Americans, brown for Hispanic

Americans, red for Native Americans, and yellow for Asian Americans (who are not as under-represented as the other groups by most criteria, but who are also exposed to various forms of negative discrimination).

5 Another Hispanic sub-group consists of those who have immigrated directly from Spain. As European immigrants who are predominantly White, and who assimilate relatively easily into mainstream US society, the members of this sub-group are not in principle eligible for affirmative action. In practice, however, they are sometimes included in the overall group of Hispanic Americans – e.g. when the latter are defined simply by Hispanic surname.

6 In the Indian context of vertical caste differentiation, members of some Dalit castes have sought to improve the position of their caste in the Hindu caste hierarchy rather than to do away with the whole notion of caste hierarchy; see Deliege (1999: 42, 73). Such an aspiration is probably due to grave doubt that the hierarchical system as a whole can ever be dismantled, rather than to any strong conviction that hierarchy is appropriate. In the US there is no overarching hierarchical system within which under-represented groups might hope to improve their relative position; Blacks and other US under-represented groups therefore want to get rid of the whole system of White supremacy. Increasingly, Dalits and Adivasis are taking the same position vis-à-vis "caste-Hindu" supremacy in India.

7 See, for example, Rao (2002: 56), who cites the case of the Telengana Madigas concerned about the much higher share of reserved SC seats going to the coastal Malas in Andhra Pradesh.

8 In the case of marriage between a White and a non-White person, the convention in the US is to assign the offspring to the non-White group; but this assignment may be problematical when a child happens to "look White." In the case of marriage between members of two different non-White groups, the following question arises: to which group should the offspring be assigned? Increasing numbers of Americans are declaring themselves to be "multiracial."

9 See Deliege (1999: 11).

10 This is, of course, all the more true of Hispanic Americans who have immigrated more or less directly from Spain.

11 See Deliege (1999: 14–15).

12 See US Census Bureau, *2001 Statistical Abstract of the US*, Tables 686, 678, 679, and 685.

13 See Sharma (1990) and Deshpande (2001) for evidence on the relative socio-economic level of Dalits and Adivasis. Because the census of India has not collected data on castes or sub-castes (except for those on the official SC list) since 1931, there is little hard evidence available for OBCs.

14 The few exceptions are in secondary schools, not in higher education.

15 High reliance on standardized tests makes access to supplementary preparation for such tests (private tutors, training courses aimed at improving test scores, etc.) all the more critical to an applicant's chances of success, adding to the competitive disadvantage faced by those with few resources.

16 See Dreze and Sen (1995: 90–1).

17 The figures are based on US Census Bureau, *2001 Statistical Abstract of the US*, Table 15.

18 See Chapter 1, pp. 10–15.

19 But, in the case of higher educational institutions, see Chapter 9 (pp. 136–40) and Chapter 10 (pp. 147–51).

6 A comparative analysis of the likely consequences of positive discrimination in the US and India

1   Here, as in the rest of Part I, I am alluding to PD policies only in the spheres of education and employment. The reservation of legislative seats for Scheduled Castes and Scheduled Tribes in India has no close counterpart in the US, and it raises rather different issues – for example, concerns about quality of performance are much less salient in the case of political representation.

Part II: Introduction

1   Recall that I define the term "ethnic group" broadly to include any group whose members share a common race, caste, tribe, religion, and/or ethnicity.
2   Policies of positive discrimination in US university admissions have been the target of a series of lawsuits beginning in the mid-1990s; see the link to "Recent legal decisions on affirmative action" at Anderson (2003).
3   Hereafter, for simplicity, I will use the term "university" to denote strictly undergraduate colleges as well as higher educational institutions that offer both undergraduate and more advanced degree programs.

7 Positive discrimination in admissions to higher educational institutions

1   Only at a university that selects its students from a larger number of applicants can there be any meaningful content to a policy of positive discrimination.
2   I have borrowed these terms from Bowen and Bok (1998).
3   Indeed, these may be the only institutions actually practicing positive discrimination in admissions. This is true of admissions to undergraduate programs of US colleges and universities: according to Kane (1998: 432), only the top 20 per cent practice positive discrimination.
4   This argument has been made by, among others, the student interveners in the University of Michigan cases; see Anderson (2001: 20).
5   See my discussion of the Bakke and Michigan cases in Chapter 1, pp. 9–10.
6   See Loury (1976, 1977) for a pioneering effort to analyze the relationship between differential access to social capital and racial inequalities in the US.
7   In helping to offset UREG student deficits of social capital, PD provides a form of compensation for past injustice; so argument 6 is related to argument 1. I have separated the two arguments because the former focuses primarily on the welfare of individual students, whereas the latter focuses on the welfare of society as a whole.
8   In this way, PD in higher educational admissions can serve to some extent as a substitute for PD at the job level, just as more equal access to good primary and secondary education may serve as a substitute for PD at the college or university level. This is all to the good; for the lower the level at which PD operates, the less is the risk that it will conflict with relevant criteria of merit.
9   There is not a little irony here: the presumption that PD explains much of the success of UREG members reverses the explanatory paradigm typically used to explain the success of non-UREG members, in which innate ability and individual effort are highlighted and situational advantage is discounted. This suggests that the presumption is grounded (like the negative stereotyping discussed just above) in an underlying predisposition of non-UREG members to view UREG members as innately inferior when it comes to academic ability. Such a predisposition is surely

held by some – perhaps many – non–UREG members; to the extent that it is, the devaluation problem cannot be attributed simply to PD.

10 Where PD preferences take the form of seats reserved for UREG members who do not gain admission to a university in a competition open to all applicants, as is most often the case in India, then it may be possible to distinguish plainly between those UREG students who owe their admission to PD and those who do not.

11 Loury (1997) shows clearly that among UREG members, only those who actually get selected by virtue of a PD policy benefit from the inferences about competence that can legitimately be drawn from the situation; those UREG members who would have been selected in any case, as well as those who are rejected, lose by such inferences. Among non–UREG members the direction of legitimate inferences is just the reverse: all but those who are rejected due to PD end up gaining by the inferences.

12 Even if many UREG students have been admitted with lower academic qualifications, by virtue of PD, it does not follow inexorably that the retrospectively rejected UREG students – much less all UREG students – "do not belong on campus." Universities may in principle, and do in practice, serve a variety of educational objectives as well as broader social goals, many of which do not require that a student body be formed solely on the basis of who is most qualified academically. Academic qualifications are surely an important consideration in admitting students to a higher educational institution, but they are by no means the sole legitimate basis for doing so. Any stigmatization of UREG students as undeserving of their place on a selective university campus should not therefore be attributed simply to positive discrimination; it must at least also be attributed to a very narrow conception of a university as strictly academic in function. In this case, it should be possible to reduce – if not to eliminate – the stigmatization of UREG students in the context of PD by bringing university community members to a greater awareness of the multifaceted goals of higher education.

13 Coate and Loury (1993) were the first to develop a theoretically rigorous analysis of the adverse consequences of PD-induced patronization (in a workplace setting).

14 Faculty are entitled to draw statistical inferences based on their understanding of admissions procedures; but they have a responsibility not to let general inferences about groups affect the way in which they educate individual students. To the extent that they fail to live up to this responsibility, surely the consequences should be attributed mainly to inappropriate faculty behavior rather than to positive discrimination. On the other hand, it is fair to conclude that if the application of a PD policy leads to the admission of a cohort of students who are (on average) less well prepared for the academic demands of a selective university than those who would be admitted without PD, then the task of educating the student cohort to any given level of academic performance will be more challenging. Under these circumstances, the universities involved will have to be prepared to invest more resources in the educational process than would be required in the absence of PD.

15 But these kinds of measures – especially test scores – are far from ideal indicators of realized academic achievement, since they can be strongly influenced by non-academic factors such as test-taking skill.

16 A university adds most to the education of the population by taking in and educating those who will increase their human capital most by attending the university. Although the principle of "diminishing returns" implies that there is more of an educational return to a dollar spent on education if the person to be educated has more to learn, this principle is likely to be dominated – at least in the relatively selective universities where PD in admissions has the most impact –

by the principle of "building on the best," which implies that the academically best-prepared applicants are likely to get the most out of an elite university education. Note that the advantage conferred by past academic achievement is confined to the accumulation of human capital. For social capital accumulation – the building of career-aiding networks and connections – past academic achievement is irrelevant. Indeed, pre-university levels of academic achievement are likely to be correlated with pre-university endowments of social capital; so students entering a university with relatively low levels of academic achievement will on average have more to gain from university attendance in the way of social capital than their peers who are academically better prepared. (This is precisely the thrust of argument 6 in favor of PD in admissions.)

17 This second range is of course not as wide, since those at the lower ends of the societal distribution are not likely to be in a position even to apply to a university.

18 See the discussion of alternative types of PD admission policies in Chapter 4, pp. 61–6.

19 The US Educational Testing Service has actually experimented with such a procedure to identify "strivers" among applicants taking the Scholastic Achievement Test; but they have shied away from reporting any such results: see Lemann (1999a: Ch. 23, 1999b).

20 Even if PD, by insulating UREG applicants or students to some extent from competitive pressures, does have some dampening effect on their incentive to work hard, this does not mean that their motivation to achieve in their educational activities will be any less (on average) than that of their non-UREG counterparts. This is because UREG members typically have less social capital to deploy than non-UREG members. Since UREG youths cannot count on benefiting much from social connections in seeking admission to good universities and access to good employment opportunities, their life chances are likely to depend to a greater extent on their educational achievements – unless, of course, the type and context of PD are such as to virtually guarantee their advancement.

21 See Gurin *et al.* (2002) and Milem (2002) for presentations of the argument, as well as reviews of the evidence, for the educational value of a diverse student body.

22 On the role of the university in a multicultural society, see Cantor (1998).

23 See Anderson (2000, 2002) on the importance of residential segregation as a source of social segregation.

24 Where PD is a university policy rather than a government-mandated policy, one might ask whether universities have the right to impose their own notion of societal goals as a reason for practicing PD. The answer is that public universities (because of their public funding), and also private universities (insofar as they too benefit from public funding), have a responsibility to promote contributions to the betterment of society at large, beyond what may be considered their primary objective – the advancement and dissemination of knowledge.

25 Gender or geographical region of residence would possibly provide additional dimensions of diversity helpful to achieving viewpoint diversity; but they are unlikely to substitute in this respect for ethnic diversity.

26 There remains one possibly troubling implication of any argument for PD as a means to improve the educational experience of all students. This argument implies that UREG students admitted via PD to selective universities are admitted not because of their own actual or potential accomplishments but, instead, in order to benefit other students. It is true that the argument casts PD beneficiaries in the creditable role of educating other students. Still, all that appears to be required of them to serve in this role is to be present on campus. This is likely to

feed into problems of devaluation of UREG achievements of the kind raised in argument 12 against PD.

8 Toward an empirical assessment of claims of benefits and costs from positive discrimination

1   In particular, if a significant proportion of retrospectively rejected UREG students drop out and fail to graduate, then the magnitude of the costs of claim 12.2 would be higher, because many students admitted via PD would then be shown "not to belong on campus" in a very significant sense.
2   One might suppose that evidence on whether PD admission policies actually serve to increase or to diminish the accuracy of appraisal of applicant qualifications (claim 3.1 vs. claim 9.1) would be highly relevant to a test of claim 3.2 vs. claim 9.2. Thus, evidence that PD helps appraisal accuracy should enable one to reject the cost claim 9.2; and evidence that PD hurts appraisal accuracy should serve to reject the benefit claim 3.2. However, the claims at issue here involve perceptions, not reality; and on "hot-button" issues of this kind the connection between perception and reality is notoriously tenuous.
3   As Anderson (2000: 297) has persuasively argued, the view that UREG members are cognitively inferior arises from an underlying predisposition of non-UREG members to attribute poor UREG student performance to innate weaknesses rather than to situational disadvantages. Doing away with PD would improve the average academic performance of UREG students relative to non-UREG students at the more selective universities; but it would also result in a significant drop in attendance of those universities by UREG members and hence a significant drop in the numbers of UREG graduates entering high-status occupations. The continued under-representation of UREG members in these high-status spheres would itself be taken as evidence of their cognitive inferiority, given the underlying predisposition of non-UREG members to hold this view. Thus it seems likely that the removal of PD would serve mainly to shift the locus of "evidence" for UREG cognitive inferiority from relatively poor performance at selective universities to the under-representation of UREGs at these universities and in prestigious occupations.

9 Affirmative action and enrollments in US universities

1   These figures are from US Department of Education, National Center for Education Statistics, *Digest of Educational Statistics*, Table 187.
2   These figures, and those in the next sentence, are from Bowen and Bok (1998: 9–10).
3   The SAT was for many years known as the "Scholastic Aptitude Test." In 1995 its name was changed to the "Scholastic Assessment Test" in an effort to dispel the impression that it measures some kind of natural-born ability.
4   More precisely, Kane (1998) found that in the case of the top quintile of colleges (where each quintile represents an equal number of entering students), UREG status is worth about 400 points in (combined) SAT score, or two levels of GPA (e.g. from B to A−); this makes admission rates for UREG applicants about 10 per cent higher than for Whites.
5   These numbers are based on data provided by Bowen and Bok (1998: 295, Table A.2); they apply to the entering class of 1976. Data from the *Digest of Educational Statistics*, Table 182, indicate that freshman enrollment numbers have not changed much since then.

6 See, for example, Sandalow (1999) and Anderson (2000), who points out Bowen and Bok found that Black enrollment would drop even more – to 1.6 per cent, 2.4 per cent, and 3.8 per cent at their three levels of selectivity – using math rather than verbal SAT proportions; and Bowen and Bok ignored possible disincentives for Blacks to apply in the absence of AA. Cherry (2001: 216) cites evidence that without AA, enrollments of UREG students at the University of Michigan in 1994 would have dropped from 14 per cent to 5 per cent – a much sharper drop than that estimated by Bowen and Bok for colleges at their third level of selectivity, in which Michigan is included.

7 See US Department of Education, National Center for Education Statistics, *Digest of Educational Statistics*, Table 207.

8 Student attrition over the course of four years of study would tend to reduce this ratio, but the tendency of some students to stay in college for more than four years tends to raise the ratio; in rough terms these effects are likely to offset each other.

9 See Bowen and Bok (1998: 376–7, Table D.3.1).

10 These estimates are supported by the actual experience of the University of Texas and the University of California at Berkeley law schools: after they were prohibited from using UREG status as an admission criterion, the number of Black and other UREG students admitted dropped dramatically; see Cunningham and Madhava Menon (1999).

11 The figures are from US Department of Education, National Center for Education Statistics, *Digest of Educational Statistics*, Table 208; note that they include not only entering students but all continuing students.

12 There are other academic criteria that are also used, especially in US four-year colleges – e.g. quality of high school, difficulty of high-school courses taken, and academic honors and awards.

13 See, for example, Kane (1998: 433–5) and Holzer and Neumark (2000: 510).

14 Dickens and Kane (1999) conclude that a color-blind admissions process based on a broader range of admissions criteria can actually generate Black–White test-score gaps nearly as large as the gaps in the whole Black–White population.

15 Bowen and Bok do not identify the five colleges, in order to respect promises of confidentiality, but they do note (1998: 17 n4) that they include three private universities and two co-educational liberal arts colleges whose 1989 matriculants had average SAT scores of at least 1,240; according to the criteria they used for distinguishing selectivity groups (1998: 337), this excludes all the colleges in their third level of selectivity.

16 This point applies more generally: for a variety of tests of all Black and White 17-year-olds, Hedges and Nowell (1998) found declining test-score gaps over time; however, they found that Black under-representation at the highest SAT levels has not changed.

17 The same pattern (but with even greater differentials) is found among students in Bowen and Bok's 1976 entering cohort; compare the figures for the two years in Bowen and Bok (1998: 422, Table D.6.9).

18 Many analysts have made this observation; see, for example, Bowen and Bok (1998: 42).

19 See Malamud (1997) for a comprehensive review of the ways in which conventional measures of socio-economic status overstate the SES of Blacks relative to Whites.

10 Reservation policies and enrollments in Indian universities

1 Most of the empirical evidence on the consequences of India's reservation policies that I present in this part of the book involves only SC and ST students. To

present and analyze such evidence in the case of "other backward classes" (OBCs) would require a much more detailed state-by-state investigation, since the situation of OBCs varies widely across the different states of India.

2 Data on student enrollment are presented in the annual reports of the Ministry of Human Resources Development, Government of India, New Delhi.

3 These figures are drawn from Rao (2002: 47, Table 1).

4 According to official census of India data, the SC and ST shares were 15.5 per cent and 7.8 per cent in 1981 and 16.5 per cent and 8.1 per cent in 1991.

5 The information in this paragraph is drawn from Chanana (1993: esp. Table 4) and *Selected Educational Statistics, 1996–97* (Ministry of Human Resources Development, Government of India, New Delhi, 1997).

6 Detailed data on the educational attainments of SC and ST members (as well as the rest of the population) have been gathered by the decennial Indian censuses since 1961, but the SC and ST data have been made available only for the 1961, 1971, and 1981 censuses. In the case of the 1961 census, data on graduates of higher educational institutions are available only for urban areas; I estimated the overall 1961 figures by multiplying the 1961 urban figures by the 1971 ratios of total to urban graduates.

7 Among the few exceptions to the rule of reserved SC and ST seats at centrally controlled institutions are centers of "postgraduate" (graduate-level) studies that have received special exemptions, such as the All-India Institute of Medical Sciences in New Delhi and the National Institute of Advanced Studies in Bangalore. The SC reserved seat percentage has been 15 per cent all along; the ST percentage was initially set at 5 per cent but was then raised to 7.5 per cent in 1982.

8 See Mendelsohn and Vicziany (1998: 142–5).

9 One should also note the role of educational institutions set up specifically to cater to SC and/or ST students – for example, colleges run by the People's Education Society, which was founded by Dr. B.R. Ambedkar in Maharashtra to promote the education of Dalits. While such schools have certainly played a very positive role in increasing the quantity and quality of educational opportunities available to disadvantaged students in certain areas, the number of higher educational institutions of this kind is very small in an all-India context.

10 The percentage figures in this and the next paragraph are based on Government of India, Department of Education figures cited by Chowdhary (1998: Tables 4 and 5).

11 The discussion in this paragraph relies heavily on Chanana (1993) and Rao (2001, 2002).

12 The five long-standing IITs are in Bombay (Mumbai), Delhi, Kanpur, Kharagpur, and Madras (Chennai). In the mid-1990s a new IIT was opened in Guwahati.

13 These ratios are based on admissions data compiled by Rao (2002: Table 2).

14 Rao (2002: 56) discusses, as an instructive example, the case of the two major Dalit castes in Andhra Pradesh – the Malas and the Madigas. The former are mainly agricultural laborers with a sense of superiority over the latter, who work with animal hides. The Malas have always had considerably greater access to schooling, and they now capture the lion's share of reserved seats in higher education, as compared to the Madigas.

11 Affirmative action and academic performance in US universities

1 Thernstrom and Thernstrom (1997: 392) reported also that among full-time first-year undergraduates enrolling from 1984 to 1987, 57 per cent of Whites and only 34 per cent of Blacks earned a degree within six years.
2 The other academic qualification most widely used by admissions offices is high-school GPA, which tends to correlate positively – but not very closely – with SAT score.
3 As noted at the end of Chapter 9, p. 143, the Black-White SAT-score gap has diminished over the past several decades; but it remains substantial.
4 Thus, for example, Thernstrom and Thernstrom (1997: 407) report evidence of a strong correlation between SAT scores and graduation rates at UC-Berkeley; though their own figures suggest that this correlation applies only to scores up to 1,200. Vars and Bowen (1998: 460–3) report a positive correlation between graduation rates and SAT scores for a cohort of students who entered eleven highly selective colleges in 1989.
5 One is tempted to infer that Harvard, in keeping the SAT gap relatively low, does a much better job than Berkeley of admitting Black students capable of meeting the demands of its undergraduate program. But the difference in SAT gaps may also be explained by differences in the quality of the Black students attracted by the two schools.
6 It is not surprising that the average White student goes to a college with a closely matched median SAT score, because White students typically constitute a large majority of the students whose median score defines that of the college they go to. What is noteworthy here is that the average Black student goes to a college with a significantly higher median SAT than his/her own SAT score.
7 About 7 per cent of students transfer out of the college they enter and end up graduating from a different college; this percentage does not vary much across ethnic groups. A much smaller number of students take more than six years to graduate.
8 See Bowen and Bok (1998: 380–1, Tables D.3.3 and D.3.4)
9 Although Lempert et al. (2000a) gathered data from students who graduated from the Law School as early as the 1970s, they did not have graduation data by race from before 1983.
10 Mean values for all the variables in their database are given in Datcher Loury and Garman (1985: 296, Table 1).
11 Many others have also found that under-represented minority students "underperform" in GPA attainment relative to White students with similar SAT scores. For example, Kane (1998: 443), drawing on data from a nationwide sample of high-school graduates of 1982, found that Hispanic-American as well as Black students attain lower GPAs than White students – controlling for their SAT scores. Note this implies that, even if there were no AA policies in effect, UREG students would on average compile poorer academic records at college than non-UREG students for two reasons – not only because they would still enter college with lower average SAT scores (as noted in Chapter 9, pp. 140–3), but also because their academic performance would on average be weaker at any given average SAT level.
12 See, for example, Wightman (1997).
13 Bowen and Bok (1998: 77); in this regard they cite the work of Klitgaard (1985: 162–4).
14 One might infer also that admissions officers fail to take these difficult-to-measure characteristics adequately into account, or else they would have admitted those

Black applicants who are least handicapped by them. This inference presumes, however, that admissions decisions are made with the goal of maximizing the recorded academic performance of admitted students. In fact, admissions officers may take a longer or broader view and credit applicants with the potential for achievements other than high grades and academic honors.

15 Most of the explanations suggested in the next paragraph would not apply to the historically Black colleges; but they do apply to all of the more highly selective colleges and universities at which AA is most salient.

16 Claude Steele has undertaken pioneering research on what he first described as "stereotype bias"; see Steele and Aronson (1998).

17 Ferguson (1998) finds evidence of this kind of phenomenon at the secondary school level.

18 The disadvantages of a mismatch are perhaps greater if a student is under-qualified rather than over-qualified; but over-qualified students surely forgo educational opportunities from which they could have benefited at a more challenging institution.

19 Thernstrom and Thernstrom (1997: 403–5) did undertake a "crude but illuminating" test of the role of social class in explaining relatively poor Black academic performance, pointing to the fact that Black students' relatively poor SAT scores cannot be explained by their lower levels of family income or parental education. This test, however, does not go far enough in ruling out competing explanations for differences in Black academic performance in colleges of different selectivity.

20 More precisely, Kane (1998: 440-8, incl. Tables 12-5 and 12-6) found that a 100-point increase in college median SAT is associated with a 3 per cent higher graduation rate and a roughly 1 per cent lower GPA (0.03 fewer GPA points).

21 See Kane (1998: 447–8); in correspondence with the author, Kane has also cautioned against interpreting his results as evidence of a positive selectivity effect on graduation rates.

22 As Thernstrom and Thernstrom (1999b) noted in a highly critical review of Bowen and Bok (1998), the C&B database utilized by Bowen and Bok included data from several HBCs; so they could – and should – have included HBC students in their analysis and drawn some inferences about the effects of shifting Black students from HBCs to elite White-dominated colleges.

12 Reservation policies and academic performance in Indian universities

1 This hypothesis was conveyed to the author by Velaskar in an e-mail message dated 24 January 2002.

2 The Vimukta Tribe students in Patwardhan and Palshikar's sample tended to do better than SC and ST students in examination marks, but their drop-out rate was higher.

3 According to Kirpal and Gupta (1999), only 2,250 students (including less than 100 SC and ST students) are admitted annually from among roughly 80,000 applicants – an admission ratio of 2.8 per cent.

4 See Kirpal (1978) and Kirpal et al. (1985, 1985–86).

5 Kirpal and Gupta's data show that, among the IITs, IIT-Kharagpur enrolls a disproportionately high proportion of SC and ST students, and it also graduates a significantly higher proportion of them than do the other four main IITs. The overall figures cited in the text thus overstate the success of SC and ST students at the IITs in Bombay, Delhi, Kanpur, and Madras – which are the most prestigious among the IITs.

6 See Kumar (1997) for a very useful analysis of the role of the English language in Indian educational inequality.

7 These are the only such studies of which I am aware.

8 Wankhede notes that these neo-Buddhist students had to claim Hindu status in order to get access to government-funded special facilities (such as a hostel) designated for Hindu SCs.

9 According to an e-mail communication from Velaskar to the author dated 24 January 2002.

10 The fact that many beneficiaries of higher educational reservations among SC and ST graduates benefit from additional reservations in postgraduate studies or in public employment means that their career attainments may somewhat overstate the effects of their initial access to reservations. Even when this is the case, however, one must recognize that the ability of such SC and ST members to succeed in advanced studies or in jobs in which they have benefited from reservations may be due to the fact that they first gained access to higher educational institutions that provided them with the preparation and training needed for such success.

13 Affirmative action and career accomplishments in the US

1 Such useful contacts and networks tend to run along race and class lines, and as long as Whites continue to occupy a disproportionate share of the high-status jobs, Black students will be relatively disadvantaged.

2 The figures in Table 13.1 are restricted to full-time workers in order to make comparisons more meaningful; only 4 per cent of the male graduates and 22 per cent of the female graduates in Bowen and Bok's sample did not work full-time. Bowen and Bok did not gather earnings data for their 1989 entering cohort, since too little time had elapsed for those students to enter careers.

3 As noted in Chapter 9, pp. 139–40, at least 90 per cent of the University of Michigan Law School minority students would not have been admitted without AA preferences.

4 The differences in the earnings of minority and White graduates from the 1970s and 1980s were due in part to the fact that a higher percentage of Whites were working in (more lucrative) private practice rather than in government service, and partly because Whites tended to earn higher salaries in private practice.

5 It is tempting to conclude from the Lempert *et al.* finding about the unimportance of quantitative entry credentials in predicting the ultimate career success of UM Law School students that such credentials are given far too much attention in law-school admissions decisions; indeed, one might even regard them as an insidious mechanism for arbitrarily favoring White over equally competent minority applicants. The evidence in the case of UM Law School graduates, however, does not mean that such credentials are generally irrelevant to career success. What it does imply is that, in the high range of scores characteristic of UM Law School students, observed differences in the scores do not matter much.

6 Datcher Loury and Garman themselves concluded that "The principle cost of attending more selective schools for mismatched Blacks is the lower probability of graduation and the subsequently lower earnings for those who fail to complete college." Their own results show, however, that this cost is essentially offset by the higher earnings of those who do graduate (Datcher Loury and Garman 1995: 307–8).

7 These regressions control for many more student characteristics than SAT score. Bowen and Bok (1998: 143, Table 5) show that in most SAT brackets, for Black as

well as for White male and female students from the 1976 entering cohort, the higher the selectivity category of the college they attended, the higher were their 1995 earned incomes. Moreover, the findings to this effect are especially strong for Black male and female students in the lowest SAT bracket – below 1,000 – who are presumably the ones most "mismatched" when they attend colleges in the two highest of the three selectivity brackets in the "College and Beyond" (C&B) sample.

8 This finding includes the net effect of college selectivity on degree completion.

9 The cut-off point for Hoxby's top three ranks of colleges was somewhere between the second and third levels of selectivity in Bowen and Bok's (1998) sample of colleges.

10 The conditions that enable a college to provide students with a higher-quality education may also raise the students' career aspirations and levels of motivation, thereby stimulating them to make better use of the available educational opportunities.

11 It should be noted that this line of criticism does not apply to evidence in which data for all minority students are at issue, but where the analysis controls for student-entry characteristics like SAT scores. Since the point of the criticism is that minority students who do not owe their admission to AA are better prepared for higher education than AA beneficiaries, controlling for student entry characteristics has the effect of separating the two groups.

12 Moreover, in their reply to critics, Lempert *et al.* (2000b: 594–6) actually removed from their overall sample those under-represented minority students who appeared likely to have been admitted without any AA preferences; they then carried out multivariate regression analysis of the career achievements of the remaining students and obtained virtually the same results as with their full sample.

13 See Chapter 9, note 15.

14 Bowen and Bok found (1998: 43) that the differential was greater for students at the less highly selective among the colleges for which they had the requisite data.

15 See, for example, Gosman *et al.* (1983), as cited by Anderson (2000: 297).

16 This excellent point is made by Lempert *et al.* (2000b: 593–4) in reply to their critics.

17 See, for example, Sandalow (1999) and Thernstrom and Thernstrom (1999a).

18 That the 1989 cohort of entering students graduated at a higher rate than the 1976 entering cohort, as observed by Bowen and Bok's study of selective colleges (1998: 376–9, Tables D.3.1 and D.3.2), is probably due in part to such grade inflation.

19 Of all the research on the effects of college selectivity discussed in this paper, only that of Dale and Krueger (1999) is exempt from this limitation, because they had access to data on students who were accepted by highly selective colleges but chose to attend less selective colleges.

20 Moreover, Elizabeth Anderson has pointed out (in a private communication) that if this presumption is wrong, and Black students admitted to the lowest-selectivity C&B colleges are actually significantly stronger in terms of academic qualifications than White students admitted to all four-year colleges, then the claim that the Black students do not benefit from attending such a C&B college becomes harder to sustain.

21 See the discussion of Lempert *et al.*'s (2000a) research near the end of Chapter 11, pp. 183–4.

14 Further evidence on the effects of affirmative action in US universities

1 See, for example, Cox (1993).
2 Most of the references in this paragraph were compiled and cited by Conrad and Sharpe (1996); see also Ready (2001) for references to additional relevant studies.
3 Anderson (2000: 290–2, 298) emphasizes the importance of measuring the impact of affirmative action in terms of such a "value-added" criterion rather than simply in terms of a comparison of minority and White performance.
4 This point also addresses a criticism made by Thernstrom and Thernstrom (1999b: 1621), to the effect that the relatively high level of Black graduate civic participation Bowen and Bok discovered might simply reflect the fact that the admissions officers at the "College and Beyond" (C&B) schools placed a heavy premium on evidence of such an inclination on the part of minority applicants with otherwise rather weak credentials.
5 Thus Shelby Steele, a widely published African-American critic of affirmative action, has said: "As everyone in the academic world knows, people who are not at the top of their profession try to compensate for that by doing a lot of community work" (quoted in Gose 2000: A48).
6 The two studies – Bowen and Bok (1998) and Lempert *et al.* (2000a) – also provided some anecdotal evidence about the effects of ethnic diversity on learning, drawn from personal interviews with some of the members of their survey samples.
7 One of Gurin's colleagues, Sylvia Hurtado, has also published closely related work independently of Gurin; see, for example, Hurtado (2001).
8 *Gratz et al. v. Bollinger et al.*, 529 U.S. (2003) and *Grutter et al. v. Bollinger et al.*, 539 U.S. (2003); see the discussion in Chapter 1, pp. 9–10.
9 See, for example, US Supreme Court Justice Clarence Thomas's heartfelt dissent from the majority opinion supporting affirmative action in the 2003 UM Law School case (*Grutter et al. v. Bollinger et al.*, 539 U.S. (2003): opinion of Thomas, C.).
10 See, for example, Sandalow (1999: 1902–3).

15 Review of the findings on the consequences of positive discrimination policies in university admissions

1 I will therefore address the various claims in the same order as I did in Chapter 8, pp. 124–33.
2 My estimates are for the year 1989; but there is no reason to believe that these enrollment patterns in selective colleges changed much in the subsequent decade – at least until AA programs in a few major public selective schools (e.g. the University of California) were ended in the late 1990s.
3 To the extent that AA policies do contribute to the test-score differentials, they do so both at non-selective and at selective colleges – because they tend to redistribute UREG students with middling test scores from the former to the latter, which lowers the average test score for UREG students enrolled in each of the two categories of colleges.
4 PD policies may of course indirectly generate benefits for UREG members who are not among the immediate beneficiaries, via their effect on the variety of benefits that can potentially ensue from PD.
5 The evidence for graduation rates is not as strong as for earnings and satisfaction; for one thing, there is evidence that Black students are more likely to graduate from a historically Black college than they are from a more selective, predominantly White college. It is not at all clear, however, that the expected long-run

economic return is greater for a Black student who chooses the former over the latter.

6 It should be noted that the enhancement of career opportunities for SC and ST students in India is due not only to the access that PD provides to reserved seats in high-quality educational institutions; it is also due to reservation policies in public employment, where many Indian PD beneficiaries end up working. PD policies in education are, however, essential in opening up these employment opportunities; for they enable far more SC and ST students to meet the minimum job qualifications for a good public sector job than would otherwise be the case.

7 It is true that in India, UREG students admitted to reserved seats are most often readily identifiable. It is also true, however, that UREG students who would have been admitted even in the absence of a reservation policy are often included among those occupying reserved seats, in which case they cannot easily be distinguished from PD beneficiaries.

8 The issue of whether to recognize (other) caste groups as groups for which census and other periodic survey data should be aggregated has proven to be a very contentious one in India, pitting those who believe that the compilation of caste-based data would aggravate caste consciousness against those who believe that the reality of caste divisions should be acknowledged and studied. The former position has prevailed ever since India's independence; the last time the Indian census collected data on caste affiliation (except for SCs and STs) was in 1930, under British rule.

9 The rankings under "Effects via NEF" in Table 6.1 suggest that the benefits of these kinds may actually be greater for African Americans than for Native Americans.

10 One would hesitate to draw such a comparative conclusion if the UREG proportion of the population were very different in the two countries; but the proportion represented by SCs and STs in India – the major PD beneficiaries – is roughly comparable to that of all three UREGs in the US.

11 The above conclusions about PD policies in higher educational admissions, mixed as they are, accord well with assessments made by other scholars of PD policies in the US and India. In a detailed review of AA policies in the US, economists Holzer and Neumark concluded that:

> The educational performance and labor market credentials of minority beneficiaries are weaker than those of their white counterparts. But evidence of weaker performance in the labor market among these groups is much less frequently observed or is less credible...Affirmative action offers significant redistribution toward women and minorities, with relatively small efficiency consequences.
>
> (Holzer and Neumark 2000: 558–9)

Galanter, author of the most comprehensive study of reservation policies in India from a legal perspective, wrote that:

> compensatory discrimination has been a partial and costly success. Although few direct benefits have reached the vast mass of landless laborers in the villages, compensatory discrimination has undeniably succeeded in accelerating the growth of a middle class within these [SC/ST] groups – urban, educated, largely in government service. Members of these groups have been brought into central roles in the society to an extent unimaginable a few

decades ago...Even this kind of crude characterization of the overall impact
of policies is not possible in dealing with measures for OBCs...

(Galanter 1984: 551)

Writing much more recently than Galanter, social scientists Mendelsohn and
Vicziany concluded that:

Important benefits have indeed been provided to many thousands of individual Untouchables, and much unwarranted discrimination in public
employment and higher educational institutions has been overcome.
Moreover, the emergence of quite large numbers of accomplished and
professionally experienced Untouchables cannot be discounted as a leavening
agent for the larger Untouchable population.

(Mendelsohn and Vicziany 1998: 146)

12 The same point has been made by a prominent South Indian scholar and public
servant:

It is surprising that the Government of Karnataka has not bothered to make
an assessment of the impact of reservation policy on various castes and
communities in the field of education and in the wider socio-economic
sphere. No attempt has been made, even by scholars, to throw light on this
subject...Though such a study will almost certainly be controversial as well as
difficult to conduct, its relevance from the point of view of policy and social
science research methodology cannot be overstated.

(Thimmaiah 1997: 146)

13 Together with two social scientists at the Indian Institute of Technology (IIT) in
Bombay, I tried in 2001 to initiate a systematic study of the career paths of SC,
ST, and (a control group of) other IIT graduates. Regrettably, our research
proposal was ultimately not approved by the relevant authorities – most probably
because of the political sensitivity of the topic.

16 Concluding observations on policies of positive discrimination

1 See Weiner (1983: 37–8) for an elaboration of this point.
2 Holzer and Neumark (2000: 561) make this point.
3 Patwardhan and Palshikar, although supporters of means tests designed to prevent
well-off UREG members from receiving PD benefits, do agree that the criterion
for reserved seats should not be based simply on poverty (which is widespread
among most Indian communities). Instead, they argue (Patwardhan and Palshikar
1992: 105) that eligibility for PD preferences should go to ethnic communities
that have suffered past and present discrimination, connected to the stigma
attached to their members and to psychological attitudes and social behaviors
ingrained in both the discriminators and those discriminated against.
4 Note that an intermediate policy between preferential selection in admissions to a
higher educational institution (with significant costs to displaced non-beneficiaries) and investment in primary and secondary education (with much higher
costs, spread much more widely) is investment in increasing the capacity of the
educational institution – and the scope and effectiveness of developmental
programs for marginal students. This policy option would permit such students to

benefit from higher education without displacing non-beneficiaries; and it would carry lower costs than investment in primary and secondary education, spread more widely than in the case of purely preferential policies.

5 The financial aid provided to PD beneficiaries by an educational institution can take the form of outright grants (scholarships) or the (much less costly) alternative of subsidized loans, which beneficiaries are expected to pay off later by drawing on the higher earnings that their education presumably makes possible.

6 See Table 6.1, which compares the expected net benefits from PD policies for each affected UREG within each country. Differences between UREGs within a given country are attributable primarily to differences in UREG characteristics, for the characteristics of PD policies and of the societal environment tend to be much the same within a single country.

7 See Cunningham *et al.* (2002) for similar proposals.

8 See, for example, Patwardhan and Palshikar (1992). They recommend that "As individuals climb several rungs of the social ladder with the assistance of reservation and other facilities and become part of the educated upper middle class, their children should be deemed ineligible for such benefits as they are no longer socially handicapped" (Patwardhan and Palshikar 1992: 108).

9 See Sivaramayya (1996).

10 This is precisely the problem with the so-called "X per cent" alternative to affirmative action in admissions to state universities in the US, which calls for the admission of the top X per cent of graduates from any high school in the state in order to assure a reasonable amount of racial/ethnic diversity. The fact that African Americans, Native Americans, and Hispanic-Americans tend to be concentrated in a relatively small subset of a given state's high schools, because of the typically high degree of residential racial/ethnic segregation in the US, means that the top 10 per cent of students in those high schools will belong predominantly to one of these UREGs. The X per cent rule thus assures that each UREG with significant representation in the population of the state will be fairly well represented in admissions to state universities. The admitted UREG students, however, are likely to be weaker academically than those who would have been admitted under an affirmative action preference program, because they come from relatively impoverished families and neighborhoods that cannot provide their children with high-quality education.

11 See Chatterjee (1983) for a rigorous decision-theoretic analysis of preferential selection policies, which addresses precisely the question of how to determine the optimal magnitude of the preference.

12 One cannot rule out a priori the possibility that a PD policy – by recognizing hidden capabilities of UREG applicants – will actually improve the accuracy of applicant assessment (as in argument 3 for PD). In this case PD beneficiaries will, on average, be capable of performing as well as non-UREG peers with stronger conventional qualifications. It stands to reason, however, that even in this case there will be some magnitude of preference beyond which the performance level of PD beneficiaries will fall below that of peers selected without any such preference.

13 Even though there is logically a one-to-one correspondence between the size of a quota and the size of a preferential boost, there is a real policy difference between aiming to select a fixed number of UREG applicants – irrespective of the magnitude of the implicit preference needed to do so – and giving a preferential boost of a certain size to each UREG applicant (see Chapter 4, pp. 62–3).

14 The superiority of sensitive over mechanical PD selection processes was at the heart of the US Supreme Court 2003 rulings on the University of Michigan affirmative action cases, in which the Court upheld the law school's qualitative and

individualized admissions procedures but struck down the undergraduate point-based procedures (see Chapter 1, pp. 9–10).

15 It is better to use the term "preferential boosts" in this context, since the term "preferences" is often applied to any selection system in which some applicants are given an advantage, including a quota system.

16 See Chapter 4, note 2, for a minor exception to this rule.

17 Another important sphere for PD in India is political representation; but, as noted earlier, the issues raised by positive discrimination in this sphere are quite different from those raised in education and employment, and I do not pursue them in this book. In the US, government contracting is also an arena for positive discrimination – but a less significant one than employment or education.

18 To the extent that graduate/post-graduate education involves the performance of work (e.g. the teaching of undergraduates), this logic also implies that PD policies are more desirable at the undergraduate level.

19 Indeed, preferential PD in the sphere of higher education serves as a form of developmental PD with respect to the sphere of employment, for it enables UREG members (who would otherwise not have had this opportunity) to gain skills that make them more competitive in the job market.

Bibliography

Aikara, J. (1980) *Scheduled Castes and Higher Education: A Study of College Students in Bombay*, Pune: Dastane.

American Anthropological Association (1998) *American Anthropological Association Statement on "Race,"* available online at www.aaanet.org/stmts/racepp.htm (accessed 14 October 2002).

Anderson, E.M. (2000) "From normative to empirical sociology in the affirmative action debate: Bowen and Bok's *The Shape of the River*," *Journal of Legal Education* 50: 284–305.

—— (2001) "Defending affirmative action," *Against the Current* 94: 19–22.

—— (2002) "Integration, Affirmative Action, and Strict Scrutiny," *New York University Law Review* 77: 1195–1271.

—— (2003) "Race, gender, and affirmative action: resource page for teaching," available online at www-personal.umich.edu./& tildeeandersn/biblio.htm (accessed 30 June 2003).

Association of American Medical Colleges (1995) *Minority Students in Medical Education: Facts and Figures IX*, Washington, DC: Association of American Medical Colleges.

—— (1996) "Minorities underrepresented in medicine are consistently more likely to work in underserved areas," Association of American Medical Colleges Press Release, Washington, DC (22 May).

Astin, A.W. (1993) *What Matters in College? Four Critical Years Revisited*, San Francisco: Jossey-Bass.

Balagopal, K. (1990) "This anti-Mandal mania," *Economic and Political Weekly* 25: 2231–4.

Banerji, B.K. (1990) "Merit in services," *Seminar* 375: 47–50.

Bardhan, P. (1999) *Political Economy of Development in India,* New York: Oxford University Press.

Behrman, J.R., Constantine, J., Kletzer, L., McPherson, M.S., and Schapiro, M.O. (1996) "The impact of college quality choices on wages: are there differences among demographic groups?", Discussion Paper 38, Williams Project on the Economics of Higher Education.

Bergmann, B. (1996) *In Defense of Affirmative Action*, New York: Basic Books.

Berreman, G.D. (1975) "Race, caste, and other invidious distinctions in social stratification," *Race* 23: 385–414.

Beteille, A. (1981) "The problem," *Seminar* 268: 10–13.

—— (1990) "Is job reservation a good policy?", *Seminar* 375: 41–2.

—— (1992) *The Backward Classes in Contemporary India*, Delhi: Oxford University Press.

Bound, J. and Freeman, R.B. (1992) "What went wrong? The erosion of relative earnings and employment among young Black men in the 1980s," *Quarterly Journal of Economics* 107: 201–32.

Bowen, W.G. and Bok, D. (1998) *The Shape of The River: Long-Term Consequences of Considering Race in College and University Admissions*, Princeton, NJ: Princeton University Press.

—— (1999) "Response to review by Terrance Sandalow," *Michigan Law Review* 97:1917–22.

Bunzel, J. (1988) "Affirmative-action admission: how it 'works' at U.C. Berkeley," *The Public Interest* 93: 111–29.

—— (1996) "Race and college admissions," *The Public Interest* 122: 49–58.

Cantor, N. (1998) "A Michigan legacy: ensuring diversity and democracy on campus," *Michigan Alumnus*, University of Michigan (Summer).

Carter, S. (1991) *Reflections of an Affirmative Action Baby*, New York: Basic Books.

Chanana, K. (1993) "Accessing higher education – the dilemma of schooling: women, minorities, Scheduled Castes and Scheduled Tribes in contemporary India," in S. Chitnis and P. Altbach (eds) *Higher Education Reform in India*, New Delhi: Sage Publications India.

Chandola, M.V. (1992) "Affirmative action in India and the United States: the untouchables and Black experience," *Indiana International and Comparative Law Review* 3: 101–33.

Chang, M.J. (2001), "The positive educational effects of racial diversity on campus," in G. Orfield (ed.) *Diversity Challenged: Evidence on the Impact of Affirmative Action*, Cambridge, MA: Harvard Education Publishing Group.

Chatterjee, B.B. (1983) "Social costs of reservation in higher education: a decision theoretic view," *Journal of Higher Education* 9: 77–89.

Cherry, R. (2001) *Who Gets the Good Jobs? Combating Race and Gender Disparities*, New Brunswick, NJ: Rutgers University Press.

Chitnis, S. (1972) "Education for equality: case of SCs in higher education," *Economic and Political Weekly* 7: 1675–81.

—— (1981) *A Long Way to Go: Report on a Survey of Scheduled Caste High School and College Students in Fifteen States of India*, New Delhi: Allied.

—— (1984) "Positive discrimination in India with reference to education," in R.B. Goldmann and A.J. Wilson (eds) *From Independence to Statehood: Managing Ethnic Conflict in Five African and Asian States*, London: Frances Pinter.

—— (1986) "Measuring up to reserved admissions," in V.P. Shah and B.C. Agrawal (eds) *Reservation: Policy, Programmes and Issues*, Jaipur: Rawat Publications.

—— (1997) "Definition of the terms Scheduled Castes and Scheduled Tribes: a crisis of ambivalence," in V.A. Pai Panandiker (ed.) *The Politics of Backwardness: Reservation Policy in India*, New Delhi: Konark Publishers.

Chowdhary, K.C. (1998) "Dalits in higher education: cooption or domination," *Journal of Higher Education* 21: 437–51.

Coate, S. and Loury, G.C. (1993) "Will affirmative-action policies eliminate negative stereotypes?", *American Economic Review* 83: 1220–40.

Cohen, C. (1995) *Naked Racial Preference: The Case Against Affirmative Action*, Lanham, MD: Madison Books.

Conrad, C.A. and Sharpe, R.V. (1996) "The impact of the California Civil Rights Initiative (CCRI) on university and professional school admissions and the implications for the California economy," *Review of Black Political Economy* 25: 12–59.

Cook, E. (1995) "Race and UC medical school admissions: a study of applicants and admission in the UC medical schools," testimony to Assembly Judiciary Committee, California State Legislature, 4 May.

Cox, B. (ed.) (1993) *Resolving a Crisis in Education: Latino Teachers for Tomorrow's Classrooms*, Claremont, CA: The Tomas Rivera Center.

Cross, T. and Slater, R.B. (1997) "Why the end of affirmative action would exclude all but a very few Blacks from America's leading universities and graduate schools," *Journal of Blacks in Higher Education* 17: 8–17.

Cunningham, C.D. (ed.) (1997) "Proceedings of the conference on rethinking equality in the global society," *Washington University Law Quarterly* 75: 1561–76.

Cunningham, C.D. and Madhava Menon, N.R. (1999) "Race, class, caste? Rethinking affirmative action," *Michigan Law Review*, 97: 1296–1310.

Cunningham, C.D., Loury, G.C., and Skrentny, J.D. (2002) "Passing strict scrutiny: using social science to design affirmative action programs," *Georgetown Law Journal* 90: 835–82.

Dale, S.B. and Krueger, A.B. (1999) "Estimating the payoff to attending a more selective college: an application of selection on observables and unobservables," Working Paper 7322, National Bureau of Economic Research.

Daniel, K., Black, D., and Smith, J. (1997) "College quality and the wages of young men," Research Report No. 9707, Department of Economics, University of Western Ontario.

—— (2001) "Racial differences in the effects of college quality and student body diversity on wages," in G. Orfield (ed.) *Diversity Challenged: Evidence on the Impact of Affirmative Action*, Cambridge, MA: Harvard Education Publishing Group.

Datcher Loury, L. and Garman, D. (1995) "College selectivity and earnings," *Journal of Labor Economics* 13: 289–308.

Davidson, R. and Lewis, E. (1997) "Affirmative action and other special consideration admissions at the University of California, Davis, School of Medicine," *Journal of the American Medical Association* 278:14.

Deliege, R. (1999) *The Untouchables of India*, Oxford: Berg.

Deppe, M.J. (1989) "The impact of racial diversity and involvement on college students' social concern values," paper presented at the Annual Meeting of the Association for the Study of Higher Education, Atlanta, November.

Deshpande, A. (2001) "Caste at birth? Redefining disparity in India," *Review of Development Economics* 5: 130–44.

Dickens, W.T. and Kane, T.J. (1999) "Racial test score differences as evidence of reverse discrimination: less than meets the eye," *Industrial Relations* 38: 331–63.

Dirks, N. (2001) *Castes of Mind: Colonialism and the Making of Modern India*, Princeton: Princeton University Press.

Drake, Michael (1994) "Remarks to the Board of Regents," presentation to the University of California Board of Regents, 17 November.

Dreze, J. and Sen, A. (1995) *India, Economic Development and Social Opportunity*, Delhi: Oxford University Press.

Dubey, S.N. (1991), "A comparative analysis of issues in affirmative action policies in India and the USA," *International Social Work* 34: 383–402.

Duncan, G. and Hoffman, S. (1984) "A new look at the causes of the improved status of Black workers," *Journal of Human Resources* 18: 268–82.

Dworkin, R. (1998) "Affirming affirmative action," *New York Review of Books*, 22 October and 5 November.

Ferguson, R.F. (1998) "Teachers' perceptions and expectations and the Black-White test score gap," in C. Jencks and M. Phillips (eds) *The Black-White Test Score Gap*, Washington, DC: Brookings Institution.

Galanter, M. (1984) *Competing Equalities: Law and the Backward Classes in India*, Delhi: Oxford University Press.

Garcia, L.T., Erskine, N., Hawn, K., and Casmay, S.R. (1981) "The effect of affirmative action on attributions about minority group members," *Journal of Personality* 49: 427–37.

Ghorpade, M.Y. (1990) "The rationale," *Seminar* 375: 14–17.

Goodwin, N., Nelson, J.A., Ackerman, F., and Weisskopf, T.E. (2003) *Microeconomics in Context*, Boston: Houghton-Mifflin.

Gose, B. (2000) "Measuring the value of an Ivy degree," *Chronicle of Higher Education*, 13 January.

Government of India (1981) *Report of the Backward Classes Commission*, New Delhi: Controller of Publications.

Guha, A. (1990a) "The Mandal mythology," *Seminar* 375: 51–3.

—— (1990b) "Reservations in myth and reality," *Economic and Political Weekly* 25: 2716–18.

Gupta, D. (2000) *Interrogating Caste: Understanding Hierarchy and Difference in Indian Society*, New Delhi: Penguin Books India.

Gurin, P. (1999) Expert Report for *Gratz et al. v. Bollinger et al.*, no. 97–75321 (E.D. Michigan) and *Grutter et al. v. Bollinger et al.*, no. 75–75928 (E.D. Michigan).

—— (2000) Supplemental Expert Report for *Gratz et al. v. Bollinger et al.*, no. 97–75321 (E.D. Michigan).

—— (2001a) Supplemental Expert Report for *Grutter et al. v. Bollinger et al.*, no. 75–75928 (E.D. Michigan).

—— (2001b) "Evidence for the educational benefits of diversity in higher education: response to the critique by the National Association of Scholars of the expert witness report of Patricia Gurin," Working Paper, University of Michigan.

—— (2001c) "Evidence for the educational benefits of diversity in higher education: an addendum," Working Paper, University of Michigan.

Gurin, P., Dey, E.L., Hurtado, S., and Gurin, G. (2002) "Diversity and higher education: theory and impact on educational outcomes," *Harvard Educational Review* 72: 330–66.

Hacker, A. (1995) *Two Nations: Black and White, Separate, Hostile, Unequal*, New York: Ballantine Books.

Hearn, J.C. (1984) "The relative roles of academic, ascribed and socioeconomic characteristics in college destinations," *Sociology of Education* 57: 22–30.

Hedges, L.V. and Nowell, A. (1998) "Black-White test score convergence since 1965," in C. Jencks and M. Phillips (eds) *The Black-White Test Score Gap*, Washington, DC: Brookings Institution.

Heilman, M.E., Block, C., and Lucas, J. (1992) "Presumed incompetent? Stigmatization and affirmative action efforts," *Journal of Applied Psychology* 77: 536–44.

Henriques, J. and Wankhede, J.J. (1985) "One step forward, yet two steps behind: a study of wastage and stagnation in education of SC-ST in Maharashtra," report submitted to the Ministry of Education, Government of India, New Delhi.

Herrnstein, R.J. and Murray,C. (1994) *The Bell Curve: Intelligence and Class Structure in American Life*, New York: Free Press.

Hoffman, S.D. (1984) "Black-White differences in the returns to higher education: evidence from the 1970s," *Economics of Education Review* 3: 13–21.

Holzer, H. and Neumark, D. (2000) "Assessing affirmative action," *Journal of Economic Literature* 38: 483–568.

Hoxby, C.M. (1998) "The return to attending a more selective college: 1960 to the present," Working Paper, Harvard University.

Hurtado, S. (2001), "Linking diversity and educational purpose: how diversity affects the classroom environment and student development," in G. Orfield (ed.) *Diversity Challenged: Evidence on the Impact of Affirmative Action*, Cambridge, MA: Harvard Education Publishing Group.

Ilaiah, K. (1990) "Reservations: experience as framework of debate," *Economic and Political Weekly* 25: 2307–10.

—— (1996) *Why I Am Not a Hindu*, Calcutta: Samya.

Indiresan, P.V. (1982) Article, *Indian Express*, 28 June.

Indiresan, P.V. and Nigam, N.C. (1993) "The Indian Institutes of Technology: excellence in peril," in S. Chitnis and P. Altbach (eds) *Higher Education Reform in India*, New Delhi: Sage Publications India.

Jaffrelot, C. (2002) *India's Silent Revolution: The Rise of the Lower Castes in North India*, New York: Columbia University Press.

James, E. (1989) "College quality and future earnings: where should you send your child to college?", *American Economic Review* 79: 247–52.

Jenkins, L.D. (1998) "Preferential policies for disadvantaged ethnic groups: employment and education," in C. Young (ed.) *Ethnic Diversity and Public Policy: A Comparative Inquiry*, London: Macmillan.

—— (1999) "Competing inequalities: the struggle over reserved legislative seats for women in India," *International Review of Social History* 44: 53–75.

Kahlenberg, R. (1995) "Class, not race," *New Republic*, 3 April.

Kane, T.J. (1998) "Racial and ethnic preferences in college admissions," in C. Jencks and M. Phillips (eds) *The Black-White Test Score Gap*, Washington, DC: Brookings Institution.

Karlekar, M. (1975) "Higher education and the Scheduled Castes," *Journal of Higher Education* 1: 178–87.

Keith, S., Bell, R., and Williams, A. (1987) "Assessing the outcome of affirmative action in medical schools: a study of the class of 1975," document no. R-3481-CWF, Santa Monica, CA: Rand Corporation.

Kirpal, V. (1978) "Higher education for the Scheduled Castes and Scheduled Tribes," *Economic and Political Weekly* 13: 165–9.

Kirpal, V. and Gupta, M. (1999) *Equality Through Reservations*, Jaipur: Rawat Publications.

Kirpal, V., Swamidasan, N., Gupta, A., and Gupta, R.K. (1985) "Scheduled Caste and Tribe students in higher education: a study of an IIT," *Economic and Political Weekly* 20: 1238–48.

—— (1985–86) "Wastage among Scheduled Caste and Scheduled Tribe students," *Journal of Higher Education* 11: 111–16.

Klitgaard, R. (1985) *Choosing Elites*, New York: Basic Books.

Komaromy, M., Grumbach, K., Drake, M., Vranizan, K., Lurie, N., Keane D., and Bindman, A.B. (1997) "The role of Black and Hispanic physicians in providing health care for underserved populations," *New England Journal of Medicine* 334: 1305–10.

Kumar, D. (1990) "The problem," *Seminar* 375: 12–13.

—— (1992) "The affirmative action debate in India," *Asian Survey* 32: 290–302.

Kumar, K. (1997) "Educational inequality and language," in R.P. Sinha (ed.) *Inequality in Indian Education*, New Delhi: Vikas Publishing House.

Lemann, N. (1999a) *The Big Test: The Secret History of the American Meritocracy*, New York: Farrar, Strauss & Giroux.

—— (1999b) "Tinkering with the test," *New York Times*, 13 September.

Lempert, R., Chambers, D., and Adams, T. (2000a) "Michigan's minority graduates in practice: the river runs through law school," *Law & Social Inquiry* 25: 395–505.

—— (2000b) "Michigan's minority graduates in practice: answers to methodological queries," *Law & Social Inquiry* 25: 585–97.

Lerner, R. and Nagai, A.K. (2001) "A critique of the expert report of Patricia Gurin in *Gratz vs. Bollinger*," Center for Equal Opportunity, Washington, DC.

Loury, G.C. (1976) "Essays in the theory of the distribution of income," unpublished Ph.D. thesis, Massachusetts Institute of Technology.

—— (1977) "A dynamic theory of racial income differences," in P.A. Wallace and A. Lamond (eds) *Women, Minorities and Employment Discrimination*, Lexington, MA: Lexington Books.

—— (1987) "Why should we care about group inequality," *Social Philosophy and Policy* 5: 249–71.

—— (1997) "How to mend affirmative action," *The Public Interest* 127: 33–43.

—— (2002) *The Anatomy of Racial Inequality*, Cambridge, MA: Harvard University Press.

McWhorter, John H. (2000) *Losing the Race: Self-Sabotage in Black America*, New York: Free Press.

Malamud, D. (1997) "Affirmative action, diversity, and the Black middle class," *University of Colorado Law Review* 68: 939–99.

Mendelsohn, O. and Vicziany, M. (1998) *The Untouchables: Subordination, Poverty and the State in Modern India*, Cambridge, UK: Cambridge University Press.

Milem, J. (2002) "The educational benefits of diversity: evidence from multiple sectors," in M.J. Chang, D. Witt, J. Jones, and K. Hakuta (eds) *Compelling Interest: Examining the Evidence on Racial Dynamics in Higher Education*, Stanford, CA: Stanford University Press.

Mills, N. (1994) "Introduction: to look like America," in N. Mills (ed.) *Debating Affirmative Action: Race, Gender, Ethnicity, and the Politics of Inclusion*, New York: Dell.

Mukarji, Nirmal (1981) "Perspectives of a policy," *Seminar* 268: 14–19.

Murray, Charles (1994) "Affirmative racism," in N. Mills (ed.) *Debating Affirmative Action: Race, Gender, Ethnicity, and the Politics of Inclusion*, New York: Dell.

Nesiah, D. (1997) *Discrimination with Reason: The Policy of Reservations in the United States, India and Malaysia*, Delhi: Oxford University Press.

Nickens, H.W. and Cohen, J.J. (1996) "Policy perspectives: on affirmative action," *Journal of the American Medical Association* 275: 572–4.

Nigam, A. (1990) "Mandal Commission and the Left," *Economic and Political Weekly* 25: 2652–3.

Parikh, S. (1997) *The Politics of Preference: Democratic Institutions and Affirmative Action in the United States and India*, Ann Arbor, MI: University of Michigan Press.

Parmaji (1985) *Caste Reservations and Performance: Research Findings*, Warangal, AP: Mamata Publications.

Pascarella, E.T. and Terenzini P.T. (1991) *How College Affects Students: Findings and Insights from Twenty Years of Research*, San Francisco: Jossey-Bass.

Patwardhan, V. and Palshikar, V. (1992) "Reserved seats in medical education: a study," *Journal of Education and Social Change* 5: 1–117.

Penn, N. (1986) "Affirmative action at work: a survey of graduates of the University of California, San Diego, Medical School," *American Journal of Public Health* 76: 9.

Radhakrishnan, P. (1990) "OBCs and central commissions," *Seminar* 375: 22–5.

—— (1996) "Mandal Commission report: a sociological critique," in M.N. Srinivas (ed.) *Caste: Its Twentieth Century Avatar*, New Delhi: Viking Press.

Ramachandran, V.K. (1997) "On Kerala's development achievements," in J. Dreze and A. Sen (eds) *Indian Development: Selected Regional Perspectives*, Delhi: Oxford University Press.

Rao, S.S. (2001) "Equality in higher education: impact of affirmative action policies in India," unpublished draft paper, Jawaharlal Nehru University, New Delhi.

—— (2002) "Equality in higher education: impact of affirmative action policies in India," in E.F. Beckham (ed.) *Global Collaborations: the Role of Higher Education in Diverse Democracies*, Washington, DC: Association of American Colleges and Universities.

Ready, T. (2001) "The impact of affirmative action on medical education and the nation's health," in G. Orfield (ed.) *Diversity Challenged: Evidence on the Impact of Affirmative Action*, Cambridge, MA: Harvard Education Publishing Group.

Rothman, S., Lipset, S.M., and Nevitte, N. (2003a) "Does enrollment diversity improve university education?", *International Journal of Public Opinion Research* 15: 8–26.

—— (2003b) "Racial diversity reconsidered," *The Public Interest* 151: 25–38.

Rudenstine, N.L. (2001) "Student diversity and higher learning," in G. Orfield (ed.) *Diversity Challenged: Evidence on the Impact of Affirmative Action*, Cambridge, MA: Harvard Education Publishing Group.

Sachchidananda (1977) *The Harijan Elite*, New Delhi: Thomson Press.

—— (1990) "Welcome policy," *Seminar* 375: 18–21.

Sandalow, T. (1999) "Minority preferences reconsidered," *Michigan Law Review* 97: 1874–916.

Shah, A.M. (1991) "Job reservations and efficiency," *Economic and Political Weekly* 26: 1732–4.

Sharma, O.P. (1990) *Scheduled Castes, Population and Literates*, New Delhi: Kar Kripa.

Sivaramayya, B. (1996) "The Mandal judgment: a brief description and critique," in M.N. Srinivas (ed.) *Caste: Its Twentieth Century Avatar*, New Delhi: Viking Press.

Smith, J.P. and Welch, F.R. (1986) *Closing the Gap: Forty Years of Economic Progress for Blacks*, Santa Monica, CA: Rand Corporation.

Sobel, J. (2002) "Can we trust social capital?", *Journal of Economic Literature* 40: 139–54.

Sowell, T. (1990) *Preferential Policies: An International Perspective*, New York: William Morrow.

Srinivas, M.N. (1962) *Caste in Modern India*, Bombay: Asia Publishing House.

Steeh, C. and Krysan, M. (1996) "Trends: affirmative action and the public, 1970–1995," *Public Opinion Quarterly* 60: 128–58.

Steele, C.M. (1992) "Race and the schooling of Black Americans," *The Atlantic* April: 68–78.

Steele, C.M. and Aronson, J. (1998) "How stereotypes influence the standardized test performance of talented African American students," in C. Jencks and M. Phillips (eds) *The Black-White Test Score Gap*, Washington, DC: Brookings Institution.

Steele, S. (1990) *The Content of Our Character: A New Vision of Race in America*, New York: St. Martin's Press.

Takaki, R. (ed.) (1994) *From Different Shores*, 2nd edn, New York: Oxford University Press.

Thernstrom, S. and Thernstrom, A. (1997) *America in Black and White: One Nation, Indivisible*, New York: Simon & Schuster.

—— (1999a) "What we now know," *Commentary* 7: 44–50.

—— (1999b) "Reflections on *The Shape of the River*," *UCLA Law Review* 46: 1583–631.

Thimmaiah, G. (1997) "Karnataka Government's reservation policies for SCs/STs and OBCs," in V.A. Pai Panandiker (ed.) *The Politics of Backwardness: Reservation Policy in India*, New Delhi: Konark Publishers.

Thomas, E. and Shavelson, R. (2001) "Analysis of report of Wood and Sherman, addendum to National Association of Scholars brief," Working Paper, Stanford Institute for Higher Education Research.

Vakil, A.K. (1985) *Reservation Policy and Scheduled Castes in India*, New Delhi: Asish Publishing House.

Vars, F.E. and Bowen, W.G. (1998) "Scholastic aptitude test scores, race, and academic performance in selective colleges and universities," in C. Jencks and M. Phillips (eds) *The Black-White Test Score Gap*, Washington, DC: Brookings Institution.

Velaskar, P.R. (1986) "Inequality in higher education: a study of Scheduled Caste students in medical colleges of Bombay," unpublished Ph.D. thesis, Tata Institute of Social Sciences, Bombay.

—— (1998) "Ideology, education and the political struggle for liberation: change and challenge among the Dalits of Maharashtra," in S. Shukla and R. Kaul (eds) *Education: Development and Underdevelopment*, New Delhi: Sage Publications India.

Wales, T. (1972) "The effect of college quality on earnings: results from the NBER-Thorndike data," *Journal of Human Resources* 8: 306–17.

Wankhede, G.G. (1978) "Social determinants of occupational mobility: a case study of Scheduled Castes in Maharashtra," unpublished M.Phil. thesis, Jawaharlal Nehru University, New Delhi.

—— (2001) "Educational inequalities among Scheduled Castes in Maharashtra," *Economic and Political Weekly* 36: 1553–8.

Weiner, M. (1983) "The political consequences of preferential policies: a comparative perspective," *Comparative Politics* 16: 35–52.

—— (1993) "Affirmative action: the international experience," *Development and Democracy* 4: 1–15.

Wightman, L. (1997) "The threat to diversity in legal education: an empirical analysis of the consequences of abandoning race as a factor in law school admission decisions," *New York University Law Review* 72: 1–53.

Wood, T.E. and Sherman, M.J. (2001) "Is campus racial diversity correlated with educational benefits?", National Association of Scholars, Princeton, NJ.

Yadav, K.C. (1994) *India's Unequal Citizens: A Study of Other Backward Classes*, New Delhi: Manohar Publishers.

Index

ability to function in a multicultural
society 111, 114, 121–2, 130, 200–2,
214, 218, 221, 223, 224–5
academic environment, match to 164–7
academic performance 223, 245–6;
Indian universities 168–78; indicators
126–7; questions about evidence for
188–93; US universities 156–67
academic qualifications of enrolled
UREG students 206–7; India 151–3;
US 140–3
accuracy in appraisal of applicant
qualifications 47–8, 54, 71, 109–10,
114, 115–19, 218; *see also* average
academic qualifications, cynicism,
resentment
actors 16
Adivasis (Scheduled Tribes or STs) 5, 18,
20, 39–40, 206, 222; academic
performance 168–78; characteristics
80–6 *passim*, 94–6; history of PD
policy 11–14, 15; public support for
PD policy 21–2, 23, 28–31; university
enrollments 146–55
admissibility index 117
advanced degrees 180, 213
affirmative action (AA) 3–4, 7, 8, 22, 247;
and career accomplishments 179–93;
current state of policy in US 16–18;
further evidence on effects of
194–204; history of 6–10; sources of
differences in policies between India
and US 18–20; and university
enrollments 134–45; *see also* positive
discrimination, United States
affirming society's commitment to
reduce continuing disadvantages
45–6, 54, 74, 114, 133, 217–19, 224
African Americans (Blacks) 5, 18, 19,
39–40, 101, 221–2; characteristics
80–6 *passim*, 94–6; history of injustice
25; history of PD policies in US
6–10; university enrollments 134–6,
137–8
Aikara, J. 152, 169–70, 172
allocational inefficiency 32
Ambedkar, Dr B.R. 11, 12, 20, 28, 175,
260
Anderson, E.M. 26, 248, 253, 255, 257,
258, 259, 264, 265
Andhra Pradesh 174
anti-Brahman movements 10–11
appraisal of applicant qualifications 223,
258; accuracy 47–8, 54, 71, 109–10,
114, 115–19, 218; inaccuracy 51–2,
56, 72, 110, 115, 219, 223, 258
Article 46 of Indian Constitution 12
arts programs 146
ascriptive politics 252; *see also* divisive
identity group politics
Association of American Medical
Colleges 195, 196
Astin, A.W. 197–8, 201
average academic quality 126–7, 209–10,
225, 244–5; decrease in 110, 115,
209–10, 219, 223; increase in 110,
114, 209–10, 218, 219–21
average quality of individuals selected 48,
52, 54, 55
average test scores 141–3

B.J. Medical College, Pune 149, 153,
170–1, 172, 174, 176–8
Bakke case 9, 110
Balagopal, K. 31
bar exam 183
Bardhan, P. 89
Behrman, J.R. 186

National Board of Medical Examiners
(NBME) exams 182–3
Native Americans 5, 7, 18, 19, 25, 39–40,
101, 221–2; characteristics 80–6
passim, 94–6; enrollments in higher
education 134–6
need for ethnicity focus 60, 61, 78,
98–101, 101–2, 103, 231;
determination of 72–3; effect on PD
outcomes 73–4
negative discrimination 4
negative stereotypes: dispelling 47, 54,
114, 132–3, 216–17, 218; exacerbation
of 52, 55, 112, 115, 132–3, 216–17,
219
Nehru, J. 11–12, 20, 248
Nehru Medical College 170
Nesiah, D. 247, 248
Neumark, D. 195, 266
Nickens, H.W. 204
Nigam, A. 31, 35, 36
Nixon, R.M. 8, 22
non-Brahman movements 10–11, 20
non-UREG resentment 32, 52, 55, 115,
132, 216, 219, 223
nuanced approach to selection 117–18,
239; *see also* sensitivity of selection
process

O'Connor, Justice S. Day 9–10
Office of Federal Contract Compliance
Program 7
organizational performance 71, 74;
arguments against PD 51–2, 55;
arguments for PD 47–8, 54; *see also*
educational mission
'Other Backward Classes' (OBCs) 5,
14–15, 18, 20, 39–40, 101, 207,
221–2; characteristics 80–6 *passim*,
94–6; eligibility for PD 235; Mandal
Commission 14–15, 20, 23, 39, 207,
237, 248; no history of oppression 31;
public support for PD 22, 23–4
overall PD displacement impact 68, 75,
78, 90–2, 98, 99

Pacific Islanders 236
Palshikar, V. 37, 39, 147, 149, 153, 154,
170–1, 172, 174, 176, 226, 249, 250,
262, 267, 268
Parikh, S. 25, 247, 248, 252
Parmaji. 151, 174, 249
Pascarella, E.T. 179–80, 184

Patwardhan, V. 37, 39, 147, 149, 153, 154,
170–1, 172, 174, 176, 226, 249, 250,
262, 267, 268
Penn, N. 195
People's Education Society 175, 260
perceptions of fairness of admissions
processes 114, 115, 132, 216, 218, 219;
see also cynicism, resentment
performance quality 60, 61, 78;
determination of 69–71; effect on PD
outcomes 71–2; likely consequences
of PD in US and India 98–101, 102,
103; *see also* academic performance
perseverance 117
physical appearance 80–1, 83–4
political representation 11, 12, 14, 17–18,
34, 269
Poona Pact 1932 11
poor performance and frequent failure
52, 55; academic performance 112,
115, 125–6, 208–9, 219
poor tailoring 32, 35–6, 50, 55, 115, 127,
219, 223; *see also under individual
arguments*
positive discrimination (PD) 4, 229–46,
247; adapting arguments and claims to
higher education context 108–14,
115; arguments and claims in favor
45–9, 54; arguments and claims in
opposition 49–58; consequences for
educational admissions 205–26;
current state of PD policies 16–18;
debate over *see* debate over PD; as due
compensation or reverse
discrimination 41–5; eligibility of
UREGs 18, 235–8; extensions of
policies 104; history in India 10–15;
history in US 6–10; impact on
university enrollments 107–8; optimal
choice of 234–44; policy
characteristics 59, 61–6, 78, 86–9, 91,
96–7, 99, 234–5, 238–42; rationale for
in favor of ethnic identity groups
229–34; sources of differences in
policies in US and India 18–20;
spheres of activity for 242–3, 269; *see
also* affirmative action, reservation
policies
positive discrimination (PD)
beneficiaries: academic qualifications
206–7; estimates of total number
205–6; extent of support for 66, 70,
76, 78, 79, 88–9, 91, 97, 99, 240;

Singh, V.P. 15, 23, 39
skin color 80–1, 254
Slater, R.B. 137
Smith, J.P. 179
snowballing demands for group
preferences 51, 55, 115, 125, 207–8,
219
social capital 27–8, 49, 54, 72, 74, 245,
249; university admissions and spread
of 111–12, 114, 128, 187, 211–12,
218, 222–3, 224
social concern 197
social environment, match to 164–7
social harmony 54, 55, 57, 114–15,
218–19
social mobility 175–8
societal elite *see* integration of societal
elite
societal elitism, degree of 68, 76, 78,
89–90, 91, 98, 99
societal environment, characteristics of
59, 68, 78, 89–92, 97–8, 102, 234
societal goals 54, 55, 57–8, 123–4
societal salience of ethnicity 68, 73, 76,
78, 78–9, 89, 91, 97, 99
societal well-being 54, 55, 108–9, 114,
115; *see also under individual arguments*
society's commitment to reducing
continuing disadvantages, affirming
45–6, 54, 74, 114, 133, 217–19, 224
society's leadership, legitimacy of 46, 54,
114, 133, 217–19
socio-cultural background 173–4
socio-economic disadvantage 240; extent
of 67, 70, 78, 84, 91, 95, 99, 231
socio-economic status (SES) 36, 234;
academic performance 163–4, 165–6,
172–4; creamy layer and university
enrollments 143–5, 153–5; ethnic
identity vs 229, 230–2; social mobility
175–8
Sowell, T. 33
specialization 176
spheres of activity for PD 242–3, 269
Srinivas, M.N. 174
stagnation 169–70, 171
standardized tests 118; average scores
141–3
Steele, C. 253
Steele, S. 33, 265
stereotype bias 162, 262
stereotype threat 71, 253

stereotypes, negative *see* negative
stereotypes
stigmatization 55, 55, 253; extent of 67,
71, 73, 78, 85–6, 91, 95–6, 99, 231;
university admissions and 113, 115,
130–1, 203–4, 214–15, 219, 224, 256
structural diversity 200–1, 202
subcultures 162
support for PD beneficiaries, extent of
66, 70, 76, 78, 79, 88–9, 91, 97, 99,
240

Terenzini, P.T. 179–80, 184
Thernstrom, A. and Thernstrom, S. 135,
142, 143, 144, 156–7, 158, 159, 163,
165, 183, 188, 204, 250, 261, 262, 264,
265
Thimmaiah, G. 267
Thomas, Justice C. 249, 265
Thomas, E. 201
tribe 4

under-appreciation of true capabilities
and achievements 53, 55, 113, 115,
130–1, 214–15, 219
undergraduate enrollments 135, 136–9,
142
underperformance 161–2, 261
under-represented ethnic groups
(UREGs) 5, 39–40; characteristics 59,
66–7, 78, 191–2, 234; comparative
effects of PD benefits in US and India
98–101; criticism of average
performance data 188–9; deceitful
efforts to claim UREG status 51, 55,
115, 131, 147, 215–16, 219;
differences in US and India 80–6, 91,
94–6, 99; eligibility for PD 18, 235–8;
estimates of total number of PD
beneficiaries 205–6; exacerbation of
inequalities among 50, 55, 115, 127,
153–5, 210, 219; relative success of
PD policies for different UREGs
221–2; status and job performance 47,
54, 114, 129, 194–5, 212–14, 218;
university enrollments 134–6, 146–7;
see also positive discrimination
beneficiaries, *and under individual
UREG groups*
United States (US) 3–4, 5, 105–6, 242,
244–5; academic performance in
universities 156–67; career
accomplishments 179–93;

Lightning Source UK Ltd.
Milton Keynes UK
UKOW04f0426220814

237369UK00006B/53/A